# Media, Markets, and Democracy

The mass media and free press should serve people both as consumers and as citizens. Critics claim that government interventions in media markets prevent audiences from getting the media products they want. Political theorists assert that a free press is essential for democracy. The critics' claim is incorrect and the theorists' assertion is inadequate as a policy or constitutional guide. Even if markets properly provide for people's desires or preferences for most products, Part I of this book shows that unique aspects of media products systematically cause markets to fail in respect to them. Part II shows that four prominent, but different, theories of democracy lead to different conceptions of good journalistic practice, good media policy, and proper constitutional principles. While implicitly favoring a theory of "complex democracy," Part II makes it clear that the choice among democratic theories is crucial for understanding what should be meant by a free press. Part III explores one currently controversial issue – international free trade in media products. Contrary to the American negotiating position relating to media products, both economic and democratic theory justify deviations from free trade.

C. Edwin Baker has since 1981 been a professor of law at the University of Pennsylvania and since 1986 the Nicholas Gallicchio Professor. He has also taught law at the University of Chicago, Cornell University, University of Texas, University of Oregon, and University of Toledo and taught communications policy at the JFK School of Government at Harvard. He was a staff attorney at the ACLU in 1987–88. In addition to more than forty scholarly articles on free speech, equality, property, philosophy, economics, and the media, he is the author of two books, *Human Liberty and Freedom of Speech* (1989) and *Advertising and a Democratic Press* (1994).

COMMUNICATION, SOCIETY AND POLITICS

*Editors*

W. Lance Bennett, *University of Washington*

Robert M. Entman, *North Carolina State University*

Politics and relations among individuals in societies across the world are being transformed by new technologies for targeting individuals and sophisticated methods for shaping personalized messages. The new technologies challenge boundaries of many kinds – between news, information, entertainment, and advertising; between media, with the arrival of the World Wide Web; and even between nations. *Communication, Society and Politics* probes the political and social impacts of these new communication systems in national, comparative, and global perspective.

# Media, Markets, and Democracy

C. Edwin Baker
*University of Pennsylvania*

PUBLISHED BY THE PRESS SYNDICATE OF THE UNIVERSITY OF CAMBRIDGE
The Pitt Building, Trumpington Street, Cambridge, United Kingdom

CAMBRIDGE UNIVERSITY PRESS
The Edinburgh Building, Cambridge CB2 2RU, UK
40 West 20th Street, New York, NY 10011-4211, USA
10 Stamford Road, Oakleigh, VIC 3166, Australia
Ruiz de Alarcón 13, 28014 Madrid, Spain
Dock House, The Waterfront, Cape Town 8001, South Africa

http://www.cambridge.org

© Cambridge University Press 2002

First published 2002

Printed in the United States of America

*Typeface*   Minion 11/13 pt.      *System*   QuarkXPress [BTS]

*A catalog record for this book is available from the British Library.*

*Library of Congress Cataloging in Publication data*
Baker, C. Edwin.
Media, markets, and democracy / C. Edwin Baker.
p.   cm. – (Communication, society, and politics)
Includes bibliographical references and index.
ISBN 0-521-80435-3 – ISBN 0-521-00977-4 (pb.)
1. Mass media – Marketing.   2. Mass media – Political aspects.
3. Democracy.   4. Freedom of the press.   I. Title.   II. Series.
P96.M36 B35 2001
302.23 – dc21                                          2001025498

ISBN   0 521 80435 3   hardback
ISBN   0 521 00977 4   paperback

For all journalists and all activists and all scholars
who work to make the mass media
better serve democracy

# Contents

# Preface

Conservatives in the United States often disagree over media policy. The conflict reflects a frequently observed division between a cultural, traditionalist conservatism and a pro-property, free-market libertarian strain. Many in the first group see the mass media as a leading force in the moral decay of American society. Bad taste is rampant. Portrayals of sex and violence are seen as possibly the two most ubiquitous features of the mass media. One conservative refrain, going back long before Vice-President Spiro Agnew characterized media executives as "pointy-headed liberals" and journalists as "nattering nabobs of negativism," sees the national media as deeply elitist and unjustifiably liberal.

From this traditionalist conservative perspective, the media needs reform. Somehow society – consumers or corporate executives or government – needs to restrict bad content. Of course, the word "censorship" is hardly popular, but at least such content should not receive government support – think of Senator Jesse Helms leading the charge to withdraw support from the National Endowment for the Arts for its support of vulgar performance art and from museums that exhibit obscene or sacrilegious art or the desire to gut the "liberal" Public Broadcasting Corporation. Moreover, objectionable content should be labeled. Even better, it should be removed, at least from all spaces easily accessible to children, a strategy that has received hesitant support from the Supreme Court, although the Court still maintains the principle that any such effort is unconstitutional if it operates to "reduce the adult population . . . to reading [or hearing or seeing] only what is fit for children," and the Court has resisted mandated cleanups of the Internet.[1] Maybe objectionable content should be subject to additional limits and maybe liability should be imposed for any harms caused.

Others on the right reject paternalism. Freedom is the key. Government should keep its hands off. Democracy and liberty both entail a free press. This pro-market, pro-property strand of conservatism arguably is central to the regime of deregulation that (with various, usually pro-industry, exceptions) has swept telecommunications and broadcasting both in the United States and globally during the past quarter century.

The left is equally conflicted – as well as in its usual state of disarray. Media are mostly owned by capitalists and the left instinctively *knows* that this creates a problem. Many on the left think it obvious that this ownership combined with other problems with markets makes a major contribution to why their message does not play more effectively in the public sphere. Moreover, unlike the libertarian right, the left is not in general burdened by any belief that freedom means uncritical support for private property and free markets. Thus, given their normative commitments and their empirical observations, many on the left conclude that intervention is needed. Nevertheless, in the media context, unlike other realms of social life – such as welfare, health care, labor policy, race policy, or the environment – the interventionist left is relatively unclear about what type of intervention is needed. This programmatic failure has a variety of causes. One problem is that many on the left have neither, for whatever reason, thought carefully enough about the nature of the problem with existing media nor related a program of reform to any carefully formulated normative ideals, such as an affirmative theory of democracy.

The interventionist left's lack of program may also reflect, in part, the influence of the other branch of the left. This other branch includes those who, in the media realm, are most offended by (and most fearful of) the censorious inclinations of cultural conservatives. These freedom-loving leftists, while unhappy with capital's ownership of the media and, in most arenas of social life, favorable toward egalitarian governmental interventions, are very hesitant to approve governmental interventions in this area. These leftists know that a free press and free speech must be part of their liberatory program – as Brandeis once put it, as both an end and a means.[2] They know that historically these freedoms have been crucial for the left in its struggle for equality and human dignity.[3] Inevitably, interventions will be censorious, controlled by those in power merely to maintain their cultural, economic, or political hegemony, or they will be ineffectual for whatever legitimate goals exist.

Although most readers will soon find it easy to see my political bias, there is something to be said for the viewpoints of each of the four groups. Both the cultural conservative and the interventionist leftist are right to see the media often doing harm or performing inadequately. Importantly, however, there is often room for disagreement about which media content is harm-causing, and certainly the reform programs of these two groups often differ. Likewise, the libertarian conservative and the freedom-loving leftist are right to want to protect press freedom. Here, however, a point of the interventionist leftist is well taken. Not only government but also capital can threaten press freedom. Or, more precisely, the market will not only fail to cure many inadequacies of the media but can also function in ways that reduce freedom. But this is getting way ahead of the story.

I do not directly enter into the debate between these four groups, although the extent of wisdom in each position should become clearer as the discussion proceeds. For me, and I expect for many readers, paternalism (sometimes) seems fine for children but very questionable for adults. Moreover, democracy is a basic norm that merits respect, and a *free press*, whatever that means, is surely a key element of democracy. The question of this book is, for one who accepts those premises, what does lack of paternalism and a commitment to democracy mean for media policy. Would a rejection of paternalism require the government to keep its hands off the media? Does a commitment to democracy require the same?

Part I of this book answers no to the first question, but in doing so it requires a close look at the economics of the media. Part II answers no to the second question, but the answer depends on the conception of democracy that a person accepts. If, however, I am right that both answers are no, what type of interventions are appropriate? Both Parts I and II offer some suggestions based on the economic and democratic theories described. Finally, Part III illustrates these themes by applying the earlier analyses to one issue, policies concerning international free trade in media products. I conclude with a claim about digital technologies and the Internet – that however much they transform the world, the issues and analyses of this book remain crucial for thinking about media policy.

This book is a revised, edited, and updated version of three articles published between 1997 and 2000: "Giving the Audience What It Wants," *Ohio State Law Journal* 58 (1997): 311; "The Media That Citizens Need,"

*University of Pennsylvania Law Review* 147 (1998): 317; and "An Economic Critique of Free Trade in Media Products," *North Carolina Law Review* 78 (2000): 1358. I received help and inspiration from a host of people, only some of whom I am now able to list, while writing the articles and then transforming them into this book. I especially want to thank Yochai Benkler, Jamie Boyle, Mike Fitts, Oscar Gandy, Lani Guinier, Fritz Kubler, Jason Johnston, Carlin Meyer, Gerry Neuman, Jim Pope, Margaret Jane Radin, and Carol Sanger. In addition, Michael Madow has been invaluable as a sounding board and reader of drafts, saving me from many factual and conceptual errors and trying to save me from others. Patisserie Claude and Les Deux Gamins have provided coffee and a welcome place in which much of this has been written. I have gained from the opportunity to present portions of the book in various venues, including workshops at either the law school or communications department of University of Chicago (2000), New York University (2000), Yale University (1999), Stanford University (1997), University of Pennsylvania (1995), and University of Oregon (1995). I have also benefited from being permitted to present portions of the argument at the Mass Communications Section of the Association of American Law Schools Annual Convention (1999, 2000); Conference: Prospects for Culture in a World of Trade (Canadian Consulate & NYU, 2000); Convention of the Union for Democratic Communications (1999); Commodification of Information Conference (Haifa, Israel, 1999); Cultural Environment Movement National Convention (Athens, Ohio, 1999); Symposium on American Values, Angelo State University (1998); Law and Society Annual Conference (Glasgow, 1996); luncheon seminar at the office of FCC Chairman Reed Hunt (1996); and Critical Legal Studies Conference (Washington, D.C., 1995).

## PART I

# Serving Audiences

Economics-minded critics of government intervention in the media realm raise a constant refrain: interventions are paternalistic and treat viewers as "helpless or obstinate."[1] Interventions assume that viewers are "incapable of wise choice."[2] A free society must treat audiences as perfectly able to know and choose what they want to read, watch, and listen to. Market incentives lead media producers to provide audiences with what they want.

In his classic article arguing for deregulation of broadcasting, former FCC chairman Mark Fowler explained that the government "should rely on the broadcasters' ability to determine the wants of their audiences through the normal mechanisms of the marketplace."[3] As with any other product, "[i]n the fully deregulated marketplace, the highest bidder would make the best and highest use of the resource."[4] Fowler summed up this view of the media with his famous remark that "television is just another appliance . . . a toaster with pictures."[5] Fowler's deregulatory perspective swept through policy-making circles in the United States. It became received wisdom in executive, legislative, and judicial branch thinking about media policy.[6] In the last decades of the twentieth century, deregulation of the media (and much else) became a global phenomenon. I argue here that this approach is fundamentally wrong.

My primary concern is with the creation and provision of media content. The pervasive antiregulatory refrain, however, has recently been equally loud in the related context of the infrastructure for delivering communication content.[7] It was overwhelmingly evident in the passage of the Telecommunications Act of 1996, adopted as an act "to promote competition and reduce regulation."[8] A virtually unquestioned market orientation was conspicuous. For example, the initial Senate

3

report described the bill's purpose as "to provide a pro-competitive, deregulatory national policy framework."[9] Senator Hollings' additional views emphasized that "competition is the best regulator of the marketplace." The only two dissenting senators did not disagree on this point. They observed that "[d]eregulation has a clear and consistent track record" but complained that, as reported out of committee, the deregulatory bill did "not go far enough" and did "not guarantee free and open markets."[10]

The chorus favoring deregulation within the media realm often repeats standard conservative defenses of free markets. Yet, in the context of the media, this view has added rhetorical appeal. First Amendment values lead even some interventionist liberals to reject government paternalism in respect to speech. Nevertheless, despite the lure of equating freedom of the press with free markets, constitutional law does not mandate such an equation.[11] Although the First Amendment ought to restrict purposeful suppression of speech, it should not and has not restricted structural interventions designed to improve the quality of the press.

Still, maybe critics of intervention are right to emphasize the strong antipaternalism aspect of the First Amendment. If interventions are paternalistic, if they attempt to displace readers', listeners', and viewers' own choices, then maybe interventions are contrary to basic First Amendment values. The critics argue that, in respect to media content, surely the government ought to let the public get what it wants – and this, the critics assert, means leaving the issue to the market.[12] An advocate of intervention might plausibly argue that people often do not know what they want or that they should receive what (someone else thinks) they need – government does this for children in the schools. Both positions have nuanced versions, but I put this debate aside. Rather, in Part I of this book I assume that people's choices ought to prevail but argue that this will not occur in an unregulated market. Thus, Part I critiques the underlying assumption of the market advocates' argument, namely, their claim that the market gives people the media they want.

Before beginning, however, I must make a confession. The first three chapters apply the most conventional of economic analyses. This is problematic on a number of grounds. For example, the key concept of the conventional analysis, "efficiency," is *inherently* indeterminate in the policy context of choosing legal rules.[13] In a conventional analysis, determining the efficient rule or policy depends on assuming some distribution of wealth and some set of preferences. The economist's normal approach of assuming the existing distribution of wealth is conceptually unavailable when the content of the existing distribution is precisely what the choice of a legal rule or policy places at issue. The choice of a rule (or a disposition of a legal dispute) affects the parties' wealth and, often, influences people's preferences toward favored or approved options. Thus, as a positivist analysis, typical versions of law and economic methodologies are systematically incomplete; the efficiency criterion is often indeterminate. In contrast to the overt inadequacy of this law and economics analysis as positivist theory, a positivist class-based theoretical addition makes for potential descriptive completeness. When alternative results would both be "efficient," the class-based theory could predict that the law will choose the solution that adds to the ruling economic class's wealth or power. Likewise, a normative egalitarian theory would also be determinant, but would recommend the opposite. Analytically, however, law and economic analysts effectively adopt the ruling-class orientation when they assume, as a starting point of analysis, that value is determined by a person's "willingness to pay" with the wealth she has available absent the contested rule. In contrast, the poor would be comparatively favored if the analysis adopted as its criterion of value the amount a person would require before selling a benefit if it were supposed that she initially held it. This second starting point would proportionately increase the wealth of the poor more than the rich, making it possible for her to value the item more. For example, a poor person might be able to pay only $500 for a potentially life-saving operation for which a rich person would, if necessary, pay a million dollars. If, however, both had an initial right to these medical services, the amount they would require before giving up the right might be virtually the same. That is, given an efficiency goal of trying to locate a right or benefit in the hands of the person who values it the most, the first criterion favors the rich by making it seem that she values the matter at issue the most while the second comparatively favors the poor (but not as much as would an egalitarian standard).

None of the foregoing denies, and this book implicitly assumes, that welfare economics can be extraordinarily useful in examining relevant aspects of the legal order. On the other hand, this economic analysis can be equally dangerous to the extent it dominates consideration of legal issues. The analysis's linguistic commodification of all valued elements of human existence may contribute to making such commodification intellectually and socially acceptable. As Chapter 4 observes, human flourishing requires many elements of life to remain uncommodified.[14] The analysis's reductionist orientation regularly treats as assumptions particular answers to precisely the issues most in dispute.

Different methodologies are essentially different languages. Although the same question can be approached and the same "best" answer can often be reached using different languages, the different languages vary in their ability to shed light. No single language can do all that others do even if a given insight is seldom (if ever) available in only one language. A particular language may be out of place in a particular context. Each is a tool and should be used to the extent it is useful; while it makes some things clearer, it is likely to obscure other important matters. The danger of hegemony arises when a particular language either implicitly or explicitly claims to be the only way to reach insight.

Probably the most important issues the legal order faces today are normative; they relate to proper distributions of wealth and power and to what preferences or values should prevail in various contexts. These issues are inevitably seriously contested and the perspectives that different groups bring to bear on them differ, often profoundly. The methodologies that are often most important for responding to these contested issues – and hence methodologies that should be at the core of any policy-oriented education – are ones that aid in seeing different perspectives and that aid in the self-reflective development of these perspectives. If the reductive allure of economic problem solving causes neglect of these more difficult methodologies, we are all losers.

Despite these reservations, Part I is relentlessly economic in analyzing the capacity of markets to give people the media they want. In part, this emphasis is valuable because of the clarity it casts on numerous important issues of media policy. Because my conclusions diverge from those that many free-market advocates believe economics recommends, I hope this approach is also useful in speaking directly to defenders of the market on their own turf.

## CHAPTER 1

# Not Toasters: The Special Nature of
# Media Products

Economics-oriented critics of government intervention in the media realm typically rely on oversimplified economics. Under certain purportedly normal circumstances, the market provides firms with an incentive to produce and sell the product as long as the product's cost (e.g., its cost of production and distribution) is less than the purchaser will pay, that is, as long as marginal costs are less than marginal price. The market thereby leads to a preference-maximizing production and distribution. This I call the "standard model."

The standard model is subject to a host of general critiques mostly related to why the market will fail or will be dysfunctional.[1] As one example of the latter, note that market competition creates an incentive for a market enterprise (e.g., capital holders) *to gain power* in relation to other resource owners (e.g., labor or other competitors) as much as it creates an incentive *to produce goods efficiently*. The power struggles between stakeholders, however, are primarily over distribution and do not produce any goods. As such, they waste resources as well as often generating unjust distributions.[2]

Of course, no one ever claims that the market works perfectly. Still, despite its problems, many find the standard model relatively adequate, at least enough so that it provides a presumptive reason to rely on "free" markets. For present purposes, I assume that the market *generally* works relatively well – for example, it effectively and efficiently leads to roughly the right production and distribution of cars or can openers. My claim is that, whatever the validity of general critiques of the market, the standard model applies especially badly to media products.

The standard model's persuasiveness depends on the following assumptions. (1) Products are sold in competitive markets and are sold at their marginal cost. (This will mean that their market price will equal their marginal cost, which will equal their average cost, which implicitly requires that at this point their marginal cost is rising.) (2) Product's production and normal use create relatively few serious externalities (i.e., relatively few major benefits not captured by or costs not imposed on the seller-producer). (3) The most significant policy concern is satisfying market-expressed preferences.

Even if these assumptions are true enough in general, my claim is that they do not apply so well to certain categories of products of which the media are an example. Media products are unlike the hypothesized "typical" product, such as a car or can opener, in four ways that are relevant here. Each difference complicates any economic claim concerning the wisdom of reliance on markets.

## FOUR FEATURES OF COMMUNICATION PRODUCTS

First, media products have significant "public good" aspects. A public good is an item for which one person's use of or benefit from the product does not affect its use by or benefit to another person. National defense or public parks are goods that, once provided, many can use without interfering with others' use.[3] Similarly, many can watch the same broadcast or read the same poem once it is created. Economic definitions of "public good" usually emphasize two aspects: "nonrivalrous use," which is the aspect that I am primarily concerned with here, and "nonexcludability."[4] Typically, utilities or other "natural" monopolies exhibit this "nonrivalrous use" public-good quality in their infrastructure, for example, in the gas lines, water mains, or telephone lines (other than the final connection to the house). Multiple consumers can use this infrastructure with no or very modest extra expense. To the extent that adding an additional customer does not increase the cost of this infrastructure, which is usually true until crowding requires larger lines or mains, the infrastructure exists as a public good. If this infrastructure is a major part of the delivered product's cost, the marginal cost of serving that additional consumer will predictably be substantially less than the average cost. That is, the marginal cost of supplying the new user could approach zero while the average cost of the infrastructure to each user, that is, its total cost divided by the number of users, stays much higher.

This situation creates a problem. If the product is priced at its average cost (or priced higher if a seller exercises monopoly power), some consumers will be unwilling (or unable) to pay that price, even though they want the products and would be willing to pay the added cost created by their usage. Charging the average cost results in underproduction. On the other hand, charging the marginal cost, as efficiency considerations normally recommend, fails to produce enough revenue (selling price times the number of purchasers) to cover the product's cost. The market will not support production if the seller must provide the product or service to all customers at the marginal cost of supplying the last customer. At that price, the seller would not recover the cost of the required infrastructure.

To gather, write, and edit news or to create and produce video entertainment, the media incur huge "first-copy costs." This economically significant element of media products' cost is like the utility's infrastructure or, better, is like national defense. There is no limit to how many can benefit from the producer's expenditure on first-copy costs or analogous costs, such as the expense of broadcasting.* Writing the story or sending out the broadcast signal costs the same no matter how many people "tune in." Adding a marginal consumer does not affect these costs. As long as these public-good costs are a large enough part of the media's total cost,[5] charging potential audience members the average cost leads to inefficient exclusions. Charging the average cost excludes people who would pay more for the story or broadcast than it actually costs to include them among the recipients. Alternatively, setting the price at the marginal cost, that is, the cost of supplying it to

---

* Economists often identify this factor as the cause of the current dominance of one-newspaper towns. A monopoly newspaper pays only one set of first-copy costs (and requires a single infrastructure) in serving the whole city. By adding customers, it constantly reduces its average cost. See James N. Rosse & James N. Dertouzos, *Economic Issues in Mass Communication Industries* (Stanford: Department of Economics, Stanford U., 1978), 55–78. Any competitive equilibrium would be unstable, usually requiring two papers roughly equal in circulation. See Randolph E. Bucklin et al., "Games of Survival in the US Newspaper Industry," *Applied Economics* 21 (1989): 631, 636. Despite this theoretical account, until a long-term decline began just before the end of the nineteenth century, competition generally prevailed among local daily newspapers. Thus, Rosse more precisely suggests that the "fundamental long-run cause of newspaper failure is loss of effective market segmentation." James E. Rosse, "The Decline of Direct Newspaper Competition," *Journal of Communications* 30 (1980): 65, 67. Although Rosse does not explain this loss, the decline in effective segmentation could result from the changed incentives that occur when advertisers become the primary purchaser of newspapers' efforts – that is, as they become the paper's primary source of revenue and profit. To the extent that daily newspapers' primary product becomes readers sold to advertisers rather than product sold to readers, the main product differentiation for daily newspapers selling to mostly local advertisers will be geographically rather than content based. See C. Edwin Baker, *Advertising and a Democratic Press* (Princeton: Princeton U. Press, 1994), ch. 1.

the last purchaser, creates insufficient incentives to produce the media product.

Firms sometimes avoid these consequences by engaging in "price discrimination" – charging different purchasers different prices and thereby tapping the "consumer surplus" that some consumers would receive if they were charged only the marginal costs. Whether there are sufficient opportunities for price discrimination to lead to a value-maximizing level of production (hopefully without producing monopoly profits) is an empirical matter that will vary with the product and market in question. I assume in much of the discussion that follows that providers of media products cannot uniformly engage in sufficient price discrimination to eliminate this problem. Moreover, even when reasonably adequate levels of production could be achieved because of the availability of relatively costless price discrimination, price discrimination introduces an additional policy-based fairness issue. When and why should some consumers have to pay more than others for the same good, thereby reducing or eliminating their potential "consumer surplus," in order to achieve distribution to others who willingly pay the marginal cost but would not pay the higher price necessary to cover infrastructure or first-copy costs? This is a central issue in many rate-setting disputes. It can obviously also raise controversial issues in the media context – for example, was it fair for an early Congress to charge some mail users a price higher than the cost of serving them in order to subsidize the cost of communication for other users, namely newspapers?

Second, media products often produce extraordinarily significant positive and negative externalities. Externalities typically refer to the value some item has to someone who does not participate in the transaction. If one or more persons, often numerous unorganized people, would potentially pay to have the transaction occur, then the externality is positive; it is negative if they would potentially pay to have it not occur. For example, people care whether their reputation is ruined or advanced, whether people they meet are boring or cultured, and whether they are murdered or aided by the person they pass on the street – and these are among the phenomena whose occurrence can be significantly influenced by *other people's* media consumption. Likewise, many people value a well-functioning democracy. They are affected by whether the country goes to war, establishes parks, or provides for retirement and medical care – and hence can be greatly benefited by other people's consumption of quality media or harmed by others' ignorance or apathy produced by inadequate consumption or consumption of misleading, distortive, and demobilizing media. Furthermore, the political or corporate corruption that the threat of media exposure deters is a benefit that the press cannot effectively capture – there is no story – to sell to consumers. In each case, people other than the direct media consumers would pay if necessary to have the beneficial effect occur or to avoid the harmful effects. Later I suggest that many media policies, ranging from libel laws to reporters' privileges or postal subsidies given to newspapers or direct grants for public broadcasting – and much, much more – can be understood as in part designed to increase positive or to reduce negative externalities.

Third, media products are unusual in that often two very different purchasers pay for the transfer of media content to its audience. The media enterprise commonly sells media products to audiences and sells audiences to advertisers. Of course, multiple parties being "affected" by a transaction, each thus being a potential but often not an actual payee or purchaser, is not an unusual phenomenon – that basically defines an "externality." However, in the media context this multiple set of purchasers represents not merely potential purchasers; and the payment from advertisers in return for what is sold or delivered to audiences plays an unusually large and relatively routinized role. Selling to both audiences and advertisers has especially significant consequences and adds special complexities. For example, what is the right level of production of television programming? The "value" of a television broadcast is its combined value for the audience and the advertiser – in economic terms, the amount they would be willing to pay. To the extent that the broadcaster only collects from the advertiser, the broadcaster apparently receives an inadequate incentive to spend money on programming. From this observation, some economists conclude that our society drastically underinvests in television broadcasting.[6]

Having multiple purchasers creates other issues. For example, advertisers in effect pay the media firm to gain an audience by providing the audience with something the audience wants, although not necessarily what the audience most wants. A portion of the advertisers' payment often goes to having the editorial content better reflect the advertisers' interests. There is a potential conflict between advertisers' and audiences' interests in the media content.[7] A century ago many papers routinely accepted "reading matter," material prepared by advertisers that promoted their products (or sometimes their political goals) but that was not identified as advertising. Advertisers wanted this material presented as if it were editorial content, not advertising, while (presumably) the public would have preferred identification of the source. Typically the public wants and expects the news and editorial content in the news media to embody the journalists' and editors' independent professional judgment. The market brings this audience interest to bear on the journalistic enterprise to the extent that the enterprise can better sell its publication if it gains a reputation for independence. However, in the case of "reading matter," the market did not suffice to induce source identification or to create journalistic independence. In 1912 Congress responded by prohibiting the practice for any paper receiving second-class mail privileges.[8]

A fourth aspect of the media relevant to media economics involves why or how audiences value media products. In the standard economic model just presented, people seek products that satisfy various existing preferences. When people purchase media products – as when they seek education or advice from psychological, legal, or spiritual advisors – they are often seeking information or guidance for the very purpose of forming preferences. People often want a media product for what I call "edification," which includes education, exposure to wisely selected information, or wise opinion and good argument. This feature of media is difficult to embody fully within the terms of standard economic analysis. Even if a market can properly allocate resources to fulfill preferences for preference formation activities, a market for this type of product will have unusual features. When a person wants to develop "better" preferences, values, or outlooks, she puts her present outlook or preferences into question without a clearly formulated alternative to put in their place. Thus, her own preferences do not give her a complete standard by which to measure whether her purchases provide the right thing. Her preference might well be to choose a context in which she expects to get the best guidance – a context that may or may not be consistent with market purchases.

This dilemma is not entirely resolvable. How does a person know whether the person she became after seeing the psychologist is who she wants to be or whether her changes would have been better with a different psychologist? Furthermore, from what perspective does she evaluate – from the views she now has, those she had earlier when she chose the psychologist, or the views she would have had if she had chosen a different psychologist? The answers may very well not be the same, so which perspective should she privilege? Of course, even when people do not know precisely what they want, they can still have rules of thumb for guessing whether they are likely to get it. They may know the seller's or producer's general reputation for expertise. In addition, they may have reasons to presume the seller or producer exercises independent judgment and to believe that this supplier uses this independence to try to serve the purchaser's interests – reasons purportedly underwritten by professionalism in education, law, psychology, or the priesthood. These concerns provide a catalyst for the press to portray itself as independent and an explanation for most people's outrage at any evidence that advertisers influence media's editorial content. In addition, some people may also use as a rule of thumb indications that the seller shares or, at least, has familiarity with and responsiveness to the purchaser's basic values or perspectives. This sharing supports the hope that she will receive desirable guidance in formulating new preferences and values. In the media context, this might lead to preference for media with a particular partisanship. Moreover, one response that a person could rationally choose is to have society (government) create nonmarket methods of providing these edifying products.

Finally, people value media products for various reasons. Audiences want media products (sometimes the same media product) for entertainment or for specific information, as well as for "edification." Attributes that make a media product good for one purpose may not be those that make it good for another. This diversity in functions introduces complications for the notion of the audience getting what it wants, complications that are often exacerbated due to the multiple purchasers – audiences and advertisers. Audience members' knowledge about how well a media product serves differing purposes often varies. Advertisers, on the other hand, may wish to control – or have a veto over – particular attributes. For example, an advertiser may be interested in a movie's or story's transformative and informative roles, especially the product's slant and its capacity to persuade on issues related to the advertiser's corporate interests. In contrast, the audience may evaluate the media content mostly in terms of its potential to entertain. This focus might make some sense if the audience is best situated to evaluate this characteristic. In consequence, the advertiser may pay for, say, a pro-Pepsi informational slant, about which the audience is unaware or unconcerned as long as the slant does not affect the movie's entertainment value. Thus, predictably, advertisers pay for "product placements" where their products are presented within the apparently nonadvertising content.

More generally, when content serves multiple functions to different degrees but where the audience members' ability to assess its contribution varies from one function to another, a person is likely to choose on the basis of functions about which her ability to assess its contribution is better. In this circumstance, the market creates increased opportunities for manipulative or ideologically distorted content. If the audience values both the media's entertainment and edification roles strongly, but if information in respect to a program's contribution to edification is harder to obtain or evaluate, the audience may choose a media product on the basis of its entertainment value in the hope that the different dimensions correlate. This audience strategy reduces the cost to the advertiser in having its editorial choices prevail. For example, tobacco companies might "pay" (i.e., threaten to withdraw advertising) for the editorial slant they wanted in popular women's magazines – no negative stories about smoking. Their capacity to pursue this strategy increases if the slant did not overly influence the magazine's fulfilling the role most easily and actively evaluated by the audience. However, such payment is, in effect, censorship.

The point is merely that the combination of multiple purchasers (audience plus advertiser) creates multiple allegiances. Influence tends to flow in particular directions – toward the larger purchaser, the purchaser with greater knowledge of how well the media are serving its interests, and the purchaser whose purchase is most sensitive to how well the media serve its interest in relation to the specific issue in question. Having an audience that values the product in multiple ways but with different degrees of knowledge about how well it performs each is a context that enhances the opportunity for the other purchaser, the advertiser, to influence content away from what the audience wants in the dimensions about which the audience finds knowledge most difficult to obtain.

In sum, each of these four special features of media products can lead to results contrary to what the audience wants – what it would pay for. The next three chapters more carefully examine these features in terms of how they often lead the market to deny the audience what it wants or, in economic terms, lead to inefficient use of resources.

## COPYRIGHT: AN ILLUSTRATION

Drawing out policy implications of these four attributes of communicative products could explain much of copyright law. I do not attempt that here, but some examination of how copyright responds to these attributes is useful later on and serves as an illustration of some of their implication.

Once produced, media content is a public good. No one's consumption (e.g., reading, viewing, discussing) prevents anyone else from consuming the same content. Maximum value results from allowing consumption without charge for the content, although a consumer should pay for any marginal cost involved in access. The problem is that if content were *freely* appropriatable by any consumer, although this pricing (i.e., a zero price) would not exclude any audience members who value the content, this regime would provide no economic incentive for creation and would fail to encourage production.

Enter the regime of intellectual property, probably the most overt legal response to the public-good aspect of media content. Copyright law creates private property rights in content so that authors and creators will receive a reward adequate to induce production. Complexities of copyright law are (or, at least, are supposed to be) a response to its utilitarian aim of influencing both production and distribution in a manner that maximizes the availability and valued use of intellectual content. The Constitution gives Congress the power to grant rights in intellectual creations not in order to recognize some asserted natural right of authorship but in order "to promote the Progress of Science and useful Arts."[9] Copyright properly aims to recognize private property rights only to the extent that they "contribute" more to production of valuable content than they "cost" in terms of restricting access to and use of that content. This goal explains, at least in part, copyright doctrines such as "fair use." Ideally, fair use benefits audiences by allowing free use whenever free use adds more value than it "costs" in terms of reduced incentives to create and distribute. Similar economic balancing of gains and losses due to propertizing intellectual content can explain why copyright only attempts to protect the "unique expression" of the idea and not the idea (or fact) itself.

Thus, arguably, copyright's maximizing policy is relatively nonideological in merely aiming to efficiently promote "science and the useful arts," that is, to make more content more widely available. On closer examination, however, it turns out to be significantly more complicated.

Specifics of copyright law favor the production of some types and some ways of producing content over others and affect who has access to it. Whether copyright favors creating and distributing the content that society most values – whether it maximizes value – is often unclear. The question involves all the problems discussed in this and the next two chapters. Despite the standard economic argument for intellectual property rights, economic arguments opposed to all restrictive rights and in favor of zero pricing are imaginable and, depending on circumstantially variable empirical factors and people's values, could be persuasive. Much commercial production of content would continue without legal protection of intellectual property rights. Moreover, the commercial production for which copyright provides an incentive, that is, production for profit, competes to a degree with noncommercially produced content (e.g., ideological speech that people spread for political reasons or amateur productions where the joy or pride of expression provides a primary motive for production). Possibly, the absence of copyright, by dispensing with the advantage it gives commercial production, would encourage a culture in which noncommercial communications were more dominant. The policy issue is whether this culture would by any relevant measures be richer than the existing commercial culture created by the mass media. The problem is how to compare and evaluate the worlds that would be produced by the alternative legal regimes.[10] That problem, in fact, is the general issue of the next three chapters.

Different content creators line up on both sides of a debate about extending or limiting copyright protection. All creative works borrow from potentially copyrighted past creations. Often noncommercial creative "borrowers" favor less restrictions on their partial appropriations, whereas most commercial producers favor greater protection in order to maximize their return on content they own.[11] Still, because a prime role of copyright is to create effective distribution channels, sometimes even audience-oriented, non-profit-seeking creators have an interest in a commercially effective copyright. A writer or advocate may be personally unconcerned with economic rewards, wanting to make her creation maximally available out of a desire for influence or fame, but still want an effective copyright in order to induce a publisher or distributor to make her work available.

Copyright not only favors commercialization but also tilts production toward particular types of content. First Amendment lawyers will recognize this as troublesome. Copyright is a speech-related law that involves content discrimination.[†] Here, however, I want to examine the bias in terms of the policy issues that copyright's lack of neutrality raises. Existing copyright law allows privatization of only some aspects of content. It covers, for example, only the "unique expression," not facts or ideas. If privatization serves its intended purpose of creating production incentives, this coverage means that copyright directly encourages investment in creating and distributing "unique expressions" while only incidentally and presumably less effectively encouraging investment in uncovering, developing, or communicating "facts or ideas" (although, admittedly, patent and trade-secret law encourage investment in developing some commercially relevant categories of new information). This bias is potentially dramatic. For example, the distinction could encourage greater investment in unique entertainment content (expression) and less investment in news content (facts). Of course, other factors may be more central, but this bias is illustrated by media expenditures. In 1995, the annual newsroom budget of the *Washington Post*, the paper that brought us Watergate, was reportedly about $70 million, while the quite forgettable 1995 movie, *Waterworld*, reportedly cost about $175 million, although this figure includes more than just content creation (e.g., an approximately $30 million marketing budget).[12]

Even within news production, copyright rules influence expenditures. They favor unique or flashy presentation as opposed to expenditures on gathering hard news, especially news that is expensive to obtain. It should not be surprising that market competition leads television stations to advertise the images of, and pay high salaries to, appealing "anchorpersons." These personalities, like the copyrightable words, are a "unique" element that an owner can exploit commercially.

[†] The Supreme Court claims to invalidate most content discriminations involving protected speech content. But see C. Edwin Baker, "Turner Broadcasting: Content Regulation of Persons and Presses," *Supreme Court Review* (1994): 54. Whether copyright is a content-based regulation is an issue that has troubled some commentators. The best formulation is Brennan's. He claims that the traditional approach is: "any restriction on speech, the application of which turns on the content of the speech, is a content-based restriction." *Boos v. Barry*, 485 U.S. 312, 335–36 (Brennan and Marshall, concurring in part and concurring in the judgment). Obviously, one cannot know whether a writing violates another's copyright without looking at its content. Thus, copyright rules are content-discriminatory on their face. Even if that were not recognized, clearly copyright's purpose is to protect the copyrighted content and thereby to favor creation of such content over any content whose value copyright does not protect (or content whose creation copyright prohibits absent permission by some copyright holder). And the Supreme Court treats facially content-neutral laws as content-based if the law has any purpose to affect content. See *Turner Broadcasting System v. FCC*, 512 U.S. 622, 642–43 (1994).

Then, as newscasters' salaries increase, the networks fire senior professionals and generally engage in cutting the costs of news production.[13]
And this bias favoring anchor personalities has additional consequences. James Fallows has forcefully attacked the deleterious effect on
democracy of the media's constant cynical emphasis on the competitive, horse-race aspects of politics rather than on its substantive aspects.
He concludes that having a star personality "report" on the top current
story twists the content of news in a way that contributes to this misdirected media focus because, usually, this star figure does not have
expertise or reportorial knowledge of the specific issue but has general
expertise on issues such as how the issue will play politically.[14]

Although 40 percent of viewers report that the anchorperson is their
reason for viewing a particular network news program,[15] that does not
necessarily mean that the bias toward expenditures on anchorpersons
rather than news represents audience preferences, much less that a
democratic society would self-consciously choose to promote this tilt.
Rather their report may result from competitive factors created by the
existing legal and market structure. First, the anchorperson may be their
reason for choosing among programs, not their reason for watching
the news. As for it being a determinative factor in that choice, this
may reflect the extent of broadcaster expenditures both on making
this element appealing and on advertising to promote viewer interest in
this element. These broadcaster efforts may, in turn, make "economic"
sense. Anchorperson personalities and their expressive delivery, not
facts and ideas that other stations can freely appropriate, are the station's
unique goods. The station or network's exclusive position in respect to
a given anchorperson gives it a reason to promote the merits or appeal
of its anchor as a reason to "tune in." This incentive replicates the pecu-
liarities of the legal order's privatization rules. Unsurprisingly, systems
operating under different copyright rules, as well as systems where
broadcasters are less driven by market pursuit of profit, are likely to
make very different choices of what type of content – anchor personality or informative factual material – to emphasize and to spend money
on creating.

Privatizing facts or ideas in order to encourage their discovery or
development is hardly an appropriate corrective. Although in special
circumstances this is arguably acceptable (e.g., with patents, although
here only certain commercial uses are privatized), generally most people
rightly see ownership of ideas and facts as offensive. Because a person
comes up with an idea or uncovers facts hardly suggests that she should

be able to stop another from independently doing the same and then telling others about it. Even when the second person learns something from the originator, the notion that she cannot then repeat it, or reformulate it and then include it in her own messages, is contrary to how thinking and discussion occur and contrary to how cultures develop. Granting the originator control over "copying" and repetition gives her a virtual property right in the recipient's mind and speech. Of course, a person may agree or contract to keep a confidence. The default rule, however, is and should be that repetition is limited only by discretion, not by law.[16] Economic arguments, ranging from avoiding enforcement costs to reducing transaction costs in making efficient use of information, also argue against routine privatization of facts and ideas.

Various responses by media entities or government can reduce the negative consequences and underproduction related to lack of copyright protection for facts and ideas. The media may successfully nurture desires for speedy news and, more important, for reliable news. They may be able to teach audiences to correlate these attributes with news organizations that themselves engage in (some) investigations. This process of individualization of media entities would give these entities some incentive to spend money on finding facts and developing ideas. Or the government (and others) could heavily subsidize development of desired information and ideas, which then could be communicated by the media. Government-supported research universities, prestige-based reward systems within those universities, direct government sponsorship of research, and noncopyrightability of governmentally produced intellectual works serve as examples. Public officials' news conferences and press releases, and similar techniques used by various private sources, create and make available considerable information without concern for the lack of copyright protection – although with obvious, questionable content tilts.[17]

Still, the basic points remain. Communications can often be cheaply provided for everyone after being originally produced, but this provides insufficient incentives for production. The intellectual property regime responds to this problem but inefficiently restricts access. It also encourages production of some content more than other. Responses to differential underproduction provide only partial cures, and the cures contain their own tilts. Inevitably, the audience gets what the law encourages, not some "uncontaminated" version of what it wants. No "free market" could provide otherwise.

CHAPTER 2

# Public Goods and Monopolistic Competition

## PRODUCTION OF A PUBLIC GOOD

As discussed in Chapter 1, copyright is a form of propertization in the economically peculiar realm of communications. Propertization of traditional commons, for example, where sheep or cattle grazed, supposedly solved problems of overuse leading to subsequent underproduction. Owners have an incentive to husband their property to create maximum value. Copyright, however, cannot be expected to be such a perfect solution precisely because of the public-goods aspect of media content. At least without adequate price discrimination, market-based firms predictably provide inadequate amounts of those goods whose use is nonrivalrous. Private firms will not provide some media content that an audience wants – content whose value as measured by willingness to pay is greater than its cost. In these cases, no price exists at which the media product can be profitably sold even though its value to potential consumers is greater than the cost of supplying them. Another routine feature of such goods is underproduction. In order to cover the cost of a media product, it must be sold at a price that prevents some people from purchasing, even though they would be willing to pay at least the marginal cost necessary to provide them with the media content.

A simple example based on three hypothetical media products in a two-person society, summarized in Table 2.1, can illustrate these problems. For each product, the cost of producing the first copy is assumed to be 10, while reproducing and distributing a copy to person B has a minimal cost, here assumed to be 1. Then I assume three different demand functions. With the first, the product could be produced and sold to each person for 6. Even here, if a third person was added who

Table 2.1

|  | Cost | Demand[a] | | |
|---|---|---|---|---|
|  |  | Product 1 | Product 2 | Product 3 |
| Copy 1/person A | 10 | $9^b$ | $12^b$ | 9 |
| Copy 2/person B | 1 | $6^b$ | 5 | 5 |
| Profitable selling price |  | 5½ to 6 | 10 to 12 | — |
| Surplus (value-cost) |  | $15 - 11 = 4$ | $12 - 10 = 2$ | — |
| Potential surplus |  | $15 - 11 = 4$ | $17 - 11 = 6$ | $14 - 11 = 3$ |

[a] Hypothetical product 1 shows a *successfully marketed* declining marginal cost product; 2 shows that markets may *underproduce or distribute* this type of product; and 3 shows that markets may *fail to produce* a valued product.
[b] Purchasers at the profit maximizing selling price; hypothetical assumes seller's inability (or inadequate ability) to price discriminate.

valued the good at 2, the producer seller could not afford to sell to each person for 2. That is, in a free market, the producer would not supply the third person even though she values the product at more than the cost of supplying her.

In the second hypothetical, the good could be sold to person A at a price between 10 and 12. Production at this level produces a societal gain, a surplus of 2, which, depending on the selling price, goes either to the seller or buyer or is divided between them. This surplus represents the amount that the good is valued by the buyer over the cost to the seller. However, the good cannot be sold to both persons at a price of 5 each because then the seller's total revenue, 10, does not cover the cost of two copies ($10 + 1 = 11$). Since the value, 5, of the good to the unserved person B is much greater than the cost of producing it for her, 1, the result is underproduction – a failure to distribute the product to this second person.

In the third hypothetical, the media product cannot be sold at all without a loss. Person A would only pay 9 for a good that cost 10. Selling to both parties at a price of 5 would generate revenue of 10, which would not cover the cost, 11, of supplying the two persons. However, production for and distribution to both persons could produce a social gain. It would produce what people want – a value of 14 at a cost of 11 – but the market is unable to arrive at this result. In the real world, instances taking the form of each of the three hypotheticals can be expected to be common. Thus, both inefficient underproduction and inefficient nonproduction of media content are inevitable.

Nonproduction, underproduction, and inadequate distribution of media content might be avoided if owners could perfectly price discriminate. Price discrimination is where the seller sells to different purchasers at different prices reflecting the amount that the specific purchaser is willing to pay. For example, in the third hypothetical, if the seller could sell copy 1 to person 1 for 9 and copy 2 to person 2 for 5, the seller would have an incentive to produce the good – it would be able to generate a profit of 3. This solution is sometimes available. Some degree of price discrimination is common in the media realm. Consider, for example, media firms' ability to sell both hard and paperback books, often made available at different times; to distribute video content through different "windows," first in theaters, then pay television, then video cassette rental, then free television; or to divide the audience into groups who will pay different subscription rates for the same magazine. Still, often *inability* to price discriminate is desirable. In the standard model of market competition discussed earlier, price discrimination is not necessary to achieve efficient results. Rather, it merely involves a seller's exploitation of its monopolistic position to transfer wealth from purchasers to itself. More relevant here, price discrimination inevitably is only partially effective. In the media context, the problems of underproduction and inadequate distribution will inevitably continue even if some degree of price discrimination reduces the problem. Thus, intellectual property as a form of ownership combined with reliance on markets, given the public-good quality of media content, cannot be expected to stimulate adequate production.

## MONOPOLISTIC COMPETITION[1]

The preceding section described how media firms are sometimes unable to profitably market a media product even though the product's value to consumers is greater than its cost to the firm. There is a crucially important wrinkle. The introduction of a competitively successful product can exacerbate the problem, leading consumers (the audience) to get even less of what they want. Sometimes the new product that prevails competitively can reduce social value as compared with the product(s) that it replaces. When this happens, market competition itself increases inefficiency.

Table 2.2

|  |  | Product A | | | Product B |
|  | Cost | Demand at Time 1 | Demand at Time 2 | Cost | Demand at Time 2 |
| --- | --- | --- | --- | --- | --- |
| Copy 1/person 1 | 10 | 9[a] | 9 | 11 | 8[a] |
| Copy 2/person 2 | 1 | 6[a] | 5 | 2 | 7[a] |
| Profitable selling price |  | $5\frac{1}{2}$ to 6 | — |  | $6\frac{1}{2}$ to 7 |
| Surplus (value-cost) |  | $15 - 11 = 4$ | — |  | $15 - 13 = 2$ |
| Potential surplus |  | $15 - 11 = 4$ | $14 - 11 = 3$ |  | $15 - 13 = 2$ |

*Note:* Introduction of product B has the effect of slightly reducing the demand for product A, reflected in the change in demand from time 1 to time 2.
[a] Purchases under a profitable sales strategy; hypothetical assumes seller's inability (or inadequate ability) to price-discriminate.

A simple example, summarized in Table 2.2 and expanding on the illustration used earlier, illustrates this possibility. This hypothetical assumes the new product B – for example, a newspaper with additional sections desired by person 2 but without the biting or partisan content especially liked by person 1 – is somewhat bulky, explaining its some-what higher cost for copy 2 as compared with copy 2 of the old product A. This new product more equally satisfies the preferences of the two people, being more liked by person 2 and less liked by person 1 (i.e., it has a flatter demand curve). For present purposes, the key feature of this hypothetical is that the availability of the new product B reduces slightly the demand for product A. This effect is obviously quite plausible. This change in demand could, and in the hypothetical it does, make producing and selling product A no longer profitable *even though* product A is *still* valued by its audience at an amount more than its cost. Most troubling, production and distribution of product A would still create a greater social surplus than does product B *even though* product B replaces it in a competitive market.

This is merely a hypothetical. Obviously people are not always worse off when a new media product drives out of existence another inferior or more expensive product or set of such products. The general point here is that there is no way of knowing in the abstract when relying on the market will be beneficial – when the market will enable consumers to get closer to what they want as they see it. Specifically, market success does not show that people are better off, as they see it, with the new product. Which product is better depends on the specifics of demand curves. Still, some observations are indicative of when it is more or less likely that the product that prevails in the market actually frustrates people's desires. For example, although I do not try to offer an economic proof here, it can be shown that usually the competitively successful but economically unjustified material will have relatively uniform but broad appeal – a comparatively flat demand curve. In contrast, the economically justified, audience-satisfying material that a free market fails to produce often is material with relatively strong, unique appeal – creating a more steeply declining demand curve.

Most often the negative effects of monopolistic competition described here is embodied in the nonexistence (or reduced distribution) of some media products that the audience wants. In these circumstances, the net effects of market competition is to reduce audience satisfaction. Consequences also include reduced media pluralism and, often, reduced responsiveness to minority tastes – a reduction not justified on economic (i.e., willingness to pay) grounds. This effect is further examined in Part III in the context of international trade. Here, I examine this effect in combination with an additional feature of most media markets – advertising support of media.

### ADVERTISING-SUPPORTED MEDIA[2]

Introduction of advertisers adds a second set of purchasers whose preferences for media content at least potentially diverge from that of the media's audience. Although people often want access to advertising[3] and although advertising lowers the price of media products to consumers, advertising has additional, more negative consequences. Often advertisers want different editorial content than do readers or viewers, and their impact on which media prevail can conflict with preferences of the public. Most commentators, including many economists,[4] believe that the proper role of the press is to provide editorial content that responds to the interests of the public, not the public plus advertisers. However, even if the relevant standard is maximizing value from the combined perspective of the preferences of audiences and advertisers (as pure economic theory presumably suggests), the result produced by the market may not be economically efficient. More relevant here, it may not give the audience what it wants (which is a

24

combination of low prices and desired content). The basic claim developed here is that the prevailing advertiser-supported media may be like product B in Table 2.2. It may drive out the more valued media content, as illustrated by the change between time 1 and time 2 in respect to product A.

Initially, note that the most optimistic scenario is implausible. This pollyannaish account suggests that advertisers merely contribute financial support to give audiences what they want (plus ads, which they also often want). True, advertisers' concerns and audiences' preferences will overlap because advertisers want to obtain audiences for their advertising messages. That, however, is only one of the advertisers' concerns. Their additional concerns about editorial content will sometimes override or at least modify the first consideration. As the media's dominant paymaster, advertisers influence media enterprises to give audiences editorial content that advertisers want them to receive – sometimes, simply messages that support the advertisers' products. Advertisers also influence media (i.e., they pay, either directly or indirectly) to avoid content that disparages the advertisers' products or political agenda, to avoid offending potential customers in a manner that could spill over into offense at the advertiser, and to contain content that puts audiences into a "buying mood" or that predictably creates a receptiveness to ads. Although often proclaiming editorial or creative independence, most media executives recognize that people or entities who pay can and will influence content. The consequent influence of advertisers corrupts democratic justifications for the media. More relevantly here, it partially undermines the media's market incentive to give audiences the informational and cultural content that the audiences want.

In response it might be argued that advertisers' interests are not inherently illegitimate, that they ought to be taken into account. If offered a choice between cheaper media products made available by advertisers' participation or more expensive content solely responsive to audience preferences, people will mostly choose, *as the market shows*, the first alternative. That is, pure market accounts often argue in favor of all potential purchasers having the influence that their expenditures justify and argue that, if people want, they can buy ad-free (or locally produced) media products. Although if cost is ignored people may prefer content that advertisers did not influence, this market perspective notes that in the real world these people may prefer influenced content, given its cheaper cost.

25

Commentators who emphasize unique values of news, informational, cultural, or other media products routinely characterize advertisers' influence as corrupting. Although I am sympathetic with and, in the next chapter, describe economic arguments supporting this conclusion, here I stick to the pure market approach as outlined earlier. From this perspective, the question is always, Are people getting what they want, given the cost?

Typically, neither the media nor advertisers want the audience to know of an advertiser's influence on nonadvertising content. This advertiser influence conflicts with the media's claim to provide the public with professional judgment and independence. This is a pivotal value. A physician would find it bad for business if her potential patients knew that a pharmaceutical company's payment influenced her choice of which medicine to prescribe. Likewise, a publisher predictably finds it damaging if the public knows or, more relevantly, believes that it routinely bows to advertisers' directives. The public, however, often finds it difficult to determine whether it is receiving a "noncorrupt" product – which is one reason for wanting professionalism in journalism as well as in medicine. This informational inequality between the public and the advertisers makes the situation ripe for systematic market failures. Sometimes, an audience will not receive what it wants (and would pay for) because its lack of information results in it paying anyhow.

Although advertisers are concerned with editorial content, their primary concern, what they primarily pay for, is "audience," usually a somewhat targeted audience. Advertisers may target the audience geographically (local newspaper advertisers want local audiences), economically (usually at least somewhat upscale, because advertisers only benefit from those who can pay for their product), demographically (often an advertiser's product has a bigger potential market among a particular age or gender group), or interest-based (sellers of golf products want to reach golfers). Thus, possibly advertisers' most important impact on the media is to increase the prevalence of media content relevant to their favored audiences. The two main results are that the media system is biased toward content connected to marketable products and services and is tilted away from content valued by the poor. Although easily observable in magazines and television, this targeting and the resulting content biases are found in all media receiving significant advertising support.

Newspapers' primary source of revenue comes from selling readers to advertisers rather than newspapers to readers – which explains why some papers, especially weeklies, profit by giving their papers away. The business model of most newspapers is to sell to all people whom their advertisers want within a particular geographic area. This revenue source makes their primary incentive to provide a package that has the broadest, even if shallow, appeal within the area, with one caveat. If relatively poor and poor minority audiences are not good markets for the advertisers' products – a Bloomingdale executive once characterized them as our shoplifters, not our customers[5] – newspapers may slight material of special interest to these groups. The incentive to have very broad appeal, however, creates at least some disincentive to provide material for which a comparatively small group would pay a higher price, but which would be offensive or a turnoff to another audience segment. Of course, if the cost of writing and printing (i.e., the ink and paper) specialized material is not too high and, as long as the content is not bothersome or offensive to others, the publisher can often profitably create the special sections that fill the modern newspaper.[6] These sections attract some additional readers and appeal to advertisers who target that particular subset of readers. Nevertheless, the gain from selling a larger audience size to advertisers reduces any incentive a newspaper would otherwise have for any product differentiation that limits its mass appeal.

This advertiser-rewarded, mass-appeal orientation supports development of "objectivity" as newspapers' ruling journalistic norm. A purportedly objective style offends few people and leaves more people reasonably, even if less intensely, satisfied than would, for example, a partisan style. As a ruling norm, however, objectivity tends toward reduced product differentiation; in a sense its economic point is that it tries to reach all potential, advertiser-valued readers. Reduced product differentiation combined with the public-good aspects of newspapers – that is, the first copy cost that stays the same no matter how many purchasers the paper gains – leads to monopoly papers. If costs per reader go down the larger the audience, the paper with the larger audience can be priced cheaper for what it produces. And if the products are roughly the same, the consumer is likely to buy the cheaper version, that is, the larger circulation paper. This process leads directly to monopoly. The actual historical trend toward increased monopoly daily newspapers in American cities surely reflects multiple causes. Still, both the increasing rule of objectivity as the journalism's dominant norm and the increase of monopoly papers correlated throughout the late nineteenth and twentieth centuries with the steady increase of advertising revenue as a contribution to newspaper revenue.

These developments, probably at least partly caused by the increased role of advertising, can have profound social consequences. Despite advertising's beneficial effect of reducing a newspaper's cost to the public and thus increasing the potential appeal of the individual paper, its effect of reducing product differentiation and partisanship could contribute to the observed reduction of the total audience for newspapers. It would do so, for example, if many people only find appeal in the more differentiated paper. This loss of audience and reduction in partisanship could, in turn, lead to less political participation. Not only is newspaper reading a major stimulant for voting and political participation, but partisanship itself may play a crucial mobilizing role in political life. Partisan media may make politics seem both more accessible and more meaningful than it seems under the gray tones of objectivity. Moreover, monopoly newspapers' failure to target poor, often minority audiences, is arguably one cause of comparatively less political participation by these groups.[7]

Of course, advertising's effect on content diversity is variable. It helps pay for content especially appealing to those audiences targeted by advertisers, thereby potentially increasing an advertiser-specified diversity in some media, such as magazines, while undermining partisan and some types diversity in other media, such as newspapers. Because both effects involve reducing the price the media charge audiences for advertiser-supported content, the question remains: does the influence of advertising give audiences what they want? In fact, does its give them even more of what they want, because now they do not have to pay all the costs?

The answer is unclear. Many common criticisms of advertising are far too simplistic. For example, consider the claim that advertising adds to the cost of the product (which must cover the advertising cost) while manipulating the audience to buy this higher-priced good. That is, the claim is that advertising merely rips off consumers by making *them* pay higher prices for the advertised products, thereby making them pay for being manipulated into making the purchase. On the contrary, by increasing the market for the advertised product, advertising sometimes leads to a reduced price to the consumer. Moreover, advertising supplies people with information. And because advertising benefits the advertisers more if their product is one people will want again if they first try it, arguably advertising focuses on and supports the better products.

Finally, if, after the advertising, people value the product more than they would otherwise, they may be getting something that they value more than they would without the advertising – so the advertising arguably increases their satisfaction.

Other effects of advertising support are more complex. Media products that succeed due to their advertising revenue will often depress demand for other media products, sometimes causing them to fail. Within monopolistic competition, these failing products typically have a declining average cost and often have, at best, limited ability to engage in price discrimination. But audiences may still value these no longer commercially viable media products: the audience may value the products more than the products cost to produce. Thus, the introduction of advertising-supported products could be like product B in Table 2.2 and could cause the economic situation of the nonadvertised media product to change like that of product A did from time 1 to time 2. When this happens, the net result is that some media products fail, consumer surplus declines, and the public gets less of the media that it wants.

Descriptively, the success of advertising-supported media will probably result in failure of more differentiated, competitive daily newspapers, of some general audience magazines, and of some more targeted media such as magazines that appeal to groups whose interests do not overlap with use of any particular set of consumer products. Thus, the impact of advertising is to disfavor media content appealing to groups whose members are comparatively poor or whose unifying interests or activities do not implicate particular categories of consumer products. Disfavored content is likely to include that which is aimed at politically defined groups. For example, comparatively few advertisers find the *Nation* to be a particularly good advertising vehicle. A feminist journal, especially if aimed at an age- and class-non-specific, multicultural audience, might have a large potential audience but be hard pressed to find its advertising "niche."[8]

Chapters 3 and 4 note other possible critiques of the influence of advertising on content. The point here is that non-advertising-based media that do not exist because of competition from advertising-supported media sometimes could have produced a greater consumer surplus than is generated by the prevailing advertising-based media. Whether this is true in any particular instance cannot be determined a priori. However, there are reasons for worry. For example, in the competition that leads to only one daily newspaper existing in an area, the prevailing paper is likely to be less product-differentiated than the multiple papers that it replaces. Its demand curve is likely to be flatter (although broader) than the demand for competing papers that uniquely appeal to discrete portions of the audience. This characteristic provides some reason to expect that the competitive winner is like product B in Table 2.2. It creates less consumer surplus – provides the audience with less of what it wants – than would newspapers that would otherwise exist. The same may be true in a range of cases, such as advertisers' greater support for magazines like *Women's Golf* than for failed versions of magazines more like the *Nation* or *Ms.* if the intensity of demand for the latter is more variable among its potential readers.

## RUINOUS COMPETITION: TOO MANY PRODUCTS, TOO MUCH FAKE DIVERSITY[9]

Monopolistic competition can generate too many products as well as too few. In the preceding examples, the loss of consumer surplus from failed products was not brought to bear on the decision making of the firm that introduced the new product, for example, the advertising-supported product. The result can be an economically unjustified limitation on diversity. But the opposite, wasteful competition, can occur. The producer of a new product has no incentive to consider its impact on the demand for, and hence revenues produced by, surviving competitors. The surviving competitor must now spread its first-copy costs over fewer customers, meaning that it generates less surplus from each sale. If the *decline* in the surplus produced by resources still used by the competitor is more than the surplus (profit plus consumer surplus) produced by the new product, the result is wasted resources.*

---

* Rather than dissipating monopoly profits among the competitors, some arrangements allow one "winner" to gain all the reward. Markets so structured often attract numerous more or less equivalent "competitors," each of whom "spends" resources on trying to win, with the same result as discussed in this paragraph – a dissipation or waste of resources. Michael Madow identified this process as occurring in the context of "star creation," and proposed that by denying a property right in one's image, that is, denying a "right of publicity," the law could not only increase the availability of cultural resources to new creators and entrepreneurs, but could reduce (but not eliminate) the incentive to engage in the economically wasteful effort to become a star or sports hero. See Michael Madow, "Private Ownership of Public Image: Popular Culture and Publicity Rights," *California Law Review* 81 (1993): 125, 205–25. This is also a primary mechanism producing waste identified in Robert H. Frank & Philip J. Cook, *The Winner-Take-All Society* (New York: Free Press, 1995), 167–89. Winner-take-all markets also create a heightened incentive to spend resources on defending one's status as winner or tearing down efforts by others –

This situation can easily occur. The public may receive only marginally more benefits from a number of virtually identical products than it received from a single product. The total cost of providing multiple products may, however, be much greater than the cost of providing only one. For example, both NBC and ABC evening news might cost roughly the same to produce, but if the programs are sufficiently similar, the public might receive virtually the same value, an evening news program, whether or not the second exists. Despite publishers' attempts to differentiate their products, the same may be true for a group of five or six fashion magazines.

If everyone receives (without requiring additional use of resources) the benefit from the creation of "public good X," a competitor's expenditure on providing a virtually identical good benefits no one; it merely wastes resources. But if this competitor can be profitable – by taking audience away from the other seller – it has no reason to take account of this "waste." For example, if the public can get the same content or services from a single wire that passes in front of its house that it can get from a second wire (and if greater use of a single wire involves no, or minimal, added cost), the resources devoted to providing the second wire presumably provide no benefits. (Of course, sometimes monopolists will be so wasteful or will charge such excessive prices and thereby exclude those who would benefit from access that introducing the potentially wasteful competitor – for example, the second wire – will benefit the public.) The same was suggested for the news programs just described. Still, without price discrimination, an enterprise must charge either consumers or advertisers a price at least sufficient to recover its costs. A monopolistic producer may charge much more. If entry is difficult to prevent, these monopoly profits may attract competitors. If we assume that the competitor's product is not substantially different from the original monopolist's, its entry may not give the audience any more of anything it wants. Rather, the new entrant will merely take customers from the original firm, thereby reducing its monopoly revenue (and profits) by an amount sufficient to cover the entrant's costs plus any

mechanisms that often include advertising. These efforts, these expenditures, do not produce value but only determine who receives it. Frank and Cook argue that this type of market has become increasingly common. One of their most interesting policy observations is that, in order to decrease the personal incentive to participate in this type of market – to be the top executive, the movie star or model, the sports hero – much higher income taxes for very high incomes, whether or not the 91% rate that existed when John F. Kennedy took office in 1961, would increase "efficiency" or social wealth. Ibid., 58, 121–23, 212–17.

profits it garners. The result is inefficient – many more resources are spent on producing roughly the same value. Still, as long as both firms obtain enough customers to cover their costs, this competition could become an equilibrium, unstable but potentially continuing for a long period of time.

The situation can be illustrated by a variation of Table 2.3. From the consumer's point of view, the ideal in situations such as the one described here would be to have a single, efficient monopolist that does not pocket monopoly profits. Such behavior by a monopolist could result either from effective regulatory pressure, firms' strategic pricing behavior aimed at heading off competition, or firms' non-profit-maximizing decisions to favor public service or professional standards. This ideal media enterprise would either price the media content as low as possible or spend monopolistic profits on improving quality. For example, a public-spirited, family-owned monopolistic newspaper might give the newsroom a bigger budget, with more resources available for investigative journalism, thereby devoting potential profits to public-service elements of journalism. A regulated cable monopoly could choose or, more likely, be required to equip and support public-access facilities or provide universal cable service within its operating area even though doing so reduces profits. These unprofitable expenditures may be economically justified in terms of what people would potentially pay, even though a monopolist unable to fully price discriminate would not be able to realize the benefits. Under these scenarios, audiences could lose from the introduction of competition. Competition would take the potential "monopoly profits" that the monopolist "spent" on consumers and instead use them to cover the costs of producing duplicative media content (the television network example) or duplicative wires and associated operating costs (the cable example).

The Federal Communications Commission's *Carroll* doctrine,[10] although now mostly repudiated, allowed the FCC to deny a license application for an unoccupied place on the spectrum. The FCC, of course, should not deny a license merely to benefit existing licensees, but the *Carroll* doctrine recognized that sometimes licensing a new broadcaster in a community could produce ruinous competition that would be harmful to the public – like the introduction of "good B" in Table 2.3. Given that the various broadcasters must share the same advertising base, and especially if a new entrant's programming categories largely duplicate those of the established licensees, the new

## Table 2.3

| | | Product A | | | Product B |
|---|---|---|---|---|---|
| | Cost | Demand/ Value at Time 1 | Demand/ Value at Time 2 | Cost | Demand/ Value at Time 2 |
| Copy 1/person 1 | 11 | 6[a] | 6[a] | 1 | 1 |
| Copy 2/person 2 | 1 | 5[a] | 5[a] | 1 | 1 |
| Copy 3/person 3 | 1 | 5[a] | 5[a] | 1 | 1 |
| Copy 4/person 4 | 1 | 4[a] | 3 | 8 | 4[a] |
| Copy 5/person 5 | 1 | 4[a] | 2 | 1 | 3[a] |
| Copy 6/person 6 | 1 | 3[a] | 2 | 1 | 3[a] |
| Copy 7/person 7 | 1 | 3[a] | 2 | 1 | 3[a] |
| Profitable selling price | | 3[b] | 5 | | 3 |
| Consumer surplus (value-revenue) | | 30 − 21 = 9 | 16 − 15 = 1 | | 13 − 12 = 1 |
| Profit (revenue-cost) | | 21 − 17 = 4 | 15 − 13 = 2 | | 12 − 11 = 1 |
| Total surplus (value-cost) | | 30 − 17 = 13 | 16 − 13 = 3 | | 13 − 11 = 2 |
| or (Consumer surplus + profit) | | 9 + 4 = 13 | 1 + 2 = 3 | | 1 + 1 = 2 |

[a] Purchasers at a profitable selling price; hypothetical assumes seller's inability (or inadequate ability) to price discriminate.

[b] Either 3, 4, or 5 would be a profitable selling price producing a profit of 4, 5, or 2, respectively. A monopolist might price at 4 (getting the maximum) profit, but 3, modeled here, is also possible for reasons noted in the text.

*Key assumption*: Introduction of product B has the effect of slightly reducing the demand for product A between time 1 and time 2. Often product A will survive with a reduced audience, although sometimes only with cost cutting on copy 1 (not illustrated here), creating a degradation of the quality of product chosen by persons 1, 2, and 3.

The policy goal is to maximize surplus, that is, profit plus consumer surplus, which also can be said to best give the audience the media that it wants. In this illustration, at time 1, total surplus = 13; at time 2, total surplus = 5 (consisting of 3 for product A and 2 for product B or a total of 5). The introduction of product B can be expected to be successful even though it causes a net decline both in total surplus value produced and in total profits.

entrant's primary effect might be to reduce the established stations' revenue and hence their programming budgets. The resulting decline in service could produce a loss to the public that is greater than any gain from new, presumably low-cost programming presented by the new licensee. Of course, there is no market mechanism to indicate when this occurs. Hence, government officials cannot easily evaluate existing licensees' self-interested claim that granting the new license will have this effect. Still, the criterion of giving the audience what it wants, or the statutory charge to the FCC to engage in public interest regulation,[11] arguably requires an attempt.

For roughly the same reasons, monopolistic ownership of all local broadcast channels can sometimes produce more beneficial results than competition.[12] Assume three stations and three programming categories where 70 percent of the audience strongly prefer programming type A, 20 percent type B, and 10 percent type C. If the three are competitors, each is likely to provide type A, with each on average gaining one-third of 70 percent (23 1/3 percent) of the audience. For each, this 23 1/3 percent is a better prospect than providing programming of type B or C, where it can only hope to get either 20 or 10 percent of the audience. But if a monopolist controlled all three channels, having no incentive to compete against itself, it could introduce a different type of programming on each channel. This programming strategy maximizes its total audience by reaching those viewers who prefer B and C but do not bother to watch A. Whether the monopolist would actually adopt this strategy presumably relates both to the cost of the alternative programming and the degree of inelasticity of audience demand for their preferred programming. If it does, consumer welfare is better served – monopolistic ownership gives the audience more of what it wants. In contrast, competition produces a wasteful use of resources – too many virtually identical products.

Local government's grant of an exclusive license to a single cable company has been repeatedly challenged, with some success, on First Amendment grounds as an unjustified restriction on speech.[13] An alternative First Amendment analysis argues that the government should be able to create a cable franchise monopoly just as it can create a monopoly telephone service but, if it does so, it is constitutionally required to impose public-access or common-carrier-type obligations in respect to all or at least some portion of the system's carrying capacity.[14] Putting aside the constitutional issue, however, it is clear that this power by local governments can be abused but that, under some circumstances, the practice has a completely sound public-policy justification. Competition can reduce consumer welfare and give the audience less of what it wants. If system overhead, especially cable hardware such as the wires, is a large part of the system's cost, and if stringing two sets of wires by each house significantly increases that expense, adding a new competitor could significantly increase the costs that cable audiences' payments must cover. Ultimately, the single audience must now pay all the costs of two companies and two sets of wires. If regulation effectively forces the single operator to engage in efficient behavior and to return its potential monopoly profits to the public, either in the form of lower rates or public-service programming (e.g., local public-access, governmental, or educational channels), the monopolistic cable operator would provide the public greater benefits than could be obtained through competition.

Of course, some wastefully duplicative costs could be eliminated if all cable systems could use the same wire (e.g., a fiber optics line installed, owned, and leased by the phone company). An important principle is at stake here. Fair usage of this line is more likely if operated on common-carrier principles, which would be easier to police if the phone company had no incentive to favor its own cable products. First the FCC and then Congress imposed this regulatory separation by forbidding phone companies from providing their own cable content to the public. Nevertheless, industry convinced several lower courts that this approach borders on irrationality.[15] The telephone industry, during a period of high-stakes, big-bucks lobbying, "convinced" Congress that deregulation and competition is best served by eliminating this separation.[16] Still, a general principle in communications policy should be that ownership of content should be separated whenever possible from monopoly or near monopoly distribution channels, with the latter operated on something like common-carrier principles.[17]

Putting aside the possibility of common-carrier use of one wire, the optimal arrangement cannot be determined in the abstract. Actual examples exist where, for short time periods, competition between cable companies produces either better service, better program offerings, lower prices, or all three. These examples, however, hardly speak to the likely long-run scenario.[18] The benefits may be short-term effects of a struggle to become the monopolist; most situations of "overbuilding" have resulted in eventual sale of one system to the other. The same indeterminacy also exists as to whether phone companies, if allowed to carry cable programming over their wires as common carriers,[19] will eventually carry all cable programming, including that of competing program packagers, or whether a two-wire world will persist. Likewise, whether either wire or satellite broadcast video programming will eliminate the other as a competitor or whether each has product differentiation advantages that will cause both to survive is uncertain, just as it is uncertain whether new delivery mechanisms will replace over-the-air broadcasting, whose spectrum may then find better uses.

Wasteful competition assertedly can also arise in respect to local newspapers. Given the modern decline of differentiation between local dailies, a single newspaper may serve a community better than competitive papers. A significant portion of each newspaper's expense goes to producing the public-good element, the so-called first-copy costs, such as news gathering, editing, and layout. The potential revenue base from audience and advertisers stays roughly the same whether there are one or more papers. Hence, the amount a paper can devote to the first copy, which is crucial for product quality, should decline as the available revenue is split between multiple papers. In contrast, a single monopoly paper has a (potentially) larger audience and advertising base from which to derive revenue, which it could use to keep its price down, to provide a larger editorial budget, or both. Exploitation of a monopolistic position to increase profits may, however, be a more common response. Still, if the monopoly paper is more committed to journalism than to maximizing profits, this revenue should enable it to produce a better product than it could if faced with competition. Despite viewing the case as atypical, Leo Bogart notes that the *Philadelphia Inquirer* expanded its editorial staff after the failure of the *Bulletin*.[20] And although similarly avoiding endorsement of monopoly papers, William Blankenburg suggests that "if news-editorial quality can be equated with expenditures, then it's better to have a single large daily than two half its size."[21] Nevertheless, Robert Entman finds the empirical research to be quite inconclusive.[22]

Clearly, the issue is complicated. Earlier, I argued that monopolistic competition that leads to one newspaper prevailing could result in less papers than people want and could have a debilitating effect on political participation. Here, the claim is that it could lead to too many. The better account turns partly on contextual empirical matters and partly on the difficulty of describing, much less measuring, what is meant by "serving a community better."[23] Many media commentators have argued that competition regularly produces papers that are observably better, although in ways that are hard to quantify, and that competition between papers, producing at least some degree of choice, should be counted as inherently good.[24] One empirical investigation found that a typical competitive paper devoted more resources to its editorial product and maintained lower per-copy prices than did the typical monopoly paper – a result that may reflect the monopoly newspapers' tendency to take out huge profits rather than to lower prices or increase the newsroom budget.[25] For reasons described in Part II, even though the possibility of wasteful competition exists in this area, probably the better guess is that audiences and citizens would both benefit by more competition among daily newspapers.

## A SOLUTION AND NEW PROBLEM: PRICE DISCRIMINATION

The discussion so far has assumed the inability to (adequately) price discriminate. Only this inability leads to underproduction of media content (or of any other item with sufficient public-good elements) and to the possibility that monopolistic competition will drive out more valuable content and replace it with content that is less valuable from the perspective of consumers. This assumption should be relaxed. Media owners have always engaged in some degree of price discrimination. They serialize a story in a newspaper or magazine, then sell it as a hardback novel, and then as a cheaper paperback. Newspapers in effect sell cheap per person, for example, when multiple (sometimes poor) readers share a single copy, but sell at a higher per-person price when only one person (or one family) is the reader. Magazines sell at different subscription rates depending not merely on the reader's value to advertisers but also on the purchaser's willingness to search for a cheap rate. These are all examples of price discrimination – and the list could go on and on. In each, those willing to pay more usually do pay more. Technological change also often increases opportunities to price discriminate. Movie producers always engaged in some price discrimination. They charged different prices in different geographical areas, to different age groups, at different times of the day or week, and at different times after release. But new marketing "windows" have increased this capacity. The producer can show the film first in theaters and then move it through various additional distribution channels: pay television, video sales and rentals, free television, and maybe "on-line." Although price discrimination will never be perfect, its occurrence surely reduces some inefficiencies described in this chapter.

Taking price discrimination into account, however, adds a new complexity. Opportunities to price discriminate vary among communications products. Variation occurs both between mediums and between products within a medium. Price discrimination itself has desirable consequences. First, there should be less underproduction of media products that are best able to price discriminate. Second, sometimes products succeed only due to price discrimination. But variations have potential negative consequences. Those products that price discriminate soak up more of audience demand than they would otherwise. Their success (or greater success) can cause a downward shift in the demand for other products, often leading those other products to be unprofitable. The price discriminating products will be like product B in Table 2.2, putting many product As out of existence. Frequently, these failed products will still be economically justified even though no longer commercially viable given their (comparative) inability to price discriminate. Like product A at time 2, their production could still generate a surplus of value over cost. The net result is that many products that would have created a relatively high proportion of consumer surplus (they had relatively steeply declining demand curves) are driven out of existence by their comparative inability to price discriminate. In contrast, price discrimination converts consumer surplus (or lost low-priced sales) into revenue, leaving little consumer surplus. Those media products that require successful price discrimination to prevail (thus producing only minimal profit) will often generate comparatively little social surplus – little gain for either the producer or the consumer. In other words, although price discrimination can increase efficiency by extending the reach of products that people value, the competitive effect of a differential capacity to price discriminate can cause an overall decline in social welfare – and in people getting the media they want.

Media products' comparative capacity to price discriminate is an empirical matter. The slant – what types of media content will be favored and what will be disfavored – cannot be determined a priori. Still, hazardous as it may be, some broad speculation is possible.

First, the persistent opening up of new delivery channels for video products – basic and pay cable channels and VCR technology combined with rental and sale of videotapes to consumers – is likely to have increased the capacity to price discriminate in these media as compared to print. If so, this would cause audiences to receive an increasing supply of video products and a decreasing (possibly inefficiently small) supply of written material.

Second, some types of content within a given medium may be more susceptible to differential packaging and hence increased price discrimination than others. Due to its limited time salience as well as its relative lack of copyright protection, news and factual content may be less subject to price discrimination than is fiction or fantasy material. On the other hand, news content can be immediately sold by wire or on line, quickly broadcast, then sold in a newspaper and maybe a weekly magazine, and finally used in a documentary or integrated into a book. Still, there may be a bias within news production. News content that is most susceptible to use in multiple channels, as opposed, for example, to complex stories unfit for appealing, expressive (and copyrightable) video presentation, may be most valued. Again, there may be too little an incentive for print-oriented investigative journalism.

Third, the activity of price discrimination – marketing the material through different channels or windows – itself often requires large investments. Whether creating a window is worth its cost largely depends on how much additional revenue the window produces. The obvious consequence is that "blockbusters" are generally better positioned to price discriminate than products whose smaller audiences are less likely to benefit from paying the cost of using all potential windows.[26] The predicted result is that the most popular media products are likely to become even more dominant – inefficiently dominant – in the modern world. More diverse media content that audiences also want – that is, content that audiences value more than it would cost to produce – is likely to be increasingly underproduced.

Fourth, to the extent that price discrimination involves using different "windows," increasing price discrimination is usually cheaper and more convenient if the owner of the media product operates within all of the various channels. Media mergers purportedly create "synergies" by allowing the merged firm to utilize more windows in marketing a media product. This capacity only dubiously relates to the public good. One major problem is that this new capacity contributes to the likely undue dominance of the products of these merged firms – with "undue" meaning contrary to the goal of maximizing what audiences want – as a result of their superior ability to price discriminate. The same point applies with respect to media products marketed internationally (see

Part III) because these additional foreign markets typically allow sales at a different price than in the home market.

In sum, the ability to price discriminate not only increases the portion of any social surplus created by a good that goes to the seller as opposed to the audience; it also may reduce some "inefficiencies" in the production and distribution of goods with significant public-good aspects. Nevertheless, the variable ability to price discriminate is likely to exacerbate other market distortions. In particular, it is likely to favor the inefficient homogenization of the communication realm, increase the domination of blockbuster products, increase the domination of large firms, and disfavor smaller, culturally more diverse media products.

## CHAPTER 3

# The Problem of Externalities

The most commonly recognized reason for markets to produce "inefficient" or non-wealth-maximizing results is "transaction costs" that prevent some costs and some benefits from being brought to bear on the actions or decision making of market participants. The consequence of this failure is often described as an externality. Pollution is a standard example of a negative externality; a beautiful landscape freely observable by the public exemplifies a positive externality. If negative impacts of an activity are not brought to bear on the decision making of the actor, the predictable result is too much of an activity. The converse is true for positive externalities; if positive effects are not brought to bear, not made into an incentive, the result is too little of the activity. Failure to bring these effects to bear can also lead the actor to behave in a less than optimal manner (e.g., to fail to install a cheap and effective pollution control device).

"Giving the audience what it wants" can only sensibly mean doing so within some cost constraint. Usually the person who invokes the notion means that the audience should get what it wants *given its willingness to pay the cost.* Many people would like to see Broadway-quality productions at their neighborhood theaters, but this observation is not thought to demonstrate that giving audiences what they want requires making this opportunity available to them for the cost of a movie ticket. "Giving the audience what it wants" means giving it a Broadway-quality production only if the audience is willing to pay its real or actual cost. An externality, however, is a real cost or benefit, only one that is not brought to bear on the transaction. Because of this, the seller either over- or undercalculates the product's cost. When the seller overcharges because of not deducting for positive externalities, the market supplies too little of the good. When she undercharges because of not adding the costs created by negative externalities, the market provides too much. Thus, in trying to determine whether media markets operate to give audiences what they want, the analysis must come to grips with externalities prevalent in these markets.

For net externalities to be positive means that the media product produces value for which the media firm does not receive payment. Essentially, the market gives the firm insufficient incentives to produce. The audience pays for the benefit to itself but is deterred from purchasing by being required to also pay for benefits to third parties. In this circumstance, "failure to buy" does not necessarily mean that the audience does not want the content; at least, it does not in any economically meaningful sense of "want." Rather, it only means that the audience does not want the content at the improperly high price. In contrast, if the firm did receive payment for the externality from the third-party beneficiary (or from someone else, such as the government), it could profitably sell the media product at a lower price, predictably leading the audience to get more of what it wants. Likewise, negative externalities permit artificially low prices – the audience pays for only a portion of its real cost. Purchases do not mean that the audience wants that content – only that it wants the content when charged less than its real cost. And if these positive and negative externalities are significant, "good" content may be priced way too high while "bad" content may be priced way below its actual cost to society. We get too little of one and too much of the other *from the perspective of respecting consumer choices*.

These are purely abstract economic observations. Two concrete aspects of most externalities in the media context merit special comment before proceeding. First, many externalities to be discussed represent noneconomic values or activities; to think of them in economic terms, that is, as externalities, seems awkward, especially for those who resist the pervasive market rhetoric of economic analysis.[1] Nevertheless, any economic analysis that ignores these considerations has only pseudo-objectivity and, in fact, provides misleading information. Moreover, because I want to critique free-market analysis on its own terms, I use this rhetoric, although later I question its appropriateness. Second, media externalities often involve the system of freedom of expression. Many, probably most, of the media's effects on third parties occur *through* their effect on its audiences' beliefs, perspectives, and preferences – or, as sometimes described, through a "mental intermediation." Third-party harm or benefit occurs only because audience members respond to the media one way rather than another. Liberal premises concerning respect for people's agency normally require treating the audience member as ultimately responsible for her behavior. These premises, arguably embodied in the First Amendment, require that people's admittedly real and legitimate interest in what other people read or hear does not give them authority to force these others to read $X$ or prohibit them from reading $Y$.[2] Preventing harm (or obtaining gain) is not always a permissible basis for prohibiting (or mandating) behavior.[3] People have a First Amendment right to engage in certain harm-causing behavior. Acceptance of this view of the First Amendment, however, would still not stop the state from implementing policies designed to increase media products' positive externalities and to decrease or otherwise respond to their negative externalities.

This chapter considers media content's effect on third parties – costs or benefits to people other than the immediate audience.[4] Although I offer no empirical evidence, I expect my attempt to catalog and describe these externalities, both positive and negative, will convincingly support the view that third-party effects are massive. If so, markets cannot be expected to operate efficiently within an otherwise unchanged legal order – that is, cannot be expected to provide the audience with what it wants. This discredits the claim that "the fully deregulated market-place [leads to] the best and highest use."[5]

Here I catalog major categories of positive and negative externalities, leaving the primary discussion of actual or possible legal or policy responses to Chapter 5. Still, I can note now that it turns out that most existing and commonly proposed media-specific regulations or "interventions" can be understood as reasonable attempts to respond to one or another of these externalities. Thus, these regulatory actions and related media policies clearly cannot be condemned wholesale as paternalism or as interference with people getting the media they want. The market cannot be routinely expected to do as well by the audience as intelligent regulatory intervention.[6] The question in most cases is (partly) empirical – what are the externalities, both positive and negative; how important are they; and do particular regulations lead to their "distortive" effect being blunted? The empirical analysis, however, will seldom be conclusive. These externalities are not only virtually impossible to measure. Often their significance, even their valence, is disputable. Therefore, whether any particular regime gives the audience what it wants will likewise be continually contestable. Although empirical information is helpful, the evaluation is inherently political.

43

## THE CATALOG

This section considers ten generic categories of effects that the production and distribution of media content have on people other than the paying audience. These externalities greatly affect whether market production of media content will correspond to the content that would be produced if the audience (combined with advertisers) paid its real cost. Obviously, there is no natural classification scheme for externalities. Only its usefulness for some purpose gives a classification any value. Here, the constructed classification is somewhat arbitrary, with categories sometimes overlapping, and the overall scheme inevitably incomplete. Still, the catalog encompasses many, perhaps most, of the third-party effects that presently do or arguably should impact media policy. The categories are effects that involve:

1. The quality of public opinion and political participation.
2. Audience members' interactions with other people.
3. Audience members' impact on cultural products available to others.
4. Exposing and deterring abuses of power.
5. Other behavioral responses to the possibility of media exposure.
6. Nonpaying recipients.
7. Positive benefits to people or entities wanting their message spread.
8. Messages' negative effects on those who do not want the attention.
9. Gains or losses to media sources.
10. Costs imposed or benefits created by information-gathering techniques.

### THE QUALITY OF PUBLIC OPINION AND POLITICAL PARTICIPATION

Media consumption often leads people to become more (or sometimes less) informed, as well as more or less active as voters or political participants. One study showed that the decline in newspaper reading accounted for from one- to two-thirds of the decline in voting between 1968 and 1980.[7] The quality and extent of a media consumer's voting and political activity can dramatically affect other people. Even opinion polls reporting people's opinions, which are often influenced by media consumption, can influence others' behavior, including decisions of political elites who often respond to these polls. Moreover, nonconsumers of media content often have their opinions affected by people whose views were influenced by their own media consumption. These political consequences of media consumption constitute a major externality.

The point is simple. Individuals are tremendously benefited or harmed if the country makes wise or stupid decisions about welfare, warfare, provision of medical care, the environment, and a myriad of other issues. These harms or benefits depend on the extent and quality of *other* people's political participation. The media significantly influence this participation. In this way, each person can be tremendously advantaged (or disadvantaged) by other people's media consumption. People's media consumption produces huge externalities.

People value (or disvalue) not only good (or bad) political decisions made in response to public opinion that is partially generated by media content, but people also value and are committed to living in a vibrant and successfully functioning democracy. People manifest these commitments in various ways, including the symbolic, material, and institutional resources that they allow to be spent on supporting a vibrant democracy. Those who hold this value should have an interest in the quality of media content for reasons beyond their own consumption and their desire for a press to inform their own opinions. That is, people who want to live in a well-governed democracy are the third-party beneficiaries (or victims) of the extent and quality of other people's media consumption.

Media can, of course, mislead as well as inform, can present venal as well as wise argument, can encourage bad as well as good values, and can dampen as well as incite political participation. Holding other factors constant, one study found that heavy viewers of *television* news are less well informed about news than other people.[8] Escapist literature or "action" news can divert attention away from crucial structural issues and direct it toward trivial events. This orientation can undermine the quality of politics. Maybe this is why considerable evidence indicates that, despite poll surveys of self-perceptions, newspapers, not television, are the main source of the public's actual knowledge of current events.[9] More obviously, everything from negative political ads, to false information, to demagogic partisanship, can pollute political discussion. In other words, the externalities can be dramatically negative as well as positive.

Despite these relatively uncontroversial abstract points about the potential positive or negative externalities, often media content's concrete characterization is contestable. Not everyone would agree that reading the *Nation* produces good political externalities – just as I have doubts about the benefits of Rush Limbaugh. This contestability does not, however, lessen the extraordinary importance of these externalities. Many social scientists and economists apparently prefer to study and analyze empirical facts whose characterization is seemingly unproblematic, objective, or even normatively neutral, even if only by definitional fiat, and where the only difficulty is getting solid data. Nevertheless, an honest approach to policy must recognize that often factors whose characterization is very contestable are the most significant and important to study.

### Audience Members' Interactions with Other People

The media's impact on political culture is only one of its many spillover effects. All people interact, sometimes voluntarily, sometimes not, with other people whose behavior, for better or worse, has been influenced by the media content they have consumed. For this reason, everyone has reason to be concerned and can be affected by other people's media consumption.

For example, social science evidence clearly indicates that, at least under existing conditions, media portrayals of violence increase the likelihood that some audience members will engage in violent behavior toward others.[10] This effect, however, is only the tip of the iceberg. The image of the world and the real or purported information that the media present influences audiences' behavior in situations ranging from their sexual and intimate interactions to their purchasing behavior and their public or private compassionate responsiveness to others' difficulties. A heavy diet of watching television apparently corresponds to increased fear of the world and reduced willingness to come to the aid of an endangered stranger.[11] People's consumption of some religious, pornographic, advertising, racial, or other media materials may contribute to their being more or less appealing romantic or sexual partners – or influence their exercise of power in hiring decisions or assigning jobs. Group defamation can harm those portrayed by influencing audience members' attitudes and then their subsequent behavior toward members of the portrayed group,[12] although an additional, nonexternality concern is the direct, potentially devastating injury experienced by some members of the audience.[13]

Media consumption also influences the factual, cultural, and emotional resources that a person brings to an interaction. A third party will find it is more difficult to discuss the war in Bosnia with someone who has not heard of Bosnia. More generally, media consumption influences whether an interaction with another will be experienced as interesting or boring, helpful or unproductive. Media consumption can also be what some social scientists call a solidarity good[14] – creating solidarity between people that each member of the "in" group values, such that the first person values the fact that another person also consumes the first person's preferred product.

Starkly put, no one is an island. Among people's most important – dangerous, injurious, fulfilling, challenging – experiences are those they have with others. It matters whether the other is an interesting and insightful conversationalist, a skillfully acting associate, a caring person, or alternatively, a rapist, bully, or bore – and the other's media consumption influences these characteristics. A person's media consumption can have a major positive or negative value for other people with whom she interacts, value for which these third parties often would, at least in theory and in the absence of transaction costs and ignoring possible opposition to commodification, be willing to pay heavily in order to obtain. Economic theory asserts that this theoretical willingness to pay must be taken into account if people are to get what they want. Of course, it is often both empirically impossible and normatively inappropriate to attribute responsibility for specific behavior to specific media content. Nevertheless, media content undoubtedly contributes significantly to the culture that makes particular behavior more or less likely, more or less thinkable and thus doable, as well as affecting the meaning or significance of that behavior when it occurs. Other than, maybe even more than, its direct value to its audience, the media's greatest value may be for third parties. Even if they do not consume the media content themselves, they can be wonderfully or gravely affected by the media's influence on its audiences' "construction of reality" and on their resulting behavior.

## Audience Members' Impact on Cultural Products Available to Others

The point in the preceding section was that $B$'s media consumption affects $B$'s interactions with $A$. Note, however, that $B$'s consumption also affects the media (and other goods) available to $A$. Purchases of particular cultural products – say, rock-and-roll music or opera compact discs or a quality newspaper – increase the demand for media goods of that sort. This increased demand can be beneficial or harmful to A. If A likes B's favored culture or newspaper, B's purchases benefit A – at least they do if the increased demand leads this culture or paper to become more widely and cheaply available. (Of course, the opposite can also occur if, for example, too many Bs seek the limited number of tickets for live performances.)

Here, media content's public-good aspect is relevant. More demand usually allows spreading the cost of producing media content over more people. Rather than increasing its price, greater demand usually makes media content more cheaply available. Satisfaction of people's cultural preferences is in this way "subsidized" by others having the same preferences. Of course, if a person values not the cultural product itself but rather its "eliteness," she could be disadvantaged if her otherwise preferred content becomes cheaper and more widely consumed. In either case, other people's media consumption can either beneficially or negatively affect her opportunities to satisfy her cultural preferences.

Similarly, media content can affect, positively or negatively, its audience's creativity, productivity, or group identity and diversity. These effects on audience members can in turn influence the options available to nonaudience members – cheaper "goods" if audience members become more productive, useful or more interesting artifacts if audience members become more creative, and more diverse life options if media nurture diversity. Alternatively, nonaudience members may have to pay higher taxes for an expanded police-state apparatus if audience members become more dangerous. These consequences occur even for third parties who do not personally interact with those who consume the media products.

## Exposing and Deterring Abuses of Power

Professor Vince Blasi highlighted the "checking" function of speech and of the press as a key rationale for constitutional protection.[15] This function involves both the media's power to expose governmental misdeeds, hopefully leading to correction, and their ability to deter those misdeeds by increasing the likelihood of exposure. Constitutionally, protecting the institution that performs this function is an appropriate aspect of constitutional design. The merit of this design follows from recognizing the value of a structure that checks abusive or corrupt uses of governmental power plus awareness that those to be watched should not be trusted with the unrestricted power to muzzle the watchdog.[16]

Still, the general value of checking corrupt or abusive uses of power applies beyond a concern with government. Wherever power exists – in business, for example – the fact or potential of media exposure is valuable.

In an unusual but especially dramatic example, Amartya Sen argues that no matter how bad the drought, no matter how poor the country, no major famine has ever occurred in a democratically governed country that has a free press.[17] Food always exists but people's lack of money with which to purchase it can create a catastrophe. The presence of a press to publicize the existence of the drought and potential famine, at least within a country that subscribes to democratic values and tolerates competitive, oppositional political parties that potentially can take advantage of any failure of response, is all that is necessary to get the needed response. Under a media spotlight, apparently no democratic government will resist the need to act. If necessary, the government moves food to the stricken region and, more important, adopts income (or distribution) policies[18] that assure availability of food to the potentially starving groups.

A market cannot be expected to bring these "checking" benefits adequately to bear on media decision making. If the press deters misdeeds, everyone positively affected by the absence of the misdeeds benefits. "Deterrence" means, however, that the media has no "exposé" – no product – to sell to its audience and hence no opportunity to internalize the benefits it produces. The deterrence can be correctly described as either a (positive) externality or a pure public good – that is, not only is its use nonrivalrous but beneficiaries are nonexcludable. Similarly, when a press exposé occurs, the public in general, not just the audience that purchases the exposé, benefits to the extent that the exposé stimulates a corrective response by either the wrongdoers themselves or by voters, prosecutors, and others with power. Even for the purchasers of media content, their benefit is largely independent of their purchase. Of course, media enterprises do benefit some from their exposés. The long history of chasing the "scoop" makes this clear. Still, even when the media can "sell" an exposé[19] (or sell more papers generally because of its enhanced reputation), usually these sales will dramatically underinternalize the benefits. The economic prediction must be that, to the significant detriment of the country, the market will encourage the media grossly to underproduce these benefits. The public will predictably receive less of this investigative journalism than it would want if it did not have to pay for the benefits that go to nonbuyers.

Market dynamics not only underproduce these benefits, they also distort priorities. Quality journalism and expensive investigative reporting presumably perform the "checking function" better than slipshod, underfunded, or nonexistent journalism. Nevertheless, the gain that the media firm receives is directly related not to the quality or importance of the "checking" effects but to the cost of its production and its appeal to a paying audience. The result is that the value of exposés to the media will not simply be less than but will not even correlate well with their value to society. The corruption leading up to the savings-and-loan scandal was just not as easily exploitable as exposés about presidential candidate Gary Hart or President Bill Clinton's actual or alleged sex life. News media's comparative overemphasis on street or violent crime as compared with white-collar crime and serious misbehavior reflects in part the comparative expense of producing the reports and their comparative expected sale value. Predictably, those exposés that broad audiences find most tantalizing or narratively accessible and that media firms find cheapest to assemble will be comparatively overproduced. The much-praised *60 Minutes* overtly illustrates this dynamic, with segment combinations chosen in part to give a balance of audience-maximizing appeal, and individual stories chosen (and distorted) depending on the show's ability to make them accessible without too great an expenditure of resources. James Fallows argues that because of overpayment of prominent screen journalists like Mike Wallace, producers cannot spend too much of these stars' time on allowing them to fully understand any complex story, thereby presumably reducing the quality of the journalism.[20] Other recent magazine-style television journalism often further heightens the misallocation of journalistic resources by an even more overt emphasis on sensationalist exposés. Of course, this observation does not condemn those formats. Rather the point is that media firms, in large part because they cannot adequately capture the positive benefits of investigative journalism, will disproportionately underproduce the most valuable investigative material.

## OTHER BEHAVIORAL RESPONSES TO THE POSSIBILITY OF MEDIA EXPOSURE

Potential media coverage does more than deter misdeeds. Potential subjects of exposure often change their behavior, in good ways and bad, in light of possible coverage. This is a major worry of privacy advocates; a person will not read that revolutionary book, join that organization, seek help for a drug problem, watch the explicit video, or otherwise engage in experimentation if exposure is possible. On the other hand, others seek exposure and behave accordingly. Demonstrators sometimes mold and time expressive activities to stimulate media coverage believing the activity will attract and hopefully play favorably under a media spotlight.[21] Allegedly, a major incentive for some terrorist activities is the hope for media exposure.[22] The possibility of press coverage can also change the expression and sometimes the policy position of media-savvy legislators or other officeholders. At some point in the nineteenth century, members of Congress apparently stopped addressing each other in their debates as much as they addressed their constituents.[23]

Given that media coverage has these behavioral effects on people other than the purchasers of the product, a question remains whether particular predictable consequences will be good or bad. They can be either. The possibility of being "on the record" changes expressive practices of legislators, demonstrators, and others and sometimes can change substantive outcomes. The media, however, have little economic incentive to take account of these positive or negative behavioral consequences (i.e., costs or benefits) because they are "external" to the media's market-based decisions.

## NONPAYING RECIPIENTS

A profit-oriented media enterprise's decisions to produce and sell content often depends on its ability to require those who receive and value the content to pay. To the extent the enterprise cannot force payment, it underproduces what people want. However, people often avoid paying. First, many effectively receive media content through interactions with audience members who have paid. For example, a person may ask her friend: "Joe, what of interest was in the paper today?" Even if Joe values giving responses, and the possibility of this dialogue is one reason he paid, his friend also values Joe's having gained the information but she pays nothing. Second, people gain access to abandoned copies. At one point in my life, I chose coffee shops on the basis of whether they offered free refills and abandoned copies of newspapers. When the original purchaser pays only for herself, subsequent users are nonpaying beneficiaries – recipients of positive externalities. However, sometimes what from one perspective looks like free riders receiving a positive externality actually involves a form of price discrimination crucial for a product's success. Libraries (and many other purchasers who intend shared use) make purchases representing an implicit judgment of the value of the good for those who will share its use. Both cases, unintended beneficiaries of others' purchases (creating positive externalities) and price discrimination by a purchaser standing in for multiple intended beneficiaries (increasing efficient publication), illustrate media content's character as an economic "public good" as discussed in Chapter 1. In any event, many nonpurchasers gain access to media content. Depending on its quality (e.g., its accuracy or importance), the positive externalities due to nonpaying recipients can be substantial, leading to an underproduction of this media content.

The dimensions of this phenomenon follow some predictable patterns. For example, reading abandoned newspapers generally increases during hard times and is generally more common in comparatively poor communities. If during a particular time period people are less wealthy or if papers are more expensive, readership of abandoned papers (or joint purchases of a single copy) may increase. The typical English national newspaper in the 1970s had two to three readers per copy. In contrast, radical unstamped English working-class papers in the 1830s are thought to have had roughly twenty readers per copy, while at midcentury the more expensive stamped radical papers may have been read by fifty to eighty persons per copy.[24] Today, in their attempt to justify higher advertising rates, papers that charge readers for copies often assert that they obtain a much higher readership per copy than do free weeklies or shoppers.[25] Although mediated by increased advertising revenue, the nonpayment by these readers reduces the firm's incentives to produce. If the most common multiple users are the poor, the market is especially likely to underproduce valued content favored by the poor.

In a different vein, content creators are themselves possibly the most socially significant category of nonpaying (or underpaying) users. Out of almost logical necessity, content creators draw on both general and particular past content creations in their current works. Almost any "valuable" past communicative content (whether or not commercially created) becomes subject to their "appropriation," appropriated in the sense of being the subject of their comment, parody, or integrative use. All current cultural creations as well as all conversation – think of how intimates' private conventions grow out of their prior interactions – use prior communicative artifacts as their building materials. Even if an author pays for a "copy" in order to gain access to prior ideas and particular expression, absent copyright protection she seldom pays the full value of its integration into her own current work. Legal devices like copyright allow the original creator to receive some of these benefits – that is, copyright internalizes those benefits by forcing subsequent users to pay. But copyright is always Janus-faced; the incentive it creates to produce also "inefficiently" restricts further creative uses by restricting the materials' cultural availability. Standards like copyright's "fair use" are at best rough compromises between these two conflicting goals, efficient encouragement *of* and efficient use *in* creations, both of which must be *fully* served in order to encourage efficient media production. Or, in economic terms, the ideal might be perfect costless price discrimination – an unrealizable goal that copyright law poorly approximates.

## POSITIVE BENEFITS TO PEOPLE OR ENTITIES WANTING THEIR MESSAGE SPREAD

Publicity can expand or blunt demand. The media help create celebrities and pariahs. Media stories can stimulate or discourage acceptance of values that various people want accepted or rejected. A media review can foster or hamper the economic success of a restaurant, a movie, or virtually any other product. Here, however, I primarily consider cases where people value media attention, leaving the converse to the next heading.

Positive attention should be considered an externality as long as the media does not internalize the value to the party portrayed. Individuals, advocacy groups, governments, and businesses often desperately seek the media's favorable attention, while trying to avoid the opposite. Frequently people or entities pay directly for favorable presentations about themselves, their products, or their views. When direct payments are admitted, the resulting favorable content is typically called "advertising." When direct payments are for content that purports to be the media's own, the result is reasonably characterized as "corruption" of the media. As Chapter 1 discusses, this practice of putting "reading matter" in papers was relatively common during the late nineteenth century, but was subsequently outlawed for newspapers and later for broadcasters.[26] Similar legal requirements require disclosure of the fact and amount of consideration paid by an issuer of a security to any person or enterprise presenting a description of the security.[27] Note, however, that these laws and norms prohibit certain ways in which the media would internalize what are otherwise externalities. They require the media to ignore certain costs or reduce the media's incentive to provide certain benefits. (This does not mean that these laws and norms are not justified economically – just as laws against fraud can be justified economically.)

Currently common but controversial versions of "hidden" advertising include product placements, which occur mostly in film or other video productions, and computer-generated background "billboard"-type advertising images that can be superimposed over real space in broadcasts of actual events – apparently quite common in the broadcast of sports programs.[28] The boundary between acceptable advertising and corruption is subject to constant cultural negotiation, with commercial pressures obviously pushing to expand the realm of the acceptable. The issue erupted in two seemingly dissimilar contexts during one week in January 2000. CBS blocked out an actual NBC-sponsored sign in Times Square and replaced it with a CBS logo in its millennium broadcast. CBS's Dan Rather split with CBS executives and, after the fact, called the substitution of the CBS ad "a mistake." Although noting that "there is no excuse for it," Rather admitted that at the time he "did not grasp [its] possible ethical implications."[29] Even more protest occurred that week after *Salon* disclosed that the government essentially paid – that is, it gave credit against the broadcasters' obligation to broadcast public-service announcements – for the networks' inclusion of government-approved antidrug messages in their entertainment programming. Predictably, both the networks and the government defended this presumably propagandistically effective practice. Others reacted more like Andrew Schwartzmann, a leading public-interest media lawyer, who labeled the practice as "craven" and "an outrageous abandonment of the First Amendment."[30]

The public-relations industry, now bigger than the press itself, is in significant part a side effect of people's and firm's concern with media treatment. Clients directly pay the public-relations firm but often indirectly pay media enterprises for favorable treatment. Their payment to the media can take the form of covering most of the media's expenses in gathering and using (favorable) information. The person or entity provides press facilities, news conferences, press releases, video news releases, and other similar materials and services. Here, again, there is plenty of room to contest the line between properly informing the public and engaging in improperly hidden advertising or improper manipulation of audiences. For example, where do video news releases – prepackaged news material made available by public-relations firms or corporate public-relations departments to be shown as the station's own editorial material – fall? Are they any different from press releases that newspapers have long published verbatim? Similarly, the FCC has struggled with the question of whether broadcasting rules regulating advertising apply when a toy manufacturer "gives" a network cartoon programming that features characters that the manufacturer markets.[31] By reducing the cost of creating a media product, these and most other public relations activities are essentially a transfer payment buying favorable media treatment.

Often, however, the media bestow major positive benefits – favorable reporting about a person, group, place, or product – without either direct or indirect payment by the beneficiaries. These significant gratuitous benefits are a major plus for these groups and individuals, a positive externality of media content that is not internalized into the media's decision making.

## MESSAGES' NEGATIVE EFFECTS ON THOSE WHO DO NOT WANT THE ATTENTION

Media attention can also harm those whom it portrays. Either accurate or inaccurate information, either fair or unfair comment, can ruin a restaurant or politician. The market does not routinely bring these harms to bear on the media's editorial decisions. Of course, the situation changes if the media have routine transactions with the negatively described (or potentially described) person or entity. Implicit payments or explicit bargains are then much simpler. The journalist can offer to keep the source confidential in return for information. The media entity may soften or avoid the negative portrayal of its important advertisers in implicit return for continued advertising or of government officials or agencies in return for leaks or privileged access. Nevertheless, explicitly accepting payment for not running or for changing a story is typically characterized as corrupt. An "independent" press is not supposed to engage in such transactions.

Theoretically, the possibility of market transactions permit media companies to partially internalize costs imposed by its unwelcome portrayals. A media entity could compare the value the injurious content adds to its journalistic product with the amount the negatively portrayed party would pay to exclude the content. Unless charging for not running the content is illegal (e.g., as "blackmail"), the media entity could offer nonpublication in return for an adequate payment. It could then choose the most profitable course. If it published, the foregone potential payment would be treated as an "opportunity cost." Nevertheless, actual journalistic practices (possibly because of high transaction costs or, even more, the value of the media entity's reputation for "independence") rule out routine versions of such transactions. Full marketization requires calculation of how much audiences do (or would) pay for the newspaper to eschew such deals; in a sense, these implicit payments for independence represent amounts people would pay to resist full commodification. In other familiar legal terms, these audience payments are made in "restraint of trade." In any event, the market's predictable failure to lead the media to internalize these costs imposed on the subjects of their news arguably makes the news "inefficiently" negative. If the media had to pay both the cost of gathering the information and the cost imposed on the negatively portrayed "victim" rather than only the first cost, they would publish much less negative news.

Distinctions between different negative portrayals – for example, between accurate and inaccurate portrayals or between accurate newsworthy and accurate nonnewsworthy portrayals – are economically and socially important. Media entities have market incentives to avoid inaccurate portrayals. Audiences may pay less for poor-quality information. This incentive for accuracy, however, underdeters inaccuracy because it only internalizes one cost created by the "bad" information – the cost borne by the audience, not the additional harm to the person or entity described. This market failure might be partially remedied by, for example, the liability imposed by defamation law. Likewise, a possible economic explanation of the privacy tort is that it requires the media to act in a manner that internalizes the costs imposed on the exposed individual. Where there are no uncaptured positive externalities of the publication (suggested by the characterization of the content that violates privacy as "non-newsworthy"), internalization would likely lead to nonpublication, at least where the costs imposed are significant (roughly suggested by the tort's requirement that publication of the offending content be "highly offensive"). This defense of application of tort law, however, may proceed too fast. Without exploring all the counter arguments here, not internalizing these costs may help achieve the result that would occur if the media entity could internalize various, uncaptured positive externalities. Fear of liability for defamation, for example, could impede the media's performance of the checking function, which produces substantial positive externalities. Even violations of privacy could further the feminist goal of greater public discussion of matters in the supposedly personal realm and in other ways promote more desirable distributions of power and knowledge.[32]

One particular response to noninternalized negative effects on the people or entities portrayed merits particular attention. Many groups – both private and governmental – have an interest in the public only receiving sanitized news concerning their activities. They can advance this goal by collecting and writing their own accounts and then distributing these accounts as press releases. Media enterprises then sell this freely obtained content to audiences, possibly because audiences do not know what they are getting or, equally relevant for the current point, because audiences just do not value greater accuracy (as to these issues) enough to pay the added cost of more investigative journalism. In other words, public relations, discussed earlier as a means to obtain positive portrayals, can also be a means to implicitly pay the media for avoiding negative portrayals.

Thus, "press-release" journalism reduces a significant negative externality created by negative portrayals. Nevertheless, press-release journalism can be objectionable. Distributive or fairness considerations may argue that the media usually should not be deterred from presenting accurate information. Moreover, not publishing negative portrayals may be "inefficient." For example, it would be if it leads to a failure to produce major (uncaptured) positive externalities such as those associated with the media's political and "checking functions." If the media entity were able to capture these positive externalities, "real" investigative journalism might be much more profitable than press-release journalism. Not internalizing investigative journalism's negative consequences for the subjects of its reports could be a second-best result when its positive externalities are also not effectively brought to bear on media decision making. Here, as elsewhere, professional journalistic standards may provide a reasonable solution to predictable failures of the market.

## Gains or Losses to Media Sources

Sources stand to gain from their interactions with reporters. They may obtain desired publicity for their views, desired personal recognition, a sense of empowerment, a route to future media access, or an opportunity to impose harms on their enemies or competitors. There are also potential costs; most obviously, the media may injure a source by disclosing her identity, leading to retaliation or embarrassment. The reporter and, subsequently, the publisher or broadcaster offer these benefits and create the risk of costs in exchange for information that, depending on its quality, may benefit the media entity by giving it a better story to publish or broadcast – that is, a better product to sell to a public. Even if no cash is involved (although sometimes it is in so-called checkbook journalism), as with any voluntary exchange, this exchange is usually mutually beneficial – that is, efficient from the perspective of the media and the source. This mutuality presumptively justifies reliance on the market, that is, these negotiated agreements. Still, this dyad merits special attention. Contract law is neither a natural phenomenon nor, as contract breaches demonstrate, something that parties necessarily experience as mutually advantageous at the time for performance. Rather, contract is a governmentally established institution that regulates when, if, and how the government will enforce an agreement.

Failure to obtain "efficient" levels of disclosure by sources might occur if the law denied the opportunity to enter into effective binding agreements between sources and reporters. Any limit on this opportunity might be predicted to reduce the availability of information from sources. Consider, however, two examples, one where the government forces the press to break its promise, and the other where it forces the press to keep the promise.

Being able to promise anonymity helps a reporter "pay" for information; the media internalize a major potential cost of a publicity-shy source. The government's claimed right to demand that a reporter testify and expose the source[33] limits the reporter's ability to give persuasive assurances, thereby reducing the availability of information.[34] The blockage arguably leads to an inefficient reduction in news production. Of course, the law could create a "reporter's privilege" – a right not to testify or not to disclose the identity of a confidential source – not given to other members of society. This special right could be seen as a government subsidy of the press. The law grants the reporter a right, a resource. Thus, the question might be whether society wisely grants this subsidy.

Of course, characterizing a "reporter's privilege" as a subsidy follows only from a particular conception of the baseline – for example, a generalized duty to testify even when the duty would substantially deter creation of socially valuable information such as a client's statements to her attorney. This characterization of the baseline is not an analytic but a policy matter; arguably, the baseline should be that the reporter has this privilege. This view distinguishes the reporter *in this context* from other citizens. She possesses the information covered by the privilege only because of being a journalist. Unlike most members of society, the reporter's professional activity creates a real social value in the capacity to offer anonymity. To the extent denial of the privilege deters sources, those seeking courtroom testimony as well as the public lose. And to the extent that the constitutional guarantee of press freedom represents a commitment to protect this business, a plausible view is that this constitutional commitment requires that this information about the source's identity, which is generated by the press, belongs to the "press."[35] Recognizing a reporter's "special" testimonial privilege does not give the press something that otherwise was the government's, but only gives it something created by its own constitutionally protected activity. From this perspective, required testimony amounts to a negative externality of the court system.

The preceding paragraph argued that the press's ability to grant anonymity merits protection. Similarly, a simplistic economic analysis suggests that a press enterprise should be able to contractually promise confidentiality.[36] The availability of contract provides the news organization with a tool to create, without cost to outsiders, something of value to give the source in exchange for information. Without this, information might be lost to the press and, thereby, to the public. Exemptions from liability when the media violates its promise by publishing the source's name, for example, on the ground that liability should never be imposed on the truthful publication of information,[37] would inefficiently lead to reduced production of news. The claim is that freedom of contract (just like property rights – consider copyright) is an essential condition for maximum and efficient production of information.

A more textured account, however, must consider the effect of contract liability on journalistic practices and on the *quality* of information produced.[38] For example, does the unavailability of liability disempower journalists as opposed to editors, for example, because it prevents reporters from committing the enterprise to the decision about publishing a source's name? Or, alternatively, would the potential availability of contract liability lead media enterprises to centralize more power in editors, whose permission would be required before a reporter was allowed to promise confidentiality? This development would disempower reporters. And given the answers to these questions, what would the effect be on the quality or nature of news produced?[39]

Without legally enforceable contracts, journalism has functioned fine. Reporters have long offered and sources have long relied on promises of confidentiality. Thus, it is worth considering what is gained (or lost) by adding the opportunity to contract. Consider when the source is most likely to demand a *legally binding* promise. This will most likely occur if the source reasonably fears that the media entity will have strong journalistic reasons to breach the promise. The press will have these reasons if it concludes that the source's identity is itself important news (e.g., because the source had attempted to manipulate the press into publishing misleadingly negative information about a political opponent).[40] Thus, the *New York Times* now has a policy that it will not honor its promises if the source has provided the paper with "lies and false documentation."[41] If this is the typical situation when a source would be deterred without a contractually binding promise, the analysis favoring contract falters. If non-enforceability silences this source the most obvious "loss" is misleading or "corrupt" information. In contrast, enforceability deters publication of politically relevant and truthful exposés about unethical attempts to manipulate the media and, thereby, the public. The negative externalities of "bad" information merely add to the undesirable nature of these results. Thus, the ability to contract here may increase the information obtained from sources but pollute its quality. The economic analysis that merely looked at "quantity" is seen as unwisely simplistic. Audiences *may* be benefited by making these promises unenforceable if the result is that "bad" information is less prominent. Common-law doctrine could develop the principle that, in light of First Amendment values, contracts are unenforceable as contrary to public policy if they restrict disclosure or publication of information needed to serve the public interest. To avoid content evaluation of the press's publication decisions, its publication of the information could be taken as conclusive of whether the public is served thereby. Merely relying on contract and the market cannot be said here to be clearly the best way of giving the audience what it wants.

## Costs Imposed or Benefits Created by Information-Gathering Techniques

The journalist's information gathering activities sometimes directly create benefits or, more often, impose costs. The "speeding" reporter may damage property or injure people in a rush to obtain a story. Of course, the recognized applicability of general laws to reporters' activities is the legal means to internalize this cost on a reporter's decision making – the car accident produces civil or criminal liability. However, general laws (i.e., laws not specifically directed at communicative activities) often do not cover harms caused merely by a reporter's presence and her questioning. She may, for example, intrude into privacy or interfere with personal, business, or political relationships. After safely rushing to be first to interview the crime victim, the reporter can be painfully intrusive, whether or not later publication occurs, with publication merely being an additional upsetting invasion. Consider the reporter who, after a mother kills her two young children and then herself, goes next door with camera rolling. Knowing that the parents are not at home, the reporter tells the murdered children's young playmates about what happened in order to get their reaction on film.[42]

The impact of gathering news is more routine than suggested by vivid examples like the speeding or insensitive reporter. People who know they are being monitored, especially if they know they are being recorded on audio- or videotape by the press, will often change their speech or other behavior from that which they would otherwise prefer. Although the federal government does not bar recording of conversations as long as one party (e.g., the reporter) consents,[43] many states outlaw tape recording unless all parties consent.[44] If without consent and without a legal remedy a person is recorded, any later pain, embarrassment, or loss caused by the exposure of the taped message is a cost externalized onto that subject. When the person consents or is told about the recording in circumstances where her continued speaking amounts to consent, her changed behavior is still an effect. If consent was simply the best option in the circumstances but still undesired, the reporter still imposes a cost not internalized on the press.

For third parties, the changed behavior of the subjects of news gathering can count as either a benefit or cost depending on whether or not they prefer the change. The mere presence of reporters can negatively affect the content and openness of discussion at a board meeting or among a group of people trying to decide how to respond to some issue. Televising a trial might affect a jury's attention or attitude toward the case; the received view is that televising jury deliberations would be inappropriately intrusive and probably distortive. Alternatively, the presence of reporters or news gatherers (and of recordings) can be beneficial. "On the record" board discussions may be fairer or wiser in their output. In other contexts, a reporter's presence can provide an unpopular group with increased safety or an activist organizer with increased status. In one of the original cases bringing the issue of reporters' privilege to the Supreme Court, local Black Panther officials had invited a reporter to their headquarters at a time of an expected police raid, presumably in the hope that the reporter would either document or, by his presence, deter police misconduct.[45]

Sometimes ongoing relationships between a reporter and her subjects, or general background property or tort rights such as a right of exclusion implicit in ownership of private property,[46] or other unique features of situations allow rough internalization of many effects of the activity of news gathering. Still, routinely the activity of news gathering creates benefits and costs – and generates changes in behavior – that are independent of later publication and that are not internalized into the media's decision making. In these cases, the media do not pay the full costs or receive the full benefits of news gathering. Audiences will receive more of some content than they would if the press had to pay all costs of its news gathering. And audiences receive the reverse, less content than they should, when reporting creates uncompensated benefits, for example, better or fairer conduct of public affairs at public meetings or more safety for dissidents. Not taking into account these externalities distorts media content in particular ways, possibly toward more sensationalism and away from coverage of public affairs and dissent.

CHAPTER 4

# The Market as a Measure of Preferences

In a perfectly working marketplace, people engage in exchanges so as best to fulfill their existing preferences – as expressed by market exchanges and given their willingness and ability to pay. Market advocates assume that people's willingness and ability to pay within a market properly identify and measure consumer preferences. Only if this assumption is valid can unimpeded markets be expected to give people what they want; only then is the consumer really sovereign. This chapter critiques that assumption.

Significantly, people express preferences not only in the market and not only through market behavior. Indeed, people often express preferences simply by saying they prefer something, and what they will say they prefer often changes as the context changes. People also express preferences by choosing to spend time engaged in one activity rather than another. Indeed, the market is incapable of identifying a preference that requires avoidance of the market. That is, the market's willingness-and-ability-to-pay standard is merely one way to identify and measure preferences. What is identified and measured is an artifact of the method used, and other methods are possible. A system could refuse to credit any expression that does not survive discussion and reflection. Another system might measure preferences on the basis of how much a person would be willing to pay under circumstances in which everyone begins with equal wealth. Both these systems let the person be sovereign, counting only her expressions of preferences. Both offer a method of identifying and, at least in the second case, of measuring preferences, but both get results very different from the market's.

No neutral or logical principle indicates that one or another identification or measure of preferences is more accurate, legitimate, or "real." Society's (or an analyst's) determination of which expressions to credit depends on the purpose of the identification and measurement. The choice can always be, and often is, contested. That is the stuff of politics. Presumably, the measure that a society chooses to credit will vary depending on the issue or context. Moreover, the response to these contexts often turns on society's conception of the qualities of a person that the society treats as most significant, either in general or in that context. With these observations in mind, I consider three types of possible objections to reliance on market identification and measurement of preferences: (1) market measures are sometimes misguided because they are too commodified and ignore preferences for noncommodified communications;[1] (2) relatedly, market measures only identify expressions made in one context, and that context should not be privileged; and (3) the market's criterion – willingness and ability to pay – is often inappropriate largely because it is insufficiently egalitarian. If the market does not properly identify or weigh preferences, there can be no reason to expect that it will effectively give people what they want.

## COMMODIFICATION

Market exchange commodifies the good exchanged.[2] For purposes of the exchange, each party treats the item she gives up solely instrumentally. That is, she uses the item as a means to exercise power over the other.[3] She uses it and values it solely as a means to get a performance from the other. And the other gives the performance only because of receiving the "payment." The fact that both prefer the outcome to the prior status quo does not prevent the exchange from being a mutual exercise of power of each over the other.

The social role or value of some goods may be perverted or undermined merely by being distributed through commercial exchange rather than being subject only to being earned or bestowed.* Although people often spend large sums of money on preparation for a sports or intellectual competition, the very point (and value) of winning the first-place award is that, in the final instance, it is "earned," not purchased. The trophy customarily has a unique and usually higher value to the

---

* Slightly different is the belief that certain activities of creating and certain created goods are perverted if produced merely on the basis of market demand, whether or not those goods are then thought appropriately distributed by the market. This observation relates to one rationale for treating many occupations that sell "speech," such as psychiatry, law, teaching, or the priesthood – and journalism – as professions. Satisfying preferences hardly explains why professionals sometimes must complain about their audience "killing the messenger."

person who has won than to a stranger. Certainly its value is as a historically or narratively identified object rather than as an "anonymous" object available for use; market exchange inevitably changes and often defaces or erases that history or narrative.[4] Similar things are often said of love. Some people's primary objection to commercialized sex is a fear that commercialization will pervert or undermine the social salience of a noncommodified conception of love. For somewhat different reasons, society resists the commodification of the vote, elected office, or life-preserving body parts.

Some aspects of communication obviously resist commodification. Possibly one of the most defining characteristics of human life is speech aimed at agreement – or, more generally, conversation. The premise of this activity is either the gift relation or the notion that both are mutually engaged in a shared activity. The activity of exercising power, implicit in exchange transactions, is inconsistent with the enterprise of discursively reaching agreement. Nor is it present in the mutuality of conversation or bestowal of an informational or entertainment gift on the other. To use sociological terms, much of people's communications occurs within the lifeworld, the premises of which are inconsistent with regulation by the economic subsystem.

Other communications are unproblematically commodified. The press has always been at least in part a business, as have theater, film, and television.[5] Most mass media are products generated by the economic order. Still, it is clear that people can lose something of great value when entertainment and culture become *too* commodified or too routinely commodified. George Gerbner, former dean of the Annenberg School of Communications, regularly observes that the age of commercial television is the first time in human history that children learn about themselves and the world primarily by listening to corporations with something to sell rather than to people with something to tell. Family storytelling or a town's participatory ritual celebrations or reenactments differ from their commercialized counterparts. The differences are threefold. First, opportunities for the practices are distributed differently – opportunities to engage in the noncommodified version are more democratically available. Second, their overt content is likely to differ for various reasons. Third, even if the overt content were to remain the same, the experience of receiving (and providing) the content can differ dramatically. A plate or bottle of wine has different significance for a person if won in a competition or received as a gift than if purchased from a seller. The same is true of a story.

Commodification changes, sometimes worsens, the experience of receiving access to culture and entertainment.

Thus, it is no surprise that many people resist commodification of some communications. Calling teaching an act of love expresses the more general thought that in at least some social interactions (e.g., in conversation) people ought to give others the benefit of their insight.[†] Doing so shows respect or care for the recipient. In giving, actors routinely and not improperly make choices partly on the basis of their view of the recipient's needs, although the recipient can always say no. The structure thereby honors the autonomy of both parties. In contrast, the market systematically responds to the recipient's own perceptions (possibly influenced by advertising) of her preferences. Nevertheless, the recipient will often prefer the noncommodified context. This preference is often part of the explanation for why people sometimes, not always, resist commercializing conversation. Restating this at a societal level, the claim would be that various cultural resources ought to be available to people not based on their willingness and ability to pay its market price, maybe not even available through market transactions, but through social interactions defined by solidarity, honesty, giving, and willingness to search for answers.

Although trade secrets, patents, and other legal devices help commodify *some commercial* uses of facts and ideas, a sense of the unseemliness of copyrighting facts and ideas illustrates cultural resistance to commodification – a characteristic also present in the invocation of "fair use" to resist liability for many noncommercial uses of copyrighted

---

[†] A perverse case of commodification is the student who does not talk in class out of fear of giving away her "good ideas." This case can be contrasted with the activist who seeks to give away "good," public-interest-oriented ideas. Academics are used to students being charged tuition for the receipt of the professor's speech. Nevertheless, many of these academics felt strangely uneasy in the late 1960s about the students who complained that they were not getting what they paid for when professors canceled a class as part of a political protest – uneasy, I believe, because the complainants reminded them that their class was in at least some respects a commodity. Likewise, many, but not all, faculty think it unobjectionable for a student to bring a nonpaying friend to class (unless the friend's presence is disruptive or there is inadequate physical space). Many instructors would not even object to a nonpaying person sitting in all semester, especially if it were a large lecture class. Although the institution treats classes as a commodity, the instructor, who is not paid on the basis of the number of paying students, resists this orientation. When I realized this as an undergraduate, I became quite despondent at the thought that I (i.e., my parents) were paying for credits or degrees, not for an education that was apparently available for free – I could simply attend. The economic perversity of my reaction reminds me now of the standard movie story line of the guy paying the hooker and only wanting conversation, not sex, with this eventually leading to love(?) and sex without payment. See *Leaving Las Vegas* (Metro-Goldwyn-Mayer/United Artists, 1995).

materials. The widespread existence of and support for free public libraries and public theater can also be seen as fighting the commodification of a common culture.

Whether or not true, a popular belief is that the best cultural content will be an expression of talent, possibly even of genius, and that production following these artistic dictates often will be inconsistent with production of commodities for the market. Similar is a belief that journalism should express integrity and professional craft unperverted by the market. I will not here defend these views or discuss their implications for media policy. These assertions suggest, however, that maybe a good society would provide space or opportunities, presumably meaning a subsidy, for the creative expressions either of all people or, at least, of specially identified professionally committed people or specially identified "talented" people. To the extent people prefer such a society, their preferences speak more to public policy and cannot be effectively registered or implemented by the market.

These observations about people's desires for noncommodified communications should be obvious. Less obvious is why it matters for policy purposes. The question is: why not merely allow people to choose? Virtually all people sometimes prefer commodified, sometimes noncommodified, cultural content. Both commodified and noncommodified communications have value. Each has its proper domain – one in the economy, one in the lifeworld. The two coexist. Why will people's choices not lead to an optimal mix? Just as history has shown in relation to sex, neither commodified nor noncommodified entertainment or discourse is likely to disappear. Of course, commodified and noncommodified options often compete for people's time and resources.[6] When commodified forms become cheaper, they will be chosen more often. But this variation is not a reason to object; presumably, more preferences are satisfied when costs go down. The market is left to work in its domain. On this voluntarist view, the observation that commodification is sometimes unwanted is admitted but is not found to show that the market, when used, fails to give people what they want. People seek out whichever type of information, entertainment, or other communications they prefer whenever they want. Thus, the observation that people sometimes prefer noncommodified communications should be irrelevant for policy purposes.

Against this claim of irrelevance, I consider three possible objections. First, the view about coexistence can be too optimistic. Second, even if it is not, policy choices that cannot be made by the market but inevitably set the parameters on which the market operates significantly affect the balance between commodified and noncommodified communications in ways that people may or may not want. Third, noncommodified communications may require resource support that the market is ill-equipped to supply.

Coexistence assumes that the social environment reflects a summation of many individual choices. However, sometimes individual choice can create a "domino" effect that moves toward particular results. A particular choice can be "contagious" in the sense that one or a few people's choice places great pressure on others to make the same choice.[7] Likewise, sometimes one or a few people's choice determines the outcome in a manner that makes other people's contrary choice irrelevant. The choice of one or a few hunters to shoot an endangered species can eviscerate the effectiveness of all others' choice to refrain from shooting in order to preserve the species. The same might be true if one person sets off her backyard nuclear weapon while everyone else in the community chooses not to use theirs. Allowing individual choice rather than deciding outcomes politically does not normally work best to maximally satisfy preferences when choices are "determinative" in this way.

Why and when a domino or determinative effect occurs is the crucial question here. Sometimes this effect may occur because a particular structure – for example, the market – enforces it within the realm that the particular structure operates. When a person relies on market sales for livelihood, she must replace the resources she used to produce the items she sells. If she is unable to sell at a price at least equal to the replacement cost of her inputs, she loses her livelihood – goes bankrupt. The possible selling price, however, is partly determined by the competition. If another seller introduces new, more "efficient" practices that allow him to sell at a price lower than her replacement cost, given her current practices, she must either change her practices or go under. Thus, the market enforces a domino effect in the direction of efficient practices – a point observed by grand theorists ranging from Marx to Weber and the feature hailed by many conservative defenses of the market.[8] Much earlier in *The Prince*, Niccolo Machiavelli made a similar point. The structural context can require the Prince to adopt behavior not generally praised by the ethicists. Unless the Prince acts in the strategically most effective manner, however, he will lose out to one who does.

Even if domino effects often powerfully influence decisions of producers within the market, this "system effect" does not control whether people enter into the system. The "household" or lifeworld decision of whether to enter – as well as what to buy when one enters as a consumer – is not controlled by the mechanism described here. People are free (of at least this mechanism of market competition) when deciding whether to purchase a commodity within the market or, alternatively, to seek noncommodified goods or practices outside it. The mere existence of the commodified option should not cause a domino effect unless there exists a "natural" tendency to commodify, a "debatable ideological postulate . . . that utopian non-commodifiers can[not] afford to endorse."[9] Of course, whether some commodification will lead to the activity or good being progressively seen more and more as a commodity, with the result that the noncommodified relation eventually becomes unsustainable, is a vital question about cultural processes. But there seems to be no reason why this would be so. Opportunities for noncommodified relations to creation, distribution, and consumption of content can coexist with commodification. More generally, culture does not appear to work in a domino or determinative fashion. It typically reflects the summation of each person's choices.[10] Of course, people are subject to persuasion; cultural leaders and innovators exist and can be very influential. Still, as Radin noted, without implausible assumptions about a universal tendency for imitative commodification, the fact that one person seeks or consumes commodified culture does not require and, maybe, does not even create great pressure for others to do so.[11] Thus, at least in the extreme form, this domino-effect argument should be rejected.

The voluntarist thesis, however, must maintain more than that commodified and noncommodified media and cultural experiences can coexist. It must show that individual choice leads to the right or preferred proportion of each. There is little reason to expect that this will be true. Clearly legal rules, as well as consumer choice, shape the result by determining how difficult (or rewarding) it is for a person to choose either commodified or noncommodified communications. An expanded scope of copyright, for example, can both increase the availability of (some) commodified communications and restrict opportunities for (some) noncommodified communications. At the extreme, if all words were copyrighted and there were no fair-use rights, no noncommodified conversation could occur. Less extreme was the *Washington Post* and the *Los Angeles Times*'s lawsuit to stop an on-line conservative discussion group from posting clippings of *their* stories, which were then used as the basis of the group's discussions.[12]

Defamation law can also affect the comparative cost and, hence, prevalence of commodified and noncommodified communications. If Justice Potter Stewart had been right that the Constitution protected newspapers from libel judgments in contexts in which it did not protect private individuals,[13] the scenario could be imagined where a person would be subject to liability for reading or summarizing a defamatory story to her partner at the breakfast table but the newspaper, from which it was read, would be insulated from liability. The pressure toward choosing the commodified form is obvious under such a legal regime. (Under existing law, both media and individuals can be libel for repeating someone else's defamatory statements.)

The point is that legal rules always provide part of the background framework on which both enterprise's productive decisions and people's individual choices, especially their market choices, take place. Given the capacity of the background legal regime to affect choice, no references to what individuals choose under a particular market regime can show the extent people prefer commodified or noncommodified communications or culture. At best, actual individual choices merely show what people prefer *given those rules, that is, given policy decisions made independently of the market*. With different background rules, consumers' choices, their apparent preferences, would be different.[14] Hence, the market by itself cannot be assumed to maximally satisfy preferences. It cannot resolve the question of which legal regime or context of choice best gives people what they want. That is, voluntarist choice within a legal regime cannot make the choice between legal regime. Rather, the only obvious institutional method of finding and weighing evidence of preferences for noncommodified versus commodified communications is collective decision making, most obviously discursive political choices, that register these preferences by adopting legal frameworks that do or do not facilitate noncommodified options.

The voluntarist claim also does not consider the propriety of policy decisions concerning whether to make resources available for noncommodified communications. The meaning of noncommodification lies in part in the goods or activities not being allocated by, or overtly participating in, the market. There can be degrees of removal from the market. At one extreme, for some activities – storytelling within the home, for example – people may simply make individual choices about their time and efforts (if one assumes that storytelling, or noncommodified theatrical performances or singing, does not violate copyright or some similar "commodifying" rule). By comparison, public broadcasting, storytelling as a community activity held at schools or libraries, free public concerts in the park, and public access to video production facilities and cable public-access channels are all noncommodified to a degree but all also require resources, from paid employees to facilities and equipment, that are secured through market transactions. This reliance on economic resources makes the value of noncommodification relevant for public policy. Collective-action and free-rider problems as well as distributive issues prevent gifts or other voluntary nonmarket allocations from supporting these noncommodified activities to the extent that individuals would wish. Because the market cannot adequately register and respond to preferences for noncommodified media or culture, reliance must be placed on collective, usually governmental processes. Desires for noncommodified communications may be great and socially significant. Reliance merely on the market will lead to their drastic undersatisfaction.

## DISTRIBUTION

A market distributes goods based on people's willingness and ability to pay. It "weights" preferences on the basis of the money placed behind them. Obviously there could be other weightings, hence other distributions, and, consequently, other preferences being satisfied. There are three main points here. First, there is nothing objectively either accurate or just about weightings based on the existing distribution of wealth; there is no reason to believe that it measures the "real" strength of preferences. Second, this is not the only possible weighting. Third, this weighting is particularly objectionable if the underlying distribution of wealth is objectionable.

On the third point, it seems to me unquestionable that the existing distribution of wealth in the United States is incredibly unjust. Given this injustice, those outcomes that result from relying (as do market practices) on this distribution as the starting point are presumptively unjust – or, in the language I have been using, are not what people would want under an acceptable distribution of wealth. This point discredits reliance on markets for determining the production and distribution of media products – *but no more than it does for any other product.* Despite my claim of unjustness, society largely accepts the existing distribution of wealth and its use to distribute most goods. Thus, this section considers only distributional concerns that have special relevance in the media context.

The first point, however, still needs emphasis. "Willingness and ability to pay" counts preferences of the wealthy more than those of the poor. Nothing about the liberal idea of respecting (or satisfying) people's preferences implies the propriety of this weighting. Nothing about being wealthy implies that a person's preferences are stronger. No premise that the economy ought to satisfy people's preferences requires the conclusion that a rich person's $240 French dinner (with a "good" wine) fulfills three times as many preferences as a poor family's $80 spent on food staples intended to last a week. Of course, economists do not make such a stupid claim. They mostly eschew interpersonal comparisons, there being no logically or objectively correct way to compare different people's preferences. Still, any assertion that the market gives people what they want implicitly accepts money as the criterion for making comparisons.[15] This criterion, however, is no more a correct measure of collective preferences than would be many others, including subjective evaluations. There is no reason to believe the market criterion best provides for fulfilling preferences – for giving people what they want. Once this fallacy is recognized, other possibilities open up. Indeed, for various practical and normative reasons, society *often* uses the medium of money to determine who gets what. All democratic societies, however, reject the market criterion in many contexts. When they do, their alternative mechanisms of distribution still generally respond to some expression of preference or desire but in effect weigh preferences by other standards.

## PRINCIPLES OF DISTRIBUTION

No society believes that all goods are properly distributed on the basis of willingness and ability to pay. Democratic societies always treat some goods as properly distributed on a basis of equality or need (or merit of some sort). The vote, citizenship, life-sustaining organs, and various negative liberties are possible examples. Many democracies guarantee at least minimal levels of public education, food, shelter, and health care to all members. Usually, receipt of police and fire protection is distributed for free on a somewhat egalitarian basis. In response to an argument that "would permit the State to apportion all benefits and services according to past tax contributions of its Citizens," the Supreme Court asserted that "the Equal Protection Clause prohibits such an apportionment of state services."[16]

According to Michael Walzer, "[t]he social contract is an agreement to reach decisions together about what goods are necessary to our common life, *and then to provide those goods for one another.*"[17] He goes on to claim that "[t]here has never been a political community that did not provide, or try to provide, or claim to provide, for the needs of its members as its members understood those needs."[18] His account emphasizes that the goods considered essential to membership and that are distributed on a more egalitarian, nonmarket basis vary with the culture of the particular democracy.[19]

These observations leave the question, What distributive principles should apply to media products? Most democracies use a combination of market and nonmarket devices. Historically, some government publications, public libraries, and, more recently, public broadcasting provide media content beyond what people receive through the market. This combination of market and nonmarket provision makes sense for two reasons: first, as is emphasized in Part II, the significance of assuring an independent-minded media and of preventing censorship counsel in favor of supporting a wide variety of different forms of media creation and distribution.

More relevant here is the second reason. Media products serve different functions: they educate, inform political participation, foment and energize civic and political participation, provide a forum for public debate and dialogue. Media content influences public officials directly but also indirectly through influencing the views or opinions of citizens; and it helps create and provides a significant part of the culture in which people live. But the media also serve a wide second set of functions. They amuse, entertain, and divert. They promote private consumption of commercial products and provide information relevant for people's private consumptive activities – and this list could continue. A market measure of preferences might be perfectly appropriate for media content that primarily serves an entertainment function. And there is no legitimate reason to prevent people from receiving (properly priced) media that the market will provide. On the other hand, remember that the vote and education are purportedly distributed more egalitarianly. A democracy could rationally conclude that media content crucial to people's democratic participation or their continued education ought be provided on a subsidized and egalitarian basis. Likewise, access to culturally important media arguably should not depend solely on ability to pay.[20] Basically, society concludes that market responses to preferences are appropriate for a wide range of goods but also concludes that a more egalitarian response is appropriate for goods that relate to a person's status and capability to be a full member of the community. Media products fit into both categories. A mixed system of responses is called for.

Distributing different media content on the basis of different principles, particularly given the legal order's role in making the distinction between categories, creates a potential constitutional difficulty. In *Turner Broadcasting System v. FCC*, the Supreme Court apparently treated a concern with content as a constitutionally inappropriate basis for structural regulation of the media.[21] That view, however, is out of line with both history and Court precedent.[22] Content concerns have been central to governmental media regulation and interventions since the beginning of the republic. In 1792, Congress, following late colonial practice, provided for mail subsidies for newspapers out of a purported concern with promoting the distribution of a particular content category – the news.[23] In the twentieth century, the government gave licenses to broadcasters in a manner designed to produce types of dialogue or content that the government considered valuable.[24] Currently, both newspapers and broadcasters exist under media-specific rules regulating ownership that are designed to have a beneficial impact on content available in the communications environment.[25]

The Court's episodic impulse to treat content-oriented regulation by the government as contrary to basic First Amendment principles largely reflects, I believe, the ubiquitous use of content-based regulations to suppress or censor speech. Suppression contradicts both egalitarian and liberty-based democratic premises. Because the government seldom wants to suppress all speech but rather wants to suppress speech of a particular content, forbidding content discrimination often eliminates suppression and censorship. The evil, however, is suppression. Content discrimination by the government, when not involving suppression, is common and can be desirable.

Of course, categorization of content is not simple. The same material can serve multiple functions for one recipient or serve different functions for different members of its audience. The distinction between politics and entertainment, between politically salient and politically irrelevant communications, is notoriously slippery.[26] Still, for many legitimate and practical purposes, this and related content distinctions are continually made by both individuals and governments. Content discrimination seemed implicit in the law granting cheap postal rates for publications that are "published for the dissemination of information of a public character, or devoted to literature, the sciences, arts, or some special industry."[27] Here, the Supreme Court concluded that the Post Office was severely limited in its authority to deny that material fit the category. However, in selecting books to assign in class or to purchase for the public library, the necessity of choice does not permit this escape. Content concerns are equally central in selecting artistic or cultural projects to receive governmental support.

## MEANING OF EQUALITY IN THE MEDIA CONTEXT

If egalitarian premises are to determine the availability of media content, the egalitarian standard needs clarification. Clarity turns out to be deceptively difficult largely because different groups often prefer different media products. By comparison, equality for voters was easy: each person has a right to vote in districts with approximately equal populations.[28] But what policies provide for all people equally in the media context?

Equality in respect to some types of goods means getting roughly the same dollars' worth of the goods. Thus, equality in school finance might be understood as each school district having the same amount of money to spend per student.[29] But even in public education, equal per-student expenditures is only one possible meaning of equality. Maybe a state provides for equality if each school district has the capacity to raise the same per-student revenue by adopting the same tax rates – "district power equalization." Or maybe equality requires that each student (or each group of students), no matter how much it costs, gets equally educated (as measured either by their potential or by some absolute standard). The proper notion of equality depends on the specific "right" or value at stake in education finance. Even greater complexities exist in the media context.

First, it might seem that when a poor person and a rich person spend $1, fairness requires that each get a media product that costs $1 to provide. However, advertisers often skew the result.[30] Advertisers pay for media intended for their targets – usually, the comparatively affluent – to a much greater extent than media designed for the poor. An affluent person may be charged $.40 – or nothing – for a media product that costs $1 because advertisers will pay the extra $.60. Because poor people have less to spend on the advertisers' products, their value to advertisers is less. Thus, media enterprises must charge much closer to the full cost for media products directed at the poor – maybe $.95 for a $1 product. When price discrimination is possible, media firms often charge the poor more than affluent customers for the same content. Magazines and newspapers, which benefit by being able to present advertisers with high-profile audience demographics, offer low-price or free "sample" subscriptions in wealthy neighborhoods while charging the higher "regular" prices in poor neighborhoods. Newspapers purposely design their content to discourage purchases by poor people. Television drops shows that attract huge audiences if their demographics are wrong – too old, too rural, or too poor. The net result is that even beyond their having greater wealth with which to buy media products, wealthy people have their preferred media subsidized by advertisers.

This skewed subsidy is strikingly unfair, especially if media content involves a person's role as a citizen and not merely as a consumer. In *Harper v. Virginia Board of Elections*,[31] the Supreme Court struck down a poll tax.[32] The Court thought that charging the rich and poor *the same* in order to enter the voting booth denied equality given that the same "price" burdened the poor more than the rich. But access to media content may be a prerequisite to meaningful exercise of the franchise.[33] Thus, while *Harper* implies that media content oriented toward and available to the poor should be subsidized, reality in an advertising-dominated world is the reverse.

*Harper* suggests the more substantive notion, recommended earlier, that society ought to make equal provision for all people's access to politically salient media products. So I return to the question, does this equality mean that each person should have roughly the same amount to spend on her preferred media products?

For many goods, an equal amount to spend would be the obvious meaning of equality. Equality is arguably satisfied if each person has the same amount to spend on a car, on food, or on education. Even here, one might be concerned about this interpretation. Consider, for example, a Los Angeles resident as compared with a New York City subway rider; or a very large, active person or a diabetic with special food needs as compared with a physically small, inactive individual. Consider the person with special educational needs. Sometimes, the most meaningful notion of equality relates to the level of need fulfillment.

In the media context, the economics of public goods complicates the analysis of equality even further. The more consumption is nonrivalrous, the more the good's availability to a single person will reflect not just her expenditure but the aggregate expenditures of all those who want it. For example, putting aside copy costs, if each person gets to spend $1 and if a thousand persons each use that dollar to buy the results of an investigative journalism effort, then each receives a $1,000 investigative report for her dollar. But if only ten people want that investigative journalism, then each can expect only a $10 product for a dollar expenditure. Clearly, a person in the broad mainstream benefits most from equal amounts to spend on nonrivalrous goods, which includes most media products. "Culture" and news is more lavishly provided for such a person than for others. This inequality in result, of course, still embodies one possible concept of equality: each person gets an equal amount to spend.

The lack of equivalence, however, suggests a second conception. Equality could mean that each person gets to have the same amount spent on producing media content that she desires. The first conception gives each person the same amount *to spend*, the second gives each person a product on which the amount *is spent*. These two conceptions would be operationally equivalent except for the "public-good" aspect of media products. But given this public-good element, the first is a form of equality of opportunity: anyone who wants some content, say mainstream content, has the same opportunity to get it as anyone else. This form of equality, however, dramatically rewards people for being in the mainstream. The second conception is a form of equality of outcomes or equality of results, a much more radical standard. Imagine, for example, if society spent the same amount on creating products oriented toward the political or cultural concerns of gay and lesbian people and of heterosexual people, such that gays' cultural needs were provided for to the same extent as those of straights. Which standard treats people equally? The question is not rhetorical. Different conceptions of equality are available and each requires a defense that is convincing *in the given context*.

In addition to the second conception's radical nature and, if rigorously applied, its impracticality, there are possible normative grounds to favor the first and object to the second. An assimilationist or melting pot perspective is very consistent with each person controlling the same resources spent on media content, because the result, given the public-good quality of media expenditures, is to push people's choices toward the mainstream. Similarly, in one influential conception of democracy, democratic interest-group pluralism as described in Chapter 6, the degree to which a group prevails should depend roughly on its size. From this perspective, the advantage that the standard of equal amount to spend gives to the mainstream is not objectionable. It is just tough that people with relatively unique tastes have them satisfied less. It would be unfair, possibly elitist, for members of small groups to get more resources *per person* devoted to their preferred media than do members of large groups.

Other powerful normative arguments, however, suggest a role for equality of outcome – that is, equal amounts spent on preferred media products. Will Kymlicka observes that individuals typically require a relatively stable cultural context for identity formation, for maintenance of self-respect and self-confidence, and for having meaningful life options. People's capacity for effective choice normally depends on membership in a cultural community with a cultural heritage; coercive assimilation can have literally deadly results, leading to increased rates of suicide and destroying people's very sense of agency.[34] Cultural structure is a vital *context* of choice.

Given these observations, Kymlicka then draws on John Rawls' claim "that we should have social conditions needed to intelligently decide for ourselves what is valuable."[35] Because people cannot intelligently examine and choose options except from within "a rich and secure cultural structure," the Rawlsian liberal must "be concerned with the fate of cultural structures."[36] Rawls reasons that "parties in the original position would wish to avoid at almost any cost the social conditions that undermine self-respect."[37] Kymlicka argues that one such condition is "loss of cultural membership."[38] For this reason, liberals such as Rawls should see membership in a viable community with its own cultural heritage as a "primary good" concerning which inequalities are a matter of injustice.[39] Its value as a primary good lies "in its capacity of providing meaningful options for us and aiding our ability to judge for ourselves the value of our life-plans."[40] The relevance of this observation is, of course, hardly limited to Rawlsians. These considerations lead Jürgen Habermas, for example, to conclude that a liberal version of the system of rights must ensure "*strict equal treatment*, directed by the citizens themselves, *of the life contexts* that safeguard their identities."[41]

Treating cultural structures as Rawlsian primary goods suggests that justice requires that they be distributed equally (unless inequality benefits the worst off). But equality cannot mean merely making a single dominant culture equally available to anyone who wants to join. This would be like the view, properly critiqued by feminists, of equality meaning equal opportunities for both men and women to assimilate to the dominant male norm. Such interpretations "misconstrue the universalism of basic rights as an abstract leveling of distinction."[42] Empirically, most people find that their own background culture is the context for their subsequent choices,[43] even if these choices sometimes consciously deviate from the person's cultural tradition – choices that, when added to those of others, will change that tradition. Because a cultural structure, not income, is here the Rawlsian "primary good," equality in relation to this primary good requires something closer to equal amounts spent on one's culture – the outcome equality notion.

The same conclusion follows from adopting a second theory of democracy. A Habermasian "dialogic" or what in Chapter 6 I label a "complex" theory of democracy emphasizes respect for and the adequate development of any seriously advanced (reasonable?) view.[44] Presumably, media products should equally serve different groups' democratic or civic visions and discourses. This objective suggests something like expenditures that equally provide for the different visions, not equal per-person expenditures. Equal expenditures supporting each perspective best keeps alive a cultural pluralism. Thus, this conception of democracy and the related positive valuation of cultural pluralism both suggest that a person should not be disadvantaged merely because she is different. Society ought to be concerned that people's basic participatory needs for media content are equally satisfied.

To conclude, democratic theory clearly supports at least some egalitarian tilt in satisfying preferences for media content. This tilt should apply more strongly the more the media content in question serves political, educational, or cultural roles. Still, despite normative arguments for the more radical interpretation in the media context, the demands this "outcome" interpretation makes on the community may be too great. It would be somewhat unfair as well as unworkable to follow stringently this conception of equality.

Consider two reasons to limit the claim that treating media goods as a Rawlsian primary entails the claim that members of smaller identity groups have a right to have as much be spent on products tailored to their needs as is spent on goods for members of the mainstream, resulting in much higher per-person expenditures for their preferred media goods. First, the egalitarian claim follows only because this good is a primary good – a resource necessary to make individual choice meaningful. Once provided at a level that satisfies this need, satisfying further preferences for group-oriented media is not a primary good but merely something desired for which a person might want to use her resources. Of course, the level of media production necessary to serve this egalitarian demand will be a contested matter that a society must reflectively decide for itself. Nevertheless, the egalitarian claim does not require further expenditures on group-specific cultural or political content, although responsive to desires to which some group members may be dedicated. At this point a person is justly left with making expenditures out of whatever wealth she has in an appropriately egalitarian society.

Second, the argument for expenditures on culturally group-specific media required for individual identity formation and for the opportunity for meaningful individual choice leads to somewhat fuzzier conclusions than may have been suggested so far.[45] People are not just in one group in which their identity develops. Even at a young age, a person has sexual, maybe class, and various other identities. The empirical content of Kymlicka's claims needs more examination; however, it is likely that, just as the borders between various groups and subgroups are not clear, the specific need for support of media oriented toward any particular nonmainstream group will also be unclear. The point here is not so much to limit the normative argument made for equality of outcome but to raise questions about the capacity to identify with clarity the media, including mainstream media, that serve the individual's interest in having a meaningful context of choice. The conclusion may be that the egalitarian argument justifies greater per-person expenditures on media directed toward meeting the cultural needs of people in nonmainstream groups but the proper amount of increased expenditures has no clear measure. The argument justifies merely a presumption toward some greater per-person expenditures.

In conclusion, normative theory suggests that strong reasons justify diverging from market measures of preferences for media content. Even the most radical "outcome equality" argument for responding to preferences for media content has normative force and, in some circumstances, should provide a rough policy guide. However, different arguments apply to different media goods and at different levels of provision. No single standard for weighting preferences for media content can be justified, a conclusion that apparently calls for a mixed system of market and nonmarket provision.

## IDENTIFYING PREFERENCES

The standard claim on behalf of the market is that it responds to people's real preferences; it provides audiences with what they want. Even if the existing distribution of wealth were a fully appropriate criterion for weighting people's preferences and even ignoring the economic dysfunctions considered in Chapters 2 and 3, a critic could claim either that the market does not properly identify people's preferences or that satisfying these market-identified preferences is for some other reasons (e.g., paternalistic reasons) inappropriate. Here I explore the first claim.

### Which Expression of Preferences?

Markets measure preferences only when a person makes purchases. That context, however, is not the only time or only way a person expresses preferences. As noted earlier, some preferences are even inconsistent with this manner of expression – if the preference is for a non-commodified good, for instance. A related but separate observation is that a person will express different preferences in different contexts: a person expresses a preference in the ballot booth, in conversation after reflection, or by giving a list to Santa Claus. These expressions need not be consistent. Both the ranking and intensity of preferences about the same items often vary across modes of expression. A person may rank three equally expensive goods in one order as shown by her market behavior, in another after discussion if not required to publicly disclose her views, and in a third order if she must express the rankings publicly. A person may choose differently if now choosing something that she will receive in the future than she would if the decision were delayed until then or if she were to receive it now. A person may express a preference in making a New Year's resolution and a different preference the next day when she breaks the resolution. These examples show that her preference can change either over time or with a change in context.[‡] None of these expressions need be dishonest or inaccurate. They differ in part because the person considers different matters in each context. But none of the expressions is necessarily more "real" or accurate or

---

[‡] Larry Tribe famously noted that some pigeons would peck a button to force a delay in getting food if the delay results in more food but that, without the button option, the pigeons would choose to obtain the smaller amount now. People are more advanced – they can create such forced-delay buttons, which provides one interpretation of the role of the Constitution. Lawrence H. Tribe, *American Constitutional Law*, 3d ed. (New York: Foundation Press, 1999), 22–24. For example, people may value freedom of speech in the abstract – they would peck the more-free-speech button – but are often tempted now to abridge speech freedom. Still, there is no obvious reason why something people impulsively want now is worse than what they previously but calmly thought they should receive. Until additional premises show which expression should be favored, they are just different choices at different times in different contexts. Constitutionalism, like the market, is not justified until a reason to favor one of these expressions over others is offered.

honest than any other. A person could rationally identify more with, or wish more for the opportunity to make, one or another of these expressions. Her choice about the expression with which to identify will depend on the issue or context.

Most societies privilege different expressions of preferences depending on the issue or context. Sometimes, choices must be expressed publicly: a criminal defendant must make her plea in open court; often members of a deliberative body must publicly indicate their vote. Other times, society counts only choices expressed anonymously or secretly, as in many balloting systems. Some expressions of preferences can become binding on the basis of impulse, as is usually permitted with market decisions. Alternatively, sometimes society structurally favors reflection. Either to reduce influence of sellers on buyers or possibly to promote reflection and deliberation, the law makes some purchase decisions revocable for a period of time, privileging later over earlier expressions. Promoting reflection and deliberation is also the purported, legitimate reason to require waiting periods, spousal or parental notification, or mandatory exposure to certain information before getting an abortion.[46] (The constitutional critique of these requirements relating to abortion did not object to the goal of promoting reflection but rather questioned whether that was the real reason for the requirements, a logical objection given that the requirements did not seem well designed to advance this goal.) The legal order counts other expressions of preferences, for example, the waiver of certain constitutional rights, only if the person is adequately "informed" or has the opportunity to receive the advice of a professional, whose professional status purportedly assures that her own market gain or personal interests are not the basis of the guidance she offers.

Whether a market works well depends in part on which expressions of preference should count. A perfectly functioning market tautologically responds properly to *market-expressed* preferences.[47] However, people identify and reveal preferences in many different ways and at many different times and in many different contexts. Cass Sunstein emphasizes that influences on the expression of preferences include social norms, social meanings, and social roles.[48] Even the presence of a rejected option can influence which of the other options a person will favor.[49] Lee Bollinger observes that "[w]e will make different choices and behave differently depending on the context in which the choices are made."[50] Bollinger's primary argument for governmental interventions in and limited regulation of the media is his implicit affirmative answer to the critical question of whether "people may reasonably want to guard against, or to moderate, certain inclinations they know they have by altering the context in which they will exercise choice."[51]

On one day, a person may vote for higher taxes and public expenditures and open a personal savings account. After reflection or discussion, she may have concluded that savings and investment are vital both individually and for the country. The vote may reflect civic commitment and altruism. Notwithstanding these views, the day before she may have showed civic commitment and solidarity by joining with her peer group in demonstrating against higher taxes. And the day after, she may impulsively charge an expensive rug to her credit card, creating a debt quite inconsistent with her dedication to saving. An observer might say that there is no inconsistency; her preferences merely changed. It is equally likely, however, that each expression would recur at the present moment in its appropriate context. A person may express (and may know that she expresses) different preferences when voting, when showing solidarity, and when engaged in market purchases. Thus, the observer might better conclude that her preferences are more complex than originally supposed. This conclusion, however, quickly devolves into the correct point that preferences depend on contextual factors. A market expression only identifies "what she wants at that moment *while acting in the market*," not "what she wants."

A possible claim is that a person's behavior or, more precisely, a certain type of her behavior – market purchases – shows her *true* preferences. In contrast, verbal expressions often reflect other factors, such as self-deception, conformity to a superego, strategic calculations, or conformity to social and role norms. However, this claim seems arbitrary. First, verbal behavior is not necessarily determined by these other factors and market behavior sometimes is. An explanation is also needed for rejecting identifying the real person with her superego or social roles. More important, why should one particular subjectively honest expression be privileged over the other and taken as real? Why should the move impulsive or more self-centered behavioral expression be privileged over more deliberative, self-reflective behavior? Some justificatory argument is needed. Identifying the "real" preference probably cannot be disentangled from why an observer is trying to make the identification – for example, for psychoanalytic reasons, for marketing purposes, for self-identification, or for normative theory. That is, "real" may properly mean different things for different purposes. If so, the question might be: is one or another context more basic? Surely people believe that multiple contexts should be part of life. Again, the point is that privileging one over another, without argument or reason, is arbitrary.

The choice of which expression to privilege likely reflects the commentator's conception of what it means to be a person. Some people consider capacities for reflection and deliberation as among the most defining and distinctive attributes of being human. If they do, they presumably would give these qualities and their expression priority. Even if reflection and deliberation are important, persuasive arguments suggest that at different moments, maybe in relation to different matters, people ought to privilege impulsive expressions. Impulse may be better for choosing among ice cream flavors than among political candidates. I no longer remember which intellectual icon my mother quoted as saying that reason is fine for unimportant decisions but that feeling and intuition ought to prevail for something as important as choosing a career or a spouse. (Not that she convinced me!) Alternatively, maybe a person needs to achieve a wise integration of methods of identifying and expressing preferences, commitments, or values. Or maybe, even if all methods of indicating preferences are fundamental to being a person, rationally defensible ordering principles could resolve (some) conflicts. For example, since a person's wealth is dependent on the legal order, and since ideally the choice of legal rules that create the legal order occurs in contexts in which all people are implicitly equal, arguably political expressions have logical and normative priority over market expressions.[52]

Societal structures are created by human behavior. Perhaps the existence of a structure that registers preferences could be taken as evidence that people believe that the registered expression ought to have priority. Where the market presently prevails, maybe people consider market expressions basic. In areas where governmental choices now prevail, maybe people consider political expressions as basic and market expressions as epiphenomenal. This account, however, has problems of positivity and circularity. It reifies the status quo. Although some aspects of the existing order surely reflect people's commitments, other aspects are the legacy of injustice and domination. In any event, people should still have the right to change their conclusions; that is part of what both dialogue and politics are about.

The propriety of privileging any particular expression of preferences is always contested. Surely different forms of expression should prevail for different issues and in different contexts, but people will disagree about which ought to rank highest in particular contexts. The choice is a matter of individual and collective self-definition and commitment. For individual self-definition, no structure determines the expressive forms to which she subjectively most heavily commits. However, because of its partial dependence on legal rules, determination of which expressions shall prevail socially is *inherently* a matter of collective choice. All arguments that identify democracy with self-government or self-determination suggest that, as to this fundamental question, dialogue, reflection, and democratic expression ought to rule. In other words, granted that the audience ought to get what it wants, whether people best or more accurately indicate the media content they want by their expenditure decisions in a market, by their political behavior, by some combination of the two, or by other means has no logical answer. Presumptively, however, the prevailing answer as to which expressions of preferences to valorize ought to result from and be open to revision by democratic processes. Moreover, any choice to valorize one set of expressions provides no justification for suppressing others.

## Preferences about Preferences

The problem of determining which expressions should prevail is pushed further by asking, Do people always prefer their existing preferences to prevail? Fulfilling preferences is an inadequate or under-specified description of people's goals. People have preferences about their preferences. A person can want to be a certain type of person even though she is not (yet) that person.[53] She can both want a cigarette and want to be a person who not only does not smoke but who also does not even want to smoke. She can want to be a person who easily talks to strangers but, because she is not yet that person, does not now want to talk to a stranger. These are not merely conflicting preferences, like wanting to go tonight both to the opera and to the Yankees game. Rather, this situation concerns the person's view of the merits of having one of her "real" preferences.

The same can be true of groups. A community can want to become a certain kind of people. There exists in the collective case, however, an obvious danger that the sought-after frame is really an attempt by some to impose their current orientation on others – which provides one reason to distinguish policies that encourage or subsidize change from those which coerce individual conformity and punish deviance.

People value media content for serving different purposes. Broadly, media content serves to entertain or divert, to energize or engage, to educate or inform, and to transform. The same media content may do each. More often, particular content serves particular functions much more than others. And, at different times, a person is primarily concerned with one or another these functions. Of course, she usually would not object if the content she seeks for one reason also contributes to other functions. However, content chosen for one purpose sometimes will disserve a person's other goals.

Probably the best standpoint for evaluating how well media content "entertains" – the first function listed – is how well it satisfies present preferences. Of course, even a person's concern with entertainment may not be quite so flat. Sometimes, at least some people feel entertainment is inadequate unless it leaves a puzzling, potentially transformative, aftertaste. Moreover, a person can value purported entertainment in peculiar ways. She could attend the string quartet's performance not so much because she currently takes pleasure in it, but because she expects attendance will help develop her capacity for a richer or deeper (or merely different) pleasure than those she now experiences, or attend in the hopes of learning to enjoy that which she thinks is enjoyed by people who are like the person she wants to become. Still, market expressions may be the most appropriate identifiers of "what entertainment she wants."

The other listed purposes of the media – to energize, to educate, to transform – are easily viewed in a more dynamic fashion. She may value First Amendment protection of street protests in part because these demonstrations result in her being confronted with expression she would otherwise choose to avoid but with which she believes she ought to be confronted[54] (as well as because she wants to have the right to demonstrate recognized). Similarly, a person often values media content in part because of changes in herself that she expects her consumption will prompt. "What the person presently wants" is an odd standard for evaluating material whose value lies in changing the person's preferences.

Coerced educational paternalism should apply to kids, if anyone. Respect for people's agency argues in favor of having an individual's preferences or choices control even in respect to media content whose principle value lies in its transformative functions. The adult should be free to choose when and if she wants to be educated or transformed and free to choose the materials or instructors or activities that she believes will best perform these roles. However, she often knows that she is not now in a position fully to know what it is that she wants to know or to become.

Given this lack of knowledge, she might, within the market, carefully choose media or media providers that on the basis of reputation or her past experience she predicts will be the wisest guides of change.

This market behavior, however, is not the only self-chosen alternative. Instead, she might rationally privilege certain nonmarket mechanisms that provide easy access to transformative media content. That is what she did when she favored First Amendment protection of demonstrations. Likewise, instead of or in addition to market purchases, she might rationally support government subsidies for public radio or the National Endowment for the Arts. Because a person knows how she typically behaves in markets or because she is not confident of her ability to make wise market decisions or because she understands troublesome structural tendencies of markets, she might rationally conclude that government subsidies of nonprofit entities, special structural rules that refashion market entities, or other forms of government intervention will predictably result in her better obtaining the transformative media content that she desires.

## MARKET-GENERATED PREFERENCES

Preferences are never entirely exogenous to social processes or structures. Preferences encouraged by any particular social structure, however, bear no automatic relation to the preferences that a person wants to develop. Therefore, a capacity to make choices about one's preferences requires opportunities to make choices about the social processes or structures that will, themselves, influence those preferences. These choices could be either individual or collective. Individually, a person can choose whether to participate in particular social processes – she can always decide to live in the Alaskan woods or not to go to singles' bars or to watch only public television. Collectively, people can choose legal arrangements for structuring these social processes or for financially supporting particular processes. Of course, empirically, the capacity to deliberately make either type of choice may be severely limited. Still, this capacity is essential if people's preferences concerning their preferences are to be given scope.

In addition to family, friends, school, and work, the media are among the powerful determinants of people's values and preferences. Moreover, market and nonmarket media tend to differ in characteristic ways in their effect on preferences, largely because different incentives influence the design of their content. Two obvious policy issues are, first, whether, out of a concern for the preferences that will be created, people should favor more commercial or more noncommercial media; and, second, whether regulation of either is desirable. An intelligent policy response requires, first, an examination of the different incentives operative on each category of media and a description of the differences these will have on the preferences favored. Then people should engage in a more self-definitional appraisal of these differences.

This task is largely beyond the scope of the present discussion. Still, partly to show that the choice is an important one – and one that cannot be avoided in assessing the adequacy of the market in giving people the media they want – and partly to engage in preliminary thought about desirable choices, I want to consider aspects of preferences likely to be favored by alternative structures.

The market creates incentives to generate particular preferences. The incentive is for the media to create preferences valuable, first, to the owners of the media and, second, to advertisers and others who pay the media to encourage these preferences. This normally means that the media will encourage preferences for its own content and for the goods and services sold by advertisers. Some consideration of this bias should help people in deciding whether they want – out of concern for the type of person they will be – to rely solely on the unregulated market in media products or rather whether they want the state to regulate or supplement the market in some ways.

Advertisers employ media to stimulate preferences for their firms' products. Although the products vary, this orientation toward product promotion is in itself a particular and significant structural bias. Although talking more of the ads themselves than advertisers' influence on the media's own "independent" content, Steve Shiffrin observes: "Advertisers spend some sixty billion dollars per year to disseminate their messages. Those who would oppose the materialist message must combat forces that have a massive economic advantage.... The inequality of inputs is structurally based."[§55] Michael Schudson, despite

---

§ Shiffrin's characterization of this as a market failure may be debatable, but he is certainly correct that the bias is structural and that collective rejection of this bias could be a justification to limit "commercial speech," even though individually based speech of the same content is allowed (and constitutionally protected). The bias toward materialist messages is illustrated by comparing the amount spent on "marketing" candidates and products. In 1996, all of the candidates for president and Congress, together with their supporters (often "soft" money), spent an estimated $2 billion on their campaigns. Meanwhile, in 1995, a single company, Proctor & Gamble, had an ad budget of $2.78 billion, followed by Philip Morris at $2.58 billion. See R. Craig Endicott, "Leading National Advertisers," *Advertising Age* (Sept. 30, 1996): S3; David E. Rosenbaum, "In Political Money Game, The Year of Big Loopholes," *New York Times* (Dec. 26, 1996): A1.

his signature iconoclasm illustrated by his skepticism about advertising's direct effectiveness and his doubts about the wisdom of those in the advertising industry, describes advertising as "capitalist realism."[56] He emphasizes that advertising's ubiquitous cultural contributions help create or naturalize particular sets of attitudes, including those that see salvation in the product. This bias is structural: the only way human choice can affect it is by collective decisions to regulate or modify the market structure. Thus, although the Supreme Court thought it appropriate to regulate commercial speech to promote its truthfulness or its capacity to inform, Justice Rehnquist, following arguments much earlier elaborated by John Stuart Mill,[57] thought society should also have the right to regulate commercial speech as a means of exercising control over promotions that reflect nothing other than incentives generated by the market structure.[58] For instance, he argued that the government should have the right to regulate the *commercial* promotion of preferences for prescription drugs as well as for liquor and cigarettes. Just as regulating individual choice is often paternalistic, so is the denial of people's right to choose collectively whether to regulate the market and market-based expression.

Along with audiences, advertisers are also customers of the media. As such, advertisers' preferences influence media firms to provide content they want. Their influence on the creation of audiences' preferences operates directly through their advertising messages, but also indirectly through "corruption" of the journalistic or creative process of providing nonadvertising content. Both influences have characteristic biases. As for the nonadvertising editorial content, advertisers typically prefer the following: content that is not critical of their products or their corporate activities; content that encourages a buying mood (which often means an uncritical mind-set); content that does not alienate any relevant group of potential customers; and formats and content that appeal to or create audiences that advertisers see as appropriate for their marketing goals.[59] In terms of both advertising and nonadvertising content, advertisers are paying market-based media to encourage people to be a certain type of person – a person who constantly wants more material goods or commercially provided services and who, when faced with characteristic life problems, responds with purchases as the cure-all for every dilemma. Patent medicines were once "able" to cure any malady. Even if modern ads are sometimes more subtle, their message continues to be how their product solves the most pressing problems confronting people with money to spend. Joseph Turow effectively describes the typical advertising format: "[I]t portrays a world of the intended audience, a problem in that world, and actions that show how the product can solve the problem."[60]

The shallowness and potential dangerousness of this advertiser-sponsored view of the world should be obvious. I do not here try to critique this culture or set of preferences or even further defend my claim that these are the preferences that advertisers encourage. The point is that if people have preferences about what preferences they will have, they have reason, as John Stuart Mill and Justice Rehnquist have pointed out, to consider the merits of legal intervention in this process.

The media themselves also have market-based incentives to create particular preferences, most obviously for the media products that they sell. They have an incentive to create these preferences up to the point where the (marginal) cost of creating them is as much as the gain from creating them. Of course, because media can have any content and that content could encourage any type of preferences, this incentive to create preferences for the media product might seem benign – unless we want a less mass-media-oriented society, a view that inspires some people as indicated by the substantial support for an annual turn-off-your-TV week.[61] Nevertheless, remember that the matter under discussion here is the narrower issue of describing and evaluating the media's incentive to use their resources to encourage the existence of particular preferences. It turns out that the market structure creates three, sometimes cross-cutting tilts to the preferences that the media have an incentive to create.

First, everything else being equal, any firm has a greater incentive to encourage more cheaply stimulated or cultivated desires or preferences. If generating an appreciation for a type of informational or cultural item is difficult, the expenditure on creating the desire is less likely to be worth the cost. Thus, the firm will spend more promoting Homer Simpson than Homer; more on *Buffy the Vampire Slayer* than on *To the Lighthouse.*

Second, different media products have potential appeal to differently sized audiences. To the extent that the total costs of the promotional campaign are roughly the same, the incentive will be greater to promote an interest in the media product with the larger potential audience. Authors often find it disillusioning to learn their publisher will only promote their book after it has already proved its popularity. Promoting niche products can be profitable, but usually only where the payoff is high, for example, because of a high selling price, or where the promotional costs are low or especially cost-effective, for example, because the targeted audience is concentrated and easy to reach or is very easily aroused. More generally, the incentive is to encourage preferences for the large-audience products, which often translates into an incentive for the media enterprise to encourage preferences for the lowest-common-denominator content. That is, the market gives the firm the most "bang for the buck" for "dumbing down" the audience and the culture.

Third, a profit-oriented enterprise must consider its ability to capture the entrepreneurial benefit resulting from any demand it creates. Colgate-Palmolive can capture much more of the desire for Colgate toothpaste than it can of a desire for more healthy tooth brushing. Even if ads for the second would stimulate more gain for toothpaste companies as a group (or for society), unless Colgate can turn the pro-tooth-brushing ads into self-promotion (e.g., by appearing to be a responsible company) or unless it has a very high percentage of the toothpaste market, it usually will be better off investing in creating the first preference – a preference for Colgate toothpaste. And certainly it would have no interest in promoting effective rinsing of the mouth with tap water even if that turned out to be a more effective means of dental hygiene. The firm needs to control access to the product for which it creates a desire. Similarly, a copyright holder can capture more income by encouraging a desire to watch *Mean Streets* than from a desire to go for a walk down the mean streets on a sunny afternoon. The Walt Disney Company benefits more from people enjoying Fantasyland than from enjoying their own imaginative fantasies (particularly if their fantasies do not require specific Disney-supplied props).

To a significant degree, the first two tendencies operate only under the dominance of this third factor. A firm gains little from creating even cheaply aroused or large-scale preferences unless it is positioned to profit from their existence. Thus, the market incentive is to create preferences for monopolized qualities of products rather than for generic aspects of life. There is no incentive to generate desires (or capacities) to engage in activities or to have preferences unrelated to the advertisers' salable products or services or unrelated to expressive content that the media enterprise owns or controls.

These three factors significantly influence the preferences that profit-oriented media enterprises try to influence people to have. Publishers have a strong incentive to promote desires for the latest blockbuster whose copyright they hold. In contrast, rights to most literary classics lie in the public domain. Because competitors can publish their own version, media firms have little interest in promoting desires for the classics, unless they can profit from a popular translation or a unique edition, possibly combined with a new, appealing, and copyrighted introduction. This, for example, was Verso's strategy when it had Eric Hobsbawn write a lengthy introduction to a unique upscale hardback 150th-anniversary edition of the *Communist Manifesto*.[62] Otherwise, stimulating desires for the classics is largely left to the non-market-oriented educational system.

As noted earlier, the market, combined with existing copyright law, also creates an incentive to generate preferences for a broadcaster's news anchorperson or her chatter rather than for uncopyrightable news content. This structure also provided the economic rationale for Hollywood to create the "star" system.[63] The long history of serialized stories provides an equally interesting illustration of the combination of easily aroused preferences with monopolistically controlled elements. Movie producers' repetition of film titles and key characters and broadcasters' soap operas duplicate a profitable approach pioneered by book publishers, newspapers, and then magazines. By originally creating demand for a program series the firm guarantees a continuing demand.

The key point is that the market not only creates an incentive for a media firm to produce media content that consumers desire, which is presumably good, but also an incentive to generate preferences for particular types of content, which is a much more problematic matter. In the star system, for example, the firm benefits by cultivating preferences for particular actors under contract. Even better, the firm benefits from preferences for star cartoon characters, created by employees of the media firm, since the firm does not have to renegotiate the cartoon characters' contracts or worry about their potentially embarrassing off-job activities or their untimely death.[64] Most observers concede that to become a star "requires a modicum of talent,"[65] but still emphasize that "successful [stars or performance] groups . . . are made."[66] The star system arguably teaches (or reinforces) an individualistic orientation that combines with other market incentives to replace consideration of social or structural forces in commercially produced news as well as in dramatic stories. The star system also may encourage economically wasteful amounts of individual effort toward becoming a "star" by people who will not succeed at that but who could have been very successful at something else.[67]

I have suggested three factors that influence the preferences that a market-based media fosters. If these suggestions are right, critical policy questions are: (1) Are these the preferences that people want to have? That is, if they were choosing, would they choose these preferences – for example, to be so responsive to stars on to prefer dumbed-down content rather than the classics? (2) How powerful is the market-based tendency to create these preferences? (3) What alternatives are there?

As for the first question, I obviously cannot offer an answer for people in general. Still, several observations are possible. First, because the question concerns what preferences a person wants to have encouraged, one cannot look to the market, which encourages particular preferences primarily for structural reasons rather than in response to anyone's view of what should be encouraged, to learn what preferences people want to have. Only collective, usually political, or other discursive processes can indicate an answer. Second, since a decision favoring creation of certain types of preferences or certain approaches to preference creation involves, in this context, a decision about the collective "environment," for example, about the scope of unadorned market processes, the decision affects all people. Hence, the issue seems intrinsically one where everyone should have (possibly equal) input. Foundational commitments of democracy to people's equality or agency suggest that democratic judgments are an appropriate basis for answers. Third, most tellingly, these questions about what preferences we want to create have probably been most directly faced, both as a discursive matter and in an egalitarian political manner, in decisions concerning the content of the educational system. The educational system, however, largely rejects each of the tilts that the market generates – toward cheaply cultivated preferences and exclusively materialist preferences (or those nonmaterialist preferences only obtained through purchases of commodities); toward mass appeal, dumbed-down content rather than diversity; and toward owned content rather than the classics. The premise of a liberal education, and I expect many people's self-conception, is that a person should want to be someone who appreciates a broader range of cultural phenomena at more complex levels and with higher levels of enjoyment. She should live a culturally "richer" life, constantly increasing her understanding of both herself and the world. Maybe she should be someone who (either individually or as part of political communities) makes better choices about both the social and physical world. Moreover, many people would like to be more reflective, more self-reliant, more politically energized, more responsive to the needs of others, and more interested in being informed. Many apparently want to be inspired and spurred to responsible social and political activity. Of course, many individual market-produced media products do further such visions of the self, but in each respect the market's general tilt is against creating these preferences and capacities.

I put aside the issue of how powerful the market bias is. It is undoubtedly strong but abstract discussion can shed little light on exactly how powerful it is. The final question concerns alternatives. I note that none of the policy conclusions in this book suggest suppressing or abandoning market-based media. Rather, alternatives presumably would involve government interventions both in creating non-market-oriented media entities and in influencing practices of market-based media enterprises. Because the first is discussed at various points in the book, I note here that there surely is also a heavy role for the second. Interventions could involve increasing nonmarket incentives operating within market-oriented enterprises, systematic modifications of market incentives, and possibly some regulation of advertising. For example, consider two sorts of nonmarket incentives: people's internal incentives to remain true to personal or professional values or standards; and material or status incentives granted independently of the economic marketplace. Professional organizations and journalism schools try to reinforce the first. Journalism's reputation for being a prize-oriented profession relates to the second. Government subsidies and legal policies greatly affect the extent to which these alternative incentives exist and are behaviorally effective. Thus, the efficaciousness of internal incentives could be enhanced by laws that either mandate or provide greater opportunities for alternative structures of control within the media industries. Law could make it easier or harder for journalist-owned or nonprofit foundation-owned media entities to exist. Recognizing that not only government but also owners and markets should not "intru[de] into the function of editors,"[68] the law could require that journalists have a greater say in content decisions. To paraphrase the Supreme Court, the law could prohibit the "repression of [editor's] freedom by private interests" – specifically, by corporate entities, which are "nongovernmental combinations" that should not be allowed to "impede the free flow of ideas."[69]

This section asked how people's preferences should be identified. The question led to the conclusion that, as compared with reliance on an

unadorned market, greater reliance on nonmarket techniques of identification could result in production and consumption of media content
more in line with people's actual preferences. The following observations provide the premises for this conclusion. First, alternative expressions of preferences exist – that is, expressions made within different
contexts or identified through structures other than the market. Next,
a particularly important set of preferences relate to what type of person
a person wants to be and to what type of society people want to have.
Third, the market is inadequate to the extent that people would choose
to be different from the type of people that the market, operating on
its own internal logic, would try to make them. Finally, reflective or
discursive political expression of preferences ought to be privileged, at
least for some purposes – for example, for determining the mixture
of structures that society should rely on to identify, respond to, and
partially create preferences.

CHAPTER 5

# Where To? Policy Responses

The market cannot be expected to provide the audience what it wants. Although I have not attempted empirical measurements, the divergence between what the market produces and what people want can be expected to be massive.

Each of the first four chapters supported this conclusion. Chapters 1 and 2 explained how the public-good aspect of media products leads to too little production and distribution. Chapter 2 showed that the nature of monopolistic competition in media products can lead less-valued media products to prevail competitively. Monopolistic competition tends to favor blockbuster products over more diverse and smaller media products that people often want more. Chapter 3 observed that media products produce tremendous positive and negative externalities. Market processes produce excessive amounts of media products with negative externalities and insufficient amounts of those with positive externalities. Finally, Chapter 4 observed, first, that there is no reason to expect that market mechanisms for identifying and weighing people's preferences lead to objectively correct results. It then argued that there are good reasons to think that the market as a measurement device for media preferences diverges dramatically from how people actually want their preferences measured and from how a democratic people should want them measured when "want" is properly understood. That is, Chapter 4 claims to be more realistic and more normatively defensible than a typical market perspective in understanding the way people actually do and should understand their preferences.

Thus, from the perspective of providing people what they want, media markets are subject to the following criticisms. They provide much too much "bad" quality content – bad meaning content that has negative externalities. Media markets also may produce a wasteful abundance of content responding to mainstream tastes. Otherwise, the main problem is underproduction. Markets predictably provide inadequate amounts and inadequate diversity of media content. Especially inadequate is their production of "quality" content – quality meaning content that has positive externalities. Production of civically, educationally, and maybe culturally significant content preferred by the poor is predictably inadequate. Smaller groups will often be served inadequately, either in relation to democracy's commitment to equally value their preferences or due to the consequences of monopolistic competition. Finally, the market seldom reflects people's arguably more mature or more considered conceptions of the content they want, especially of content that relates to the type of people they want to be.

These assertions of dramatic failures of markets directly conflict with the deregulatory mood that has swept the country and much of the world over the past two decades. It directly conflicts with recent moves to reduce rather than expand funding for public broadcasting, for the humanities, and for the arts. It has direct implications for postal and telecommunications policy. It weighs in on virtually all media and communications issues that the country has taken up – and implies that additional reform issues should be raised. However, no single policy will provide an adequate response to the market's inadequacies.

An exploration of some policy implications of these market failures permits the following general claims. First, despite rarely explicitly relying on the type of economic analysis developed in this book, most past media policy can be seen as responsive to these failures of the market. Second, structural regulation of media firms and government-provided subsidies have often improved on results that would have come from an unregulated market. Third, despite being comprehensible as responses to problems with the market, persuasive objections should block policies to suppress particular content, for example, because of its negative externalities.

Possibly the most easily seen problem with the market involves its failure to account for negative and positive externalities. Of course, the economic language of "externalities" is usually absent from popular discourse about media policy. Yet without consideration of these externalities, faith in markets is blind and use of economic analysis is uninformative. Once this consideration is included, much existing media law, as well as most policy advocacy, can be seen in a new light. Rather than being paternalistic, legal interventions often attempt to reduce costs not otherwise borne by the media, to impose otherwise externalized costs on the media, or to promote provision of content otherwise inadequately produced because of the media's inability to internalize various benefits.

## RESPONSES TO POLITICAL EXTERNALITIES

The content and quality of people's political participation have always been a major concern of media policy. An almost reflexive response is to suppress speech that purportedly has negative political externalities and some of these regulations have survived constitutional challenge. Nonmedia business enterprises have no moral "agency" or institutional political role. Their participation within the political culture can be seen as distortive rather than contributory. During the Progressive Era in the early twentieth century, most states and the federal government adopted laws restricting corporate political contributions, which were thought to represent corrupting profit-oriented concerns rather than people's actual political sentiments or principles.[1] And although the constitutional issue has been contentious, a closely divided Supreme Court recently indicated constitutional acceptance of these limits.[2] The Court has also allowed considerable regulation of speech within the institutional bounds of the electoral process.[3] Here, regulation involves legitimate government authority to structure the electoral process in ways needed for it to serve its democratic purposes. Likewise, free-speech doctrine permits various restrictions on false factual assertions where the speaker indicates no concern for their truth, a practice that undermines the quality of political information.[4]

Nevertheless, any legal system that respects people's agency or that protects the institutional integrity of the press will rule out censorship. Thus, the Supreme Court unanimously struck down a prohibition on newspapers' *election day* endorsements, a state law purportedly justified as preventing powerful unanswerable messages that could distort the political process.[5] The Court also will not allow limitations on the promises candidates can make or on political endorsements.[6] The Court declares most restrictions on political speech, even if reasonably viewed as having serious negative political externalities, unconstitutional.

A much different, and constitutionally more acceptable, communications policy is to promote content expected to have broadly positive political externalities. Newspapers' predicted positive influence on political knowledge was a primary public justification for the huge mail subsidy newspapers have received since colonial times – subsidies once paid for by postal charges imposed on other "speakers," usually first class letter writers.[7] Providing socially valuable information also helped justify extending mail subsidies to magazines, but pointedly not to "advertising papers," which policymakers perceived as serving only private concerns.[8] More modern examples abound. Government actions that help make "good" media content more cheaply and plentifully available to the public include provision of public libraries, expenditures on public broadcasting, grants for producing art and cultural materials and for making them publicly available, and government printing information and distributing it free or below cost. The government also subsidizes information development within research universities, within government agencies, and by specific government contract, although often these expenditures have legitimate aims unrelated to improving the political culture. The government massively but indirectly subsidizes the news media and the development of political information by its constant stream of press releases and by providing press facilities. The Freedom of Information Act (FOIA) mandates that lots of expensive-to-create information be made available on request.[9] Moreover, the charges for finding (as opposed to duplicating) governmentally held information are waived for the media and, sometimes, for various nonprofit organizations. The FOIA also directs that even duplication charges be waived or reduced when making the information available serves the public interest.[10]

Content subsidies are only one means of promoting positive political externalities. A quite different approach involves influencing the structure of the media industry and the distribution of ownership of, or decision-making control within, media entities. This approach is most easily seen in the broadcast context. Government decision making chose to allocate certain electromagnetic radio frequencies to broadcasting as opposed to solely military uses and to allocate some of these broadcast frequencies to noncommercial broadcasting rather than commercial broadcasting. Structural rules originally tried to empower diverse local owners, whom the FCC assumed would meet local informational or discursive needs – a heritage arguably revived by the recent FCC approval of creating neighborhood, low-power, or "pirate" radio stations.[11] Structural regulation of all media enterprises (and other entities), however, is implicit in the provisions of corporate, contract, and other law, a point to which I will return.

Different legal structures allow control by different sorts of people who may have predictably different personal and economic incentive systems. That is, different structures empower people who vary in the priority they give to public-service ideals; professional norms; influencing political outcomes; serving particular geographic, identity, or interest-based communities; and maximizing profit. The people in control can be crucial in an industry that constantly struggles with a tension between profit maximization and allegiances to creative, professional, and public values – a tension that can be redescribed, in part, as a tension between producing more negative or more positive externalities. A profit-maximization focus lacks any concern with negative externalities – costs that do not take money away from the enterprise. In contrast, public-service ideals, professional norms, and various other non-profit-based incentives typically amount to standards for, or goals of, reducing negative or producing certain positive externalities. A public policy concerned with giving the audience what it wants should tilt toward promoting structures that give authority to categories of people – or, more precisely, to people in roles – less dominated by a profit focus and more oriented toward maximizing social value.

A standard justification for antitrust rules is that monopolies inefficiently reduce production. In the media context, however, positive political externalities provide major additional "economic" reasons to engage in structural regulation that go far beyond traditional antitrust concerns. For example, Sweden targeted its newspaper subsidies to maintain or increase newspaper competition. Like many other democracies, Sweden believed this competition contributes to the quality and vitality of a democratic political culture.[12] Similarly, this country's Newspaper Preservation Act,[13] however inept at achieving its ends,[14] was oriented in part toward this end of maintaining multiple, diverse media voices.

The primary reason to worry about the tension between maximizing profits and maintaining journalistic standards is the belief that the second contributes more to a desirable social and political order. An increasing dominance of a bottom-line orientation purportedly damages the informing as opposed to the entertaining role of the media, especially of the news.[15] A plausible hypothesis is that different ownership structures lead to differing trade-offs between these two demands. Some research indicates, and many editors and media professionals believe, that profit considerations dominate less in independent than in chain-owned newspapers.[16] Possibly owners or publishers closer to actual journalistic practice have greater commitment to journalistic standards, possibly out of personal and professional pride. Warren Phillips, former editor of the *Wall Street Journal* and CEO of Dow Jones, spoke with pride about the importance his organization placed on its tradition of having the publisher and CEO come from the journalistic rather than the business side of the company.[17] C. K. McClatchy, a respected former editor and head of a newspaper chain, argued that "good newspapers are almost always run by good newspaper people; they are almost never run by good bankers or good accountants."[18] Local owners may have commitments to serving their community as well as to generating profits. In contrast, those further removed (and those not coming out of a journalistic culture) may take a more single-minded interest, possibly even an entrepreneurial pride, in bottom-line success.[19] If so, and if other factors are held constant, positive externalities should increase as ownership (or control)[20] moves from conglomerates (especially conglomerates not headed by journalistic professionals) to independent, local ownership or, possibly better, to ownership by journalists themselves.[21]

Many media-specific legal rules attempt to discourage concentration and increase control at the local level. The United States, like virtually all democratic countries, has long been concerned with media concentration.[22] Going beyond antitrust rules, the FCC at one time severely restricted the number of broadcast stations a single enterprise could own as well as restricting within a single community cross-ownership of various types of media outlets.[23] The FCC's licensing policy gave pluses both for diversification of control and for integration of ownership and management, which effectively favored a preferred form of local control.[24] Its chain broadcasting rules explicitly attempted to keep ultimate decision-making power over as well as responsibility for broadcast content in the hands of the local broadcaster rather than the networks.[25]

Unfortunately, many structural regulations have been either eased or abandoned due to deregulatory attacks. Corporate interests continually push to lift restrictions on ownership concentration. Their view prevailed in a lengthy report initiated during the Bush administration and issued in early 1993. Using simplistic consumer welfare economics to give a veneer of legitimacy to its analysis, the Department of Commerce favored legal changes that would stimulate greater concentration of media ownership.[26] Essentially Commerce concluded that concentration beneficially aids American firms' domination of world markets. Likewise, although President Clinton and others resisted even more dramatic cuts, the Telecommunications Act of 1996 substantially reduced limits on media combinations.[27]

Other governmental policies have had unfortunate effects. Possibly because of policy lapses, generally applicable tax laws (e.g., inheritance tax and corporate tax rules) have in the past encouraged newspaper concentration.[28] In the early 1930s, corporate lobbying dominated contrary popular policy sentiments, with the result that government policy favored corporate commercial interests in their battle with existing and potential noncommercial users over control of broadcasting.[29]

Still, the ubiquitousness of industry's ability to misdirect governmental policy should not lead to forswearing governmental involvement. Governmental structural interventions, *when they occur*, have mostly been beneficial. From a historical perspective, profit-maximizing, audience-denying industry victories typically occur only in the following situations: (1) where some type of governmental intervention is conceded by all interests to be necessary, like the initial governmental structuring of broadcasting, and, therefore, the struggle cannot be over whether to regulate but, instead, must be over the content of regulation; (2) where the victory involves defeating attempts at useful intervention; or (3) where the victory eliminates beneficial current regulation.[30] In no case would a presumption against regulation have served the public interest. Cases where media-specific structural regulation occurs but audiences would have benefited from no regulation are rare. (One exception might be copyright once it is seen as a form of media regulation, but that is mostly beyond the scope of this book.) Thus, history indicates that in practice regulation can be beneficial. The struggle ought to be over its content.

Beyond the historical examples of useful media-specific interventions noted here, more dramatic policies aimed at beneficial structural changes in media control are possible. Ben Bagdikian is one among many who argue for the benefits of journalistic employees electing (or having some veto role in choosing or dismissing) their editors.[31] Law could either require or could provide tax or other economic incentives for this arrangement. Legislation could forbid the purchase of existing media entities except by individuals or by legal entities for whom the purchased entity would be its primary business.[32] Such regulation would end the twentieth century's long trend toward greater media concentration and would encourage ownership by the people who work in the enterprise. More generally, James Curran persuasively argues that effective performance of the media's multiple political and cultural roles requires a mixed system, with public policies designed to encourage different forms of ownership and control.[33]

The list of possible subsidy and structural policies responsive to the political culture externality could go on and on. Each will be subject to refinement and to numerous (but only rarely persuasive) objections. Nevertheless, past and current examples show that this country, in accord with all other Western democracies, has never thought that reliance on the market alone is adequate. Rejection of a pure market process implicitly reflects an understanding that media potentially create significant positive political externalities and that appropriate structural regulation can increase the likelihood of these occurring.

## RESPONSES TO OTHER EXTERNALITIES

Media consumption influences its audience's behavior. Other people positively or negatively value that behavior. This situation is the focus of Chapter 3's first, second, and third externalities – audience members' interaction with other people and audience members' impact on the cultural and political products available to others. If a person's media consumption results in her becoming a stimulating conversationalist or a murderer, her friends or victims are affected. Existing and conceivable policy responses are abundant. Most of the subsidy and other strategies discussed in relation to political culture apply here. Mass media's emphasis on gratuitous violence and sex likely reflects bottom-line judgments of corporate executives more than autonomous or creative choices of writers and producers. Given that at least the emphasis on violence interacts with other aspects of culture and personality to increase the likelihood that a viewer will engage in violence,[34] a shift in ownership or decision-making control toward media professionals could lead to better media products with fewer negative externalities. Subsidy programs that support creative or professional control can also benefit nonaudience members by supporting media that are more likely to have positive cultural and educational effects. Well-designed expenditures to increase the availability of good media content could conceivably be more effective at reducing crime than comparable amounts spent on hiring more police or building more prisons. Of course, other justifications often support the same subsidy (or an overlapping set of subsidies). As Chapter 4 argued, a society might believe that, like education, access to significant and personally relevant cultural material is a primary good that should be available to all members of the society

103

irrespective of their ability to pay. Certainly, respect for audiences as moral agents is consistent with *encouraging* their exposure to collectively considered "good" speech,[35] even with convincing speakers that certain speech choices are unwise, inappropriate, and offensive.

In contrast to proposals promoting positive externalities, a different response seems almost instinctual. People often wish to ban or restrict expression that they believe encourages antisocial conduct, that is, negative externalities. Even if apparently justified on efficiency grounds, this repressive response directly contradicts most interpretations of the First Amendment – and, I argue, is poor policy. In marketplace-of-ideas theories, the proper response is always more speech. Grudging acceptance of the negative consequences is considered less dangerous than suppression. Likewise, respect for autonomy requires that a person be able to portray her views even if others experience harm from hearing her speech or are lead by her speech to engage in harmful behavior. Holmes argued if speech persuades, even proletarian dictatorship should be accepted – surely a real harm to capitalists.[36] Listeners have at least the theoretical option of rejecting the incitement or reinterpreting despicable affronts with anger at or disapproval of the speaker – or by making other legally permitted responses. Denying listeners access to speech considered "bad" is paternalistic, inconsistent with respect for their agency. Attributing the responsibility to the media – unless, possibly, where the audience's behavior is precisely what the media was trying to achieve *and* could reasonably be expected to achieve, in which case joint responsibility may be appropriate[37] – conceptually treats the reader or viewer as a mere puppet whose strings the media pull.[38] Media effects always depend on reception. Different audience members – sometimes even the same audience member depending on the context of reception – will take different things from exposure to the same cultural artifact. Particular responses or effects are clearly objectionable, but the content itself is always multivocal and its meaning and use contested.[39]

Equally important, even if suppression appears to be a quick fix, it usually is ineffective, can reinforce negative and restrictive images of its supposed beneficiaries as well as of its overbroad set of targets, often generates additional problems, and can divert attention from more useful responses. All these dysfunctional outcomes arguably resulted from the feminist campaign to use law to suppress commercial pornography.[40] Attempts at suppression on the basis of characterization of content as bad, for example, because of its portrayal of violence or sex

104

or impropriety, often mask ideological efforts to impose majoritarian or status quo views.[41] Each point provides a pragmatic reason to believe that a free-speech ideology committed to protection of dissent and to a democratic process of change should not permit suppression as a response to the negative externalities of – the harms caused by – particular content.[42]

Zoning sometimes can usefully reduce negative externalities. Children are assertedly especially vulnerable to injury by media content. Out of either paternalism (constitutionally and presumably morally permissible in regards to children) or a desire to reduce negative externalities (effects on children that lead to bad consequences for others), policymakers often propose to restrict children's access to various media products. The issue merits more attention. Often, restriction will amount to a centrist attempt to mold people according to the most conventional popular standards.[43] Arguably, such a policy contravenes basic First Amendment principles.[44] Parental control of children is, however, widely accepted. Media practices that reduce parents' capacity to exercise desired control can be considered negative externalities, and practices that increase this capacity can be desirable. Mandates for rating systems or devices like the V-chip technology *might* usefully increase this parental capacity. "Channeling" of indecency on television could give parents a time period – for instance, during adults' normal daytime work hours – when they could be assured that, even if unsupervised, their children would not have such easy access to the restricted programming.

Still, any robust system of expression must accept the principle that the adult population not be reduced to the level of children.[45] That is, content should not be suppressed. Any permissible channeling must at least leave ample time periods during which the adult audience can view any programming it wants (within the notable constraint of what the broadcasters choose to offer). Channeling that satisfies this basic principle regulates speech, but arguably does not "abridge" the relevant freedom of either the media or the public.[46] The issues then become empirical – and political. Will the proposed practice – V-chips or channeling – really enhance parental authority? Do parents actually want that enhancement? What will the practice cost? Will this regulatory response to the evils of unrestricted provision of commercial media divert attention from more meaningful responses, and so on?[47]

Both private and governmental policies encourage the media's performance of the "checking" function, Chapter 3's fourth externality.

Journalism is a prize-ridden profession. Both individual journalists and sometimes owners of media enterprises devote resources to winning privately provided "Pulitzers" and various less prominent prizes. Likewise, although investigative journalism remains expensive, some legal rules decrease the costs borne by the media, thereby increasing its production. Examples include some constitutional protection from liability for defamation, especially during discussion of public affairs, the Freedom of Information Act's subsidized provision of information, special access often given reporters, and reporters' testimonial privileges. Even if these measures are grossly inadequate to correct for the market's failure to create appropriate incentives for investigative journalism, they do externalize some costs. They amount to a rough response to the fact that media entities only receive payment for a fraction of the benefits their performance of the checking function produces.

The specifics of these "subsidies," however, can be criticized for reasons in addition to inadequacy. Their content can bias the choice of which abuses to investigate and expose.[48] Although the FOIA grants cheap access to (some) government information, nothing – for example, Security and Exchange Commission (SEC) rules – gives comparable access to corporate information. Common law as well as the constitutional protection gives media (or nonmedia) speakers more protection from liability when they defame government as opposed to the private actors. These rules and practices favor exposing governmental rather than private (corporate) wrongdoing. This bias is also evident in defamation law's fair-report privilege, which normally applies to coverage of official governmental proceedings or documents.[49] This rule arguably "subsidizes" damaging media reports about government or government officials but not those concerning corporate misbehavior. To the extent reporting follows these economic incentives, the consequence is to encourage distrust of government as compared with corporate power. The bias could even tilt against people's motivation, as well as informed ability, to use public power to promote the public good (i.e., these rules create a negative political externality).

The fifth externality concerns the media's behavioral effects on third parties (other than those considered under the checking function) due to their actual or potential portrayal through media exposure. Particular instances have differing, sometimes contested, valences. Sometimes people respond to the possibility of media coverage with behavior that benefits others – they want to be pictured as heroes so will act to save another. Sometimes they respond with behavior that inflicts harm – as does the terrorist who wants media attention. Possible legal responses are various, and often their wisdom (and constitutionality) is disputable. Policy choices include whether trials or governmental meetings should be closed and whether nonconsensual video- or audiotaping by the media should be restricted. The decision depends in part on assessments of whether these limitations will have good or bad (or minimal) effects on the participants' behavior – for example, on their frankness and honesty, their attention and thoughtfulness, their willingness to bargain properly. Likewise, either law or media self-restraint could limit media coverage of terrorist acts in the hope of discouraging such behavior. In contrast, the *New York Times* and *Washington Post*'s joint decision to publish the "Unabomber's" tract generated a controversy. Would publication encourage similar terrorist behavior in support of similar demands in the future?[50] Alternatively, some radical media critics assert that the argument that media coverage stimulates terrorism basically blames the victim. Terrorist activities may be a (sometimes rational) response to an inadequate media order that screens out views of dissident groups and facts of which the public should be aware. From this perspective, rather than suppress coverage of terrorists, a more legitimate method of reducing terrorism would be to open up access to the media in order to reduce dissidents' need to rely on terrorist acts to gain coverage of their suppressed messages.[51]

Incentives for creation and distribution are inadequate when people obtain desired media content without paying, Chapter 3's sixth externality. Subsidies could provide substitute incentives. However, the political will to respond with an efficient level of subsidies is likely always to be lacking, and the subsidy approach creates serious problems for wisely and efficiently selecting beneficiaries. Alternatively, the legal regime sometimes creates indirect mechanisms, unavailable simply through market agreements, to collect and distribute to copyright owners payments for these benefits – for example, surcharges imposed on equipment and blank tapes[52] or payments required for public musical performances. A common European practice is to impose an annual fee on radio and television receivers or a tax on their purchase to raise money to support public broadcasting. These structural interventions, as well as copyright protection – which is possibly the single most important legal device aimed at helping content creators collect for access to their creation – will be grossly inadequate to internalize fully the benefits gained by nonpaying audience members. On the other hand, except for direct subsidies, these interventions restrict the availability of a public good, creating a serious additional inefficiency. Clearly, although various policies respond to this externality, solutions are inevitably incomplete.

The seventh externality – benefits to individuals or groups from favorable media attention – generates complexly ambivalent legal responses. First, being a positive externality implies inadequate media expenditures on producing such content and the audience's not getting some content it wants. These features implicitly justify subsidies, mostly of the sort recommended earlier. In contrast, the market solution – payment for favorable coverage – directly internalizes these benefits. In theory, this market solution might be expected to lead to appropriate production and distribution. Inadequate production of favorable content is, however, probably not the most serious issue here. The often possible market solution, payment for inclusion, is typically characterized as corruption unless the favorable content is labeled as advertising. Thus, the law discourages this market behavior. For instance, it requires most media entities to identify as advertising any content that someone or some entity has paid them to present.[53] Recently, a storm of protest arose over disclosures that the federal government was itself part of the problem. The government not only effectively paid media entities to include, buried in entertainment programming, government-approved views concerning drugs, but also monitored scripts to ascertain the message's presence.[54]

Even if direct payment for favorable treatment is seen as corrupt, indirect payment is common – and takes many forms. In addition to questions of distortion and inaccurate information, possibly the most important issue may be distributive. Some individuals and groups get favored treatment, some do not. Worse, markets do not distribute this inequality randomly. Media critics continually observe that organizations with large public relations or advertising budgets – usually corporate or other elite interests – and individuals holding high political position have much greater access to the media than others.[55] This greater access does not necessarily nor consistently reflect greater public interest in their views, greater reliability of their pronouncements, or greater intrinsic importance of their insights or information. The access does not even necessarily reflect reporters' or editors' own greater interest or confidence in these sources – although media professionals' personal ideological bias concerning the relation of class, gender, race, and role position to knowledge or insight is observable and gives a content-based reason to push for more newsroom diversity.[56] Rather, corporate and elite access to the media reflects their ability to make themselves easier and cheaper to rely upon – that is, to indirectly subsidize favorable treatment.[57] Organizations that routinely put out information – most obviously government but also large corporate entities – not only pay a large portion of the expense of gathering and composing information but also often provide facilities and scheduling that conveniently and cheaply integrate into reporters' beats.

Various policy measures can be understood to respond to this distributional skew in the underproduction of favorable media attention. Most obvious are governments' usually marginal attempts to empower those otherwise least able to "pay" indirectly for media presentation of their perspective. Examples include tax exemptions or postal subsidies for nonprofits, media access schemes ranging from public-access cable channels to right of reply laws or the FCC's Fairness Doctrine, and policies designed to encourage "alternative" media.[58] These efforts, however, are frequently attacked, both legally and politically. The Court unanimously struck down a right to reply law in the print media.* The FCC has now abandoned, based both on a deregulatory ideology and a constitutional analysis, the Fairness Doctrine;[59] access cable channels have been under consistent constitutional attack;[60] postal subsidies are declining;[61] tax exemptions are limited and sometimes operate to restrict important speech;[62] alternative media are often suppressed.[63]

The appropriate policy goal should not be to fully equalize access. Real equalization of favorable media attention is not only impossible but is also misguided. No reasonable conception of equality requires that the media provide equally glowing reports of the latest ax murder and discoverer of a cure for cancer. Both media and audience attention are appropriately selective. The Communications Act's provision mandating equal opportunities for political candidates in broadcasting[64] was

---

* *Miami Herald Publishing Co. v. Tornillo*, 418 U.S. 241 (1974). The Court initially gave two rationales for its decision. The first – protection of almost absolute control by editors of what is to be published – is usually emphasized by media lawyers and academics. If followed, it would doom most direct attempts to mandate access. The Court has more recently explained *Tornillo* in terms of its second rationale, which objected that the law provided a right of access only because the paper first published a criticism, a rule that the Court characterized as punishing, and hypothesized would deter, such critical speech. See *Turner Broadcasting v. FCC*, 512 U.S. 622 (1994). This second, apparently currently accepted rationale both is subject to empirical critique – its predictions are not supported by European experience with guaranteed reply rights – and leaves open many possibilities for structural intervention providing for access.

once thought to require that all candidates, no matter how minor the party, be invited to participate in any televised debate.[65] It is obviously questionable whether this equal opportunity served the public well.[66] Thus, the Court held in *Arkansas Educational Television Commission v. Forbes*[67] that even state-owned media should have discretion to exclude legally qualified candidates from televised debates if the exclusion was for valid journalistic reasons. More generally, favorable media attention should depend on the merits. There is, however, no natural standard of "merit." Distributive issues reappear in that groups and individuals inevitably contest the importance or merit of differing foci.

Fairness (or wisdom and desirable media policy) lies not in quantitative equality but in thoughtful, intelligent, non-monetary-based, diverse choices of where and how to focus media attention. A partial response would be editorial or journalistic budgets that were adequate to avoid rank manipulation by business and government. Also desirable would be professional, independent journalists, editors, or media-content creators (and owners), whose backgrounds are sufficiently pluralistic that individual journalists' or owners' inevitable adoption of particular perspectives will not silence alternative approaches to society. That is, rather than equality, the appropriate response to the distributive concern is structural. What is needed is media independence, which requires an adequate financial base, combined with adequate pluralism. From this perspective, one of the more distressing trends is the increasing imbalance between the number of public-relations professionals as compared with professional journalists – a trend that the economics of the Internet may exacerbate.

Depending on the story's precise content and context of publication, some people will experience either truthful or untruthful media attention as harmful, the eighth externality noted. If media offer this "harmful" attention, either propagandistic publishers or interested audiences must be assumed to value the communicative content to at least some, roughly market-indicated, extent. In the case of false information, of course, audiences usually would prefer accurate coverage but may not value truth enough to pay for greater investigative care – or may not pay because they are unable to identify when care occurs. Even if in a market the audience gets the level of accuracy and harm-causing content for which it pays, the audience's calculations and, according to economic logic, the media's decisions will not include as a cost the injury to those portrayed by the content. At least, the media will not, if, as I assume for the moment, the people portrayed have no effective opportunity to pay to suppress publication and other nonlegal measures do not internalize the cost.

Tort law "remedies" provide the most obvious policy response. Damage remedies partially internalize into media decision making the harms caused by defamatorily inaccurate information about people and products. However, the actual use of tort law to internalize the cost of injury is highly selective. Tort law seldom covers even harmfully inaccurate information if the information is not about a harmed person or product[68] (e.g., a misguided weather report that harms both the resort and people by causing these potential customers not to go and spend money, inaccurate information about the economy that helps defeat an incumbent, or inaccurate praise of one's opponent or competitor). Moreover, the law seldom imposes liability if the harm to the party portrayed results from accurate information[69] or from negative opinion.[70] The tort of invasion of informational privacy has little if any actual bite,[71] although, unlike defamation law, this tort potentially imposes liability on media enterprises for harm to a person truthfully portrayed. Here is not the place to explore either the economic coherence or constitutional acceptability of these doctrines. The point is merely that they show how the legal order selectively and relatively rarely reduces negative externalities by forcing media entities (and other speakers) to internalize costs imposed on those portrayed.

Truthful exposés (and sometimes even false information) that harm *some* third parties are often considered valuable by *other* third parties. Candidate A or the seller of product B wants it known, truthfully or not, that candidate X is corrupt or product Y is defective.[72] Negative and positive externalities sometimes may roughly balance out. However, for certain categories of truthful content – true but salacious gossip or other purported invasions of privacy[73] – identifying the positive externalities (i.e., benefits to someone other than the avid reader or viewer who presumably pays, thus creating no positive externality) to balance against the negative externalities is difficult and controversial.[†] A purported

---

[†] To say "difficult or controversial" does not rule out the possibility of positive externalities of "salacious" gossip. Thus, in protecting a televised video presentation of an accident victim while bleeding and in obvious pain, the Oregon Supreme Court noted that some editors may believe that the "community should see or hear facts or ideas that the majority finds uninteresting or offensive," and this choice should be preserved. See *Anderson v. Fisher Broad. Co.*, 712 P.2d 803, 809 (Or. 1986). Any creation of categories of truthful but punishable speech is dangerous. It tends to reinforce conventional views and power relations, thereby being directly inconsistent with First Amendment premises. People's capacity to gossip may also help equalize the distribution of social power. (More problematic is the tendency for law to unequally favor "gossip"

lack of positive externalities in these cases may help explain legal distinctions between two categories of harms caused by truthful information. Truthful communications characterized as invasions of privacy, especially of private figures, presumably creates few third-party benefits (and certainly few legitimate benefits) to other third parties to balance against the harm caused. In contrast, truthful exposés of publicly relevant information – which few legal commentators believe should be a basis of liability – regularly create appropriate benefits for the exposed party's competitors or rivals and for those who interact with the exposed party. In fact, cases where obviously harmful, truthful information is not thought to be an appropriate basis for media or speaker liability are precisely cases where majoritarian views consider it appropriate for the person portrayed to be "punished" or disempowered.

Superficially, a rough balance between positive and negative externalities sometimes exists for discrediting false information. The person misdescribed is harmed, while some other candidate or competitor benefits. Nevertheless, the seeming balance is misleading. The benefit that the competitor receives is analogous to the benefit from theft or, at least, to unjust enrichment. Distributive or fairness considerations

when engaged in and valued by the powerful – like in hiring contexts.) Karst's argument that the First Amendment most crucially and appropriately protects "unreason" is suggestive of the notion that gossip is both a means of resisting dominant power and of popular participation in the creation and maintenance of norms. See Kenneth L. Karst, "Boundaries and Reasons: Freedom of Expression and the Subordination of Groups," *U. of Illinois Law Review* (1990): 95. See generally Max Gluckman, "Gossip and Scandal," *Current Anthropology* 4 (1963): 307; John Sabini & Maury Silver, *Moralities of Everyday Life* (New York: Oxford U. Press, 1982): ch. 5. Similarly, "outing" may change general attitudes as well as affect behavior. See Larry P. Gross, *Contested Closets: The Politics and Ethics of Outing* (Minneapolis: U. of Minnesota, 1993).

Still, the harms caused by truthful information can be serious and sometimes unfair. However, rather than the largely ineffectual attempts at suppression through imposition of liability, arguably the better policy response is to search for ways to decrease the likelihood that speakers (and the press) will impose these harms unwisely (e.g., merely for commercial gain). Unjustified imposition of harms might decline if journalistic (or societal) norms improved or if media professionals gained greater power to resist market pressures. Changed interests of a better-educated or more mature public could reduce market incentives to publish or broadcast personally harmful content. A needed additional policy response would be to reduce the harm the exposés cause – for example, by teaching people to have more tolerance. Surely no negative consequences should result from knowledge that a person is gay or has been raped. The practice of greater openness may, indeed, be central to reducing such harms – although the cost of this process of change is largely and unfairly borne by those currently mistreated. Still, policies directed at stimulating these changes are arguably more liberating than attempts at speech suppression – and the two types of responses sometimes work at cross purposes. Legal damages imposed for identifying rape victims or exposure of a gay's or lesbian's sexual orientation, for example, reinforces the view that these facts are somehow discrediting.

require that these benefits not count at all for policy purposes, just as the gain to the thief not count (in most circumstances). Moreover, the escalating self-protective measures that people would take, if not legally protected against damage from intentional false statements, are often socially wasteful.

The process of news gathering also creates external costs and benefits imposed on sources and on third parties, Chapter 3's ninth and tenth externalities. The earlier discussion noted that the impact of news gathering on sources, to the extent interactions between reporters and sources are voluntary, is often internalized into their decision making. The reporter and source rely on contract or, more often, its transactional substitutes to assure that the interaction is mutually advantageous, although I noted earlier that the availability of legally enforceable contracts here did not necessarily lead to either efficiency or good policy results.

The impact of news gathering on third parties – members of the public – are usually internalized by the same legal rules that apply to similar costs created by similar activities by people other than journalists. Application of trespass law to both journalists and nonjournalists is illustrative. Often, however, the regulatory goal is to stop *only* forms of news gathering that impose costs that are predictably greater than the societal gains the news gathering would achieve. Thus, state law might give reporters permission to trespass on some sort of fictional "implied consent" theory, especially when the reporter trespasses openly and without violating any explicit demands to keep out, in places where newsworthy events are occurring or have recently occurred.[74] Likewise, a state might decide or the First Amendment might require that damages be limited to injuries created by the news gathering itself, rather than including damages that result because of later publication. Truthful publication often causes injury to the person portrayed but that harm is not normally a permitted basis of liability for speech. Similarly, here, even though publication might cause injury to the party whose property had been subject to the trespass, sometimes this injury should be considered a collective benefit (or sometimes an appropriate punishment of the exposed party).[75] Possibly, publication damages should vary depending on the public relevance of the information exposed: did the trespass produce evidence of illegal corporate behavior or pictures of a person's private sexual behavior? In any event, some rules leave individual property owners to bear some or all of the "cost" of information gathering. Where they do, because this cost is not brought to bear on the media, the rules "subsidize" production of particular types of media content.

Many jurisdictions restrict use of tape recorders without the consent of all the parties being recorded. The interest protected is sometimes difficult to describe given that the law does not restrict nonconsensual publication of the full contents of conversations that the reporter hears but does not record. The ban reduces the accuracy of content that the media makes available to the public.[76] Presumably, however, the ban protects some aspect of privacy or "deniability," thereby reducing some costs otherwise imposed on the subjects of news gathering. Maybe people have better interactions if they can be confident that, without their permission, no one can broadcast or even possess an exact replica of their speech despite their still being exposed to the risk that others will repeat precisely what they said. Likewise, the government sometimes regulates coverage of legislative, administrative, and judicial proceedings. The main legitimate justification is to prevent the news-gathering techniques from having negative effects on the proceedings. (More troublingly, regulation sometimes has an eye to how coverage advantages or disadvantages the people who choose the rules).

## POLICY SUMMARY

The market will predictably not come close to providing people with the media content they want. That has been the conclusion in each of three types of critiques of the market described in Part I. Huge and vitally important costs and benefits of media content and practices are not properly or adequately brought to bear by the market on the decision making of paying audiences or media enterprises. But what are the implications of these observations? The preceding review of some media policy responses to externalities illustrates that much media law can be seen as a response to the market's failures. Even if the media generated no externalities, Chapter 4 shows that the market has no natural or logical priority as a method of identifying and satisfying people's desires.[77] Some policy responses have been already described. Here, I describe more generally three aspects of the needed directions of change and then evaluate three major, possibly responsive, policy approaches.

First, beginning with the initial discussion of the public-good aspects of media products, it has been clear that the market does not create incentives to produce enough media products or to distribute them adequately. Economic theory suggests that society should devote more resources to these activities. This point, however, can be further refined. Given the immense scale of potential positive externalities, market-based firms will produce and deliver drastically inadequate amounts of "quality" media content (with "quality" meaning here content that has significant positive externalities). Audiences could be charged much less – and would buy much more – if the media seller did not have to recover all its costs from its audience but instead received some payment from third parties (or from the state acting on behalf of third-party beneficiaries).

Second, although the incredible array of media material available in the world today might seem to belie the point, the clear expectation is that the market devotes insufficient resources to creating diverse, quality media desired primarily by the poor and by smaller groups, especially marginalized or disempowered groups. This failure reflects the intersection of three factors. Monopolistic competition often under-mines the economic success of smaller, more diverse media products that audiences still value more than the products that prevail. The nonrivalrous-use aspect of media products leads to desires for products valued by smaller groups being less effectively fulfilled by the market than the desires of equally wealthy people in larger, mainstream groups. Moveover, Chapter 4 argued that egalitarian considerations justify weighting preferences for this more diverse content more heavily than do market criteria, especially in relation to smaller groups' preferences for culturally, educationally, or politically salient media products. Finally, the market does not measure preferences for nor produce sufficient amounts of noncommodified media products. Thus, it is likely (but not certain) that self-conscious people would favor rules or subsidies that tilt production toward more diverse noncommodified media.

Third, audiences now get more "junk" than they want (with "junk" here primarily meaning content that has significant negative exter-nalities). Of course, it is often argued that if they buy it, their purchase shows that they want it. There are two reasons why this is wrong. Most clearly, this argument assumes that the product is properly priced. However, audiences pay much less than the real cost of material with significant negative externalities. They would get (and want) much less of this junk if required to pay its "real" cost (i.e., its cost after the media had internalized the content's negative externalities). In addition, the argument that people's behavior shows they want it looks at only one expression of their desires, only one part of their behavior. People may – this claim cannot be made in the abstract but must look at actual expressions – want less low-quality media content, as well as more high-quality, when expressing their desires reflectively or politically. Hence, it is plausible to conclude that audiences now believe they get too much junk even though they continue to buy it. If so, there is no reason to give priority to the market expression.

In addition, in the case of so-called ruinous competition, although people want the products they get, they sometimes could have had their preferences satisfied more cheaply or efficiently. Thus, without this market-created situation, either they or others would have gotten more of their other preferences satisfied. In this case, they in a sense get too much of certain types of material – even materials not necessarily in the junk category. Still, this effect most often applies to lowest-common-denominator-oriented material aimed at larger audiences.

There are three potential types of responses to these inadequacies of the market, of which the first and third should be employed to much greater extent than at present. First, the tendency to massively under-produce content that ought to be considered "good" or "useful" or "edifying and enriching" justifies significant subsidy programs. There is, of course, the problem of identifying whom or what to subsidize, a problem exacerbated by inevitable disagreements about what content fits the categories meriting subsidy. Possibly, subsidies should go mostly to diverse representatives of groups thought most capable of making sensitive decisions about what content is needed or to people or entities thought most likely to serve the more underserved media consumers. In any event, useful subsidies can take many forms. Possibilities include direct subsidies for non-market-controlled production of content, such as public broadcasting; mail or tax subsidies for content produced by nonprofits and ideologically oriented organizations; support for professional journalism education in the belief that this increases the supply of creators of quality content and may increase the likelihood that producers will resist mere market pressures to debase production; subsidies given through entities like national and state endowments for the arts and humanities to support both creation and delivery of diverse cultural materials; subsidies funneled through political parties or other mass-based associations; support for public libraries; and support for media literacy education that could increase the relative demand for high-quality content. Although there is room for debate, the implication of the analysis in Part I is that each of these should receive much greater governmental support than in the past, starkly contrary to recent moves in the direction of reducing public support for each.

Second, the most obvious response to too much "bad" content is suppression. Probably the most common political reaction to inadequacies of the mass media is to identify and then attempt to suppress or restrict content popularly conceived as "bad." Maybe it is merely easier to see what is bad about what exists than to imagine the benefits of receiving that which presently does not exist. In contrast to this response, the most fundamental civil libertarian premise is that suppression of freedom is seldom the wisest or most effective way to handle a social problem. This premise about the imprudence of suppression applies even more forcefully to laws that would prohibit activities, like creating and gaining access to expressive content, that some people plausibly view as aspects of their basic freedom. Here, suppression is rightfully seen as illegitimate as well as unwise or ineffective.

Virtually inevitable uncertainties pragmatically warrant great caution concerning any form of suppression. First, is a particular media effect (or content) good or bad? Often people will disagree in their characterization – otherwise censorship would hardly be controversial. Ideals of liberty and equality require democratic opportunities for collective *promotion* of majoritarian conclusions, but *suppression* of minority views overtly contradicts both ideals. Second, social science has had notorious difficulty proving media effects. Granted that effects do exist, only speculative assessments are possible concerning the quantity of various "bad" effects properly attributable to particular media content. Even given certainty that media portrayals of violence are sometimes a crucial element in the causal chain leading to some acts of antisocial violence, it is still important to know: how often? What opportunities exist to intervene in other links of the causal chain? And what is the content's value to those who do not engage in violence (or even to those who do)? These inquiries are important because any policy response to a portrayal's bad effects ought also consider any good that it produces.

Once these uncertainties are noted, an array of additional questions opens up. For some of the audience, do these portrayals lead to a revulsion against violence and, behaviorally, to reduced violence? For other people, do the portrayals lead to increased readiness to resist unjust oppression – do they, in part, promote a liberating psychology? Of course, also relevant would be whether the portrayals promote wise and effective or self-destructive methods of resistance. Will bad consequences attributed to particular bad content still occur if *that* content is suppressed but now occur due to other, nonsuppressed content? That is, will suppression be effective at reducing evils? Even if the net effect of some content is bad, how often and how much content with significant net social benefits will also be suppressed due either to line-drawing difficulties, to mistakes of categorization, or to improper agendas of people with censorial power? And how often will valuable content be discouraged out of fear that it will be misidentified and suppressed – or even out of the creator's uncertainty about what category, in the end, her creations will fit into? Whose evaluation of these costs and benefits ought to prevail?

Given the complexity and variability of responses to any specific content, the "real" problem may not be "bad" content but the failure of society to educate people adequately to be good media "readers" of violent or other objectionable content. In contrast to education and transformation, suppression could be a disempowering and ultimately less effective response to the problem of media-stimulated violence.[78] Suppression can also divert attention from more useful projects.

Or is a more serious problem – the "real" problem – the set of commercial incentives given to media creators and producers who, if given the opportunity, would have chosen to produce richer, more complex, and potentially more beneficial content? If this is the problem, suppression is misdirected as compared with policies directed at changes in the structure of incentives or changes in the rules that determine who gets to make content decisions.

Of course, these questions could be paralyzing, suggesting that people never have an adequate basis for judgment. But that conclusion should be resisted. People inevitably make affirmative choices individually to obtain certain content, not other content, and collectively to have rules that favor some content over other content. In these choices, judgment should be used. Choices appropriately reflect people's best guesses about net personal and social consequences as well as overt judgments about the quality of media content. People are likely, especially if empirically informed, to make these choices relatively intelligently. As compared to choice, suppression is not similarly inevitable. And given both the problems with suppression and its almost inevitable skew toward dominant, elite, and status quo views, both practical and normative considerations counsel against its use.

Thus, it is disquieting that the more popular policy route, the easier approach for the political entrepreneur, is to focus on (purportedly) objectionable material and to respond with calls for suppression. Positive alternatives often involve greater programmatic complexity. Promoting them requires greater, and more difficult, explanatory effort. Implementation often requires overt expenditures of resources that come from taxpayers. These features can generate opposition, especially from those with wealth or property. These features also provide opportunities to nitpick proposals and to obscure real issues. Is this in part what happened in 1993 and 1994 in the health care debate?[79] It surely occurred repeatedly in response to proposals to require greater expenditures on quality television for kids. The paucity of good children's television is obvious. But rather than attempt to create more good material for which there is an apparent consumer demand, the more vocal political response is to be repressive: first, to ban indecency; more recently, to use societal resources to manufacture V-chips and to apply "ratings" to help people engage in private censorship, despite questionable evidence that they will use the censorship technology when made available.[80] Still, sometimes affirmative rather than suppressive instincts prevail, as they did in the FCC's more recent (but inadequate) steps to implement the 1990 Children's Television Act by requiring stations to provide children three hours a week of educational programming.[81]

The third response is structural intervention. This is the most complex of the three responses. Even the category is difficult to characterize abstractly. The complexity and characterization difficulty in part reflects that the concept applies to so many, radically different things. Introducing the possibility of legally binding contracts was a structural intervention into the lifeworld that made modern markets possible. Copyright is likewise a structural intervention. Usually, proponents of any intervention could characterize it as, in effect, a subsidy for the people or content that the structural change benefits or promotes. Opponents, likewise, often characterize the same intervention as suppression. In her dissent from the Court's approval of legislation that allowed local broadcasters to demand carriage by cable systems, Justice O'Connor characterized the rules as "content-based speech *restrictions*," which she would have held unconstitutional. In contrast, she indicated that she might approve subsidies for the local broadcasters (as well as requirements that the cable operator act as a common carrier).[82] It would be very easy, however, to characterize the must-carry rules as precisely that – a subsidy for the local broadcaster paid for by the local government, which could now extract less from the cable operator.[83]

Although these observations indicate the possible arbitrariness in the characterization, as I use the terms here, "subsidy" generally refers to direct transfer of wealth, usually cash, to the subsidized party. "Suppression" refers most overtly to a prohibition on certain communications or other acts, such that the inability relates not merely to lack of wealth or resources, although it also refers to rules purposefully designed to stop particular communications even if the rules operate indirectly to achieve this aim. "Structural interventions" refer to rules that allocate (or create) authority or opportunities. In effect, structural rules are, unlike either subsidies or suppressions, an inevitable part of the social world. They operate, however, like subsidies in benefiting or enabling particular behavior. And unlike suppression, they do not prohibit any communication. Finally, like subsidies, they should have a justification or purpose other than stopping particular expressive acts even if that may at times be their effect. Thus, my claim is that structural interventions are as legitimate as subsidies, at least as long as they have some empowering objective and are not merely designed to stop unwanted expressive behavior. They should be a central aspect of media policy designed to promote better, more, more diverse, and better distributed communication content.

Thus, media policy should favor structural rules that allocate or encourage the allocation of decision-making control over content creation to people with commitments to quality rather than merely to the bottom line (e.g., the content creators themselves or decentralized control by people involved in the media enterprise). This goal, for example, supports a drastic revitalization of antitrust enforcement in the media area, with the policy being guided by First Amendment concerns that go beyond traditional market analyses.[84] It also supports the following: the long-standing FCC policy of favoring license grants for applicants whose principals live in the community or, even better, whose principals are themselves involved in management; tax policies that favor family ownership rather than sale to conglomerate interests; labor laws that favor a stronger editorial voice for media workers; business organization laws that favor media ownership by workers or nonprofit organizations; and access rules or provision of communications facilities (e.g., public-access channels) that provide greater opportunities to communicate for individuals and noncommercial entities committed to, rather than market-driven toward, their content. The recent FCC decision in favor of low-power radio, mentioned earlier, is exemplary.

These suggestions are merely a beginning. The key claims are, first, massive subsidies of a wide variety of sorts are justified. Second, rules relating to the distribution of decision-making power are appropriate objects of attention and revision, not with the goal of making media entities more responsive to the existing market (which is the typical goal of much policy discussion) but with the goal of making them more responsive to the goal of creating diverse and "quality" content. Third, in discussions about particular proposals, attention to market considerations should not divert the focus from more important normative or evaluative choices. As suggested in Chapter 4, these collective-definitional choices about how to supplement and how to sculpt the market ought to be the center of media policy.

Given the different possible ways to identify and weight preferences, the premise of satisfying people's preferences cannot be the rationale for relying on a market rather than some alternative. This choice can only be made politically. That political choice ought to be made on the basis of normative values and of a society's preferred self-conception. Neither a libertarian nor an egalitarian democrat can accept pure reliance on the market.[85] Of course, some reliance on markets surely makes sense. Pragmatic arguments for *maximal* reliance on markets cannot even be ruled out abstractly. Still, claims that welfare maximization or antielitist or nonpaternalist principles support maximum reliance on markets cannot be justified. Such ideological claims are simply wrong.

Possibly the most common complaint about intervention is that it is paternalistic. However, this complaint, not intervention, is what is really paternalistic. Paternalism lies not in subsidized government structural intervention but in refusing to treat the decision about subsidies and intervention as a matter of democratic choice. A rule of nonintervention is paternalistic in two ways. It limits people's choice to act politically, with this limitation having the systematic effect of benefiting, and often cynically designed for the purpose of benefiting, those people or entities that profit from nonintervention.[86] More sadly, unquestioning nonintervention sometimes represents a paternalistic refusal to believe in people's capacity for democratic decision making to create media more to their liking and more conducive to their aspirations.

PART II

# Serving Citizens

D emocracy is impossible without a free press. At least courts and commentators tell us so. Justice Murphy expressed the common sentiment when he stated, "A free press lies at the heart of our democracy and its preservation is essential to the survival of liberty."[1] Justice Frankfurter stated simply that "[a] free press is indispensable to the workings of our democratic society."[2] More strikingly, James Madison claimed that "[a] popular Government, without popular information, or the means of acquiring it, is but a Prologue to a Farce or a Tragedy; or, perhaps both."[3] Despite deploring "the putrid state into which our newspapers have passed," Jefferson argued that "our liberty depends on the freedom of the press, and that cannot be limited without being lost."[4]

This consensus, however, floats above crucial but more controversial matters. What type of free press does democracy need and why does democracy need it? Answers to these questions would allow the necessary follow-up questions. Are existing media adequate? Do they provide for the informational or communication needs of democracy? And if not, in what way do they fail, and what can be done? If there are inadequacies, do they reflect bad decisions made by media professionals, such that the prime need is for better, smarter, tougher editors and reporters or better training in journalism schools? Or do inadequacies reflect, at least in part, deeper structural problems? And if governmental policy correctives are necessary to make matters better, what interventions would promote a more "democratic press" – that is, a press that properly serves a society committed to democracy?

These questions implicate central issues of First Amendment theory. Agreement on two abstractions – that democracy requires a free press and that the First Amendment protects a free press – is relatively easy.

But what constitutes "freedom of the press"? Any answer requires understanding the role or purpose of the constitutional guarantee. If the Press Clause is a structural provision designed either to support or to protect a press that adequately serves democracy, this premise should guide its interpretation.

Well, those questions provide the agenda. But how to proceed? To assess the media's service to democracy requires a theory of democracy. A choice among possible theories will largely reflect why the chooser values democracy, a normative issue about which people inevitably disagree. Although variations may be infinite, three or four rough approaches may capture most people's view of the normative rationale. First, *elitist* theories of democracy often reflect the somewhat cynical view that the only good thing (although a very important thing) about democracy is that it is better than the alternatives. Somewhat more optimistically, many people value democracy as the only form of government that respects people's equality and affirms their autonomy. Democracy embodies the equal right of each person to participate in matters of collective self-determination. Thus, it respects each person as an equal in her status as a citizen and as a moral agent. It also provides a form of *public liberty* that is inextricably bound to private liberties, whose existence requires, and is required by, public liberty.[5] The legal- and political-theory literature often suggest two dramatically different ways of respecting people's equality. In a *liberal pluralist* or interest-group conception, an ideally functioning democratic system is equally influenced by the private desires of each person; a well-functioning democracy is the fairest mechanism of aggregating preferences or desires for purposes of making law and policy. In a *republican* conception, an ideally functioning democracy is open to everyone's participation in the formulation of collective ideals and public goals; democracy is an open process of defining as well as advancing the public good.

Chapter 6 fleshes out these three theories of democracy, describing premises that make each plausible and maybe even appealing. It also describes what each – the elitist, the liberal pluralist, and the republican theory – require of or hope for in the media. In addition, Chapter 6 describes a fourth approach, which I label "complex democracy," that may be somewhat less familiar, but which I defend and to which I believe our constitutional order is roughly committed. Complex democracy claims to express a more realistic empirical, and a sounder

126

normative, perspective than offered by either liberal pluralist or republican democracy. It expects the media to take on the tasks assigned by each of these theories and, in addition, to support the self-constitution of pluralist groups.* Because the media tasks assigned by republican democracy are sometimes in tension with those assigned by liberal pluralist theory, their combination in complex democracy complicates the problem of assessing media performance. It turns out, or so I argue in Chapter 9, that this complication restricts the issues that should be resolved constitutionally. Before getting to the constitutional issue, however, Chapter 7 identifies the democratic theory implicit in several prominent conceptions of journalism, and Chapter 8 considers each democratic theory's implications for media policy.

Methodologically, I should note that these four "theories of democracy" are presented as ideal types or models, not as descriptions of the views of any particular theorist. Because my concern is with justification, I have described normative reasons why each "ideal type" could have appeal even if many of the prominent theorists usually connected with some notion of democracy tried to present a solely descriptive (or scientific), not a normative, theory.[6] Moreover, in describing each model, I have emphasized factors that I find most persuasive in normatively justifying each theory. For instance, I emphasize government's need to handle technical complexity in justifying elite democracy. Other versions of this theory could, however, emphasize the inherent merit of government by wise leaders.[7]

I have drawn the categories in a way that I hope many readers will find familiar or at least understandable. Still, my specific aim is to highlight how different possible elements of democratic theory are particularly relevant for press theory. Important themes of more robust versions of a particular theory – for example, republican theory's

---

* Although the notion of a group is important for my discussion, I should emphasize now that this notion is neither formal nor essentialist; it does not assume any necessary institutional embodiment, although such embodiments will sometimes exist in practice. A group is a label that basically refers to situations where some people identify with other people on some basis – although I do not exclude the possibility of latent groups, that is, groups with which people would identify on the basis of reflection or circumstance that has not (yet) occurred. Although people sometimes identify with a group because outsiders so identify them, that is hardly necessary; moreover, a person is not a member unless she sees or will see herself as such. Membership is hardly forced; on the other hand, although groups will often have organizational embodiments from which people can be excluded, there is also a sense in which a person often can be relevantly part of a group whose other constituents do not identify her as a member.

thematic worry about the corruption of civic virtue – are sometimes ignored or marginalized if the theme seemed less relevant for the concerns canvassed here.

For other purposes, different categorizations of democracy might be preferable. For example, different theoretical goals might lead to combining elements of liberal pluralism with elitism to show that *elitism* purportedly produces reasonably acceptable results. In contrast, C. B. Macpherson once presented a "pluralist elitist equilibrium" model to do roughly the opposite – to critique an account of the democratic process based on an analogy to economic markets.[8] In my account, however, a pluralist vision can provide a quite powerful account of the point of a particular type of democratic *participation*. Partly because of the normative power of the account, I have isolated this version of pluralism and labeled it as one type of participatory democracy.

CHAPTER 6

# Different Democracies and Their Media

## ELITIST DEMOCRACY

Societies require governments for a host of reasons, many involving the need to overcome collective-action problems that would exist in a world of purely private action. Governments and legal regimes can increase the flexibility, the usefulness, and the effectiveness of a normative order that is used to resolve disputes, can help people effectively and maybe fairly coordinate private behavior, and can encourage productive or "prosocial" behavior. The question is what type of government would best perform these functions. At least one analysis suggests the answer is democracy, but democracy of a distinctly limited sort.

Good governments must routinely respond to problems that are technically complex. Governmental interventions are often most effective if implemented before people even experience a problem. Effective responses frequently rely on intricate economic and scientific analyses. Most people have neither the interest nor the ability to understand, much less to devise solutions for, the problems that government should address. Experts and specialists at understanding the economic, human, and natural environments must do the bulk of the government's decision-making work. As Walter Lippman argued seventy-five years ago: "There is no prospect . . . that the whole invisible environment will be so clear to all men that they will spontaneously arrive at sound public opinions on the whole business of government. And even if there were a prospect, it is extremely doubtful whether many of us would wish to be bothered, or would take the time."[1]

More recently, Vince Blasi questioned whether citizen involvement describes either the "reality" or the "shared ideal of American politics."

129

Blasi suggested that "occasions for involvement in public affairs [such as the necessity to stop totalitarian forces] are a cause of sadness," not a description of the good society.[2] Widespread popular involvement in government seems, to many, at best a romantic, but idle, fantasy – and at worst a disaster.* The complexity of the modern world requires that policy-oriented decision making be a full-time activity. A country can only be governed sensibly by a vanguard leadership of elites or skilled experts. Nevertheless, three practical problems come with government by these experts, technicians, or purportedly wise leadership elites. These three problems suggest that the most practical form of government, at least for more developed societies, is a limited form of democracy – one where, according to Joseph Schumpeter, "people have the opportunity of accepting or refusing the men who are to rule them" as a result of "a free competition" for votes.[3]

First, an effective government cannot rely primarily on force to gain obedience. Reliable legal orders require high levels of voluntary compliance to most of their laws, by most of the population, for most of the time. To a significant degree, voluntary compliance often reflects habit, lack of reason to deviate, or the overlap of the laws' substantive directives with behavior adopted for a person's own practical or normative reasons. Still, compliance with legal commands that require conscious conformance can be expected to be more stable and secure when people view the government as basically legitimate.[4] The problem is that, at least in a world dominated by Enlightenment values, people are unlikely to accept a self-perpetuating government of elite technicians as legitimate.

Second, some experts and technicians will be more skilled than others in responding to a society's problems. In the economic realm, as Schumpeter observed, "[n]o doubt, a manufacturer may be indolent, a bad judge of opportunities or otherwise incompetent; but there is an

---

* Lippman also argued that democratic theory falls apart given its view that human dignity depends on each person being involved in all public decisions. It would be wiser, he claimed, to recognize that self-determination is only one interest and that a government should be measured by how well it serves people's "desire for a good life, for peace, for relief from burdens." Walter Lippman, *Public Opinion* (1922; reprint, New York: Free Press, 1965), 195. He continues, arguing that "if, instead of hanging human dignity on the one assumption about self-government, you insist that man's dignity requires a standard of living," then government should be judged on whether it provides such a standard. Ibid., 197. Lippman observed that even in legislative bodies, most laws are "rejected or accepted by the mass of Congressmen without creative participation of any kind." Ibid., 183. Cf. Joseph A. Schumpeter, *Capitalism, Socialism, and Democracy* (1942; reprint, New York: Harper & Row, 1976), 247 ("[T]he people never actually rule but they can always be made to do so by definition").

effective mechanism that will reform or eliminate him."[5] The market's invisible hand (hopefully) determines which "experts" do the best job. Competition assures that ineffective solutions and inept problem solvers lose out. In governance, however, no such system works automatically. Optimistically, badly managed regimes will collapse in the long run, as arguably happened with the Soviet empire. But the long run is hardly heartening for those living at any moment. Think of the pain that could have been avoided and the gains that could have been obtained if the Soviet regime (at least, accepting common critical assessments of it) could have been replaced earlier (at least, if replaced by something better). A country needs systematic, structural means of replacing less effective, less intelligent experts with others who may do better.

Third, no one's commitment to the public good is ever perfect. Cynics suggest that, as opposed to a person's dedication to her own personal or private good, dedication to the public good is seldom evident. Outright corruption, as well as small-time advantage seeking, is endemic to government and governmental leadership.[†] No matter how idealistic the revolutionaries, no matter how patriotic the coup's new rulers, history consistently portrays them as losing their civic virtue over time and reports well-intended governments degenerating into corrupt administrations. The empirical premise, which Robert Dahl credits as central to Madisonian democracy, is that, "[i]f unrestrained by external checks, any given individual or group of individuals will tyrannize over others."[6] Reasonably acceptable government, whether or not composed of elites, depends on finding systematic, structural means to keep the level and type of corruption within limits.

Democratic elections provide partial solutions to each problem. For reasons not necessary to explore here, the legitimacy of unelected governments is widely challenged today. Simply as an empirical matter, people in the modern world are apparently much more likely to accept a government as legitimate if they perceive it as democratic. This legitimacy gain brought about by elections should improve governmental

---

[†] Advocates of limited government routinely lodge this criticism, often without noting the ubiquitousness of corruption in private enterprise as well. Of course, market competition often generates monitoring techniques that provide some discipline in the private sector. Market discipline, however, does not necessarily further the public good. Illegal or corrupt practices by private firms are often profitable and, from the point of view of the firm, efficient. One complaint about market competition is that it encourages corrupt, socially inefficient, or otherwise objectionable practices. Think of profit pressures leading firms to secretly dump their pollutants or airline competition leading airlines to ignore safety requirements.

effectiveness, especially if the elections do not otherwise seriously interfere with governance by elites.

Elections also create some circulation of elites. People inevitably experience problems that they believe the government should – but did not – help solve. Other problems, they believe, the government has caused. And the experience of problems often festers while proper, even skillful functioning is taken for granted. The accumulation of grievances eventually leads voters to replace one set of rulers with another that makes somewhat believable promises to govern somewhat better. The regular occurrence of elections also creates an incentive for leaders wanting reelection to do a better job and to avoid corruption or, at least, to avoid widespread, observable corruption. Of course, some incentives created by this system may be undesirable. Elections can create incentives for governmental leaders to look to the short-run, pleasing current voters, while avoiding needed but unpopular responses to long-run problems. On the whole, however, democratic elections provide a relatively functional method both to dislodge less effective elites and to create incentives for better performance. A democratic theorist could reasonably conclude that an effective electoral process provides the best, and perhaps the only, structural mechanism for preventing or limiting governmental tyranny and overt corruption.[7]

Democratic elections, of course, hardly exhaust the list of structural devices that might improve governmental performance. Consider allocating authority to different branches and different levels of government, structuring a competitive relation between these loci of power, and imposing process requirements on governmental operation. These are all methods that, if well designed, could facilitate the replacement of elites when appropriate, increase the incentives and capacity of elites to act intelligently for the public good, and provide potential checks on their abuse of power. Designing and explaining devices like these are major tasks of political science and are central to constitutional theory, especially in relation to the Constitution's structural provisions involving separation of powers and federalism. Nevertheless, these are partial measures. Even if one accepts elite rule as wise or necessary, democratic elections may perform the crucial tasks described here, thereby justifying this limited version of democracy.

To fulfill its mission, elite democracy requires a free press – a press to which it gives relatively specific assignments. A free and independent press can make important structural contributions that are as great or greater than many of the constitutional and administrative devices just mentioned. If corruption or incompetence of elites is the problem, exposure is at least part of the remedy. The possibility of exposure can deter corruption and create incentives for proper performance. Actual exposure can promote the orderly replacement or rotation of elites.

The press, however, need not provide for nor promote people's intelligent political involvement or reflection. Elite democracy assumes that meaningful understanding of social forces and structural problems is beyond the populace's capacity and, in any event, is marginal to its interests. Exposure of government corruption or incompetence – the watchdog role or what Vince Blasi dubbed the "checking function"[8] – is probably the most important contribution the press can make to democracy. Publication of the Pentagon Papers and, even more so, the Watergate episode, dramatically illustrates the press living up to this potential. Less dramatic exposés and, even more, a constant deterrent effect, are more routine, day-to-day features of a free press.

A separate issue becomes especially relevant in later discussions of media policy and constitutional interpretation. Is an equally important role of the press the exposure of private corruption and incompetence? Fear of elites' abuses of power could reasonably extend to private elites. Private firms exercise vast power in the modern world. A plausible policy goal is to create a press that maximally "checks" or exposes abuses of power regardless of whether the abuser is public or private, governmental or corporate. A possible implication is the need to make the press structurally independent of both government and private economic power. In contrast, as long as only exposing government corruption or incompetence remains the key concern, a press structured by private power might be equally or more willing and able to perform this function than any press resulting from government intervention.

For elite democrats, a press that checks private corruption or incompetence is desirable but should not rank as an especially high priority.[9] First, the potential danger of private evil arguably does not compare with that created by governments, which have a monopoly on legitimate violence. Only governments could do what the United States did in Vietnam or the Nazi and Soviet governments did earlier in the twentieth century, examples that led Vince Blasi to conclude that "the threat posed by the totalitarian state represents . . . the overriding problem of twentieth-century politics."[10] Second, two powerful forces potentially "check" private power: market competition[11] and, most important, government regulation and law enforcement, especially if crafted and implemented by competent, noncorrupt governmental elites. The central constitutional role of the media results from the unavailability of these forces to check abuse by government, which can only be controlled by "the power of public opinion."[12] Public opinion, in turn, can only be a force for good if it is informed of the abuses. However, the abusers in need of exposure should not be trusted to control the watchdog. Thus, Justice O'Connor is right, from this perspective, to emphasize that "the premise" of the First Amendment is that "government power, rather than private power, . . . is the main threat to free expression; and as a consequence, the Amendment imposes substantial limitations on the Government even when it is trying to serve concededly praiseworthy goals."[13]

Elite democracy has additional implications for the press. First, the media need not, arguably should not, raise serious questions about the underlying legitimacy of the country's constitutional order. As long as elites are honest and competent, the press acts properly in reinforcing the general sense of the system's legitimacy. At most, the press should focus on critical substantive issues about which elites are divided. Despite commentators' criticism of this recurrent practice as "palace court journalism,"[14] only when elites are divided is public discussion really relevant. Division raises the possibility that the currently ruling elite should either change directions or be replaced. Second, because honesty and competence of elites rather than public participation in determining the structure of society are the central democratic concern, heavy emphasis on the character and behavior of individual public figures is appropriate. To facilitate competition among and timely rotation of elites, the press should examine how well the current governmental administration responds to identifiable problems. A deeper focus on structural and other substantive issues is basically unimportant – matters best left to elites. Third, public chronicling of elite debate as well as "neutral" development of information about even uninformed public attitudes can aid elites in their own position taking. Finally, the provision of objective information about major unsolved problems in society can promote good governance in two ways. It provides elites with useful information. It also provides a basis for identifying possible elite incompetence in handling the problems, thereby stimulating both deterrence of incompetence and elite rotation.

## LIBERAL PLURALISM OR INTEREST-
## GROUP DEMOCRACY

Fourth of July speeches extol the will of the people, not the virtues of elites who govern an ignorant or apathetic population. Despite attracting some supporters among self-perceived hard-nosed or realistic academics, elite democracy has little popular appeal.[15] Sloganizing for democracy praises popular participation and celebrates a self-governing people. People have a right to rule; the popular will ought to prevail. Widespread popular critiques of existing practice bemoan the lack of voting and democratic participation. The consistency with which popular discourse takes this course suggests that deeply ingrained values are at stake in people's purported democratic commitments.

Here and in the next section, I outline two strikingly different accounts of the point of popular participation. These accounts, which I label "liberal pluralist democracy" and "republican democracy," share certain objectives. Possibly most important, both purport to explain why popular participation or, at least, real opportunity for participation is crucial for normative legitimacy.

Elite theory values democracy, in part, to maintain a popular sense of legitimacy for government. Its concern with legitimacy, however, is purely sociological. Elite theory predicts (or observes) that people feel and treat their government as more legitimate – and thus are more prepared to obey its laws – if it is democratic.[16] In contrast, for the various participatory accounts of democracy, the concern with legitimacy is usually ethical. The normative defensibility, not merely the empirical stability, of government is at stake.

A jurisprudential elaboration can help here. In rejecting John Austin's predictive interpretation of obligation, H. L. A. Hart observed that the legal order asserts that people are obligated, not just obliged, to obey the law.[17] Of course, the persuasiveness of any assertion of obligation depends on the values and perceptions of those addressed. Given value premises that are widespread in the modern world, only legal orders that respect people's right of self-government – that is, only the existence of democracy – can support the claim of obligation that the legal order presupposes. Of course, no argument will, in fact, convince all those subject to a law of the law's legitimacy or obligatory force. Some will always resist unless "obliged" to conform.

If we put aside this problem of convincing those subject to law, there is a parallel issue. Those exercising governmental power should be able to explain to themselves why they are justified in exercising power over those who object. Their best answer, I think, includes the claim that their exercise of power grows out of a practice that treats the subjects of law as intrinsically significant moral agents whose liberty and equality the legal order respects. Only such a practice justifies the lawmakers' "request," whether or not accepted by the subject, that the subject recognize herself as obligated rather than merely obliged. Normative political theorists constantly debate about what such respect for agents' liberty and equality requires. A common element in most theories, however, is that the legitimizing practice must include participatory democracy – only this process recognizes both people's right to self-determination (autonomy) and people's equality as to this right.

People inevitably interact within humanly created frameworks that create opportunities and impose constraints. Two factors lead inexorably to a normative requirement that many of these frameworks and environments be subject to law and that the laws be ultimately subject to formulation by a participatory democracy. First, the success of people's important projects often requires binding rules – for example, property rules against theft or trespassing or contract rules that allow for the creation of binding obligations – or requires the dedication of resources to particular uses. Imaginable alternatives to any possible set of binding rules will always exist. As compared with these alternatives, any particular set of rules or dedications will disfavor or burden or conflict with some people's preferred projects. Therefore, conflict over which rules or dedications should prevail will be inevitable. People's individual flourishing requires an authoritative way to settle these disputes. Second, only people's opportunity to participate in that government will respect their claim to engage in self-determination on a basis of equality. The first point requires government, the second requires that the government be democratic. Thus, the claim is that a participatory democracy is necessary for (normative) legitimacy of the framework on which people's flourishing depends.

Up to this point, liberal pluralists and republicans might agree. Both emphasize the opportunity for participation. Many also tie the right of participation to the legitimacy of government. They differ most overtly in their understanding of the point and nature of participation. Here I will describe a liberal pluralist view, returning to a republican view in the next section.

The liberal pluralist recognizes that each person has her own interest and each group has its own interest. Each person has her own conception of the good life, usually a conception respected and furthered by groups with which she identifies. Individuals' and groups' interests and values are largely exogenous to the political order. Their interests and values often conflict with those of other persons and groups – a view powerfully illustrated by the Wobbly (International Workers of the World) premise that "the working class and the employing class have nothing in common." In any event, a plurality of sometimes conflicting interests is, the liberal pluralist emphasizes, a fact. The liberal pluralist observes that a telling aspect of many elite theories (and often republican theories of democracy as well) lies in their silences. Elite theorists are concerned with problem solving. They seldom discuss class. Their public policy may ignore gender (often in ways that naturalize subordination). Elite theorists usually identify other potential lines of conflict, like race or ethnicity, only as problems to be managed in a process of teaching groups about their true commonality of interest. Because religious disagreement cannot be overcome rationally, elite democrats deemphasize the extent that religious conflict matters, or should matter, for and in public practices. If a common religion is unavailable, religion is discursively and institutionally segregated. Elitists accept religious freedom but largely ignore the religious world view. In contrast, liberal pluralism recognizes intractable diversity. Conflict among both values and interests, like conflicts among world views, is seen as incorrigible.

Liberals' theoretical response to this pluralism varies. Some versions of liberal pluralism back away from conflict. They argue that the state has no business advancing any particular vision of the good. In their view, "the liberal conception of equality ... prohibits a government from relying on the claim that certain forms of life are inherently more valuable than others."[18] In contrast, the empirical political scientist typically observes how the system manages conflicts to produce relative stability. Other liberal normative theorists consider how interests *ought* to influence results. Treating people as equals and as autonomous means that the properly functioning democracy should respond fairly to the different concerns of each.[19] These liberal pluralists argue that laws and policies should respond equally to each person's interests. In any event, because values are exogenous, all versions of liberal pluralism turn out to treat the key political issues as essentially distributional.

Liberal pluralists plausibly argue that, if properly structured, democracy provides the mechanism most likely to take into account and properly weigh all interests. Interests are detectable and influence government policy primarily due to interest-group pressures or representation. Political mobilization by each group creates political capital and gives each group leverage in the political bargaining that generates a democratic regime's laws and policies. Popular political and electoral participation provides the currency that assures that a group's interests are taken into account, hopefully in rough proportion to the group's size and the intensity of its interests. Participation protects people's rights and interests – it is "preservative of all rights."[20] This institutionalization of (properly) accounting for interests provides the normative significance, the legitimizing contribution, of democracy.

According to liberal pluralist theory, the goal of creating fair compromises or bargains between groups should guide the design of institutions (including the media). When possible, constitutional provisions should be interpreted to protect such institutions, to mandate their maintenance, and to facilitate their creation. Of course, particular conditions can undermine the pluralist democratic bargaining process, including "prejudice against discrete and insular minorities . . . which tends seriously to curtail the operation of those political processes ordinarily to be relied upon."[21] In this circumstance, pluralist democratic theory tries to devise approaches or structural devices, possibly including interpretations of constitutional provisions such as the Equal Protection Clause,[22] that either help to repair the process or mandate the fair outcome that a properly working process would have achieved. In this book, however, the relevant inquiry is to determine how the press can contribute to this pluralist democracy and to identify the media policies or Press Clause interpretations that best enhance these contributions. I momentarily postpone this inquiry, however. It can be best developed in contrast to the implications of the next version of participatory democracy.

## REPUBLICAN DEMOCRACY

According to critics, liberal pluralism's purportedly unsentimental realism is actually not so realistic. Interest-group pluralism neglects two basic attributes of most people and these attributes are central to a sounder democratic theory. First, people are not, certainly not always, narrowly self-interested. People are social, communal, and often caring and idealistic, not purely selfish and atomistic. They define themselves as beings not concerned merely to advance their personal interests. People are often motivated by conceptions of a common good and by a concern with others' welfare. Second, people's interests do not spring full blown from some inner source or even from their group identity. Rather, people expend considerable effort in formulating, evaluating, and choosing interests and values to which they then give allegiance. This task requires self-reflection, discourse, or sometimes both, and normally takes place at least partly in interaction with others.

Republican democracy treats as basic these two attributes that pluralists ignore. Whether naturally or by socialization, most people in the real world are, to varying degrees, oriented toward a good that involves a concern for others, what can be called a "common good." Furthermore, most people engage in practices – discussion, reading, and reflection – partly in order to understand or to formulate their own notions of the right and the good. Both attributes affect action within all spheres of life, but they arguably have special relevance to action oriented toward the collective order, the political realm. A person *might* focus on others' welfare when she goes shopping or when she decides what to do with her time in the evening after a long day at work and after taking care of the children. And certainly a concern for others, even people beyond the family, is evident in many people's daily activities. A concern with other people is especially likely, however, at more discrete points in time – when a person sees herself acting in, or thinking about, the "public sphere."

People's political concerns are often much more public-spirited than much of their private economic and consumptive behavior. Many people see their interests in politics as predominantly related to a concern for justice or for a better world for everyone, even if these concerns are only intermittently dominant in their nonpolitical practices. Economist friends tell me that even the mere fact of voting is hardly rational for most people, in terms of a calculation of personal advantage gained compared with effort spent on voting.[23] Nevertheless, voting can be valued and rational in itself as a self-definitional expression of being a part of a community, as a selfless performance of civic responsibility, and as a means of participating in the collective project of choosing between contested notions of the public good. Even if, in practice, the content of people's vote usually corresponds to a political scientist's external view of their narrow economic or group interests, this observation need not discredit the republican view of democracy. First, a political scientist's report of people's votes tracking self-interest is at best a statistical observation. It leaves huge numbers of votes unaccounted for – to be explained by something else, cynically, by their ignorance but alternatively by a public orientation. Moreover, the characterization of the votes as self-interested reflects the political scientist's external analysis; the voter herself may deeply believe that she is trying to advance the public good. The rich voter might actually believe in trickle-down economics. Any vote's apparent correspondence to a self-interest (or group interest) that conflicts with a broader public interest (at least, according to the observer's most likely contestable conception of public interest) could easily represent the voter's partiality of perspective, which limits her understanding of the public good. This does not demonstrate narrowness of commitment, only of execution.

The republican conception of politics is implicit in norms about what interests are properly voiced in public political speech. The practical need for the candidate's or legislator's speech to appeal to assertedly broader, common interests demonstrates that people, in fact, believe that democracy and politics should be about common or public, not merely private, goods. Narrow self-interest, purportedly observed in actual voting, should not be accepted as normative but as a problem that an ideally working democracy would help alleviate. From the republican perspective, the extent to which current politics is narrowly self-interested merely indicates the degree to which it is currently corrupt.

Thus, a central feature of democracy should be a (public) realm especially dedicated to people's formulation and pursuit of the "common good." Moreover, government should be designed to institutionalize a responsiveness to this public realm in which people consider the public good.[24] Republican democracy shares with liberal pluralism a critique of the elitist focus on merely sociological legitimacy. But where the liberal pluralist sees normative legitimacy as the result of fair distributions resulting from fair bargains, the republican sees legitimacy flowing from commitment to, and agreement on, common goods. An autonomous, moral agent ought to be self-governing, including making her own interests subject to her own reflection and commitment. This principle rules out subordination to exogenously given interests. For self-governance, a person must be able to participate in formulating, and must be able to accept, the mandates of the collective process.

In this republican view, politics is most fundamentally about discussing, formulating, and committing to common ends and then pursuing them. From both the individual and group perspective, participation is not merely or primarily an aspect of efficient or fair self-interested bargaining. Rather, participation is intrinsically valuable as part of the life of a self-defining, reflective person and people. The liberal pluralist critiqued the elitist for not seeing the need to build mechanisms into the structure of government to take fair account of true conflicts of interest, especially those concerning distributional issues. The pluralist sees bargaining over these differences, along with handling collective-action problems, as the central function of politics. The republican, however, critiques the pluralist for ignoring the people's activity of *formulating* truly "common interests." She rebukes both the elitist and the liberal pluralist for treating values and conceptions of the good as mere empirical facts advanced either by expert administration or by fair bargains.[25] A public good is found or formulated only through the deliberations of civically virtuous citizens. From this view, "the experience of democracy is not ultimately about winning but about deliberating and acting together. . . . [Democracy] is about how we equalize politically in acting together for shared purposes."[26]

For the republican democrat, the central category of civic virtue consists in a behavioral orientation toward the common good. Unsurprisingly, fear of corruption has also been a major republican theme. In the liberal pluralist account, where self-interest is accepted as the norm, the concept of corruption, or what I sometimes call "overt corruption," is generally limited to illegal or otherwise improper pursuit of self-interest. This is the behavior, for example, that press theorists hope the press's "checking function" will expose or deter. Because the republican proclaims "civic virtue" as the proper norm, she will see a much larger realm of potential corruption. Under this republican conception, in addition to the liberal idea of "overt corruption," legal pursuit of self-interest can also be a "fall from virtue" that is to be feared as a form of corruption. The scope of needed press probing will be correspondingly greater.

Further description requires a choice in how to model republicanism. So far, the account has emphasized two central themes: civic virtue and a public or common good. But the relation between virtue and the common good can be seen in alternative ways. First, even if all virtuous people were oriented toward the common good, their conceptions of the common good could vary and compete. Although a civically virtuous person must remain open to hearing and considering alternative conceptions of the common good,[27] in the end she should struggle to have her understanding prevail, even if opponents are not, and never could be, convinced. This competition can lead to "republican moments" – times of intense politics when old orders are transformed by people's struggles to have new conceptions of the public good come to dominate politically even though many committed to the old remain unconvinced.[28] Moreover, this pluralism of conceptions of the good suggest the propriety of episodic fair bargains partially realizing various different visions. Alternatively, some theorists believe (or at least theorize as if they believe) that, with sufficient deliberation, agreement on a common good would be possible among civically virtuous persons. A conception's "commonness" relates to its really being the good for all – or, at least, for all within the relevant community. Invocations of the popular notion of an "ideal speech situation" often appear to be attempts to describe a hypothesized context in which people would reach this consensus. The ethical premise that a free or autonomous person must live under laws that she helps to author and that she accepts suggests the importance of this possibility. Freedom or autonomy purportedly exists for people only when the legal order represents a truly common good that all can accept. The aim is true agreement, not acceptance of "fair" bargains.

As will be discussed later, these alternative conceptions of the common good lead to somewhat different notions of ideal media policy. Given the concerns of this book, it is analytically useful to label them as involving different conceptions of democracy. The first alternative is an element of what I call "complex democracy," the next type of democracy to be described. Here, I call the second alternative "republican" – namely, the notion of a politics aimed at a truly common good that is or would be accepted by all within a community after appropriate discourses.

John Dewey might serve as an exemplary republican democrat. He has inspired many advocates of a more participatory democracy and of a press that better serves participatory ideals. More to the point here, he argued for broad participation as a way to find and pursue what we have or need in common. In the book most cited in this connection, *The Public and Its Problems*,[29] Dewey consistently stresses "common concerns." Democracy "forces a recognition that there are common interests."[30] Unlike elitists who argue that the many do not have the expertise to rule, Dewey argues that rule by the many does not require this scientific expertise but rather the ability to "judge of the bearing of the knowledge supplied by others upon common concerns."[31] Unlike pluralist democrats, Dewey does not mention deep conflict within the public. Rather, the public's "essential need . . . [is improved] debate, discussion, and persuasion."[32] Conflict is only implied by the need for the public to prevail over elites. "No government by experts in which the masses do not have the chance to inform the experts as to their needs can be anything but an oligarchy managed in the interests of the few. And . . . [the public must] force the administrative specialists to take account of the needs."[33] Clearly, democracy must be participatory. "From the standpoint of the individual, it consists in having a responsible share according to capacity in forming and directing the activities of the groups to which one belongs."[34] This "responsible share" seems deliberative and solidaristic, in a republican sense, rather than a matter of interest-group bargaining or conflict. Future improvements of democracy, Dewey argues, must "make the interest of the public a more supreme guide and criterion of governmental activity, and . . . enable the public to form and manifest its purposes still more authoritatively. . . . [T]he cure for the ailments of democracy is more democracy."[35]

A full-blown republican theory would have relevance for the design of many structural features of a democratic order. Here, the point is that the press or the media constitute a central democratic institution. Its design ought to facilitate the process of deliberating about and choosing values and conceptions of the common good.

## COMPLEX DEMOCRACY

It is difficult to deny the existence of people's altruistic impulses. People often act selflessly to aid others and to serve varying common goods.[36] Social life as we know it would be impossible without these elements. Likewise, people surely need processes by which they can clarify both their individual preferences and their conception of more general common goods, a fact that leads to the elements of discourse most emphasized by republican theory. It is equally difficult to deny, however, that much of politics (and of life) involves bargaining, reflects self-interest, and often relates to real conflicts of values. A further complexity is involved in the many cases in which political bargaining does not reflect people's narrow self-interest but rather groups' conceptions of the good that their members favor. Here, a person may favor this good within the political or public arena not out of any personal desire for a benefit but solely because of solidaristic, even altruistic, impulses to further the group's interests. That is, there is solidarity and altruism in the orientation of the individual but conflict and bargaining at the societal level. Think of labor solidarity and class conflict.

Complex democracy recognizes both points, drawing on elements of both liberal pluralist and republican democracy. As a more "realistic" theory, it assumes that a participatory democracy would and should encompass arenas where both individuals and groups look for and create common ground, that is, common goods, but where they also advance their own individual and group values and interests.[37] Moreover, complex democracy assumes the same is true normatively. It is difficult to argue that either type of political striving is inappropriate for an ethical person or within a justifiable politics.

Individuals and groups can have both real conflicts of individual or group interests ("I or we want more country music rather than your classical 'junk'"; "you top CEO's earning 1,000 times what us manual workers get is not in our interest") and unresolvable disagreements about the common good ("as a people, we would be better off with more wilderness areas rather than the access roads you want"). In relation to these conflicts, when real and unresolvable, the political structure should facilitate fair bargains or compromises.

Conflicting group interests or conceptions of common goods, however, often have complicated histories. Republican theory as described here emphasizes that common ground or societal public goods do not spring forth preformed, but require discursive development. This same point is also true of groups' own "common goods." Groups require their own internal processes of value formulation and clarification. Processes that the republican intends to serve as discursive value formation and value clarification for society as a whole should be duplicated at the group level to serve each group's internal discursive needs. An adequate participatory democratic political order must provide institutional or structural support for discursive political processes at levels below society as a whole. These should be internal to or controlled by groups, groups that conflict with others in society. This is a crucial element of complex democracy that is not found in either liberal pluralism (which, because interests are taken as exogenous, does not require discursive as opposed to bargaining processes) or in republicanism (which, because of its emphasis on commonality, does not require pluralistic discourses).

As noted, some liberals argue that the collective treats differences fairly only if the law does not favor any conception of the good. In contrast, republicans sometimes claim that there is a truly "common" good to be found or formulated and then furthered. From the republican perspective, group assertion of distinct interests and maintenance of divergent perspectives is always a matter of concern – a sign of inadequate integration. As Todd Gitlin has argued, "[t]he question is how to cultivate the spirit of solidarity."[38] The melting pot dream looks to the time when all people's interests will be merely human interests. From a left republican perspective that seeks a politics of equality that will embody the "essence" of "Americanism," the "squandering of energy on identity politics . . . is an American tragedy."[39]

The choice, however, need not be between liberal pluralism and republicanism (as described here)[40] – or, worse still, a "partial good" imposed by an oppressive elite. In contrast to republicanism, an adequate democracy must recognize that different groups and different interests do exist. Often, such differences are probably desirable. In any event, they may be inevitable in a free society. This fact of "reasonable pluralism" helps explain, for example, the attention recently given by John Rawls to showing that his principles of justice can be defended on the basis of "an overlapping consensus of reasonable religious, philosophical, and moral doctrines."[41] Multiculturalism – the recognition and celebration of difference – could be a move toward a realistic and, most important, a more inclusive, nonoppressive conception of society. Even though there may be real "common goods," significant aspects of any single group's good will differ from that of others, just as is true for individuals. A nonoppressive society will normally have many groups that develop divergent, potentially conflicting "common goods." Inevitably, these differences and conflicts often will not be (fully) dissolved through discussion. As a result, many of these conflicting goods will not be perfectly realized. But a democratic order must encompass giving different groups – just as it gives different individuals – fair scope to develop and live their differences. And "fair scope" will presumably be a matter, at least partly,[42] for bargaining and compromise.

This distinction between the republican search for a common good and the norm of giving scope to differences can be analogized to a distinction between two arguments made by John Stuart Mill in *On Liberty*. Although Mill treated his argument for free speech as illustrative of his argument for liberty, this ignored an important difference between two arguments that corresponds to the difference between conceptions of democracy. According to Mill's argument for liberty of thought and discussion, people's actions and their concepts of the good are best founded on truth, discoverable in the long run by free speech.[43]

Like with republicans, this premise seems to suggest that differences – like differences in opinion – are ultimately only instrumentally valuable as a means to arrive at truth and that truth would be the same for everyone. Thus, Mill maintained that "no belief which is contrary to truth can be really useful," and that "the well-being of mankind may almost be measured by the number and gravity of the truths which have reached the point of being uncontested."[44] Although Mill valued liberty in part for these same reasons of experimental progress, like complex democrats, he also valued liberty because "different persons . . . require different conditions."[45] In order to give "fair play to the nature of each, it is essential that different persons should be allowed to lead different lives."[46] In the terminology used earlier, the first argument, which instrumentally values freedom of speech, aims for a melting pot, while the second argument, which values liberty (and difference) as an aspect of the good for persons, celebrates multiculturalism.

A pluralist society encompasses different groups whose separate conceptions of the good partly overlap and partly are in tension. Greater societal integration may or may not be desirable. The appropriate extent of societywide common goods and of legitimate integration should be a matter for noncoerced agreement by individuals and groups. Purportedly "common" public spheres, especially if they claim to bracket differences, inevitably manifest particular cultural content, usually that of dominant groups.[47] Any majoritarian or elite denial (or bracketing) of actual or experienced differences during a purportedly impartial or "reasoned" democratic search for a public good inevitably involves ideological oppression. A true search for more inclusive "public goods" will be noncoercive only if groups first have an adequate opportunity to develop their differing perspectives, and then have their perspectives fully voiced and given their due. Historically groups, especially subordinated groups, need the opportunity and resources to develop, examine, and articulate independently their own identity and consolidate their own strength. Only then are they in a position to consider truly common goods. Nancy Fraser is surely right that reducing the oppression of a stratified society requires flourishing public spheres of, for, and by these "subalternian" groups and thematizing rather than bracketing difference.[48] Pluralist groups need their own discursive development; they need their own public spheres and media in which they can independently develop identity and strategies. Only then can a group properly agree on the extent and content of "common goods."

This complex view combines elements of liberal pluralism and republican democracy. It assumes the reality and legitimacy of bargaining among groups over irreconcilable conceptions of the good, but also hopes for discursive development of common conceptions of aspects of the good. This vision of complex democracy generally corresponds to the democratic theory recently developed by Jürgen Habermas. Habermas argues that democracy is not a matter of merely following appropriate principles of fairness while maximizing and allocating private goods, as claimed by some interest-group pluralists (the liberal view). He also contends that democracy is not solely a matter of finding or constituting and pursuing societywide common goods (a republican account). A preferable "discourse" theory of democracy encompasses republican-type discourses aimed at ethical self-understanding and self-constitution of specific historical communities.[49] This ethical self-constitution, however, should be "subordinate to moral questions."[50] Acceptable political decisions must be consistent with, although not entailed by, principles of justice that "claim universal validity."[51] Moreover, Habermas argues that "compromises make up the bulk of political processes" – that is, politics also includes "fair" bargaining leading to compromises between groups that presumably maintain separate identities under conditions of cultural and societal pluralism.

In this account of democracy, Habermas sees politics as encompassing different types of discourses that take on different tasks. Some discourses aim at compromising interests. Others try to find elements of a shared common good. Groups or communities within the inevitably pluralistic society also retain the task of defining non-societywide, more particularistic "common goods." Thus, Habermas' account rejects republicanism's totalizing conceptions as oppressive but incorporates the republican idea of self-defining or public-good-constituting discourses as one key aspect of politics. Given pluralism, different self-defining discourses must occur at both the societal and group level. Although often not noted, this implicitly requires different "public spheres" – those in principle open to all and also those open to all who are members of, or who identify with, smaller, pluralistic groups. Finally, this account rejects liberal pluralism as founded on an unrealistically stunted conception of people and politics; but it incorporates the liberal pluralist's recognition of fundamental value conflicts and the need for bargaining and compromise.

## PARTICIPATORY THEORIES' IDEAL MEDIA

Each version of participatory democracy treats somewhat different attributes of the governing process as crucial. The optimal design of institutional structures of governing depends on the functions highlighted by the favored democratic theory. Similar observations apply to the design of the press, which, though usually privately owned, is widely recognized as an institution that plays a crucial role in democratic governance.[52]

Liberal pluralist democracy hopes to generate fair bargains as a result of groups' pressing their interests. In this process, the media should perform several tasks. First, the press should provide individuals and organized groups with information that indicates when their interests are at stake. Second, the media should help mobilize people to participate and promote their divergent interests. Note that neither function – information or mobilization – nor presumably the media structures that facilitate them are necessary for elitist democracy. Third, for pluralist democracy to work, information about popular demands must flow properly – that is, given the practical gap between citizens and policymakers, the press should make policymakers aware of the content and strength of people's demands.

For at least the first two tasks, a common media serving society as a whole likely will not suffice. Most pluralist interest groups conclude that only their own media effectively identify when their interests are at stake. Often, only their own media will develop and present information relevant to their needs and interests. Groups also need their own media for the second function. Arguably, the decline of competing partisan daily newspapers contributed to the decline of voter participation in the United States.[53] Pluralists rely on partisan, mobilizing media entities to help spur participation. Thus, they should be unalterably opposed to media monopolies. Moreover, competing media entities should not compete merely for undifferentiated shares of a single, mass audience. Audience segmentation is necessary in the pluralist vision. The hope is for separate media entities, with each entity focused on, and preferably controlled and maybe owned by, one of the various groups making up the polity (or controlled by individuals whose primary allegiance is to one of these groups).

Republican democracy has a very different vision. Two elements are crucial. First, the press should be thoughtfully discursive, not merely factually informative. It should support reflection and value or policy choice. Second, this discursive press must be inclusive. The democratic pursuit of, and hopefully agreement on, a real common good requires an inclusive public discourse. Popular involvement in democratic deliberation requires at least that "serious issues . . . be covered in a serious way" and "that a significant portion of the citizenry is actually exposed to diverse views."[54] The press ideally should be civil, objective, balanced, and comprehensive – although some slippage in the first three might be allowed if necessary in order to not overly restrict participation. Still, the republican may be ambivalent about mobilization, certainly more so than the pluralist for whom partisan mobilization, which often lacks civility, is a central currency of democratic bargaining. The republican wishes to see politics as a matter of the better argument, rather than the stronger (fair) pressure. Participation by the uninformed and unreflective is hardly a gain from the republican perspective. Nevertheless, corruption, narrow self-interest, or possibly even policy inertia can thwart realization of the common good. Thus, a mobilizing press may sometimes be needed, but it should be directed at general civic mobilization on behalf of honesty, good procedure, and responsiveness to popular demands. Segmented, partisan media required by pluralist democracy are unnecessary. They may even be disruptive, thereby impeding reflective discourse and agreement. Indeed, the republican can be happy with media entities that are dominant within a community – media monopolies – as long as these dominant media are adequately inclusive and comprehensive. But, these media are only desirable *if* sufficiently responsible, which becomes the crucial republican concern.

Complex democracy seeks a political process that promotes both fair partisan bargaining and discourses aimed at agreement. Like pluralists, complex democrats require institutions, including media entities, that assist groups in recognizing when their interests are at stake and in mobilizing their members. Segmented media can help groups participate in political bargaining aimed at obtaining their fair distributional shares of social resources. Complex democrats also require institutions, presumably including inclusive, nonsegmented media entities, that support a search for general societal agreement on "common goods." Thus, complex democracy entails a media system that performs the somewhat conflicting functions respectively highlighted by liberal pluralist and republican theories. And it requires more.

Diverse groups sometimes can agree on a societywide "common good," but sometimes choose instead to pursue their own separate vision. Agreement on a common good, however, is real only if acceptable from the perspective of each group's own needs, projects, and commitments. These, however, do not flow from obvious, objective interests. Rather, interests as well as the strategies for their pursuit often result and, if the group is self-determining, ought to result from the group's discursive reflection and potentially revisable choices or commitments. Normally, identity and commitments are best arrived at or properly affirmed through discourses largely internal to the group. Unless groups' internal needs for discourse are met, purportedly broader solidaristic or altruistic conceptions of the public good almost inevitably mask dominant groups' oppressive impositions of values. "Dissenting" or minority groups are left with the unfair choice of assimilating under oppressive conditions or appearing selfish as they deny purported common goods and pursue their own apparently narrow interests. To avoid these alternatives of oppression or marginalization, complex democracy increases the assignments given to the media. It requires media entities that support groups' internal discursive and reflective needs for self-definition, cultural development, and value clarification. All functions that republican theory assumes the media should perform at the societal level, the complex democrat expects a segmented press to perform for each group at this subsocietal, group level.

The centrality of these self-reflective and self-defining activities also points to the crucial role of media forms, such as fiction, art, and dance, that are largely ignored in the democratic vision of the elitist or pluralist. These forms of expression are not only valuable in themselves but also play integral roles in individuals' and groups' reflective and definitional processes. If preferences or interests are fixed, and the only issues are technical (elitist) or distributional (pluralist), these media forms have little democratic relevance. Art and fiction, like other consumer goods, may have social value – and some lawyers with an impulse toward favoring free speech may want to provide them with some constitutional privilege. Elitist or pluralist press theories, however, can properly disregard these forms. That conclusion changes somewhat for the republican. Even then, those fictional or artistic contents that would be truly useful in republican discourse are unlikely to be in much danger of political suppression. For a complex democrat, however, these media forms not only have major significance to groups' self-defining discourses, but also may be in danger of direct suppression or, as suggested in Part I, of inadequate economic nourishment. Dominant groups sometimes find the art or fiction of outlying groups to be exotic, while, at other times, to be unrefined and base, perhaps even threatening.

Often dominant groups see the cultural expression of outliers (or, as another example, each generation's children) as the paradigm of "unreason" – sometimes dangerous and, at best, an arousing, offensive diversion.[55] Nevertheless, complex democrats would expect these media forms to make significant democratic contributions to groups' internal discursive needs. The vibrancy of these media would provide some evidence of the health of the complex democrat's ideal media realm.

Thus, complex democrats have the most robust hopes for the media. They seek both a societywide press called for by republican theory, and a strong, partisan, segmented press called for by pluralist theory. In addition, segmented media entities should support the same value and identity clarification tasks internally for "each" individual group that responsible societywide media entities should provide for society as a whole.

The difference between the visions of the media held by each democratic theory is further exemplified by their views concerning the information that media should produce about the public itself. In a representative democracy, elections provide some, but usually quite inarticulate, information about the public. Democratic theorists would want the media to help fill the gap, sending those reports down to the public or up to the government officials that the theorist believes democracy requires. For elite democrats there is little need for the public to know about itself; and for governance, elites *need* not know much about public attitudes unless the public is disturbed enough to produce instability – even though elites may also *want* to have polling data relevant for reelection purposes. Participatory democrats, however, need considerably more information, although the specific need varies from one participatory theory to another.

Participatury theories commonly believe that the media should report public opinion to government officials, thereby prompting governmental responses. The media should also provide the public itself with knowledge about itself – so that those who disagree with the dominant opinion can contest it and so that people can have a criterion against which to measure government responsiveness. But what is public opinion? Consider two conceptions: (1) a currently widely accepted view, which defines public opinion as the sum of polling data about what members of the public, even *without reflection*, will *assert in private* to the pollster about *any matter;* and (2) the classical view, which views public opinion as what members of the public, *after reflection or discussion*, will assert, presumably in public, about a *public matter.*

For the liberal pluralist, the first notion may serve. The "polling" conception of public opinion should seem natural if interests are exogenous and only their advancement is internal to the political process. For the pluralist, a legislator engaged in political struggle, like a poker player, needs to know what cards she holds. When bargaining in behalf of her constituents, she needs accurate information concerning the depth and breadth of their preferences. To some extent, polling organizations supply this information. Conceptually, the major problem is that polls typically fail to reflect the intensity of concerns. (Different attitudes about this failure are possible, however. For example, George Gallop saw this blindness to intensity as a desirable way to "neutralize the power of pressure groups.")[56] In addition, there are always questions concerning interpreting results due to the form of the question and the stability of reports obtained without reflection. In a 1999 study conducted by the Freedom Forum, 51 percent of those surveyed said when asked that the Constitution should "be amended to prohibit burning or desecrating the American flag," but 90 percent of this group changed their mind when told that this "would be the first time any of the freedoms in the First Amendment [were] amended in over 200 years."[57] Still, for pluralists, the only doubts about polling concern the empirical question of whether polls cause more distortion, for example, by failing to measure intensities of preferences or reporting unstable or cued preferences, than they eliminate, for example, by more adequately reporting preferences of unorganized groups that are undermeasured by other means.

The republican should favor the more classical accounts that see public opinion as "the outcome generated by a body of people . . . who come together through a process of discussion, debate, and dialogue about current affairs."[58] The classical accounts understand "public opinion" as views formulated in public discussions about common interests.[59] From that perspective, polling has little to do with either identifying or measuring public opinion. Instead, polling duplicates liberal pluralism in its focus on existing private preferences, while lacking any methodological concern with reflective and discursively developed views. In the classic accounts, only the latter represent politically significant public opinion.

Overall, pluralists are generally pleased that the press provides regular reports on polling data. Publication adds political force to people's (private and usually unreflective) opinions. The reports provide information about majoritarian attitudes. This information can have political effects both directly on government decision makers and indirectly to the extent that other members of the public often conform to apparent majoritarian attitudes. For liberal pluralists, this is as it should be. In contrast, republicans will be deeply suspicious of, if not irate about, this type of reporting by the press. Their concern is that reports of polling data give too much weight to unreflective, untested private views. The object of politics should be to generate and give force to the better argument – thus, any political effect of mere polling data is inappropriate. Press coverage should further public opinion seen as a "whole-scale conversation" among citizens.[60] Further, republican theorists object to media using limited resources to focus on private preferences rather than on issues needing public attention and on the information and discussion relevant to their consideration. Complex democrats should agree with the substance of the republican objections, but recognize that the state appropriately responds in part to private needs and concerns, which are part of the data for bargaining discourses. Moreover, the media should provide information about views and debates within "outsider" or "subalterian" public spheres. Such information is essential both for the internal purposes of these subgroups and for the thinking and policies of the overriding democratic government.

CHAPTER 7

# Journalistic Ideals

Journalistic practice and ideals can reflect or be critiqued from the perspective of a particular conception of democracy. Here I examine journalism's dominant professional paradigm and the most influential current alternative. These examinations first identify the conception(s) of democracy implicit in each. Then, because I consider complex democracy most appealing – an admittedly disputable judgment – I also consider each paradigm's adequacy from this democratic perspective.

## SOCIAL RESPONSIBILITY

The Hutchins Commission's report, *A Free and Responsible Press*, provides the most influential modern American account of the goals of journalistic performance.[1] Media scholars observe that this report, or even more its restatement in the Cold War classic, *Four Theories of the Press*,[2] is virtually "the official Western view," has had "startling power and longevity,"[3] and is at the point of becoming "the unique, universal model for journalism practice and theory all around the world."[4] Published shortly after the end of World War II, the report describes a "social responsibility model" of the press.[5] The Hutchins Commission identified five responsibilities, the fulfillment of which could serve as a measure of press performance. The press should (1) provide "a truthful, comprehensive, and intelligent account of the day's events in a context which gives them meaning," a commitment evidenced in part by "objective reporting"; (2) be "a forum for the exchange of comment and criticism," meaning in part that papers should be "common carriers" of public discussion, at least in the limited sense of carrying views contrary to their own; (3) project "a representative picture of the constituent groups in the society"; (4) "present[] and clarify[] the goals and values of the society"; and (5) provide "full access to the day's intelligence," thereby serving the public's right to be informed.[6] The commission also identified three central tasks of the press's political role: to provide information, to enlighten the public so that it is capable of self-government, and to serve as a watchdog on government.[7] Fulfilling the five listed responsibilities presumably would accomplish these three tasks.

This conception of the press implicitly assumes that what a properly functioning democracy needs most from the media is "information." The press should present the day's events, a picture of all elements of society, and the day's intelligence – fulfilling the first, third, and fifth functions listed here. Thus, in 1953, Norman Isaacs, the president of the Associated Press Managing Editors Association, explained: "The one function we have that supersedes everything is to convey information."[8] Presumably, wise politics and wise decisions will follow. In addition to information, the commission also recognized the obvious importance of values. However, rather than having the press be a center of a societywide discussion of values, societal values need to be "presented" to, and "clarified" for, the public. Thus, the media's role is primarily as an educator, to enlighten the public. A professed commitment to performing this educational responsibility was evidenced by the media's own "codes of performance, which urge the media to respect accepted values and to portray the traditional virtues."[9]

The Hutchins Commission's study took place in the context of an increasing concentration of the mass media. The long trend toward media monopolies, regularly in the news in the 1990s, was clearly observable in the 1940s, and the commission advocated some government policies to promote pluralism and competition. Rather than dwell on objections to the inevitable, however, the commission treated this apparently irreversible trend primarily as evidence that the media must be responsible. "A press characterized by bigness, fewness, and costliness in effect holds freedom of the press in trust for the entire population."[10]

The commission's emphasis on "responsibility" can be understood as a pragmatic response that makes the most of the fact of largeness and monopoly. A telling feature of each of the five responsibilities identified by the commission – both those related to values and those related to information – is an easy compatibility with monopolistic media. With adequate professionalism and dedication, a single master of ceremonies, namely a monopolistic media enterprise, could apparently perform them all. Echoing declarations commonly made by owners of modern monopoly newspapers,[11] the commission asserted that power and monopoly impose obligations on media entities to present all sides of an issue and to provide the public with sufficient information.[12] Journalists' professionalism arguably qualifies them to identify the societal issues requiring attention and to gather the relevant information. Media critics should and do exist to point out lapses. The public should demand quality performance. Even then, a constant danger exists that a monopoly press will not be responsible. However, as long as journalists' professionalism, critics' watchfulness, and the public's demands lead the press to meet its responsibilities, a monopoly press poses no serious problems.

Much about the commission's vision is praiseworthy. Performing the watchdog function, providing information, and maybe teaching people proper values (enlightenment) are all that elitist democracy requires of the press. Like all democratic theories, the elitist agrees that a watchdog on government is needed. Also, the public needs to accept the results of government. For this, it should be "enlightened." And whether the government is by elites or by a republican people, decision making requires information. These are precisely the three political tasks that the commission identified. To varying degrees, however, those who support participatory conceptions of democracy should be troubled by what the commission leaves out (as well as the arguable naiveté of aspects of its vision).

Of the participatory theorists, republicans should have the fewest complaints. Like republican democracy, the social responsibility theory indicates a concern that "partially insulated groups come to understand one another."[13] Still, the top-down implication of the fourth function – presenting and clarifying society's goals and values – sounds inadequately discursive. And the emphasis generally seems to be more on providing information than on promoting discussion, even though the second function (being a "forum") may address this republican requirement of discourse. Finally, the republican may find the commission's vision inadequate in failing to call for media that support general civic mobilization. Admittedly, some references suggest an interest in participatory democracy. Still, the commission explicitly does "not assume that all citizens . . . will actually use all the material" but rather, more in line with elitist democracy, assumes that many will "voluntarily delegate analysis and decision to leaders whom they trust."[14]

"The allure of social responsibility" pales from other perspectives. It gives little structure or support to the social conflict emphasized and valued by the liberal pluralist. The commission's list does not satisfy the pluralist's demand for media that aid groups in pursuing their agendas and mobilizing for struggle and bargaining.[15] Likewise, it does not satisfy complex democracy's additional demand for media that assist groups' own internal discursive development of identity and values. The report does wish, ideally, to have "specialized media of advocacy" in addition to general media. The reason for the wish, however, is more elitist or, maybe, republican: partisan media could serve to police the fairness of the general media and provide "partial safeguards against ignoring important matters."[16]

Thus, the commission's vision embodies more an elitist or, in important respects, a republican rather than a pluralist or complex conception of democracy. Like republican or elitist conceptions, the commission's socially responsible press must assume that society contains few deep divergences in interests and perspectives. This can be seen in the assignments that it thinks the press can fulfill. Deep divergences cause different "facts" to be relevant for different groups – "responsible" presentation would require choices based on particular perspectives.[17] Given deep divergences, even the same facts will have different meanings. The media simply cannot report the "context which gives them meaning" because the relevant context will vary for different groups. In contrast, in the absence of deep social divisions, the same information and context can serve all. Reporting and contextualizing only require that reporters act professionally and that the press act "responsibly." Thus, only the lack of deep divisions (or the failure to recognize these divisions) can make notions like objective reporting, "a comprehensive . . . account of the day's events," and the notion of "the day's intelligence" appear unproblematic as ideals.[18] Only then could values be primarily a matter of "presentation" or "clarification," not conflict or at least debate. Without these deep divisions, it is possible to believe that, by "rais[ing] social conflict 'from the plane of violence . . . to the plane of discussion,'" free expression can "promote[] the *harmonious*, fruitful society."[19] Apparently, a responsible press not only defangs conflict but, in the end, exposes conflict as irrational.

Without deep divisions of interest and value, or with only divisions that do not profoundly color perceptions of facts and values, government decisions might be primarily a matter of problem solving,

possibly best performed by experts. People's individual, private preferences as well as their related informational interests may differ. Significant societal issues and relevant information, however, are largely an
objective matter. Only this assumption allows the monopolist press
to identify (as well as present) "all ideas deserving a public hearing."[20]
Politics, if any, is a matter of republican citizens coming together.

In contrast, if ideology (or experience) deeply colors perceptions of
facts and values and thereby affects what counts as relevant news, even
a "responsible" media entity is likely to present primarily issues and
information relevant to the society's dominant ideological perspective.
If conflict and divergent ideological perspectives are and should be
central to politics, monopoly media are likely to be able, at best, to *report*
differences. More likely, a monopoly public-affairs media will (even if
unconsciously) suppress differences – claiming objectivity for what is
really a partisan vision. For example, to those outside a moderate to
moderate-liberal, development-oriented stratum, the *New York Times*,
perhaps the country's best, maybe most socially responsible paper, may
seem like a wildly biased and censorious apologist for established
elites.[21] Democracy needs competing media to develop and promote
alternatives. While this does not rule out the need for some socially
responsible media entities that try to be inclusive, informative, and clarifying, both pluralist and complex democracy also require a segmented,
partisan, mobilizing press. Furthermore, complex democracy requires
these pluralistic media not merely to interpret groups to each other and
to mobilize, but also to satisfy each group's legitimate internal discursive needs.

## PUBLIC JOURNALISM

The fact that the social responsibility model is aligned more with elitist
than with participatory democracy primarily is seen in relation to what
it left out. The model emphasized providing information and being a
watchdog – or, paternalistically, clarifying societal values. Performance
of these functions should help elites in governing and aid the public in
identifying and, hopefully, in throwing out corrupt officials. However,
this vision placed no emphasis on mobilization or effective encouragement of popular participation.

The ethos of a socially responsible press is merely to provide the facts
or, maybe, the facts supplemented by context – that is, "the truth about
the fact[s]."[22] Critics, however, recognize that values inevitably deter-

mine the choice of facts. Even the ethos of responsibility is not neutral. Its practice and content inevitably amount to a value-laden conception of the press's role – values that are further implicated in practice whenever it adopts more specific interpretive frames. This press uncovers wrongdoing. It avoids being tricked. Instead, it identifies officials' hidden agendas, resolutely exposing public persons' hidden, inevitably self-interested concerns. It provides information that a moralistic public would consider discrediting. By engaging in these journalistic activities, the press necessarily participates in and helps create, rather than merely reports on, the public order. The choices recommended by social responsibility – an ethos of objectivity and the informational and watchdog roles – align the press with the generally quietistic needs of elitist, rather than the active engagements of participatory, democracy. The press facilitates elites' rational decision making while deterring and exposing violations of the largely unproblematic norms of public office.

In the 1990s, many within the profession found neither American democracy nor the American press in good health. These critics observed that journalism's established routines provoked popular cynicism.[23] Detached objectivity encouraged a sense of powerlessness about civic processes. With considerable academic and foundation support, some editors and journalists spoke of "civic" or "public journalism" as an alternative to the existing journalistic orthodoxy.[24] Central to civic journalism is the view that journalism should better serve democracy. More specifically relevant here, I want to assert that civic journalism embodies a conception of republican rather than elite, liberal pluralist, or complex democracy.

Public journalism's leading academic champion, Jay Rosen, repeatedly emphasizes that public journalism is oriented toward "citizens as participants, politics as problem solving, democracy as thoughtful deliberation."[25] The constant image is that through "deliberation" the "public" can find its "common interests." In place of narrow self-interest, public life is about *common* problems, the *common* good, *common* work, *common* ground. "Common" seems to be the key – the word is used continuously within civic journalism circles. We are all in this together. In this picture, ours is a world where there are real issues, real problems, and real choices to be made, but where there is little fundamental conflict of basic values or identifications. The people – not the politicians or journalists – know their common problems and the people ought to be involved in applying their intelligence to solving them. Thus, Frank Enton, editor of the *Wisconsin State Journal*, defines civic journalism as "helping the public find the solutions to problems," implicitly treating politics as a matter of consensual problem solving rather than conflict.[26] Journalism, according to Rosen, quoting Davis Merritt of the *Wichita Eagle*, should be based on "broad, shared values."[27] Public life needs deliberation, but apparently neither class- nor identity-based struggle. "The most basic form of politics is conversation about . . . choices and about what is really in the public's interest."[28]

This civic vision calls for new journalistic practices. Journalism should self-consciously intervene in public affairs – not on behalf of particular viewpoints but on behalf of invigorating public involvement. For example, by sponsoring open community meetings, a newspaper or broadcaster literally convenes the public for deliberation about public issues – and then it reports on those deliberations. At present, public journalists insist that they are experimental, still trying to find ways to involve the public. Rather than cataloging and evaluating its experimental practices, however, I want to note the movement's justifiable appeal. Then, I will describe some of the vision's most troublesome limitations.

The distance of public journalism from the Hutchins Commission's elitist democracy is implicit in its characterization of the press's watchdog role as important but too limited.[29] Public journalism continually indicates that journalism's special role is to *actively* serve democracy – or, more specifically, "to promote and indeed improve . . . the quality of public or civic life [and to] foster[] public participation."[30] This active involvement is probably the biggest difference between civic journalism and social responsibility. Civic journalists are not merely objective, they are proactive. They do not merely enlighten the public and instruct it on values; they rather call the people into session and provide them space to talk about common concerns.

Civic journalism's leaders correctly recognize that a useful vision of journalistic practices must be tied to a conception of journalism's function. Without excluding making money for owners and employees and providing amusement and information for audiences, they see that function is centrally to serve democracy. Then, of course, the question is the conception of democracy. Unlike some versions of liberal pluralism, public journalism properly rejects treating people and politicians as merely self-interested. It favors asserting and reporting on solidarity between people and on their common, civic interests. In many respects, public journalism tries to fulfill the democratic roles that the early Habermas saw performed by the people, although unfortunately only the new bourgeoisie, within a public sphere or public space.[31]

Like the Hutchins Commission's model, however, civic journalism's republicanism is consistent with the economic interests of a monopolistic press. If a single public interest exists, and if the political task is problem solving, then a single responsible convener of the public discussion might be ideal. Also, conveniently, civic journalism can help secure the press's financial viability, a point that its advocates do not ignore. Only if people are oriented toward civic problem solving, only if they participate in a public deliberative process, will they need to read and, therefore, to purchase the "news," the press's "value-added" product.[32] Still, critics of public journalism are wrong to see "convening the public" as merely a marketing ploy. Given the assumptions of republican democracy, professional journalists properly find out what the public thinks and wants as an integral part of a participatory democratic process.[33]

Still, civic journalism's slide into republican democracy may reflect less a considered judgment about democratic needs than an attempt to make the most of existing economic constraints. Today, monopolistic daily newspapers are the norm. These papers are unlikely to allow any journalism that threatens their extraordinary profitability.[34] As early as the late nineteenth century, an industry trade journal warned that newspaper partisanship can be suicide in a small town because it invites the opposing party to establish its own paper.[35] Arguably, the erosion of the economic basis of partisanship and the corresponding economic advantages of objectivity result in significant part from advertising. Advertising makes the ability to attract the largest audience the key to profitability. Hence, as the role of advertising in newspaper finances increased, it should be no surprise that avoidance of partisanship, except mildly on a ghettoized editorial page,[36] increasingly became the norm.[37] Thus, whatever its merits, any democratic theory that recommends partisanship is unavailable to civic journalists at least as long as they operate within the existing structure of the industry. Instead, civic journalism champions participation, which involves activism, but, as constantly affirmed, the civic journalist does not "cross the line." Even as civic journalism's proponents expose absurdities in the traditional notions of value-neutral objectivity, they continue to proclaim abstention from partisanship except for a partisan commitment to democracy and other broadly shared values.[38] They claim to "function as 'fair-minded' participants in community life whose participation focuses on non-partisan processes and procedures."[39] Journalists are to participate by "helping the public gain confidence in its own ability to reach consensus and solve problems."[40]

More sinisterly, a radical critic might charge that civic journalism amounts to ideological boosterism – a refined technique for legitimizing the existing order without challenging major injustices or structures of domination. A central motif in arguments for civic journalism is the need to respond to the current democratic distemper, the loss of faith in both the press and the political order.[41] Civic journalism seeks participation. Thus, the *Charlotte Observer* asks readers what should be done about rowdies taking over a neighborhood park. If this "journalism" successfully involves people more in civic life, it should count as a clear gain despite plausible worries that the paper would censor any radical views – the paper "said it would only print constructive suggestions."[42] Moreover, rowdies in the park is one thing. The more serious question is whether civic journalists also identify as problems and raise questions about the class structure of the city or the need for material redistributions of power. Christopher Conte notes that after the *San Jose Mercury News* encouraged readers to respond to the problem of special interests' influence on the legislature, the paper then blocked the "convened" citizens' impulses to lobby for limits on campaign spending. It viewed that response as too political. Instead, the paper encouraged its convened citizen readers to formulate a statement, which legislators could sign, concerning accountability.[43]

A few examples prove little. Still, civic journalists' consistent emphasis on common ground and common interests easily connects with their emphases on deliberation and on problem solving. As a journalism of conversation, it "favors a publicly tested consensus over the spectacle of conflict."[44] Richard Harwood, a public journalism advocate, argues that "reporters should pay attention to areas of agreement, as well as conflict."[45] As professionals, civic journalists recognize that false reporting of harmony is improper; still, the repeated emphasis is on the importance of finding common ground and a real public interest. In October 1994 a newspaper committed to civic journalism called a meeting between contending sides in a community dispute. The reporter originally assigned to cover the story first described the meeting as filled with conflict. The published version, however, was much brighter, describing how the meeting helped participants "find some common ground."[46]

From the perspective of complex (or pluralist) democracy, the visions of both democracy and press activism offered by civic journalism are at best inadequate and at worst naive and apologetic. Admittedly, civic journalism merits great praise for favoring participatory over elite democracy and for recognizing that journalism inevitably participates in, rather than merely objectively reports on, politics. These well-founded developments are revolutionary in many traditional journalistic circles. Much of the criticism of civic journalism reflects this traditional perspective and objects to precisely what is potentially good about it. But civic journalism's emphasis on commonality distorts reality and at least stunts and arguably misdirects journalism's participatory role. Values and interests are often in real conflict. Some people benefit from the oppression suffered by others. Greater involvement in a "nonpartisan" pursuit of important but uncontroversial goals – safer parks or honest legislators – or in problem-solving agendas largely defined by and consistently acceptable to community elites, although not bad in itself, should not substitute for popular struggles around issues involving real societal division. This "civic" focus becomes bad if it diverts popular challenges to injustice and inequality.

If democracy is, in part, about bargaining between segments of society with conflicting interests and about the struggle of the disadvantaged and their allies against the injustice of privilege, then a democratic order needs more partisan journalism. Particular groups, especially oppressed groups, also need more segmented or partial dialogues in which to develop their self-conception and their understanding of their own interests. Oppression consists, in part, in the impoverishment of these partial discourses. Thus, from the perspective of complex democracy, civic journalism's republicanism is at best inadequate. True, common ground is valuable. Groups do need to talk with each other about collective problems. But these are not the only, and sometimes not the most pressing, needs. At worst, civic journalism could be a technique of co-optation or legitimization that creates a false sense of participatory involvement without challenging entrenched elite interests. If so, it unwittingly serves its owners' ideological needs as well as their economic interests. In any event, complex democracy would recommend going far beyond civic journalism's republicanism and assigning additional partisan roles to the press.

CHAPTER 8

# Fears and Responsive Policies

M edia policy and constitutional principles attempt to allay fears about and serve hopes concerning the mass media. Each theory of democracy, with its thematic assignment of duties to the press, generates its own set of fears about how the media might fail. Thus, not surprisingly, each normative democratic theory has different implications for media policy. Of course, because some theories do not repudiate but rather add to other theories' assignments, neither fears nor responsive policies will always be unique to a specific theory. For example, although participatory democratic theories add citizen mobilization to the media's assignments, these theories share elitist democracy's fear that the press will be prevented from checking or otherwise unable to check government malfeasance or misfeasance. This chapter describes each democratic theory's fears about media performance and suggests potential policy responses.

First, a preliminary matter should be noted that could have implications for media policy. Do democratic media have any reason seriously to fear anything other than government? If not, maybe the government's media policy itself is the only real threat. The best principle might be simply: "Government, hands off!" Of course, fears necessarily reflect both factual assumptions and values. Factually, normal market processes may create precisely the press that democracy needs. But this depends in part on what democracy needs – the value issue. For example, if democratic institutions ought to be whatever people want them to be and if markets automatically respond to (or, better, reflect) people's wishes, then the "hands off" conclusion could follow. An alternative route to the "hands off" principle might look to history and ask: has not government intervention, always loudly defended as furthering desirable societal interests, usually been found in retrospect to have improperly interfered with press freedoms and the press's democratic roles?[1]

In this broad form, the abstract argument against intervention must be rejected. First, history can show mistakes but cannot determine whether further interventionist efforts are now merited – it only reports the failures and successes of the past. Moreover, the bleak reading of the historical record is less than obvious. After putting aside overtly censorious interventions that should be struck down under the First Amendment, and if the reading of the historical record is restricted to legislative interventions by *democratic* governments, the record may not look so bad. And certainly theory does not support "no intervention." Whether a person gets good affordable medical care, a clean environment, safe streets, or other (contestable) benefits of good government – benefits for which *she*, if necessary, would pay a lot – is determined less by the media she purchases and consumes than the media that others consume. As Chapter 3 explained, these benefits to her are not reflected in her market purchases and, therefore, are not internalized by the market into media enterprise's incentive structure. This lack of internalization leads the media to produce less democratically beneficial media content (and more harmful or inadequate content) than people want or democracy needs. In fact, some of the media's major contributions, such as deterring corruption, do not even produce a product for it to sell – which leads to further divergences between the market-generated media and the media that would best serve democracy.

People also may be committed to a democratic theory that requires media practices that a market order does not even claim to provide. For example, just as with basic educational opportunities, Chapter 4 observed that people can be committed to a relative equality of opportunities to consume and, maybe, even to participate in the creation of media products. People may even value a system that equally provides media products designed for, or tailored to, the interests of all people. But these egalitarian commitments are not realized by a market that, by design, responds to unequally distributed dollars. Moreover, markets do not provide reliable evidence of the extent of people's commitments to (or preferences for) this sort of equality.[2] Because such commitments amount to a rejection of market criteria of measurement, the market is a logically inappropriate device for evaluating the importance, relevance, and strength of such commitments. Instead, this evaluation most logically takes place discursively within a public sphere, which should lead to the commitments' subsequent political embodiment.

An ideal account of media policy might determine the democratic theory and then the corresponding conception of the press to which people are committed or would be committed after discursive reflection. This chapter takes on a more modest task. It identifies each of the democratic theories' primary fears concerning possible failures of or inadequate performances by the press and then examines the policy implications of these fears. For example, all democratic perspectives fear that the lure of profits or the competitive forces of the market could cause the press to shortchange its democratic role. Different democratic theories, however, vary in their view of when and where the short-changing occurs. Consequently, different democratic theorists vary in the policy responses, if any, that they would find congenial.

## PERSPECTIVE OF ELITE DEMOCRACY

Elitist democrats' primary media-related fear is governmental censorship that undermines the media's checking function. Even benign governmental interventions threaten eventual censorship. Worse, the mere possibility of interventions, benign or not, can lead to media self-censorship as a means to avoid unfavorable or to ensure favorable regulation. Any loss of independence is dangerous. The press must keep government at arm's length – which it cannot do once it is subject to regulation. Thus, some commentators interpret the First Amendment's Press Clause to mandate that government keep its hands off. Others add that the Press Clause gives affirmative protection to the press's institutional integrity.

Elite democrats might develop a more complex view. While the danger of government undermining the checking function is real and constant, it is not the sole threat to the effective performance of the media's watchdog role. That role could be threatened from at least two additional directions. First, journalists and editors could abandon adequate performance due to laziness, incompetence, coziness with government officials, or conflicting professional ideals. Not surprisingly, a major worry about "civic journalists" is that, in order to find "common ground" and to engage all segments of the community in solving community problems, they will sacrifice their drive to expose and willingness to offend and, instead, will get into bed with local elites.[3] Likewise, critics of traditional journalist routines, many of which reflect economic "realities," observe that these routines create incentives and dependencies that threaten the press's ability to be an effective watchdog. Journalists' relationships with government sources and their reliance on news beats focused on the most regular and productive sources of information can breed the dangerous dependencies and self-deceptions that Hertsgaard calls "palace court" journalism.[4]

Second, and possibly more relevant to constitutional issues, private centers of power can generate pressures that impede press performance. These pressures can be either internal or external to the media. Critics regularly blame the recent decimation of many papers' investigative journalism units on an increased bottom-line mentality within media enterprises. Printing news that the paper clips from wire services is much cheaper than hiring investigative reporters.[5] Either increasingly competitive market conditions or greater assertions of control by bottom-line-oriented chains and conglomerates can trigger newsroom budget cuts that leave the press without the resources to be an effective watchdog. Conglomerate ownership can also create pressures not to damage the economic interests of the nonmedia parts of the organization. The result can be that media entities become less watchful of problematic corporate or government activities that intertwine with corporate interests. Or the media owner's other economic interests can blunt reporting of problems, for example, those generated by the city's building a new stadium or convention center. Outside the press itself, institutionalized critics, sometimes derogatorily called "flak producers," can undermine press performance by making the press worry about appearing biased or inadequately patriotic.[6] A press that exposes periodic abuses of power could appear on casual observation to be "biased" against the powerful even as that press leaves the routine use of power unexamined. This perception of bias will likely be nurtured by the powerful, especially wealthy corporations and individuals, who have the easiest access to the resources needed to advance this characterization. Thus, mere performance of watchdog role can cause inaccurate portrayals of the press as having a leftist tilt. Dependency on advertising can also undermine press performance. Journalists (or publishers) who fear offending valuable advertisers may, for example, avoid reporting a local tax authority's (corrupt?) failure to fairly assess and tax a downtown department store's property.

Private and governmental power centers are the foci of reporters' beats and provide the informants or sources for their stories – as well as providing conveniently already written stories in the form of press releases. These centers operate as both locational and content sources for the press's routine news-producing activities. Some observers argue that this dependence causes today's press to be not a watchdog but rather a "guard dog" for groups with power and influence.[7] Thus, elite democrats, though settling simply for the press's watchdog role, might favor government interventions that increase the media's capacity and readiness to perform that role. Still, the checking function is most overtly threatened by government censorship. For whatever reason, elite democrats seldom develop much passion for media policies other than those protecting the press from government.

More than other democrats, elite democrats focus on the Constitution. Policy interventions seem inherently dangerous, more dangerous than they are worth. These democrats agree with Justice O'Connor's emphatic claim that "the First Amendment . . . rests on the premise that it is government power, rather than private power, that is the main threat to free expression."[8] In order to ensure that the watchdog is not muzzled by those watched, the Constitution forbids governmental meddling. The extreme formulation of this view rules out any intervention that has the effect of "distorting" the press's communication. It requires a "wall of separation" between the press and the government.[9] Even favorable specialized treatment by the government can create a dependence and a willingness to bend to gain favor, thereby undermining the press's watchdog role. The Newspaper Preservation Act[10] illustrates the problem. It gives the attorney general broad *discretionary* power to confer what is generally seen as a major benefit – approval of a joint operating agreement – on individual papers.[11] Apparently, both Knight-Ridder's *Miami Herald* and its *Detroit Free Press* ordered their cartoonists not to lampoon Attorney General Edwin Meese at the time when he had discretionary authority to decide whether to allow the *Free Press* to enter into a joint operating agreement with another Detroit paper.[12]

Of course, participatory democrats, who conclude that a country's media needs require various governmental interventions, share this concern about a loss of press independence. However, they respond differently from the "hands off" advocates. In addition to constitutionally prohibiting direct attempts at censorious interference, like the withdrawal of advertising as punishment for media criticism,[13] these democrats look for policies that, to the extent possible, reduce the danger of the problem. Often when the government provides benefits to individual units of the press, like use of a press office in the White House, courts require procedures that limit their allocational discretion.[14] Moreover, media regulations that apply broadly and do not grant discretionary official power to provide benefits or exemptions create much less of a problem. A legislative body is unlikely to strike at the press as a whole in response to the behavior of an individual entity. And, even if it would, an offending media entity is less likely to be deterred. It would itself bear only a small fraction of the total cost created by such a response. No individual public television station, for example, should worry much that its actions will cause reduced funding to the system as a whole. By structurally externalizing a "cost" (government wrath) on outsiders (other media entities), governance by mediawide rules encourages individual media entities to act with appropriate aggressiveness. Of course, increasing concentration of the media (or cross-ownership by enterprises dependent on other government favor) reduces this safeguard.

Justice Potter Stewart has been the premier judicial advocate of protecting the structural integrity of the press. He argued that "[t]he primary purpose of the constitutional guarantee of a free press was . . . to create a fourth institution outside the Government as an additional check on the three official branches."[15] Although Stewart would not give this institution any constitutional right to *act* in ways that would otherwise be lawless, he considered protection of its institutional integrity as essential to the press's constitutional role.[16] He argued, for example, that the Constitution bars the government from "attempting to annex the journalistic profession as an investigative arm of government."[17] To prevent government appropriation of journalists' work products and the consequent deterrence of sources, Stewart would severely restrict government's power to search newsrooms or to force journalists to disclose the names of their confidential sources.[18] The loss of confidential sources and secure newsrooms creates a major interference with the press's ability to gather news, including information about government wrongdoing, and increases the danger that the press will become little more than a mouthpiece for official statements and press releases.

The elite democrats' media proposals are unlikely to extend further than Justice Stewart's constitutional defense of the press's institutional integrity. Although the elite democrat sees merit in the press both explaining government policies to the public and providing elites information about the public's concerns and needs, only the press's watchdog role justifies constitutional protection, that is, protection against government. Government control and manipulation present the most serious threat to performance of this checking function. Therefore, the elite democrat is likely to be generally uninterested in media policy and opposed to most interventions. She is likely instead to favor a constitutional doctrine that is strong enough and clear enough to block suppression of the press even during pathological times – times when the checking role may be most vital because even weak-kneed judges may be inclined to approve purportedly justified interventions.[19]

## PERSPECTIVE OF REPUBLICAN DEMOCRACY

Like all democratic theorists, republican democrats share with elite democrats a concern to protect the press's watchdog role. In addition, they recognize two primary dangers to democracy that the press can exacerbate or lessen. First, they fear inadequate popular political participation. The press ought to stimulate citizen involvement. But republicans worry that, rather than talking with the public to "engage us in solving . . . shared problems," the press will "contribut[e] to a mood of fatalistic disengagement."[20] They worry that the media's "relentless emphasis on the cynical game of politics threatens public life itself."[21] Ironically, the ideals of detachment and objectivity, implicit in the Hutchins Commission Report as well as in the emphasis on the press's "outsider" watchdog role, may contribute to this disengagement.[22]

The second republican fear is social disintegration.[23] Society cannot exist as a babble of voices. A bleak vision foresees one family member watching only MTV (music videos), another watching only old movies, a third watching only the sports channel, and possibly a fourth watching only public television. New media will follow magazines in dividing and subdividing targeted audiences into smaller and smaller ethnic, age, gender, occupational, and recreational groups. Each individual will receive over the Internet a customized newspaper that she designs in accordance with her individual interests or that her "intelligent computer agent" shapes in accord with her prior reading habits or personalized directives. The advertising industry's "relationship" marketing, made feasible and cost-effective by new computer technology, increases the economic base for this radical disintegration.[24]

As this media segmentation advances, the republican fears that people will not develop any common fund of knowledge. With nothing to say to each other, they will become unable to engage in civic talk. Any common public sphere will wither and die. For example, Elihu Katz reports that when there was one public broadcaster, 65 percent of

Israelis watched the evening news and then often talked about it even across ideological divides. But with the arrival of a competing channel, people watched their "own" news. Possibly because there was less need to watch in order to participate in a common discourse, the total audience for the evening news – even though people now had a choice – dropped to about 35 percent.[25]

This fear of disintegration envisions either popular habits or economic forces causing the breakdown of central, dominant media. The nightmare intensifies as technological options and price structures change in the new world of broadband communications, including the Internet. Each separate community (or, worse, each individual) will develop its own unique interpretation of the world, its own agenda, its own basis for action. Tribal segregation within self-enclosed media worlds will contribute to an unraveling of civil society. Radical pluralism threatens not just stability but the very possibility of legitimate authority. Of course, a public that is split between 500 cable channels and that reads personalized newspapers is a far step from the national or ethnic segmentation in portions of Eastern Europe or Africa, with the apparently consequential violence and governmental collapse. Still, the Yugoslav example purportedly stands as a warning.[26] The republican sees dominant, nonsegmented media providing the necessary foundation for an effective public sphere and a truly common discourse. Society should avoid any media-driven "balkanization" of the public.

As noted, public journalism tries to respond to these dangers from within the profession. Possibly, republican media can only be created by struggles within the press, with thoughtful journalists taking the lead. Regulatory intervention may be too blunt a tool to induce appropriate performance of the media's republican discourse role. "[L]ike many other virtues . . . [press responsibility] cannot be legislated."[27] Still, structural legislation is often motivated by the hope that it will lead to better content and more responsible performance.[28]

As a radical illustration, law could require that owners permit journalists to elect their managing editors, thereby arguably reducing owners' abilities to enforce a bottom-line, decision-making orientation. Despite its radical nature, this law might be acceptable constitutionally. In *Miami Herald v. Tornillo*, a famous case that struck down a statute giving a criticized candidate a right to reply, the Court did not describe itself as protecting owners but rather as protecting editors. The law failed, the Court said, "because of its intrusion into the function of editors."[29] The Court was protecting "the exercise of editorial control and judgment" – although the hypothetical statute imagined here would be protecting editorial control from the owners, not the state. Nevertheless, the Court had previously said the First Amendment does not stop the government from protecting the press from "nongovernmental combinations," for example, corporate owners, "if they impose restraints upon [the] constitutionally guaranteed freedom."[30] The law giving journalists authority to elect their editors would be premised on the assumption that, like most workers, journalists take pride in their work. When investigative reporters were asked in a survey to rank "the rewards that sometimes result from doing 'successful' investigative pieces" in order of importance, out of five choices, 56.1 percent said that the "reformer in you was satisfied" ranked first, while only 2.6 percent chose "monetary rewards" as most important.[31] Editors and reporters rooted in journalism and empowered by law are likely to resist attempts by bottom-line-oriented publishers to erase the line between advertising and editorial efforts. Such editors might also be more likely to engage in republican discourse style of journalism. Putting this radicalism aside, however, many less dramatic legal policies can also help create the inclusive discourse that republicans favor.

Given the fear that legal interventions inherently threaten the press's watchdog role, one republican policy response might be to divide the press, leaving a "watchdog" realm untouched while creating a second realm in which regulation affirmatively promotes a common democratic discourse.[32] Historically, much broadcast regulation fits the solidaristic specifications of republican democracy.[33] Regulatory policy could indirectly encourage local broadcasters to promote republican political involvement. One strategy is to promote localism, which is the locus of actual popular participatory involvement. This was, in fact, the policy of the FCC. Although the fast-fading dominance of the networks makes it easy to forget prior policy goals, the FCC's chain broadcasting rules were a somewhat quixotic attempt to limit network power and to maintain local station control over programming.[34] Other FCC policies explicitly designed to promote localism included limits on the geographical reach of stations' signals, licensing that favored locating television stations in each community rather than creating regional stations (which would have encouraged an earlier introduction of a fourth network), and licensing preferences that rewarded an integration of (local) ownership and managerial control.

Broadcasting policy aimed at discursive inclusiveness as well as managerial localism. Congress and the FCC took steps to promote a common discourse in which many voices could be heard, not each on its own station, but all on a single media entity. Early on, Congress required that broadcasters give political candidates *equal access*, presumably fearing the power of broadcasters to shut out disfavored candidates. In response to the danger that broadcasters would shun all candidates, Congress later added the mandate that broadcasters grant candidates *reasonable access* to the airwaves.[35] Directly parallel to these two requirements, the currently defunct Fairness Doctrine had a balance (compare equal access) and a coverage (compare reasonable access) requirement. It required broadcasters both to cover important issues and to present alternative views on controversial matters of public importance.[36] These regulatory initiatives follow directly from the demands of republican democracy: important issues should be discussed in the public sphere and the discussion should be inclusive.[37] "Balance" is hardly ideologically neutral, but its purported inclusiveness is the heart of republicanism. Of course, the licensee is still a gatekeeper. The licensee decides which issues are important, whether any particular perspective or particular speaker gains access, and how the various sides are presented. In contrast to a wide open, common carriage system in which "self-appointed" representatives receive time for whatever they choose (and pay) to say,[38] the licensee's role as an inclusive but "responsible" gatekeeper tracks the republican concern that discussion be rational and civil.

Some republican democrats might even favor limited censorship to further this concern with civility. Racist or sexist speech adds little to reasoned discourse. If this offensive, uncivil speech "silences" speech by other portions of the community, restrictions arguably serve compelling democratic interests in inclusive discourse.[39] A democracy must allow forceful advocacy of any policy, even criticisms of republican democracy's inclusiveness. But the republican observes that speech that in the very act of its expression narrows discourse, as opposed to the speech that attempts to persuade, is hardly a part of a democratic dialogue. If discourse is to be inclusive, then speech that denigrates other potential participants in the debate is not helpful. Just as the Fourteenth Amendment prohibits governmental denigration of people on the basis of race,[40] such expression when voiced by private individuals or media remains inconsistent with and could impede republican discourse.

Other media policies have special prominence for republican democracy. Elite democrats can be content as long as an alert press watches for problems. The elite democrat could be skeptical, however, about the helpfulness of a freedom of information act. Would officials, to the extent that they are corrupt, obey an act's requirements to disclose documents showing their corruption? Moreover, most freedom of information acts cover many categories of information that, even if relevant for republican or other participatory democratic discourse, is unlikely to expose official corruption or incompetence. On the other hand, the spotlight of publicity potentially generated by the release of information can politicize difficult governmental decision making, causing it to be more difficult for elites to proceed rationally. Therefore, on balance, the elite democrat might decide to rely only on the strength of a strong press to confront and embarrass reticent government officials. As Justice Stewart suggested, "the Constitution establishes the contest, not its resolution."[41] Liberal pluralists may even join elite democrats here. Both might conclude that the most effective bargaining or governing often occurs behind closed doors. Disclosures on demand will be at best expensive burdens and could be dysfunctional, making arriving at needed decisions more difficult.

In contrast, the republican democrat would wonder if the loss of behind-doors bargaining is not a gain rather than a cost. Availability of information about government is absolutely crucial for popular republican discourse. Madison is to be quoted again. "A popular Government, without popular information, or the means of acquiring it, is but a Prologue to a Farce or a Tragedy; or perhaps both."[42] Thus, republican democrats must support extensive freedom-of-information acts, open meeting laws, and, perhaps, constitutional rights of access to information.

While no one advocates inefficient monopolies, republican democrats have little fear of monopoly per se. As Katz's Israeli television example suggested, a "socially responsible" monopoly press could be ideal in providing a common dialogue. Competition could even be detrimental if it encouraged uncivil partisanship or undermined participation in the common discourse. To the extent that a monopoly press is willing to make the expenditures, the existence of monopoly profits increases the press's capacity to responsibly provide service to the community. Monopoly profits could be spent on robustly fulfilling public-service obligations that the FCC could, and partly did, impose on oligopolistic broadcasters.[43] Limits on entry into broadcasting may be justified not by physical scarcity – sometimes there is none – but, as the government once concluded, by the goal of increasing station revenue in order to support good programming.[44] Creating cable franchise monopolies could be good policy if local governments are willing and able to force the monopolist to use some monopoly profits to provide "republican public goods"[45] – for example, public-access, educational, and governmental channels ("PEG channels"), as well as the resources, facilities, and support that these channels need to be meaningful. Despite cynics who cannot imagine any businessperson being anything but profit-maximizing, the primary assumption implicit in the ubiquitous criticism of chain purchases of formerly independent (monopoly) papers is that different types of owners tend to act differently. The belief is that the previously independent, often family-owned, papers normally put more resources into providing a better paper than mere economic considerations required, but that publicly traded corporations will put MBAs or, in the case of the *Los Angeles Times*, a cereal company executive in charge and allow bottom-line considerations to rule.[46] In other words, monopoly media can, and sometimes do, use monopoly profits to serve republican concerns, while competition can dissipate these profits, thus eliminating the possibility of their beneficial use.

Republican democrats' appropriate concern is not monopoly but the possible (or likely) "corruption" of monopoly, whether by market forces or socially irresponsible owners. Republicans should favor any policies that realistically promise to limit this "corruption." They should approve requirements, imposed early in the century on newspapers and more recently on broadcasters and cable systems, to identify "paid for" inclusions as advertisements, even though these requirements regulate speech on the basis of "content" and interfere with the newspaper or broadcaster's freedom to decide whether to include the message.[47] Various speaker-access provisions should have appeal. Their goal of greater inclusiveness is a clear plus for republicans. Of course, the quality and pertinence of the discourse resulting from self-nominated speakers – the people who get on public-access channels, for example – is a worry. Still, cable systems should be required to maintain public-access channels.[48] Arguably, media entities that accept advertising should be open to all public-issue advertising on a nondiscriminatory basis.[49] Right-of-reply laws also have presumptive appeal, although in the end their merit depends on the empirical question of whether these laws are more likely to deter valuable speech or to add balance to discourse.

Finally, government could fund or subsidize particular institutional structures or realms of inclusive republican discourse. Of course, all participatory democratic theories could agree on the need for subsidies or funding for public discourse, but different theories are likely to be at odds about the design of publicly supported institutions. Consider public broadcasting. Should the government fund several public systems, each representing a different ideological viewpoint,[50] or, if only a single public entity is created, should the government mandate time-sharing so as to allow pluralist groups to pursue their own agenda separately? Alternatively, should public media offer more inclusive and integrative discourse, striving for rough balance in each program? Complex democrats might favor either approach depending on the context, and liberal pluralists are likely to prefer the first. Republican democrats, however, should be strongly inclined toward the second alternative.

## PERSPECTIVE OF LIBERAL PLURALIST DEMOCRACY

Of course, liberal pluralists share with all democrats a fear of any threat to the press's watchdog role. In addition, liberal pluralists identify two primary threats to democracy resulting from a flawed media order: inadequate pluralism and corrupted pluralism (or, as I often describe them, inadequate and corrupted media segmentation).

### INADEQUATE PLURALISM

Objections to monopoly media are not hard to come by. A self-satisfied, comfortable monopolist could become a lazy and unaggressive watchdog. Or, as republican democrats fear, irresponsible, monopolized media could be either improperly ideological and biased or inadequately comprehensive in coverage and inadequately inclusive in perspectives. These complaints, however, do not assert that monopoly is intrinsically bad. Rather, they describe specific sorts of "corrupted" monopolization. In theory, a sufficient remedy is "social responsibility."

For the liberal pluralist, however, monopoly is intrinsically objectionable. Monopoly overtly threatens pluralism. John Stuart Mill once remarked on the decided advantages of hearing a message from a partisan. To arrive at the truth, he explained, a person "must be able to hear [arguments] from persons who actually believe them, who defend them in earnest and do their very utmost for them."[51] The pluralist emphasizes that each segment of society needs its own media for internal mobilization, external advocacy, and recruitment. (The complex democrat would agree but also argue that each group needs its own media for internal discourses aimed at developing, revising, and celebrating the group's own identity and commitments.) A single monopolistic media outlet cannot suffice to meet these needs of varying, often opposed, groups. Committed belief and sometimes stridency, particularistic standards of relevancy, often unique interests, and discussion within the community – not balance – are hallmarks of pluralism. Only partisan, pluralistic media entities are likely to be effective at political mobilization or at many other tasks that liberal pluralists assign to the press. Thus, even if a local daily newspaper monopoly, possibly because of its paper's stronger financial base, could provide a paper that would be "better" in some ways than any of several competing partisan papers, the liberal pluralist would still object. She predictably favors partisan competition.

The extent of liberal pluralists' devotion to competition requires further explanation. Typically, pluralists object not only to a monopoly entity within a single market but also to media conglomerates at the national or global level. These forms of concentration, however, still allow local competition, for example, between entities owned by the few multinational conglomerates. Ben Bagdikian generates grave concern with his description of the "five media corporations [that] dominate the fight for the hundreds of millions of minds in the global village."[52] Unlike the obvious reasons to object to local monopolies, it is intuitive, but less obvious, why liberal pluralists (or anyone else) consider national or global concentration of media ownership to be bad. Certainly, it is less obvious to Wall Street, which runs up the stock price of these companies, or to government lawyers who approve the mergers, or to the Department of Commerce, which concluded that the current legal order is defective in being too restrictive of media concentration,[53] or to the FCC, which has eliminated or relaxed most of the broadcast concentration rules over the past twenty-five years. Moreover, these global conglomerates or even local media conglomerates may be especially likely to promote some types of local pluralism. A profit maximization goal should induce a monopolist or conglomerate to offer diverse media products that serve different segments of the market. A single conglomerate often supports separate media entities or titles espousing radically different views and serving very different groups. This diversity expands the corporation's overall market coverage without forcing it to compete against itself.

In contrast, the existence of many owners may not translate into pluralistic diversity. If a media entity's "voice" reflects the owner's attitudes, and if most owners come from the same social class and hold similar views, pluralistic diversity is unlikely. Moreover, market forces can push even diverse owners toward providing similar content. Economists offer hypotheticals, many modeling the broadcast system, to illustrate this effect.[54] For example, assume that 66 percent of the audience only like programming of type X, 20 percent only like type Y, and 14 percent only like type Z. In a three-firm market, three competing owners can each expect to obtain, on average, a 22 percent audience share by offering programming of type X, which is more than any firm could obtain by offering either type Y or Z. Thus, competition could lead three firms to each offer a version of type X programming and to ignore 34 percent of the potential audience. In contrast, a monopolist owner of the three stations, rather than compete against herself, could offer a different type of programming on each station, hoping to capture 100 percent of the audience rather than create the danger of 34 percent having their sets turned off. Here, monopoly could produce more diversity of programming and more total audience satisfaction.

Given this predictable behavior, the democratic theorist must either explain why national- or global-ownership concentration fails to provide pluralistic diversity, or must identify other problems with concentration.[55] That is, the liberal pluralist has more work to do to identify the circumstances that provide or prevent true diversity. Still, the difference between republican democracy and liberal pluralism is clear. The republican fears segmentation that destroys a common discourse. The pluralist fears lack of segmentation and diversity, because this lack could suppress constructive conflict and undermine pluralist politics.

## CORRUPT SEGMENTATION

Lack of segmentation is not liberal pluralists' only fear. Equally objectionable is a corrupted diversity. "Corruption" here implies unreal or inauthentic interests or identities. For the media to perform their democratic role, segmentation ought to reflect audiences' "authentic" character. However, the operational meaning of "authentic" is somewhat unclear. Certainly, "authentic" need not mean essentialist. Possibly, the most that can be hoped for conceptually is a capacity to identify some cases of segmentation as corrupted or inauthentic, which does not imply the converse, an ability to identify authentic segmentation. This limited capacity to specify the crucial concept is, however, not that unusual. Despite borderline cases, some governmental administrations or regimes can be identified as "unjust" and some personal interactions as "nonconsensual." An observer unsure whether justice requires actual material equality can still conclude that a society that leaves its people to starve through no fault of their own is unjust. Whether or not consent to sex exists in a case without overt coercion, overt coercion typically negates consent. The meaning of these normative conceptions is disputed and subject to change – in fact, this is implicit in the assumption that the concepts are not essentialist. Nevertheless, some features' presence or absence may indicate that the system is not just or the behavior not consensual. Likewise, it may be possible to describe only very roughly what is meant by proper segmentation. Still, particular factors may persuasively indicate that a segmentation is corrupt – that the diversity is not properly responsive to authentic differences.

Uncorrupt or "uncolonized" segmentation would reflect, using Habermas' suggestive language, the logic and needs of the "lifeworld," not the "systems world."[56] Both markets and bureaucratic organizations, especially the state, are functional subsystems that modern society presumably needs to flourish. They provide tremendous benefits. By managing complexity, these functional systems greatly expand society's problem-solving and productive capacities.

People's everyday lives and interactions (which constitute the life-world) are routinely "steered" by interpersonal "discourses" aimed at agreement as well as by habit, which is open to discursive challenge. Such discourses respond to questions ranging from where to meet for supper or whether to invite Pat to join us to questions such as whether to participate in the city's voluntary recycling program or to favor an integrated school system. In contrast, the effectiveness of the market and the state bureaucracies in responding to complexity depends on their own steering mechanisms – money and power, respectively. These "currencies" direct the functional subsystems according to the subsystem's internal criteria – maximizing profits, efficiently maintaining control and order, or advancing other externally given ends. But the human value of these autonomously steered subsystems lies only in their ability to serve people in the "lifeworld." Moreover, their operations necessarily grow out of a lifeworld. They must feed upon culturally developed values and motivations. The functional systems respond, to some degree, to the demands of the lifeworld – that is, they fulfill needs that exist and that often are generated within the lifeworld. But they also treat the lifeworld as an environment to be managed in order to further system ends – an effect that can be described as "colonization." However, if people are to be self-determinative, these subsystems must be subordinate to, not controlling and colonizing of, the lifeworld and its cultural and discursive development.

These distinctions between the lifeworld and the autonomously operating system realms, and the importance of the lifeworld's priority, underlie my claim that media segmentation, as well as social pluralism, should grow out of and serve people's discursive needs in the lifeworld. Colonization by system realms would undermine that possibility. Understanding this colonization amounts to a theory of corruption. If people are to be self-governing, their choices, their identities, and, likewise, the segmentation of their media should not be anonymously determined by bureaucratic or market logic. Segmentation that responds to the lifeworld would produce a plurality of public spheres that reflects different groups' self-understandings of their experiences and needs. Each authentic or lifeworld-grounded group would use the media (1) to construct itself and to provide a locus of internal debate, value choice, and value clarification (points emphasized by complex democracy); (2) as a source of information relevant to the group; and (3) as an instrument for mobilization, advocacy, and recruitment.* Segmentation ideally represents each group's discursive development within the lifeworld in response to each group's identification of its needs and values.

Corruption occurs when segmentation reflects the steering mechanisms of bureaucratic power or money rather than the group's needs and values. For example, bureaucratic steering occurred during World War I to the extent that the state, acting appropriately according to bureaucratic logic, concluded that various German, anarchist, or communist publications helped to sustain groups that impeded the government's overriding interests. Therefore, the government proceeded to

---

* The first use is specifically called for only by complex democracy, while both liberal pluralism and complex democracy emphasize the second and third possible uses. One theoretical weakness of liberal pluralism arises from its need for a notion of corrupt segmentation. Because it takes interests or preferences or values as given, and sees politics as mere bargaining between groups furthering these interests or values, it lacks the theoretical resources necessary to explain the notion of "corruption" of groups' identities.

deny them mail privileges or to prosecute the publishers.[57] The First Amendment can be understood as the final line of defense against such state corruption or suppression of lifeworld segmentation.[58]

Market steering can also corrupt segmentation. As shown in Part I, the market neither necessarily nor uniformly reflects or responds to individuals' or groups' diverse concerns or interests. When it does not, any corresponding segmentation amounts to the mechanisms of system maintenance colonizing the lifeworld. This corrupt segmentation can undermine both authentic pluralist discourse and complex democracy's self-governing group life.

To illustrate, imagine five possible women's magazines.[59] Each offers a combination of news, features, information, and fictional content. Assume, however, that each emphasizes a particular theme: upscale fashion and cosmetics; women's health issues; middle-class family life and raising children; progressive women's political agenda; and the problems, needs, and interests of relatively poor, single mothers. Which of these serves authentic interests such that, if written and produced with adequate skill and appropriately priced, it would predictably secure an appreciative audience? Probably all five. Still, if magazine purchases primarily respond to people's self-examination of their needs and interests, it is very possible that the last, the magazine designed for poor, single mothers, would attract the largest following. In fact, to the extent reflective of concerns of actual portions of the population, audience size may be lowest for the first magazine and increase as one goes down the list (although arguably I unduly deemphasize the third). But consider the existing reality. In the world as it is, a format's success and comparative circulation size is more likely to correspond to the list's present order, with the upscale fashion and cosmetics magazine doing best. This rank ordering and, more generally, the domination of market system criteria may influence the content of media segmentation and, thereby, the existence of various social groups as well as the formulation of women's identities.

Why the radical divergence between the two orderings? The second ordering could reflect market forces rather than people's "real" interests – real in the sense of what the interests would be if they developed discursively within the lifeworld, independently of the system-based need for the press to be profitable. Even if the potential audience for the magazine directed toward poor, single women is larger, and their interest in such a magazine is more intense than the audience for and interest in the upscale fashion magazine, these numbers and this interest are unlikely to translate into equivalent sales, revenue, or profits for the magazine's publisher. Actually, the poverty of potential readers doubly disadvantages this magazine. The readers' lack of disposable income (and possibly their comparative lack of free time) will reduce their purchases of the magazine. In addition, advertisers do not want an audience that merely desires the advertised products. They want an audience that will buy. Poor, single mothers' comparative lack of disposable income makes their preferred magazine comparably less attractive to advertisers, thereby reducing the advertising outlays that could help pay for quality content and help keep the cover price down. This lack of advertising support means that the magazine, if it exists at all, will achieve a much smaller circulation (due to higher price and lower quality) than if advertisers valued all readers equally. Thus, the audience's poverty leads to a comparatively smaller circulation than would be appropriate using the lifeworld criterion of "authentic" audience interest.

Moreover, advertising does not simply fail to favor some media and their corresponding groups. It can undermine them. Assume that each magazine in the hypothetical list would have survived in a world without advertising. In a world with advertising, however, given comparative shopping, fewer people will buy the fourth or fifth magazine once the revenue received from advertising allows the first three magazines to reduce their price and improve their quality. As the last two lose their audience, they also lose revenue needed to pay for good writing and production. This leads to a weaker product, a further spiraling decline in audience, and possible financial collapse.

As an illustration, consider the *Daily Herald*, the only major labor-oriented newspaper in England during much of the twentieth century. It failed because of lack of advertising revenue, reflecting the poverty of its mostly working-class readers. This occurred even though, according to James Curran, "on its death bed, [the *Daily Herald*] was read by 4.7 million people – nearly twice as many as the readership of *The Times*, *Financial Times*, and *Guardian* added together . . . [and research showed that its readers] constituted the most committed and the most intensive readers, with the most favourable image of their paper, of any national paper audience in the country."[60]

Advertisers' financial involvement has further implications for segmentation. Advertisers and the media that serve them construct groups. The criteria they use in doing so have systemic, not discursive, bases. The first three women's magazines in the hypothetical list concentrate on readers likely to purchase particular consumer goods, making each magazine especially attractive to the sellers of those goods. In contrast, the diversity of consumption interests and the comparative lack of common-denominator product interests among potential readers of the progressive, political-agenda women's magazine cause it (and, hence, this possible segment) to be poorly designed for marketing. Even if its readers' disposable income and their money-backed demand for the magazine are comparable with those of the audiences for fashion, health, and family-oriented magazines, these factors are less likely to support publication. That is, some potential segments are more likely to flourish merely because they better serve specific marketing needs.

Uncorrupt segmentation should respond equally to each person's interests as experienced by the person, not as valued by the market. If it did, the fourth and fifth hypothesized magazines *might* be most prominent. People's unequal incomes and advertisers' influence predictably prevent this from happening. Of course, the real world offers a much richer subsegmentation of media audiences than my hypothetical. Many slightly different fashion magazines compete, partly for the same general audience but partly by subsegmenting the fashion market. The fault lines, however, correspond to advertising potential. Media segmentation selectively responds to interests that map onto efficient advertising strategies.[61]

Segments thrive wherever media entities can construct an audience that marketers desire. As a result, any interest or identity group whose members are not disproportionately heavy consumers of one or more product categories is comparatively undeveloped and underserved by commercial media. Even very large groups may be ignored. Welfare recipients, unskilled workers, union members, blacks, or partisans of a particular political ideology may either be comparatively poor consumers or, equally objectionable from a marketing perspective, have product interests that do not diverge much from those of the general population. If so, advertising predictably steers segmentation away from these groups. Union households, for example, are unlikely to have distinctive consumption interests. Therefore, union-oriented media are not likely to serve advertiser interests and, hence, are likely to be undernourished. In contrast, subsets of these underserved groups hold identities and interests in common with subsets of other groups – interests in sports, computing, travel, sex, fashion, marriage, masculinity, or household management. To exploit the connection between these interests and particular consumer goods, the market rewards media entities that assemble these groups. Again, constructing these segments comparatively disadvantages the larger categories noted earlier. However, even without the exacerbating and organizing effects of advertising, segmentation fails to represent true democratic or cultural cleavages to the extent that it more strongly reflects a group's affluence than its size.[62]

Of course, modern America does not lack diverse media. Within the proliferation of newsletters and smaller publications, virtually any interest can find itself addressed. The liberal pluralist concern, however, is about the *comparative* nurture or support of different segments. The advertising and wealth-influenced market largely determines the effort, both creative and reportorial, lavished on assembling and serving each segment. Many "natural" cultural cleavages are not ignored, and often marketers find them profitable to exploit. Support for "natural" or lifeworld-based segments is not automatic, though. Market-determined segmentation predictably disfavors, for example, media focusing on political ideology, non-market-valued ethnic and cultural divisions, economically poorer groups, or any life-style needs and interests not easily exploitable for marketing purposes. There is no reason to expect media-favored segments to correspond to the communities, interests, or identifications that people would choose after reflection and discussion. Corruption exists to the extent that the segmentation springs from the needs of the "systems world" rather than the pluralism of the "lifeworld."

## POLICY

Liberal pluralists should favor any policy that supports more robust media conduits for pluralist groups not adequately nurtured by the market, or that reduces systemic corruption of segmentation. They should applaud, for example, Arkansas's asserted rationale for exempting certain magazines from its sales tax – to promote "fledgling publications," especially if the fledgling publications provide content for otherwise underserved segments of society.[63] Of course, the Supreme Court was clearly right that this rationale did not fit that law. This rationale did not explain why the broad sales tax exempted all magazines except the *Arkansas Times* and, at most, two other Arkansas magazines. Still, liberal pluralists should be pleased that the Court accepted the possibility that such a rationale might save an appropriate content-based tax preference from First Amendment attack.

There are numerous governmental interventions that could promote the liberal pluralist demand that pluralist media serve the various groups of the lifeworld. Advertising tends to corrupt segmentation in some media, such as magazines, and to encourage homogeneity in others, like newspapers. Subsidies for non-advertising-supported media could increase the availability of diverse media. For example, by the middle of the nineteenth century, Congress had adopted postal rate policies that disfavored advertising and that presumably reduced its influence. Publications identified as primarily advertising vehicles were denied subsidized postal rates.[64] Even more directly, the Post Office charged more for the portion of a publication's weight devoted to advertising than for the portion devoted to other communications, thereby somewhat reducing the economic power of advertising to structure publications.[65]

Segmentation serving groups arising within the lifeworld could also be supported more directly. Lower postal rates have subsidized communications of some nonprofit groups.[66] Or the government could promote diversity by funneling media subsidies to secondary competitive papers. Sweden, for example, has long had extensive subsidy programs designed to maintain a competitive, partisan press, which the Swedes have treated as essential for democracy.[67] Similarly, Finland and Italy have been among the countries to fund subsidies directly through the political parties.[68] New York was once among the places where the law supported competition and partisanship by requiring that local government advertising (and hence advertising revenue) be placed in two papers of different parties.[69] Governmental policies could specifically aim at increasing media outlets owned by minority group members as a plausible means of promoting media that voice these groups' concerns.[70] In a controversial decision, the Supreme Court properly rejected an equal-protection challenge to FCC policies designed for this purpose, holding that the "content-based" goal of increasing the diversity of voices justified racial preferences.[71] More radical group empowerment plans are possible, such as a Netherlands-like allocation of broadcast time and resources based on citizen sign-ups that amount to voting for a particular programmer.[72]

The concern with corrupt segmentation can also be the basis for identifying some government interventions as bad. In addition to more general economic objections to tax advantages given advertising,[73] as noted, policies that increase its sway contribute to the corruption of segmentation. By allowing some advertising-targeted segments – for

example, professional groups – to treat particular professional publications as deductible business expenses, government policy favors
segmentation that reflects market logic independent of any connection with lifeworld logic. Exempting advertisers' purchases of media
space but not consumers' purchases of media products from sales
taxes, a choice made by California in 1991, increases advertiser and
reduces audience influence on segmentation.[74] In contrast, most
countries in Europe, which fully apply their value-added tax (VAT) to
advertising but only at a reduced rate, if at all, to consumer purchases of newspapers, encourage a somewhat more appropriate
segmentation.[75]

A different pluralist strategy simply favors dispersal of ownership.
Having more owners could increase instances of supporters of different groups owning media entities and orienting content toward their
groups' interests. The danger is that more owners will merely compete
for the center, in contrast to monopolists, who have an incentive to
provide different goods for each niche. Empirical evidence of these
divergent possibilities could be gathered.[76] But, irrespective of such evidence, a pluralist is likely to have considerable hesitations about relying
on any pluralism provided by outside monopolists. Her reasonable fear
is that the monopolist, even if providing diverse, segmented fare, will
blunt or corrupt partisanship. Thus, a liberal pluralist might support
the (predictably ineffective)[77] attempt of the Newspaper Preservation
Act to keep competing local daily newspapers' independent voices alive.
Strengthened enforcement of antitrust laws is a similar consistent pluralist theme. Of course, vigorous antitrust enforcement may not eliminate local monopoly, and, even if it did, competition may not suffice to
create real diversity in perspectives or content. More radically, reduced
capital gains taxes or other economic incentives could be given for sales
of media properties that increase deconcentration. For example, tax
advantages could be given for sales to entities whose assets after the purchase are still less than half of the original assets of the selling entity.
Such policies could begin a spiral of spin-offs leading to ever greater
deconcentration.

Finally, in addition to affirmative policies, liberal pluralists could reasonably balk at some policies recommended by other democratic theories. For example, if effective,[78] balance requirements appear designed
to support republican dialogue, but they could undermine a media
entity's partisanship and its service to discrete groups.

## PERSPECTIVE OF COMPLEX DEMOCRACY

Complex democracy is at least neurotic, and maybe schizoid. It exhibits all the fears held by the other democratic theories and more. Like elite democracy (and all other theories), complex democracy fears that the watchdog will be muzzled, whether by government or private power. Like republican democracy, it fears that segmentation or corrupted monopolization will undermine effective, societywide discourse. Like liberal pluralism, it fears that monopolization or corrupted segmentation will suppress or disfigure media pluralism. Finally, complex democracy additionally fears that pluralist media will be so oriented toward mobilization and propaganda that it will not aid pluralist groups in thoughtful internal discussion and debate about identity and interests. This last failure most likely would reflect inadequate market support, but could also relate to an overriding instrumentalism, especially of a group's leadership.

Probably, no one would argue that there should be only specialized, segmented media or only media oriented toward the public as a whole. And surely neither is absent today. However, the market may fail to support adequately – or to corrupt – either specialized or common-discourse media or both, justifying both the complex democrat's republican and pluralist fears. Moreover, the market and legal structure may unduly favor one type while providing inadequate support for the other. Because all these possibilities are affected by circumstance, the complex democrat must recognize that the type of media that is corrupted or inadequately supported may change. For example, the impact of electronic, interactive media obviously needs to be taken into account.[79] Nevertheless, I leave for another time a pursuit of theoretical expectations and practical issues involving the growth of these new media. Beyond the problem of market corruption of whatever pluralist or monopoly media that exist, the key policy issue for the complex democrat is, What democratic tasks are most slighted by the market or by existing arrangements? And, then, what can be done to correct the slight.

Sometimes policy advocates who purport to take up these issues fall into a simple republicanism, a tendency common among media reformers. For example, in elaborating a Habermasian conception of democracy (which closely resembles "complex democracy" as used here), Randall Rainey and William Rehg properly observe that Habermas rejects the republican's exclusive interest in consensus, provides a place for pluralist bargaining, recognizes value pluralism, and places central importance on diverse associations and other groups in civil society.[80] However, their programmatic proposal of a Corporation for Public Interest Speech and Debate seems more republican than complex democratic in inspiration. The proposed institution is much like the existing public broadcasting except for its exclusive emphasis on public-affairs programming, presumably greater insulation from distortion by corporate underwriting, and some more explicit attempts to keep it in contact with grassroots civic associations. Their republicanism and lack of structural recognition of groups' pluralistic needs, including groups' needs for partisan mobilization and internal self-definitional discourses, is evident in their emphasis on developing mechanisms to exclude bias and ideology.[81] It is also illustrated by the mandate, which they would impose on all commercial broadcasters as well as their proposed noncommercial corporations, to explore issues "in a balanced and non-partisan manner" and to provide "a reasonable opportunity for the discussion of conflicting views."[82] Although their own proposed institution could undoubtedly be very valuable, its republican-like emphasis on a common and nonpartisan discourse seems very inadequate as compared with the pluralistic needs of complex democracy. Think of all that it would exclude. Michael Moore's "angry yet hilarious" (according to Roger Ebert) documentary, Roger and Me, was an attack on greed at General Motors that, according to Vincent Canby of the New York Times, "makes no attempt to be fair. Playing fair is for college football. In social criticism, anything goes."[83] Although Canby described the film as a "triumph," it comes nowhere close to meeting Rainey and Rehg's standards of balance and nonpartisanship.

Much better from the perspective of complex democracy is Lee Bollinger's insight that different portions of the media might serve differing functions. Bollinger argues that this justifies different regulatory regimes for different media.[84] He would regulate broadcast media in order – in the terms used here – to make it more inclusive and republican, while keeping the government's hands off other media, especially print. From the complex democracy perspective, however, the problem with Bollinger's analysis is that it is doubtful that this policy would lead print to be adequately pluralist, thereby leaving one side of the complex democrats' concerns unmet. (In fairness, Bollinger's concern relating to the unregulated media was not that it be pluralist but that it be a truly unmuzzled watchdog.)

James Curran deepens Bollinger's insights. Curran observes that not only will different media sectors serve somewhat different democratic functions but that they should differ in their internal organizational principle and possibly their economic base.[85] Diversity of organizational structures reflects the need to perform different functions. Given the danger of corruption by either the government or the market, a diversity of structures and economic foundations can also strengthen the overall system. This diversity reduces the danger that corruption of a particular media sector by forces originating in either the political or economic system will undermine the system as a whole.

Programmatically, Curran identifies five sectors. The "core sector" should allow "different classes and groups to take part in the *same* public dialogue" and "promote a culture of mutuality that facilitates agreement or compromise."[86] Possibly reflecting his British heritage and experience with the BBC, he suggests that this sector could be institutionally centered around a revitalized public-service broadcasting system. Second, a very important and, Curran argues, currently troubled "civic media" sector would be a major locus of group pluralism. Among its elements could be media entities aimed at winning wider support for particular groups. These could include party-controlled, general-interest newspapers; identity-oriented media entities such as gay magazines; and organizational-oriented media such as newsletters that provide for groups' internal communication needs. Various policies could promote this diversity. For example, different political or identity groups could be given control over their own broadcast facilities or over time slots on dedicated broadcast or cable channels. A public agency, like a modified Swedish Press Subsidies Board,[87] could provide assistance to new or marginal, group-based communications media. Third, Curran calls for a "professional sector," controlled by media professionals, presumably organized democratically, that would be free of any obligations to serve any ideal other than internal professional standards. Independence from both the state and market-oriented firms would contribute to this professional sector's capacity to serve the media's watchdog function.[88] A "private enterprise" sector, Curran suggests, would be responsive to audience demand[89] and could add diversity (especially given the market's inherent right-wing tilt). Even here, however, Curran suggests that separating ownership from editorial control would improve performance. Finally, a "social market" sector would "incubate new forms of competition, rooted in social forces underrepresented in the market, as a way of extending real consumer choice and power."[90] This sector should try to cure some market distortions in the "private enterprise" sector. For example, as a response to market failures, subsidies should be provided for entities and ownership forms whose mission is to serve public demands to which the market does not adequately respond. Stringent application of antitrust rules could help prevent destruction of these entities by media conglomerates and help provide the pluralism of entities from which social market sector participants could be recruited.

Curran's proposal concerning differing media sectors has a number of merits, but from the perspective of complex democracy the proposal's most insightful quality is its recognition of the different functions that a democratic media should serve. Especially important, he implicitly recognizes the need for both the republican common discourse (embodied most directly in the core sector) and the pluralist mobilization and group-centered media (the civic sector). Curran is right to see the need to provide for a structural basis for media sectors that are less distorted by the market. He also correctly observes that this combination of structurally different media sectors is likely to perform the checking function better than the structurally simpler, pure free-market system.

Curran's schema suggests the following premises that a complex democrat should recognize for policy purposes: (1) the strongest media order does not rely on any single form of organization; (2) this order must perform diverse functions, and differing media entities, possibly organized on different structural principles or economic bases, are likely to best perform different functions; (3) although this order should not dispense with the market, government policy should nurture other structures and nonmarket entities in a variety of ways – for example, with subsidies and by making alternative organizational forms legally available and economically attractive; (4) the extent of government involvement and support should vary depending on how underdeveloped or distorted a particular sector is; and (5) the form or nature of governmental involvement or support should reflect the particular functions of the media (or, in Curran's terms, the particular sector) being aided.

Three additional points should be emphasized. First, there is every reason to expect that market forces, especially advertising, corrupt both common discourse and pluralist segmentation; moreover, the market provides inadequately in amount and quality for both. Observation should convince most people of this conclusion, but economic theory also predicts it. When properly performing its various democratic functions, the media generates significant positive externalities – that is, benefits to people other than the immediate consumer of the product.[91] The economic meaning of a product having positive externalities is that from the point of view of total social welfare, free markets will underproduce these quality products.

This observation leads to the second point. A central principle for the "neurotic" complex democrat is, Be opportunistic! Complex democrats should embrace virtually any opportunity to develop or support differing media organizations or any of Curran's sectors, except possibly the already inevitably supported private-enterprise sector. In this respect, complex democracy differs from republican or pluralist democracy, each of which has a narrow policy agenda that sees the agenda of the other as a threat. In contrast, complex democracy can easily justify supporting the affirmative goals of both.

Third, even the private-enterprise or market sector should be the focus of considerable government policy-making attention. The aim of structural rules should be to reduce the corruption of segmentation by market forces, especially advertising, to reduce the corruption of monopolization, and often (this need being a partly empirical matter) to promote diversity. Elsewhere I have discussed some possible interventions, especially relating to reducing the negative structural effects of advertising,[92] but the key point here is to recognize that structural interventions can promote the democratic contributions of the private-enterprise sector.

Ideally, policy analysis should address questions such as whether, under existing circumstances, more partisanship and segmented media or more common discourse and societywide media are the greater need. The answer would suggest where to concentrate reformist energies. Often republican, common-discourse, or majoritarian-oriented products, whose first-copy costs can be spread over many people, will have a competitive advantage over products favored by smaller groups, so-called outliers. If so, the market may disfavor pluralistic media more. In addition, if the particular version of complex democracy concludes, as I do, that society should distribute politically and culturally salient media products in a relatively egalitarian manner, like it distributes public education or the vote, special emphasis should be placed on supporting media products designed especially for the poor.

Here is not the place for a comprehensive development of specific proposals. Both economic and democratic theory, however, predict that

pluralistic media, especially those designed for comparatively impover-
ished groups, are likely to be especially underdeveloped and ought
to receive special public support. Still, as a practical matter, the key
principle for complex democracy is to pursue any opportunity to
further government support for new, noncommercial forms of media
discourse.

## CHAPTER 9

# Constitutional Implications

Different theories of democracy not only recommend different normative visions of the press; they also may lead to different interpretations of the Press Clause. In this context, possibly the most important implications of complex democracy, my preferred democratic theory, may appear modest. Yet even here the theory is not unimportant. Rather, its conclusions are anticlimactic in the way that interpreting due process as not justifying *Lochner*-style interventions was dramatically and importantly anticlimactic.[1] For the complex democrat, the Press Clause mandates very little. Here, I wish to explore those implications and consider why they are so limited.

Any actual constitutional interpretation relies at least implicitly on some interpretive theory. In my view, legally authoritative constitutional interpretation should be, and often is, "motivated conversation" – a conversation within an interpretative tradition in which the point is to understand the text(s) as part of an attempt to provide for a legitimate and workable legal order.[2] It is particularly important that the interpretation aims to be "authoritative" – leading potentially to the application of force. This factor motivates the interpretive point, providing for a legitimate legal order, which in turn operates to constrain interpretative freedom. This motivation distinguishes it, for example, from literary, historical, psychological, economic, or political interpretations. In these alternative frames, motivations for and, hence, the content of the interpretation are much more variable and open.

Past court decisions, historical institutional practice, and the original textual language constitute key conversational "participants." Current interpreters treat these materials as open-ended (i.e., requiring further interpretation or elaboration) and presumptively (although never conclusively) correct as far as they go – that is, as the reflective views of intelligent, earlier interlocutors. Although these historical, authoritative, conversational contributions do not rigidly control, current conversationalists must take them seriously and respond to their implicit claims. Additional constraints also apply to this conversation. Interpretations intended to be legally authoritative should be strongly influenced by a conception of the role of constitutions. To the extent they aim at acceptance by courts, interpretations will necessarily, even if only implicitly, also be influenced by a conception of the judicial role. Interpreters usually understand these considerations to require that constitutional interpretation be principled. Those engaged in making legally binding constitutional interpretations, in contrast not only to those engaged in literary, historical, political, or psychological interpretations, but also to those engaged in adopting legally binding legislation, should be responsive to a particular, narrowly defined set of concerns.

Interpretations of the Press Clause depend heavily on answers given to two questions. First is the question of the purpose of the Press Clause. I assume that the constitutional order protects the press because of its crucial contribution to democracy and democratic legitimacy. This should not seem strange. Freedom of "speech" might be protected as a vital element of individual liberty. A person's speech, as a self-authored activity, is a direct embodiment of the speaker's autonomy.[3] In contrast, the constitutional reference to the "press" often, probably typically, refers to institutionalized structures or legal entities. Since in such cases the term applies to institutionally structured groups of people, no particular speaker's liberty is at stake. This, as well as democratic theory generally, suggests that the value of press freedom and its relation to liberty differ from that of speech freedom. As a provider of communications, which can supply information and vision, the independent press can aid more intelligent or meaningful uses of autonomy while not being itself an embodiment of autonomy. It is as an instrument for serving this role, particularly as it relates to democratic practice, that the media should receive constitutional protection.

This conclusion – that the Press Clause protects particular institutions, media enterprises – helps explain what would otherwise be anomalies. A special newspaper tax, for example, raises a constitutional issue because of the particular corporate entity it taxes, namely a newspaper, even though the law does not specifically tax or target any specific printed "speech." Unlike individuals, institutions including the press are not to be valued in themselves but must find their value in their social contribution. The only obvious reason that the press merits constitutional protection from democratic processes is that this protection is thought to serve its role in that democratic arrangement. Thus, in order to know what specifically to protect, the interpretation of the Press Clause must, at least implicitly, embody some theory of democracy. Exploration of this variable has been central to the three previous chapters.

Second is the question of the democratic adequacy of the market. Can the market (and centers of private power generally) be trusted to provide us with the press that democracy requires or, instead, should the market be expected to fail to perform adequately (or even at times to undermine proper performance of) the tasks assigned by (the favored) democratic theory? If a sufficiently favorable view of the market is justified, prohibiting all media-oriented governmental interventions might best serve democracy. Even a less favorable general evaluation of the market might not imply that private power would undermine the press's specifically democratic tasks. The conclusion depends in part on the nature of those tasks. The market might undermine some aspects of the press's performance, as Part I argued, but not its crucial democratic roles. If so, the constitutional guarantee of a free press could be understood to block all media-specific governmental interventions, even if generic welfare considerations would justify some interventions. The argument would be that the constitutional decision is to prohibit even welfare-advancing interventions because that prohibition best protects the press's vital democratic role.

Persuasive critiques of the market's unfortunate effects on the media are legion, but this is not the place to restate the evidence and arguments. Critics sometimes emphasize an individual owner's or the ownership class's manipulative and ideological control. Other critics point to predictable distortions resulting from the normal functioning of economic markets. Sometimes it is unclear which is the problem. Did Murdoch cancel the publication of the memoirs of Chris Patten, a conservative and the last British governor of Hong Kong, for personal or political reasons? Murdoch says it was not commercially motivated.[4] Still, some observers may believe that it was, like his 1994 decision to take the BBC off the Chinese broadcasts of his satellite television service, a profit-maximizing decision based on not offending the Chinese leadership on which his media expansions in China depended. If the cancellation was a profit-maximizing decision, it is little different than the bottom-line mentality that leads corporate newspapers to eliminate 5 percent of the newsroom jobs in six years.[5]

In Part I of this book, I argued that economic theory predicts that unregulated, market-based production and distribution of media content will diverge so radically from what audiences want that the goal of providing for audience desires provides no basis for a presumption against government intervention. There remains, however, a potentially powerful reason to object. The country might decide that the press's democratic role should take precedence over merely serving consumer preferences.* And intervention might threaten the press independence that best serves democracy. Of course, the reverse could be true instead. Even if predicted to serve consumer desires best, the unregulated press might fail to perform crucial democratic tasks. If so, democracy might require intervention. Clearly, these alternative assessments depend not only on predictions about the market but also on the content of the press's democratic tasks. The perceived merits of permitting intervention necessarily reflect an understanding of what democracy requires, an evaluation of the dangers of misguided intervention, and an assessment of the market.

Market forces could conceivably cripple the press's performance of the checking function. Competitive, profit-oriented pressures could lead media entities to abandon expensive, investigative journalism and replace it with cheaper, routine beat reporting, or even cheaper "press-release" or wire service journalism. The market could tilt journalism toward stories that are the easiest (i.e., the cheapest) to uncover and, even more troubling, the easiest to explain or the most titillating. An effective watchdog would have reported early on about the massive savings-and-loan scandal, which predictably resulted from deregulation of these financial institutions. The media, however, found that early reporting was simply too difficult or boring. The contrast with welfare fraud is telling. The faces of welfare recipients make it an interesting and easily comprehended story for a bottom-line-oriented press to portray. But compare. Estimates of the cost to the taxpayer of the savings-and-loan scandal vary widely, although $500 billion is a figure commonly cited.[6] A former *Washington Post* reporter, Kathleen Day, in

---

* This supplanting of market-expressed preferences is not necessarily or even presumptively paternalistic. People might politically express a preference for a press that serves a robust democracy rather than their unreflective consumer choices. It would be paternalistic to automatically privilege their market expressions over their political expressions.

her book on the scandal, came up with a $1 trillion figure.[7] In contrast, the inspector general of the Department of Health and Human Services during the Bush administration, presumably wanting to come up with a high figure, stated that fraud (including the costs of unintentional mistakes) in the country's major welfare program, Aid to Families with Dependent Children (AFDC), might be costing $1 billion a year.[8] On which story should a watchdog press have focused? Consider which involved corruption of people in power, which involved the larger damage to public? From the level of press attention to the two stories, a reader would hardly guess that it would take over 500 years of welfare fraud to cost the public as much as did the savings-and-loan debacle.

Nevertheless, the watchdog role may be the democratic function least likely to require or benefit from government support. It is arguably best guaranteed by a sense of professionalism that exists among journalists, whose motivations and consequent behavior are only partially determined by the market. The watchdog role requires mostly skill, courage, and freedom. Exposés generally make good, profitable news. News entities will have an incentive to devote at least some resources to performing this role. Arguably, the government can do little to add to either the press's willingness or ability to perform effectively. Still, even with the watchdog role, the evidence does not unambiguously favor nonintervention. James Curran noted that despite some loss of autonomy due to an onslaught by the Thatcher government, the state-created and -supported British Broadcasting Corporation "continued to expose [the] government to more sustained, critical scrutiny" than did the commercial newspapers.[9] This example illustrates that at least some forms of government interventions or support, which removes a portion of the press from the control of the market, could contribute to effective performance of the watchdog function.

Still, intervention may be needed least for this function and can be very dangerous. Arguably, the watchdog role is the democratic function most subject to inappropriate, censorious, or "chilling" interventions. The government can unintentionally undermine the capacity for performance by, for example, requiring testimony that identifies a reporter's publicity-shy informants. The watchdog role may be even more vulnerable to purposeful attack. The government can attempt to block performance, as it tried to do by seeking an injunction against publication of the Pentagon Papers. Censorial manipulation of benefits and privileges are probably even more dangerous because they are less easily combated. Consider a local government's withdrawal of advertising from a critical newspaper,[10] or the Nixon administration's plans to obstruct a broadcast license renewal after the *Washington Post* exposed alleged Watergate-related misconduct.[11] Government leaders can also attempt to "discipline" reporters by means such as denying them prized interviews,[12] and lower-level officials exercise similar power by picking recipients of leaks and background information.

More than the history of totalitarian regimes illustrate that the watchdog role is in danger from government. Any moderately corrupt or incompetent administration or individual governmental leader has an overt, systemic, self-interested inclination to undermine its performance. In contrast, although these leaders will vary in their view of republican discourse, pluralist bargaining, or social groups' self-development, they seldom perceive any of these communicative activities as overtly threatening their status. Of course, even media content serving these functions is not safe. Any political group may wish to suppress oppositional media. Suppression could help a dominant political group retain power or improve its position in pluralist bargaining. Suppression could also reflect the group's ideological objections to outsiders' values. Still, the watchdog role is most overtly and directly in tension with incumbents' interests. Here the incentive to suppress is significant. Thus, protecting this role might require limiting government. If political branches must be watched, wisdom counsels against granting them power to control the watchdog.

Anyone with confidence in the market's benign influence – and many with less confidence but with a healthy fear of government abuse – will view government intervention as *the* major danger to the performance of the checking function. At least for anyone, namely elite democrats, who views the watchdog role as the press's only really important democratic function, this suggests sharply limiting governmental authority. A wall of virtually total separation between the government and the press may seem desirable.[13] Thus, although media-specific laws have been allowed by the Supreme Court, some commentators have viewed such laws or any special treatment of the media as presumptively objectionable. For example, Randall Bezanson argues that "[t]he government may not . . . single out the press for either conferral of a benefit or imposition of a burden."[14] For elite democrats, this result follows directly from their democratic theory. In addition, I suspect that empirically, elite democrats as compared with more participatory democrats have greater confidence in the market.

Participatory democratic theories all place more comprehensive demands on media performance. For these more extensive purposes, faith in the market, although still possible, quickly seems naive. As noted, there are overwhelming reasons to predict that markets will fail to provide the media that people want. Markets are even less likely to provide the media that participatory theories identify citizens as needing. Depending on the theory, these needs may include more educational, societal discourse-oriented, advocacy-oriented, mobilizing, or group-constitutive media than people support through their purchases in the market. These media have significant positive externalities from the perspective of one or another participatory theory of democracy. An individual's consumption of such media content is good for the people as a whole or, at least, for others within the particular consumer's "group." Because the consumer receives only a portion of the benefit, she is unlikely to spend the full value – the value to her combined with the value to others – of her having the product. Because of this underserved need for these media, participatory democrats are likely to oppose constitutional interpretations that block all media-specific governmental regulations or interventions.

Participatory theorists, however, seldom interpret the Constitution as itself mandating the needed interventions. Doctrinally, inadequate press performance is not normally seen as "state action."[15] Although one could see failure of the government to act (or its property and licensing laws that empower some but not other private actors) as the objectionable state action,[16] various practical considerations counsel against easy reliance on this interpretative strategy. Constitutional adjudication is poorly designed for crafting appropriate structural rules and media subsidies. Participatory theorists can more reasonably argue that the Constitution permits discretionary legislative authority to intervene with those subsidies and noncensorious structural rules – even content-motivated or content-based structural rules[17] – aimed at supporting the press's performance of its democratic roles. This conclusion may be the central constitutional implication of these participatory democratic theories. It is, however, mostly a nonmandate – restricting the constitutional reach of the Press Clause. In order to allow needed and appropriate governmental interventions, participatory democratic theories recommend interpreting the Press Clause much more narrowly (in this context) than elitist democratic theory suggests.

Of course, participatory theories do not ignore the press's performance of the checking function. To allow for interventions but protect against censorious restraints, constitutional doctrine should block government action that has a censorious purpose as either its end or means. In addition, to be consistent with checking-function concerns, these theories should favor invalidating government actions that undermine the integrity of the press as an institution – for example, by requiring reporters to identify their sources.[18] Constitutional doctrine should also prohibit media-specific burdens for which the government can offer no convincing benign explanation. Thus, in the case of taxes, the Court properly concludes that "[s]tanding alone," the legitimate interest in raising revenue "cannot justify the special treatment of the press, for an alternative means of achieving the same interest without raising concerns under the First Amendment is clearly available," namely, a more general tax not focused on the media.[19] Participatory democrats, however, are open to benign explanations, even for media-specific measures that burden some portions of the media. For example, the government might justify media-specific taxes whose revenue is dedicated to those media specially needed by democracy but underdeveloped by the market. Even then, however, a tax directed at particular protected content can be seen as improperly suppressive. But if directed at, say, advertising or spectrum usage, then the reallocation should be seen as a noncensorious structural rule promoting, rather than undermining, democratic media.

Thus, my initial claim is that markets and private power are much more likely to frustrate the more ambitious democratic assignments called for by participatory theories than they are to undermine performance of the checking function. If so, the preferred interpretation of the Press Clause would shift depending on the democratic theory adopted. This can be illustrated by a simple matrix (Table 9.1).

This analysis, however, moves too quickly. A more careful examination suggests that different participatory theories may support somewhat different constitutional interpretations. Still, any conclusions must be tentative. Most positions are contestable even within any particular democratic theory, although each theory at least structures the debate in its own way.

Consider the questions. Is it permissible for the government to provide people other than owners a right to publish in, or broadcast over, privately owned media, especially as to private media that are monopolistic or at least limited in number within most communities? Should it do so? Must it? The issue of (nonmedia) private speakers' right of access has been controversial. From the perspective of elite democ-

## Table 9.1

| | Assessment of Market | |
| --- | --- | --- |
| Theory of Democracy | Faith in Market | Serious Doubts about Market |
| Elite democracy (less demands on market) | Hands off[a] | Maybe hands off (interventions dangerous; gain too small) |
| Participatory theories (greater demands on market) | Hands off | Allow intervention; prohibit censorship or objectionable purposes[a] |

[a] The more probable cell from the perspective of a particular democratic theory.

racy, such a right may have little significance (although do little harm). Putting aside her general opposition to governmental intervention, an elite democrat might favor access rights if she believed that marginalized groups would occasionally have evidence of governmental misfeasance; that the evidence would have significant political effects if effectively exposed; that a right of access would be necessary to and would be effective at achieving this exposure; and that creating the right does not unduly risk undermining press performance of the checking function. Nevertheless, public access is unlikely to be simultaneously accurate, effective, and necessary for exposing wrongdoing. In the occasional case in which the report would be accurate and effective,[20] legally guaranteed access is unlikely to be necessary. Media entities are likely to make the report on their own if given the information by the group seeking access. The elitist can reasonably conclude that the main effect of such laws is to undermine the integrity of the professional watchdog – "editing is what editors are for."[21] Thus, legislation creating such a right should be unconstitutional.

Access rights are often even worse from the perspective of the liberal pluralist. These rights can threaten media entities' capacity for partisan mobilization. "Balance" is a centrist ideology. Except for intermittent strategic or rhetorical uses, balance is often the last thing that mobilizing media need. A militant black newspaper should not be required to carry the Klan's rebuttal – or vice versa. Thus, the liberal pluralist should join the elite democrat in praising the Court's decision to strike down a law that provided candidates a right to reply to newspaper criticism.[22]

In contrast, republican democrats most fear lack of inclusiveness (and, secondarily, lack of civility). Mandated balance and well-crafted access rights could further inclusive dialogue, which a society needs to reason together about potentially common conceptions of the good. Going beyond support for the fairness doctrine, republicans might even strain to find state action in broadcasting, and then find a station's refusal to accept public issue or editorial advertising to be unconstitutional. Their only worry is whether a lack of editorial management will cause unmoderated dialogue to become too unfocused, unbalanced, or uncivil.

Complex democrats should find merit in the opposing views of both the pluralists and the republicans. Society needs partisan media that are constitutive of groups and that promote group mobilization – and rights of access can undermine such media. Society, however, also needs inclusive collective discourses, a need served by access rights. Which discourse society lacks most at any time is an empirical question. No abstract answer or even analytic metric on which to base constitutional mandates is available. Hence, the complex democrat should incline toward upholding access rights created by legislation, especially legislation that leaves some media unaffected, but not incline toward imposing the rights constitutionally.[23] Or, following Bollinger and Curran's distinction discussed in Chapter 8 between different media sectors, the complex democrat might favor something like a "balance" or "diversity" requirement in legislatively identified core media, which perform a societywide discourse role, but not in media serving pluralist groups.

In *Miami Herald*,[24] the Supreme Court invalidated a right of reply statute that applied to the print media. In *Red Lion*,[25] it upheld such a legislatively authorized right in the broadcast context. In *CBS v. Democratic National Committee*,[26] it refused to find that the First Amendment required such a rule for broadcast stations. On first impression, both the elite democrat and the pluralist democrat, although for different reasons, are likely to oppose mandated access. They would agree with the Court in *Miami Herald* and *CBS v. DNC*, but not in *Red Lion*. In contrast, the republican democrat would favor mandated access. She would agree with *Red Lion*, but not *Miami Herald* or *CBS v. DNC*. Thus, both the pluralist and republican find constitutional constraints but constraints with opposite content; one approves what the other would strike down. The complex democrat alone would accept the government's decision concerning access, whatever it is. She would agree with

## Table 9.2

| Theories of Democracy | Press Clause Interpretation |
| --- | --- |
| Elite democracy | Hands off |
| Pluralist democracy | Prohibit access rights; allow structural regulations that promote partisan media |
| Republican democracy | Allow or mandate access rights; disfavor laws that promote more partisan media[a] |
| Complex democracy | Allow, but not mandate, access rights and legislation that make some media more inclusive or that promote partisan media |
| All democratic theories | Rule out censorship; also legislation aimed at suppressing media or that undermine integrity of press |

[a] Some theorists draw other constitutional implications from republican democracy. For example, racist or sexist speech hardly contributes to discourse aimed at consensus about a common good. Republicans might be tempted to uphold laws suppressing this speech, especially if this speech would make meaningful participation in a collective discourse by members of the disparaged group unlikely. See Sunstein, *Democracy and the Problem of Free Speech*, 186–87, 192, 219–20, 225–26. But see Robert C. Post, *Constitutional Domains* (Cambridge: Harvard U. Press, 1995), 268–331 (rejecting such republican arguments for control). I find Post's reliance on autonomy and his critique of arguments for suppression to be persuasive, both theoretically (see C. Edwin Baker, "Of Course, More Than Words," *University of Chicago Law Review* 61 [1994]: 1181) and pragmatically (see Kenneth L. Karst, "Boundaries and Reasons: Freedom of Expression and the Subordination of Groups," *University of Illinois Law Review* [1990]: 95), although Post here does not grapple with the propriety of the government's proper role in structuring media enterprises. My conclusion, however, might be shaped by a preference for complex democracy, which argues that fair and appropriate collective discourse can only occur when all groups are first empowered to develop their own views. The only meaningful remedy for the groups silenced by other's speech is empowerment – support of their own voices. Suppression, even of denigrating, silencing speech, in the end does not empower the victim but does limit full inclusiveness, especially of those restricted.

both *Red Lion* and *CBS v. DNC*. Although with reservations discussed later, she may reject *Miami Herald*. To modify the earlier matrix, and if we assume at least some skepticism about the market, Table 9.2 outlines these respective positions.

Although this analysis is more fine-grained and precise, it still oversimplifies. It ignores both factual contexts and attitudes toward the judicial role. For example, the Court in *Miami Herald* reasoned that the "choice of material to go into a newspaper . . . constitute[s] the exercise of editorial control and judgment," and that the First Amendment does not tolerate "intrusion into the function of editors."[27] As noted, the liberal pluralist could approve of the premise, while the republican might be unsatisfied. However, the premise that the First Amendment does not allow an intrusion into editorial control was only one of two rationales for the *Miami Herald*. The Court also objected to the law making access turn on the paper's earlier criticism of the candidate. The Florida statute "exact[ed] a penalty on the basis of the content of the newspaper," which could result in "blunted or reduced" coverage.[28] This deterrence operates like censorship. Recently, the Court faced the argument that *Miami Herald* required invalidating rules that compelled cable systems to carry content (local broadcast stations) that they would prefer to reject. Because these must-carry rules applied regardless of whatever other speech the cable system provided, the Court found that the rules could not have the deterrent effect that it said was fatal in *Miami Herald*.[29] The Court treated cable operators as media editors, but apparently concluded that the intrusion into the "editorial" role did not matter.[30] This sheds a different light on *Miami Herald*. If convinced of the empirical basis of its penalty-deterrence rational, and this is a big "if," supporters of all theories of democracy should accept the decision.

The empirical issue, however, may have a surprising cut. Experience in countries like Germany, where the right to reply has a constitutional basis, hardly supports the empirical basis of this objection. For newspapers, with their emphasis on selling news and to some extent commentary on public events and their more engrained and economically rewarded tradition of journalistic integrity, actual deterrence may be *de minimus*. On the other hand, the deterrence may be substantial for commercial broadcasters, with their strong bottom-line orientation and concern with program "flow" – the FCC during its repeal of the Fairness Doctrine produced considerable antidotal evidence of this effect.[31] If these empirical guesses turned out to be right, all democrats would think the Court wrong in *Red Lion*. Republicans and complex democrats might think that the Court was also wrong in *Miami Herald*, where it struck down the statutory access right that promoted inclusiveness or balance.

The above analysis also oversimplified *CBS v. DNC*. I suggested that only republican democrats would recognize issue-oriented speakers' constitutional right of nondiscriminatory access to broadcasters' advertising slots, the position that Brennan and Marshall adopted in their dissent.[32] Liberal pluralists, I suggested, would object because access rights could damage the media's partisan role. Without an abstract principle to determine whether the country was most in need of more partisan pluralist politics or more societywide discourse, complex democrats would follow the Court in leaving this choice for legislative (or FCC) determination.

This characterization of the liberal pluralist and complex democrat's response rings hollow in at least three situations: if the broadcast media are, and predictably will continue to be, monopolistic within their community; if advertisers or other commercial forces effectively impose a nonpartisan, audience-maximizing orientation on broadcasters so that any realistic hope or expectation that these media will become partisan advocates is naive;[33] or if legal regulations, such as the Fairness Doctrine, already preclude this pure partisan role. Under each scenario, the pluralist can conclude that the access right best empowers diverse groups to pursue their aims. The complex democrat can conclude that because these conditions have already made these media entities part of the societywide discourse, they should perform this role as inclusively (and as intelligently) as possible. Thus, given plausible empirical observations, all three participatory democratic theories can accept Brennan and Marshall's conclusion that the Constitution requires issue-oriented speakers' constitutional right to some nondiscriminatory access to advertising slots in the broadcast media.

On the other hand, some liberal pluralist or complex democrat judges might demur. Doctrinally, Brennan and Marshall must identify state action – the asserted absence of which several justices treated as the determinative factor.[34] Even given state action, the judge might abstain from creating intricate positive constitutional rights based on arguable empirical premises. This refusal might reflect less her theory of democracy or her appraisal of the market than her view of the judicial role – a rejection of a type of judicial activism. As these complexities illustrate, even though different democratic theories lead to different programmatic objectives in interpreting the Press Clause, democratic theory by itself does not determine doctrine or specific results.

Still, the capacity of democratic theory to orient, even if not determine, applications of the Press Clause is seen in many contexts. Media entities have repeatedly invoked the First Amendment in asking courts to grant them access to government facilities or government documents. These requests, typically denied, are usually founded on a claimed right of the people to be informed. The standard view, however, is that the First Amendment provides a right to speak, not a right to the resources that would make speech informed or effective. The Court has, it says, "never presumed to possess either the ability or the authority to guarantee to the citizenry the most effective speech or the most informed electoral choice."[35] This conclusion is surely right in respect to the Speech Clause.

The argument for access to information has fared no better by relying on some special media status under the Press Clause. Even if the press's institutional autonomy requires certain, special constitutional (defensive) rights, these rights do not include affirmative grants of particular resources.[36] As Justice Stewart argued, "The Constitution itself is neither a Freedom of Information Act nor an Official Secrets Act. The Constitution . . . establishes the contest, not its resolution."[37] Over vigorous dissents, the Court has denied requests for constitutionally based access to government documents or facilities except in the context of judicial proceedings. Even here, the Court's initial analysis of courtrooms' openness was based less on a right of access to information and more on a tradition of a courtroom trial as a *place* where people could gather and listen to speech. For First Amendment purposes, this led the Court to analogize the trial court to streets and parks, rather than to governmentally held informational resources.[38]

Nevertheless, the issue of access has divided the Court. It is appropriate to ask whether the disagreements reflect different conceptions of democracy. Certainly, arguments for access to information often are based overtly on the democratic importance of information. Before considering the implications of different democratic theories, however, I want to make two general observations.

Virtually everyone agrees that sometimes government should restrict access to information. Restrictions often serve individuals' interests in their own privacy, society's interest in military security, the effectiveness of the Federal Reserve Board's actions or law enforcement investigations, and possibly, the quality and frankness of courts' in-chamber discussions.[39] It is also widely agreed that some governmentally generated information should be publicly available. Modern sensibilities find it incredible that reporting on debates held in legislative sessions at one time could amount to contempt of the legislative body.[40] Given the value and legitimacy of both secrecy and information availability – the modern term is "transparency" – line-drawing problems abound. The diverse policy considerations relevant to the lines' placement suggest the possible wisdom of viewing access to information as a legislative, not a constitutional, matter. It could be addressed by statutory freedom of information acts, privacy acts, and open-meeting laws, or by intelligent executive or agency decisions.

On the other hand, bureaucratic bodies instinctually seem to desire secrecy (except on occasions when their own agenda or their members' egotism favors publicity). They are said to "classify" everything. They may perceive secrecy as advancing their flexibility, whether or not these gains in flexibility are legitimate. Officials may fear exposure of their misbehavior, failures or, most often, merely their incompetence. Information could also lead to "misguided" criticisms, forcing public officials to, in their view, "waste" time defending their action. It could stimulate premature, democratically dysfunctional lobbying. It forces public officials to defend their actions. For whatever reasons, including partial information or distortions, members of the public often react negatively to information about government actions, even though the official believes her action was legitimate, maybe even wise. In any event, deference to the political branches on the matter of secrecy is often not deference to careful policy making but to self-protective instincts. Such deference is problematic. The combination of the occasional real need for secrecy and an organization's systematic tendency to seek excessive secrecy could lead an activist court to formulate constitutional principles to guide a modest degree of judicial supervision of executive and agency discretion. A less activist court, in contrast, might rely on the ability of the press and others seeking access to "coerce" openness by generating negative publicity about those maintaining unwarranted secrecy, or to obtain legislation requiring openness. Even for the more activist court, however, democratic theory could influence the decision of whether to intervene constitutionally.

Although all democratic theories see value in popular access to information, they vary somewhat in the particular type of information to which they demand access, in the reason for valuing access, and in the centrality of broad access for their conception of democracy. Access to certain information obviously serves the checking function. For instance, rather than forming inherently compromising relations with government officials, I. F. Stone reportedly found plenty of dirt merely by using an informed and careful eye to read publicly available reports and documents.[41] My guess is that the most explosive information will either be made available without the need for a special constitutional right, as I. F. Stone found, or will be information that, absent statutory directives, even an activist judge would hesitate before forcing the government to reveal. For example, in a dramatic decision relevant to the checking function, the Supreme Court did enforce a grand jury subpoena applying to portions of Nixon's Watergate tapes.[42] But, would even an activist Court have overridden a president's claim to secrecy and ordered access to the tapes on the basis of a request by an individual or news agency?[43] Presumptively persuasive arguments usually support confidentiality. Of course, my empirical guess may be wrong – and is more likely to be wrong if courts willingly engage in *in camera* inspections and discover that the desired secrecy is not justified. But, if I am correct, a constitutional right of access to information may do little to serve the checking function. Moreover, the elite democrat could fear that mandated access will often interfere with and negatively "politicize" expert deliberation. Thus, an elite democrat should find a constitutional right of access to be quite problematic.

Participatory democrats should place greater emphasis on routine access to information. They value access to a much broader range of information than do elite democrats. Each participatory theory, however, has a somewhat different interest in the constitutional right. For pluralist democrats, information has largely instrumental or strategic relevance. Interest groups need to know when and where their preformed interests are most at stake and need assertion. Still, like the elite democrat, the liberal pluralist may conclude that sometimes secrecy supports the bargaining on which all groups must rely. Arguably normal information disclosure provides most of what the public needs, in which case the pluralist could conclude that a constitutional right is not crucial.

In contrast, a democracy that emphasizes wisely and collectively formulating attitudes, values, and conceptions of a common good, as republicans and complex democrats believe, or conceptions of a subgroup identity, as complex democrats maintain, calls for a broader range of information. Of course, given the centrality of identity and value formation, factual information may be less important for the republican than the pluralist. The republican or complex democrat could agree with Christopher Lasch, who argued that democracy depends on argument and discussion, not information (except to the extent that the information is made relevant by, and is the product of, debate). This conclusion led Lasch to argue "that the job of the press is to encourage debate, not to supply the public with information."[44] Still, the republican will be unimpressed with the need for secrecy to promote bargaining. The republican is likely to argue not only that government actions should presumptively be public but also that decisions should be made and defended only on the basis of publicly available information. The complex democrat is likely to share these views. Even if bargaining is an important part of governing, its legitimacy may depend on its transparency as well as its results, the main concern of the pluralist. A government official should never be allowed to hide behind secrecy but should always be prepared and expected to defend her actions.

Despite these differences in their concern with access to information, it is less clear how, or even whether, these various democratic theories will differ in their view of a constitutional right. Attitudes about judicial activism may dominate all other considerations. Cutting one way are doubts about the propriety of courts engaging in essentially legislative policy making under the rubric of constitutional law. Cutting in the other direction is the fact that secrecy is a matter in which trust in the routine judgment of policy-making branches, especially executive agencies, is especially problematic. Attitudes about these considerations, rather than a choice among democratic theories, may dominate a judge or scholar's conclusion concerning the legitimacy (and scope) of a constitutional right to information.

The differences among democratic theories have potential constitutional ramifications in other areas. Consider copyright. Copyright overtly limits a later communicator's freedom of speech (or writing). Especially in noncommercial contexts, individual liberty values embodied in the constitutional guarantee of free speech may require substantial limits on copyright, limits possibly encompassed in a broad doctrine of "fair use." Here, however, I want to focus only on democratic theory, especially as it relates to the interpretation of the Press Clause.

There is widespread agreement that copyright serves the public by increasing "the harvest of knowledge."[45] In this sense, like a free press, copyright is justified instrumentally by how it serves society. All agree, however, that copyright should not give unlimited rights to an "author," a view reflected in the principle that "facts" and "ideas" are not copyrightable and in the "fair use" privilege. Beyond these areas of broad agreement, people vary in their readiness to find something copyrightable and to find that a subsequent use is a violation. My suggestion is that a person's "readiness" in part reflects the democratic theory to which she is committed.[46]

Broad copyright coverage should pose few problems for elite democrats and may even serve their ends. As long as copyright does not restrict use of facts and ideas, as it currently does not, an expansive right is unlikely to interfere with the checking function. To the extent that a broad right increases the commercial rewards of writing and of journalism, it provides greater incentives for undertaking that work.[†] Likewise, a pluralist democratic theory has little objection to extensive rights. A broad right is unlikely to restrict a group's capacity either to present or to pursue its own exogenously formed interests. In contrast, republican democracy thematizes the salience and openness of cultural dialogue. Cultural as well as overtly political expression affects the community's conception of itself and of the public good. By providing an economic incentive for production and publication, copyright encourages such cultural discussions. But, by restricting creators' or discussants' use of previously copyrighted materials, copyright also narrows cultural dialogue. If, as Lasch contends, broad participation in discussions is more important than facts – or, to restate the claim, if the democratic value of a more inclusive, multivocal discussion is greater than the democratic value of the lost media commodities – then a narrower right should be favored. This conclusion, however, is arguable. It depends on both normative judgments (what discourse is valued) and empirical predictions (how different definitions of rights will affect the discourse). Still, a plausible conclusion is that narrowing some aspects of existing copyright protection would facilitate diverse public discussion and cultural explorations of common interests more than it dampens commercial incentives to produce useful communications.[47]

Here, complex democrats agree with republicans. Cultural discourses are central to democracy. Having this observation driven home may explain the movement in Alexander Meiklejohn's work. After first arguing in 1948 that the First Amendment only protects political speech, his republican sentiments predictably led him eventually to see the importance of most art and literature for political life.[48] This

---

[†] The issue here is actually more complicated, particularly in respect to influencing (distorting?) the economic incentives to engage in particular types of communicative activities. For example, lack of copyright for facts – a rule that hopefully any democrat would demand – reduces the value of investing in costly, factual investigations that may be valuable for purposes of an exposé or other democratic concerns. In contrast, for a broadcaster that is the unique employer of its anchor people, investment in promoting the appeal of their personality-centered "chatter" becomes a better strategy than investment in news gathering.

observation also may help to explain a variation among democratic scholars; some, when discussing the media, focus solely on nonfiction (with news being the paradigm concern) whereas others take a more expansive view of media content, explicitly valuing fiction, art,[49] and other cultural materials. Democratic elitists and liberal pluralists are more likely to be in the first group, republicans and complex democrats in the second. Moreover, the second group is especially likely to value these discourses when participation is popular and noncommodified, although commodified forms can provide substance to popular discussion and commodification sometimes helps to pay for higher levels of participation.

Beyond this area of agreement with republicanism, complex democracy is additionally concerned with the effect of copyright on a *group's* ability to discuss, form, and maintain its identity. This obviously requires cultural discourses. More than republicans, complex democrats especially value the opportunity of nondominant groups to explore, develop, and maintain their own identity – an interest that is undermined to the extent that mainstream actors control and constantly orient cultural discourse toward presumptively "common" concerns. Thus, complex democrats first note that existing (and likely future) copyright law protects individual authors (or their corporate employers) rather than collective creations of culture. Here, the dual concern is that law fails adequately to protect a group's cultural identity from commercial exploitation and fails to return economic resources to the group when it is exploited. This failure is evidenced by "indigenous peoples protest[ing] the stereotypical Indian caricatures used to market a sports team"[50] or any group whose "folk" stories, wisdom, and practices are commercialized (and often degraded) without compensation or return of value to the community.[51]

Possibly more important, complex democrats object that broad intellectual property rights can restrict internal cultural development and discussion by marginalized groups. Mainstream owners can often stop or restrict outsiders' use of their "owned" images for the outsiders' sometimes critical or dissident cultural purposes. Extensive intellectual property rights support this mainstream dominance. For example, these rights would allow the estate of John Wayne to ban a postcard portraying Wayne wearing lipstick and saying, "It's such a bitch being butch."[52] Image ownership not only allows owners to impose costs on other users, but it also allows owners to shut down entirely those uses of which they disapprove, often uses adopted by dissenting or marginal groups. It is no surprise that complex democrats are particularly offended by the Supreme Court's willingness to allow the mainstream U.S. Olympic Committee to block gay organizers' use of the word "Olympic" in describing an event as the "Gay Olympics."[53] Complex democracy's cultural pluralists seldom find that copyright effectively protects the discursive or cultural integrity of unpopular or politically marginal groups. Rather, intellectual property rights often impede these groups' culturally based discussions and consequently their creation of identity. Again, the empirical points are arguable. These considerations nevertheless can lead complex democrats, even more so than republicans, strongly to favor limiting the scope of traditional copyright.

As commentators repeatedly assert, democracy depends on a free press. But different conceptions of democracy are served by different free presses. This insight has direct significance for the practice of journalism. Even the most intelligent and democratically committed journalists, however, write and report within a communications order structured both by law and by the market. Both law and the market can reward but often also can impede desirable journalistic practices. At least in a society where overt censorship (and government violence) are neither legally nor publicly acceptable, possibly the factor most troublesome for press freedom are those market forces that bankrupt certain types of media entities, sometimes the very media that democracy most needs. The obvious response, even if politically difficult to enact, is legislation favoring, protecting, subsidizing, or even creating the type of media entities or communication practices required by democracy. Identifying these requirements depends on the specifics of democratic theory. Thus, as shown in Chapters 6 and 8, an exploration of democratic theory has significant policy relevance for media law and legislative reform.

Finally, there is constitutional law. The press's democratic functions provide the best perspective for understanding the First Amendment guarantee. Elitist democracy and its checking function (a value shared with all other democratic theories) have been most influential in giving the Press Clause doctrinal content that restricts government power. To the extent another theory of democracy is favored – I have implicitly claimed that complex democracy is the soundest theory – that theory may provide further content to the Press Clause. Nevertheless, the primary implication of complex democracy for constitutional interpretation is probably that the Press Clause should be read narrowly.

Complex democracy requires a constitutional reading tolerant of structural regulation of the press by government. At any given time, democracy's primary communicative needs inevitably will be disputed. Complex democracy recognizes that the market could be failing, either by providing a media too homogeneous or too pluralistic, or by corrupting the available versions of either or both. These possibilities suggest that the Press Clause should be read to allow the government to promote a press that, in its best judgment, democracy needs but that the market fails to provide. The Constitution should only be invoked in cases of obvious governmental abuse – when the government engages in censorship or undermines the integrity of media entities.

## PART III

# An Illustration: International Trade

The analyses of the interests of consumers and citizens in Parts I and II obviously have direct policy relevance for many media issues. Different illustrations are possible. The analyses not only justify large-scale subsidies for institutions like public broadcasting but have direct implications for the design of such institutions. They could also justify and direct the form of subsidies and other regulations for print media, increasing their independence from market and advertising pressures. For at least three reasons, however, I use the final two chapters to apply these analyses to the global issue of free trade in media products.

First, the trade issue's practical importance is immense. Huge monetary stakes are implicated. Cultural products are the United States' second largest export item.[1] Moreover, people in many countries consider the ability to protect their cultural industries as vital to their cultural and democratic development, possibly even to their survival as a nation. This view is not new. In the 1920s, a Canadian editorial argued that "if we depend on the [] United States . . . for our reading matter we might as well move our government to Washington. . . . The press is a stronger cohesive agent than [P]arliament."[2] On the other hand, the United States often asserts that the free flow of information, which it typically treats as connoting private media ownership and free trade, is basic to democracy.

Second, the issue is not merely academic and is not about to go away. The dominant though not universal view in both Canada and Europe is resolutely against imposing free-trade rules on cultural or media products. In contrast, the United States has pressed hard to apply free-trade principles to cultural or media products.[3] Its unrelenting pressure to establish this position almost derailed the final agreement – seven years in the making and signed on April 15, 1994 – of the Uruguay

Round of the General Agreement on Tariffs and Trade (GATT) negoti-ations.[4] Clinton apparently asserted that trade in film and other audio-visual products was "a defining issue" that would "make or break" the negotiations.[5] Other nations' commitment was so strong, however, that the United States backed down in the eleventh hour, losing on this issue,[6] just as it had a few years earlier in the 1992 North American Free Trade Agreement (NAFTA) negotiations.[7] Similarly, in the late 1970s and early 1980s, a dispute between the United States and Third World nations over free-market dominance of the world communications order was a central cause of the United States leaving the United Nations Educational Social and Cultural Organization (UNESCO).[8] Although the United States stands almost alone in its view, it is not about to give up. Not surprisingly, then, although some rounds of the dispute have been settled, the struggle continues. For example, after Canada had carefully assured that its protectionist policy would not be covered by NAFTA, the United States brought, and in 1997 won, a legal challenge before a World Trade Organization (WTO) panel and appellate board, which found Canadian laws protecting its magazine industry illegal based on older provisions of GATT.[9]

Third, this is an arena where the guidance offered by the analyses in Parts I and II could be especially insightful. Given the passions and the stakes, real-world outcomes will likely primarily reflect power politics, probably dominated by corporate interests both in and outside the United States. Nevertheless, the dominant view in the United States is that it wins all the theoretical arguments. Free trade in media products is justified as a matter of principle, not simply American economic self-interest. The analyses developed here, however, show that this view is simply wrong. Admittedly, my claim is incautious. All I can really demonstrate abstractly is that free trade can have, depending on cir-cumstances, and predictably will have both some good and some bad effects from the perspective of serving audiences or citizens. The balance of effects is inevitably an empirical issue. Still, I argue that eco-nomic and democratic theories strongly suggest that neither consumer welfare nor economic efficiency nor democratic theory support the dominant view in the United States.

The broad outlines of the competing arguments can be stated succinctly. Widely accepted premises justify the claim that free trade benefits people of all countries, especially benefiting consumers, more productive workers, and more efficient firms. While free trade disad-vantages comparatively inefficient industries within a nation, free-trade advocates argue that a country is better off in the long term with free trade. Trade forces the country either to improve the lagging sector's efficiency or, more often, to move resources now used in these comparatively inefficient sectors to economic activities in which it holds a comparative advantage. This motivating premise underlies GATT and most of the world's attempts to expand free trade. The United States contends that this conclusion applies aptly to cultural products, pressing it strongly in relation to films and television programming, but also for magazines, books, newspapers, and advertising. Americans contend that nothing economically singular about these products justifies repudiating settled free-trade premises. Deviations from free trade disadvantage consumers in the country that imposes the restrictions. Free trade gives these consumers the media or cultural products they want and leads to more efficient domestic use of material and creative resources.

If there is anything special about media products, free-trade advocates contend, it is that they provide people with expression and information. By invoking international norms concerning freedom of the press and access to information,[10] norms with strong democratic pedigrees, free-trade advocates argue that the unique nature of these products provides an independent "human rights" reason to disapprove of trade restrictions for media products. Of course, the enlightenment hope, dating back at least to Immanuel Kant, is that by creating an economically interdependent world, free trade will make war intrusively disruptive and hence an unappealing form of action.[11] But beyond this, the ideal of promoting mutual understanding on the global level provides a special reason to value free trade in cultural products. Still, as a curious historical footnote, the United States routinely invoked First Amendment values in attacking UNESCO and critiquing Third World attempts to assure a rich local and globally balanced communications order in the face of global market forces. However, the United States changed to an "economic parlance" in opposing Europe and Canada in the dispute about domestic restrictions designed to preserve national cultural robustness.[12] Maybe some American advocates feel less confident in lecturing Western Europe and Canada about what democracy means.

An alternative view posits that culture is special. Countries should have rights to protect and to promote their own internal cultures. Most American commentators reject this view, labeling it "protectionist." These commentators assume that the issue comes down to a choice between the free-trade premise of letting people have the cultural products that they want (or, equivalently, advancing economic efficiency) and the value of preserving local culture against the consumer wishes of local people. Although admitting that the concern for culture can be legitimate, the American commentators typically disparage cultural claims, usually attacking their internal coherence or exhibiting suspicion that protectionists invoke culture as a smoke screen for purely self-interested policies designed to benefit politically influential commercial interests.[13] Most important, the economic reasoning fundamental to the U.S. position normally remains unchallenged in the academic literature, especially within the legal academy.[14] Chapter 10 offers such a challenge. Although there may be substantial grounds for doubt,* for purposes of this book I accept the claim that because of the law of "comparative advantage," free trade is generally desirable. Thus, Chapter 10 offers no general critique of free trade. Instead, it provides an analysis based on the special nature of media products. The chapter applies observations

---

* See, e.g., Noam Chomsky, "Free Trade and Free Markets: Pretense and Practice," in Fredric Jameson & Masao Miyoshi, eds., *The Cultures of Globalization* (Durham: Duke U. Press, 1998), 356. For example, a common critical observation is that market competition induces firms to seek profits as much by taking wealth from labor as by increasing efficiency – the question being whether the marginal expenditure on one or the other effort produces the largest gain. A major aspect of increased freedom of international trade, which expands the mobility of capital, is to increase capital's power in its fight with labor over the distribution of wealth. This increased capacity should predictably increase the tendency toward promoting profits by these means as compared with the now comparatively more difficult means of increasing total wealth (being more productive). Thus, even those workers whose livelihoods depend on free trade can question the terms on which it takes place – objecting to aspects that increase capital's power in its struggle with workers but approving trade terms properly oriented toward exploiting the law of comparative advantage. Only this observation explains why longshoremen played a prominent role in the Seattle demonstrations during the January 2000 World Trade Organization meeting as well as in shutting down West Coast ports with job actions made in solidarity with the demonstrators. See Kim Murphy and Nancy Cleeland, "Labor Unions Revive Powerful Past as WTO March Looks to New Future," *Los Angeles Times* (Dec. 4, 1999): A18; Bill Mongelluzzo, "Dockers Return to Work after WTO Protest," *Journal of Commerce* (Dec. 2, 1999): Martine sec. 16; David Moberg, "After Seattle," *In These Times* (Jan. 10, 2000): 14. More empirically, some critics ask whether the data actually show the supposed benefits of the law of comparative advantage. For example, Carlos Rozo observes that for the twenty years before Mexico embraced a development strategy based on free trade in 1983, its economy grew at an average of 6% a year, with growth varying between roughly 4% and 11%. During the dozen years after it embraced free trade, growth slowed to an average of 2% annually, varying from −4% to 4% a year. And although trade exports rose during this period of free trade by 450%, the rate of productivity increase fell, most people's real incomes fell, and income inequality increased – precisely the results predicted if free trade improves the position of capital vis-à-vis labor, creating increased incentives to use resources in that struggle as compared with using them to increase productivity. See Carlos Rozo, "Mexico's Failed Growth Strategy," *Dollars and Sense* (Sept. 1999): 10–11.

developed in Part I, making critiques based (1) on the non-rivalrous-use aspect of most media products; (2) on positive and negative externalities created by media products; and (3) on the way that markets identify and weigh preferences for media products. In order to show that problems with the market cannot be corrected by trade-neutral domestic regulation, Chapter 10 argues that international trade can exacerbate each of these problems.

Chapter 11 argues that unrestricted free trade should be troublesome from the perspective of any theory of democracy, but especially of the various participatory theories. To the extent trade undermines the robustness of local media, the checking function can be threatened. The chapter explores the participatory theories' insight into the difficult question of what is the meaning or relevance of "culture" in this context, suggesting that culture is and should be seen from a democratic "dialogic" perspective. Chapter 11 also considers but rejects the possibility that international free trade may be newly justified by the need for a global public sphere serving needed new forms of global democracy. Finally, although the economic and democratic analyses justify a policy of "weak protectionism," they also suggest some normatively appropriate limits to cultural protectionism. However, I suggest that people's legitimate interest in restricting government's power to deny them access to media or cultural products is better considered under international human rights law than under trade law.

## CHAPTER 10

# Trade and Economics

Belief in the merits of markets has achieved considerable conceptual hegemony. Of course, general critiques are common and, I think, powerful, but I will not take them up here. Instead, relying on Part I, this chapter considers special attributes of media products that undermine the applicability of the general assumption that markets achieve proper outcomes in the context of international trade.

The standard economic (and democratic) perspective treats consumers' own evaluations of their needs and interests as "sovereign." Reliance on consumer sovereignty is questionable in some contexts, most obviously when the consumer is a child. Nevertheless, my claim is that, from the perspective of consumers' own preferences, markets predictably and dramatically fail to provide appropriate production and distribution of media products, thereby denying any real consumer sovereignty. Part I justified this claim by developing three analyses. First, markets work well, if at all, only with respect to "private goods." Because media products have substantial "public-good" aspects – specifically, the possibility of substantially nonrivalrous use of media content – markets fail to produce enough, and they sometimes inefficiently favor less-desired, media products. Second, markets work well only if goods are properly priced, that is, priced at roughly their true cost. Substantial negative and positive externalities of media products result in improper pricing. This pricing leads to excessive demand for and an oversupply of media products with substantial negative externalities and to inadequate demand for and underproduction of those with positive externalities. Third, markets work well given the premise that they properly identify and measure people's preferences. Market identification takes place only within market transactions, and measurement is based on an individual's willingness and ability to pay. Significantly, nothing is "objectively" correct or accurate about this method of identification or its results. Although all capitalist societies rely on market-based identification and measurement of preferences for many purposes, all democracies reject these methods for other purposes.[1] Many, though maybe not all, media products have important traits that are similar to those for which societies rely on nonmarket measures of people's values or preferences. This similarity makes reliance on the market questionable in many media contexts. Part I argued that these three failures of markets justify governmental interventions and structural regulation.

This conclusion, however, is inadequate as a critique of the application of international free-trade rules to media products. International trade law generally does not forbid regulation. Rather, it primarily requires "national treatment" – that is, the application of the same rules to domestic and foreign goods and no other disfavorable treatment of foreign products. If markets in both domestic and imported media products create the same problems, free-trade principles presumably would not prevent responsive regulations aimed equally at both. For example, if consumption of pornography is unacceptable, a ban on sales of both foreign and domestic pornography should not offend trade law. Trade law would only be offended by favoring the domestic porn industry. Thus, each of the three analyses must consider whether domestic and foreign media products differ in ways relevant to how markets in these goods fail. Differential treatment of foreign and domestic media products is only justified if international free trade exacerbates market failures such that the most effective legal corrective would distinguish the two categories.

## PUBLIC GOODS AND MONOPOLISTIC COMPETITION

Markets normally fail to provide adequately for public goods. As observed in Chapters 1 and 2, the low copy costs of most media products cause them to have one of the key elements of "public goods" – nonrivalrous use. Pat cannot eat the same ice cream cone that Carol ate, but when Carol watches a television show or reads a news story, Pat can watch or read the same show or story. Two important economic consequences of goods of this sort are: (1) these goods are typically not produced or are underproduced even when their production (or greater production) would provide consumers more of what they want at a price they would be willing to pay; (2) competition among goods of this type may cause the failure of (the nonproduction of) goods that would produce more value than the competitive winner. At least these effects are predictable as long as a firm cannot adequately price discriminate – that is, sell to different users at different prices, thereby exploiting the different valuation placed on the goods by different consumers.

A simple illustration – a somewhat more refined treatment is available in Chapter 2 – can clarify this point. Imagine a three person society. The third person (P3) can produce and distribute a first copy of a media product for $11 and make a copy (or otherwise make it available to an additional person) for a zero or negligible cost. Assume that the first (P1) and second person (P2) would be willing to pay $10 and $6 respectively for the product. Here, the seller (P3) can sell the good for $6 to P1 and P2, with an expenditure of $11, receiving a revenue of $12 (2 × $6), and creating a social surplus (value to consumers minus cost of production and sale) of $5 ($10 + $6 – $11).

At this point, the story has a happy outcome. But what if the demand of P2, the amount he would pay, is only $5? And assume that the seller must sell for the same price to both potential consumers. Now there is no profitable selling price at which the good can be sold. P3 cannot recoup her investment by selling to P1 for $10 or by selling to both P1 and P2 at $5 even though in combination P1 and P2 value the good at $15 ($10 + $5) and the good only costs $11 to produce and distribute to both. The potential social surplus of $4 ($15 – $11) is lost. This is the first effect described here – failed production.

The second point noted earlier concerned the possibility of a loss of social welfare due to market competition, that is, competition itself causing a frustration of consumer preferences. This possibility exists because the availability of an alternative product at a particular price could affect consumers' demand for the first product. In the initial hypothetical, two developments are all that is needed to illustrate this result. First, assume that an introduction of a new media product caused the demand of P2 for the original product to shift from $6 to $5, causing the inefficient failure of the product and the loss of consumer surplus valued at $4. This is the change from the happy to the sad story and seems clearly a possible result of introducing the new product. Second, assume that the social surplus generated by the new product is less than would have been generated by the failed product. Nothing about market competition suggests that this will or will not occur. It is a real possibility and depends entirely on the specifics of the demand function of P1 and P2 for the new product. For example, assume that the first copy of the new product costs $8, and an additional copy costs nothing, and each copy is sold for $4, and is valued by P1 at $6 and P2 at $5. This scenario produces a surplus of $3, which is less than the surplus of $4 lost by the demise of the original product.

One further observation that becomes important later concerns the *likelihood* that the competitive effect will be inefficient. This likelihood is greater when consumer surplus represents comparatively larger portions of the value of the displaced product(s) and relatively smaller portions of the value of the winning product. Two factors are often associated with this condition. First, a relatively steeply declining demand curve is likely to produce cases where the consumer surplus amounts to a relatively high portion of the value of the product. And this sharp decline is more likely when the relevant audience is comparatively small because, if we assume the highest and lowest valuation stays the same, a larger audience flattens the curve. In the preceding illustration, rather than inefficient failed production when P1 would pay $10 and P2 would pay $5, if the audience expanded to include a P3 who would pay $9 and a P4 who would pay $6, the good could now be successfully sold to all four – they would pay $5 each (a total of $20) to the seller whose total costs were $11 or only slightly more. Second, both a flatter demand curve (typically associated with larger audiences) and an ability to price discriminate allows the sale of products even when little or no surplus is produced. Thus, if the competitively winning product has a particularly large audience or engages in successful price discrimination, there are grounds to doubt that it produces (proportionately) much surplus. Thus, these products are the ones where the likelihood is highest that their success will lead to an inefficient, audience-denying result.

These economic attributes of media goods have both explanatory and policy relevance for international trade. First, consider its explanatory relevance. Media outlets observably sell their products at radically different prices from country to country.[2] Commentators sometimes disagree about how to characterize this difference. For most private goods, substantially lower prices for foreign sales strongly suggest "dumping," that is, selling at below cost. International trade law considers dumping a major "sin." The dumped good's low price competes unfairly with goods in the importing country. Trade law agreements generally outlaw dumping and often allow various defensive responses, including retaliation by the receiving country.[3] Nonrivalrous use, however, means that the exported media product is not sold below cost in that there are few significant costs of the exported product beyond those already incurred in producing it for its domestic audience. The price differential occurs because national borders segment markets, making profit-maximizing price discrimination easier. Unlike dumping, this price discrimination presumably increases efficiency by making it profitable to produce and more widely distribute goods that people want.[4]

This public-good aspect of media products also explains the commonly observed dominance of the United States in the international trade in films and television programming.[5] *If the price to her is the same,* a consumer typically prefers the stereo, meal, car, or suit on which more resources were lavished, that is, which has better inputs. Of course, specific tastes of a particular consumer sometimes override this tendency. So does the ineptness of a producer in the use of even high-quality inputs. Nevertheless, consumers seldom get this choice – that is, goods that cost a lot to produce are seldom sold for as low a price as are cheaply produced goods. Usually, the high product cost means a higher price, which requires finding a consumer willing and able to pay more. Purchasers typically make trade-offs between higher quality and lower price. At least, this point holds for most private goods.

This simple dynamic does not hold automatically for goods, like media products, whose use is nonrivalrous. For these goods, the price to the consumer is a function not just of the cost of inputs for the first copy but also the number of purchases over which the first-copy costs can be spread. Thus, the producer's opportunity to create a "better" product – one with higher monetary inputs – is tied directly to the size and wealth of the potential audience. Looking solely at domestic markets, this dynamic means that popular media products in larger and wealthier countries, most prominently the United States, will have the largest production budgets.[6]

Now introduce international trade and, for a moment, hold constant other factors, especially tastes for local content. If distributors sell domestic and imported media products at the same price, consumers in all countries generally should prefer the products created with the higher budgets. For the reasons just described, however, this will typically be products most popular in a large, rich domestic market, most obviously American products.

In reality, however, other factors cannot be held constant. Most audiences prefer their own domestic content – content in their own language and dealing with their own cultural experiences and social issues. For the country with a large and wealthy domestic audience, both the larger production budget and the domestic content preference favor the domestic product. Americans predictably consume primarily American media products.[7] For countries with smaller domestic audiences over which to spread costs, the U.S. advantage of a higher budget is countered to some extent by the local advantage of domestic content, leading to some balance between imports and domestic products. Thus, in 1983, while only 2 percent of American television programming was imported, every Latin American or European country for which there was data (except for the Soviet Union at 8 percent) reported import percentages in the double digits, ranging up to 66 percent in Ecuador and Iceland.[8] Logically, the proportion of consumption devoted to domestic media products should increase the greater the size and wealth of a country's domestic audience and the more the domestic culture and language differ from the culture and language of the primary exporting countries. Likewise, language and cultural similarities help explain observed regional trading patterns. Still, the dominant point is that larger production budgets permitted by large and wealthy domestic audiences predictably give American products a significant advantage in the export market – precisely the result reported.[9]

This predictive analysis can be taken a step further. Eli Noam offers a simplified but useful approach that can explain some of the impact of international trade on media content.[10] Noam suggests that a media producer might consider three types of content inputs: domestic ($D$), universal ($U$), and foreign ($F$). He then assumes that, on average, domestic audiences positively value $D$ and, perhaps to a lesser extent, $U$, but disvalue $F$. A foreign audience will have the reverse reactions to some of this content, disvaluing the first country's $D$ content and potentially valuing $F$ (if it is about them, thus being $D$ from their perspective) but, like the domestic audience, positively valuing $U$.[11] In creating media content, economic logic suggests that a producer should include each element until its cost becomes greater than the revenue its inclusion allows the producer to extract from potential audiences. This model predicts that media products made for domestic audiences will contain mostly $D$, some $U$, and little if any $F$. Although producers might increase the amount of $F$ in products that they believe have a potential for significant export sales, this approach has the serious disadvantage that $F$ reduces the content's value to domestic audiences (and will only be appealing in those foreign markets for which $F$ equates with $D$).

Therefore, for a producer seeking to export its creations, generally the dominant strategy is to increase $U$ and sacrifice some $D$. The amount of $D$ sacrificed should increase as the portion of revenue the producer expects to obtain from export markets rises. Moreover, export revenue should be systematically greater for producers in any country, in particular the United States, that has a natural trade advantage due to larger program budgets, which reflect the larger size and wealth of its domestic market.

Thus, America's pro-free-trade policy is not only economically advantageous. The analysis here indicates that free trade is essentially a content-related media policy that tilts American media content toward more $U$ and less $D$.[12] Of course, the precise coverage of these symbols is not obvious. Indeed, studio executives are paid handsomely for the treacherous task of predicting audience appeal. Still, the categories' coverage is not entirely opaque. Local language, complex dialogue, local humor, references to local or national history and culture, themes dealing with unresolved national issues, and even universal themes dealt with through complex weaving of national or local cultural materials tend to be heavily $D$. Although literary and film critics often praise such content, free trade disfavors it and opts for $U$ instead. Maybe the often criticized shallowness of American cultural products is less intrinsic to American creativity or tastes – for example, does the criticism apply to less-exported American theater? – than to the commercial realities of producing these products for export.

In contrast to these critically valued but market-disvalued $D$ items, most observers believe action, violence, sex, and slick production qualities have relatively universal appeal.* Thus, the predictions about content: American video products will feature these $U$ elements more than will the cultural products of countries relying less on export revenues. Foreign audiences will buy relatively large amounts of these American imports, but not because they affirmatively value this type of content; they predictably would prefer more of their own $D$. Rather, foreign audiences favor these imports because of $U$'s relative acceptability, combined with the advantage of the imports' relatively low price,[13] and the imports' use of comparatively large production budgets to infuse the content with slick and appealing production attributes.

---

* Of course, $U$ is not of one mold. It is not just sex and violence but can also include content supporting such universal values as freedom, democracy, toleration, and empathy – contents that authoritarian elites often wish to restrict.

So far, this analysis has been explanatory, accounting for the leading role of the United States (Hollywood) in the media export market and examining the impact this export trade predictably has on content. Audiovisual products in particular and media products in general compete against each other (and, to a lesser degree, against other products and activities) for audience time and money. Predictably, the success of American exports usually takes market share from and to some degree reduces demand for an importing country's domestic media products.[14] In the American market, the economic viability of products whose domestic existence depends on their also being exported allows them to take some market share from those domestic American media products that have little or no export appeal.

Of course, the results described are not intuitively bad. Nothing said yet suggests any reason to object to U.S. dominance, at least on economic or welfare grounds. To the contrary, many observers will accept the descriptive analysis up to this point but assert that any trade restriction would cause a loss not only to exporting countries but also to the people (consumers) of the importing countries. Competition always produces winners and losers. For a typical "private" good, competitive winners usually better satisfy consumer demand than did their unsuccessful rivals. Putting aside serious disruption to lives of people who lose jobs and who now may even be unemployable (which, in the dry language of economics, is a possible negative externality), producing a product that, due to competition, is no longer economically viable generally wastes social resources. The export good may be socially "efficient" – what both foreign and domestic consumers want. In addition, the enhanced opportunity for price discrimination provided by national borders should lead to more efficient levels of production of such goods. These conclusions are the mainstay of the pro-free-trade position. Nevertheless, an evaluative inquiry provides substantial reasons to worry. The second point about marketing of media products – that competition can be inefficient when prevailing products generate less surplus than would the products that it drives out of existence – needs consideration.

Assuming inability to adequately price discriminate, many media products will not be commercially viable even though their creation and distribution would be a valuable use of social resources – that is, would be efficient. These unprofitable but valued products include some of the local media products driven out by competition with foreign imports. Of course, free trade also can produce consumer benefits. People value the imported products, otherwise they would not buy or watch. The question is whether the new surplus (value as indicated by consumer demand in excess of cost) created by the imports is more or less than the value lost because valued domestic products are no longer economically viable. Because the market firm cannot *capture* these surpluses, there is no systematic reason to expect that those products that are most desired by the public will prevail. Because the market cannot *measure* these surpluses, the better result cannot be known for sure. The realistic prediction should be that sometimes particular competitive results will be and sometimes they will not be beneficial. Several observations, however, can be made about these alternative possibilities.

Both conditions described earlier for when the value lost is likely to be greater than the value gained apply in the international trade context. First, the domestic products that lose out in competition with imports will almost by definition include mostly products with smaller audiences that serve more unique interests and potentially relatively intense desires – that is, products with comparatively steeply declining demand curves. These are precisely the conditions associated with likely large losses of consumer surplus.

Second is the matter of capacity to engage in price discrimination. Effective ability and willingness to price discriminate allow products to be commercially viable up to the point that they generate no consumer or producer surplus. Two factors make major products sold in the export market particularly able to engage in relatively high degrees of price discrimination. Domestically, by using different "windows" – such as movie theaters, video cassettes, television, pay and free cable, or an original or spin-off book – a media company can increase its ability to sell the original product to different people at different prices. To the extent that the company can market each of these versions for different prices in different countries, which is the norm, this multinational reach adds significantly to the number of windows available, thereby increasing the opportunity to price discriminate.

Using different windows, however, costs money that must be recovered. The possibility of recovery increases with the size of the audience over which to spread the overhead cost of creating and using different windows. Exporting mass-appeal products, especially blockbusters, should increase both audience size and the number of windows, allowing for more effective price discrimination. Thus, marginally successful export products may exist only because of international trade's enhancement of their ability to price discriminate. The success of these exports, however, can generate an overall welfare loss in the importing country due to the resulting failure of valued, smaller-audience domestic products that are less able to price discriminate. In such situations, audiences would benefit if importing governments could burden these mass-appeal media exports' competitive opportunities.

International sales of American media products can also deny audiences in the United States media they most want, at least in the case of the only marginally successful exports. The entire analysis of this section applies. These export products' competitive success, although producing little surplus, can drive out some smaller-audience, domestic-oriented media products that U.S. audiences still want. Using the categories described earlier, fewer American products emphasizing $D$ (domestic) content will be successful because of competition with American products emphasizing $U$ (universal) content. Some informed observers conclude that this effect explains a greater prevalence of violence, action, and sex in American products than can be attributed to the domestic audience's own preferences. George Gerbner reports that nonviolent programming has higher Nielsen ratings than violent programming in the United States – a characterization supported by audience self-reports – but that violent, action, and crime programming are much more likely to be successfully exported.[15] That is, in domestic as well as foreign markets, international trade tends to displace media products with culturally specific, discursive content even when the displaced products are strongly valued by local audiences and even though they would exist if free trade were subject to appropriate restrictions. In this circumstance, free trade hurts consumers.

In sum, the "nonrivalrous use" attribute of media goods first explains the competitive success of American media products internationally. It also provides an efficiency as opposed to a dumping explanation of the differential pricing of U.S. media products in different countries. More important for policy purposes, this attribute explains why economic theory cannot predict that free trade in these products will be better at giving audiences what they want than would a well-designed system of trade restraints. Economic theory even gives substantial reasons to expect that, from the perspective of both American audiences and audiences in importing countries, international free trade will be inefficient as compared with an optimal system of restraints and interventions.

The most obvious policy response is to subsidize those categories of media products that are most likely to be economically justified but that will not survive in a free market. This economic justification for subsidies applies uniquely to local media products disadvantaged by the free-trade regime. Nevertheless, the United States has argued that European, especially French, subsidies for domestic films violate the free-trade principles that should be enshrined in a GATT agreement. Equally contrary to a defensible policy regime and even more insensitive politically, the United States apparently suggested that French subsidies would be permissible as long as the French make their subsidies equally available to American media products.[16]

Economically justified responsive policies do not end with subsidies. Because competition with imports causes the failure of some domestic products valued by consumers, these consumers could benefit by keeping out those imports that produce the smallest proportionate surplus per consumer or by having imports reach only those audiences that valued them comparatively highly. Thus, at least three types of protectionist policies can produce a net gain in consumer satisfaction – subsidies for local media, keeping out marginally valued imports, and marginally limiting the reach of other imports. Each policy works by favoring otherwise eliminated domestic products that generate significant surpluses. A country could pursue these policies with properly designed import duties or discriminatory taxes, especially if the proceeds were then devoted to local media products. To achieve the desired effect, the duty or tax ideally should be tied to audience size, for example, $x$ cents per viewer, or, maybe, to a product's sales revenue. In contrast, a flat duty per imported movie or show would eliminate mostly imports with small, even if rather intensely interested, audiences – precisely the imports most beneficial on consumer welfare grounds.

Many countries mandate "screen quotas," typically requiring theaters to show domestic films in a certain percentage of their screenings, or "broadcast time quotas," typically requiring domestic programming for a certain percentage of the broadcast day.[17] Others have similar rules requiring a minimum percentage of domestic music in radio broadcasts.[18] These rules also can be beneficial. Although they marginally reduce the reach of imports, importantly, they do so without barring any particular import desired by people in the receiving country. Moreover, house-packing imports help make a theater (or station) profitable. The rules allow this. Nothing is necessarily kept out but entry is conditioned on guaranteeing, that is, effectively paying for, screentime or airtime for local products. In this way, these quotas operate to subsidize local content. However, they still allow importing firms to determine what combination of blockbuster and more specialized imports produce the larger capturable surplus. In contrast, quotas on the *number* of imported movies or television programs would favor importing only blockbusters even if these blockbusters turn out to damage local production more and produce less surplus than importing a larger number of media products appealing to smaller audiences. Therefore, as a policy matter, screen and time quotas are far better than quotas on the number of imports. Interestingly, the theoretical analysis here leads to something like the existing media regulation in democratic regimes in much of the world – including Europe, Canada, and Israel. The claim is that these legislative initiatives make rough economic, audience-serving sense, while the free-trade goals of the United States do not.

## EXTERNALITIES

As shown in Chapter 3, media products and their creation produce huge positive and negative externalities. This leads to the production and sale of more of those media goods with negative externalities and less of those with positive externalities than audiences would want if charged the proper price. The presence of significant externalities means that unrestricted markets will not operate to give people the media they want. However, this fact does not automatically justify differential treatment of foreign and domestic media products. Free-trade principles generally allow restrictions that are uniformly applied. In this sense, free-trade principles compare roughly with the mandate the Supreme Court has discovered in the Commerce Clause of the U.S. Constitution. On its face the Commerce Clause is only a grant of power to Congress to regulate commerce. The Court, however, interprets what is called the "negative" or "dormant" Commerce Clause to bar states from overtly discriminating against out-of-state goods or activities, thereby constitutionalizing an internal free-trade regime.[19] This regime still leaves states almost totally free to impose restraints, prohibitions, or burdens on goods or activities, even if the burden falls mostly on out-of-state firms or practices, as long as the law plausibly serves a local purpose (including nondiscriminatory economic purposes) and does not facially discriminate against outsiders.[20] Like state laws under the Commerce Clause, most domestic regulations that apply equally to foreign and domestic businesses will not violate international free trade rules.

Free trade is at issue only if the best response to externalities requires distinguishing between domestic and foreign products. This would seldom occur unless the externalities of imports differed predictably and systematically from those of the domestic products that the imports supplement or replace. Even then, sometimes an available uniform policy response would be efficacious.

Whether significant differences exist between the externalities of imported media products and of domestic products that the imports supplement or replace is an empirical and contextual matter. Even if, counterfactually, under a free-trade regime different countries chose roughly the same (often American) imports, these imports likely would replace dramatically different types of domestic products. The displaced domestic products would hardly be the same in Italy or Mexico as in Saudi Arabia or Cuba. Daniel Hallin observes that commercial Mexican television focuses almost exclusively on wealthy characters while Cuban programs portray everyday lives of ordinary people.[21] These can be quite different contents for an import to displace.

Predictions of systematic differences will be speculative. Moreover, evaluative characterizations of these differences will inevitably be contested. Did the people influenced by Thomas Paine's *Common Sense* produce good or bad for others; is the impact of feminist tracts or the Voice of America on their immediate audience negative or positive for others in a given society? Given the contestable nature of these matters, the issue of who should make policy-determinative judgments becomes central. At the stage of final choice, liberal democracy must leave decisions in the hands of individuals. However, the choice of structures or legal frameworks is an inherently collective matter. Because free trade is a structure that favors some and disfavors other content, the decision whether or not to restrict free trade properly reflects a collective judgment about this content. Specifically, the decision should reflect a collective assessment of whether content favored by free trade is more associated with positive externalities and less associated with negative externalities than is the content favored by restrictions. No abstract reasons predict that externalities of products effectively favored by an international free-trade regime would be the same or better than those of domestic products. Under these circumstances, rather than relying blindly on the market, the more appropriate response is for the parties most affected to reach a judgment through the only mechanism available to them to make structural decisions: residents of each country should express their judgment through their political order.

Despite this generic theoretical argument for leaving the issue to internal politics, there is a practical reason to disempower domestic decision-making elites. As a category, imports characteristically bring in new and different perspectives. They can support greater cross-cultural understanding. Additionally, imported products can bring with them sometimes "foreign" ideas about equality, liberty, gender roles, environmentalism, or democracy.[22] Authoritarian regimes that wish to manipulate their subjects' views have reason to fear free trade.[23] But many people in a society, including those who are not direct consumers of the media products, would find such outside or dissident content beneficial, perhaps even life-changing. Larry Gross eloquently describes the transformative experience of finding as an Israeli youth an American book about American gay identity in the Hebrew University library.[24] Even people who do not themselves read or view foreign material can benefit. Annebelle Sreberny describes "cultural and media strategies of many [repressive Middle Eastern] states [as] ultimately directed toward maintaining the prevailing gender hierarchy" and the import of foreign television shows as undermining this hierarchy.[25] Women who do not themselves read or see the foreign material – whether feminist tracts or Western soap operas – can benefit from transformations the imported materials generate due to other men and women within their culture having access to it. More generally, all the reasons for distrusting even democratic governments in their domestic regulation of speech apply to their content-oriented judgments about imports. Of course, the flip side is that a communications order is always a constructed, never a "natural" or "neutral" realm. Democracy means that conscious democratic choice should have – as it always has had in the United States as well as elsewhere – a significant and legitimate role in as noncensorious construction of this order.[26]

Still, economic analysis alone is an awkward tool with which to evaluate an externality that is negative for some – for example, authoritarian elites or traditionalists – and positive for others. In its purportedly most "neutral" version, economic analysis counts each person's preferences whatever they are (although wealthy people's greater ability to pay causes their preferences to weigh more heavily, which immediately indicates one troublesome ideological feature of typical welfare economics). Normative theory, however, discredits any policy weight being given to preferences for hierarchical or undemocratic authority. The most common normative reasons for valuing economic efficiency or consumer sovereignty is either the utilitarian goal of satisfying audiences' desires or liberal enlightenment principles concerning respect for people's autonomy and equality. Neither perspective would significantly credit authoritarian elites' interest in maintaining a repressive status quo. The utilitarian would properly reject weighting hierarchical elites' views or interests based on their wealth or power. The enlightenment rights framework gives scope to individual choices and self-expressive preferences because of the moral necessity for the collective to respect individual autonomy. For policy purposes, however, this framework should reject any "counting" of preferences that are in opposition to the "liberal" reasons that justified creating a collective order and a democracy in the first place.[27] On the whole, therefore, bringing in new ideas should be considered a major plus of free trade.

Introduction of liberating content is not trade's only or even most prominent predictable content-oriented consequence. The most important prediction for policy purposes is that in many contexts imports will have more negative or less positive externalities than the local media that they replace. The earlier discussion suggested that an export's success often relates to having comparatively high levels of $U$ (universal) inputs and comparatively less $D$ (domestic) inputs than do non-export-oriented products. For the United States, as a major exporter, this means that free trade should lead internally to more content with high levels of $U$ and fewer products with high levels of $D$. Similarly, for importing countries, the imports with typically high levels of $U$ and little $D$ will to differing degrees supplement, marginalize, or replace domestic products with high levels of $D$. Of course, the labels "domestic" and "universal" encompass a vast array of variable specifics. Still, even the rough characterizations discussed earlier and a few further observations suggest policy implications.

Universal content tends to avoid cultural complexity and to exhibit simplicity in discursive structure. As noted earlier, favored elements are likely to include violence, action, and possibly sex[28] or romance on the theory that these translate comparatively easily between cultures. Although the issue is subject to some dispute, overwhelming evidence indicates that some violent media content generates overtly negative externalities.[29] If, as suggested by many critics of Hollywood, it also tends toward cultural shallowness, this adds to the objections.

Possibly more important is the displacement or marginalization of domestic content. This loss can have major significance for the diverse functions that media serve for any society or group of people. As Part II discussed, the news media should perform various vital democratic functions, including being a watchdog that exposes corruption, an information source that informs democratic decision making, a partisan stimulant for political participation, and a medium for subgroup deliberation. Quality performance of these functions can positively benefit people other than the immediate readers, listeners, or viewers. For these purposes, domestic content is usually crucial.

The concern about not displacing local media extends beyond the news and public affairs media. Neither individuals, nor groups, nor nations float free of their context. As members of traditions and groups, individuals need to confront their own historically situated problems and concerns. In addition to using a local language, domestic-oriented popular fiction and nonpolitical, nonfictional materials typically either reflect, react against, or implicitly comment on the world views that dominate within their own country or within some subgroup within the country. Cultural materials provide the discursive means and medium for individuals and groups to address issues of identity, values, and motivation. Individuals' success in addressing these issues depends in part on the existence and quality of domestic media or cultural materials. The success of these individuals can, in turn, impact profoundly all those with whom they interact. In sum, a country's own domestic media products potentially better provide (or provide in ways not duplicated by imports) domestic content that people need for a democratic political process to function well and, more generally, for their cultural discourses of identity, meaning, and value. In this regard, domestic media can have tremendous positive externalities not supplied by the imports that threaten to replace them.

These observations on differences between domestic and imported media suggest the following propositions. First, the quality and availability of cultural content, news, and other media content influence the functioning of democracy, the development and richness of people's individual identity, and the quality of their interactions with others. Second, what counts as good media content will vary among persons, among groups, and among nations. Even within a group or nation, the identification of quality will inevitably be contested. Third, imported media products can have positive qualities. For instance, they can introduce new and potentially transformative values, perspectives, and cultural resources that can be particularly important for individuals or groups that are oppressed or marginalized by the dominant local culture.[30] Fourth, imports often embody less culturally valuable and less culturally specific material. Some imports – for example, those

emphasizing violence – predictably produce significant negative externalities.[†] Of course, domestic media products can generate negative
externalities as well, but, if my analysis is correct, this result is somewhat less common than with imported entertainment. Fifth, imports
often will replace domestic media products that are more oriented
toward crucial local needs, the needs noted in the first point. Sixth, a
substantial portion of the value of these domestic products lies in the
benefits that nonreaders and nonviewers gain from their availability and
consumption by their compatriots. That is, the displaced media would
have generated large positive externalities. Finally, although depending
on empirical matters such as the extent and significance of unrestrained
trade's impact on the externalities described, unrestrained trade in
media products is likely to reduce consumer welfare in the importing
country. In other words, implementation of free-trade principles could
prevent audiences from getting what they want had products been
priced on the basis of their real costs. If so, welfare-maximizing results
require governmental interventions, including local subsidies and possibly well-designed trade restraints.

Trade restraints, of course, vary in desirability and legitimacy.
Imports can be liberating and transformative. Restrictions can be motivated by a desire to maintain systems of domination. On the other hand,
democratic, vibrant societies require robust domestic media content.
Restraints on imports can protect and promote these essential domestic products. Happily, legitimate and illegitimate interests to a considerable degree are furthered by different policies. First, illiberal aims of
maintaining oppressive elements of a country's political or social order
are mostly furthered by overt exclusions – censorship or blockage of
specific content-based categories of materials.[31] Unless this censorship
is imposed on a massive scale, these content-based exclusions are
unlikely to further the legitimate, liberal policies of trade regulation.
They will do little to protect the local media's economic base. Second,
properly designed subsidies can greatly benefit local media. Likewise,
taxes or duties that target but only marginally burden imports or
devices such as screen or airtime quotas that preserve space or markets

---

[†] Note again the caution that these statements always require. Did violence partly inspired
by Thomas Paine create negative or positive externalities? Because of the differences among
different viewers'/listeners'/readers' reception of media materials, the same violent content
can have very different effects. Because of different evaluations of the "same" behavior in
different contexts and by different people, effects often receive very contested normative
characterizations.

for domestic products do not bar liberating outside content. These practices forcibly exclude nothing.

This distinction between policies serving the legitimate and illegitimate interests has two consequences. First, the next chapter suggests that human rights law may be a better and more targeted international response to the illegitimate policies than is trade law. Second, this distinction creates the possibility that, with will and wisdom, a nation can choose only appropriate restrictions. Given the economic justification for these preferences for local media, the ideal becomes not free trade, but rather intelligent interventions. Of course, protection of state sovereignty guarantees neither the needed will nor the needed wisdom. (My impressionistic conclusion is that the quality of the response depends much more on the democratic credentials of the "protectionist" nation than on its general attitude about trade and free markets.)

The justification for discriminations against imports becomes stronger the greater the threat imports pose for domestic media. This creates an interesting asymmetry. A country like the United States – and, today, possibly only the United States – cannot rely on these potential externalities to justify any burden on incoming materials. Where domestic media are not materially threatened, the main consequence of imports – particularly imports containing domestic content of the exporting country – is to increase cultural diversity and to add to discursive possibilities within the importing country. In contrast, for countries whose domestic media, or relevant portions of them, are threatened, the economically justified role of tariffs, discriminatory taxes, or time/screen/place quotas (but not categorical exclusions of imports) recommends something close to one understanding of the existing international trade regime: an exception for cultural products from international agreements imposing free-trade principles. A normatively plausible (but politically unlikely) "generally applicable" international trade rule might allow such discriminations only when imports in a particular media category are over some specific level, say 25 percent of domestic consumption. Otherwise, free-trade principles should apply. In the United States, imports do not come close to reaching this level in any media sector. In other countries, they often do. For example, in Canada, U.S. magazines have often captured roughly 80 percent of the market during periods when free trade prevailed. Steven Wildman reported that in eight leading countries of Western Europe, American films obtained from 92 percent (United Kingdom) to 45 percent (France) or 30 percent (Italy) of the market.[32] While the United States imports only about 2 percent of its television programming, in most countries over 25 percent originates from the outside.[33] Thus, a rule such as that suggested earlier would prohibit restrictions in the United States but allow them in most other countries.

In any event, rules that reduce imports' competitive advantage that results from their ability to spread huge first-copy costs over more customers and to engage more effectively in price discrimination often will be welfare advancing. Therefore, countries other than the United States should not negotiate away their prerogative to burden or restrict this trade. They need this authority to better structure their media industries and to promote domestic media products. The analysis here, however, does not indicate whether this is best achieved by a broad cultural exemption in international trade agreements or, as some countries have recently begun to think, new international instruments that affirmatively speak to countries' right to develop without retaliation their own cultural policies, including trade restrictions.[34]

## NONMARKET MEASURES OF PREFERENCES

Free-trade advocates assume that the criterion of people's willingness and ability to pay within a market properly identifies and measures consumer preferences. Only if this assumption is valid can unimpeded markets be expected to give people what they want; only then is the consumer really sovereign. However, Chapter 4 described three reasons to object to exclusive reliance on the market as an identifier or measurer of people's preferences for media products. First, the market does not properly measure preferences for noncommodified communications. This matter is important for policy purposes because legal rules, including legal rules such as copyright that especially support commodified communications, influence the comparative cost or availability of commodified and noncommodified communications. The second observation generalizes this first point. The market only registers one type of expression of preferences, those revealed in market transactions. However, nothing makes these expressions objectively more truthful or valid than other expressions, which may conflict with the market expressions and which all democratic societies sometimes favor over market expressions. Finally, the market weights preferences based on willingness to pay. Nevertheless, not only is there nothing logically correct or accurate about this weighting but, again, all democracies sometimes choose other, for example, more egalitarian weightings in some circumstances. Chapter 4 argued that democratic political decision is generally the most appropriate way to determine whether, in a particular context, legal rules or other government policies should favor reliance on the market measure. In the communication context, however, there are strong pragmatic reasons to rely on a mixed system. In this chapter, the question is whether the reasons for sometimes resisting the market's identification and weighting of preferences justifies deviation from free-trade rules.

A positive valuation of noncommodified expression may justify support through subsidies. Thus, this valuation provides a reason to object to an interpretation of free trade that limits a country's freedom to subsidize favored local expressive forms. In addition, sometimes, particular legal rules favor commodified over noncommodified expression or vice versa. Copyright, for instance, generates such tilts. Stronger intellectual property protections often reduce opportunities for or increase the cost of noncommodified expression. Thus, a positive valuation of noncommodified expression justifies opposition to many aspects of expansive intellectual property regimes. In contrast, the desire to globally exploit commodified intellectual property has led media exporters to push for international agreements that mandate expanded global protections. More generally, the same corporate entities that push for increased international trade in cultural or media products also favor rules that may restrict noncommodified expression. Nevertheless, this issue is at most relevant background to, not a direct aspect of, free trade. Trade itself neither increases the cost of nor reduces the opportunities for noncommodified expression. Still, a positive evaluation of noncommodified communications has implications for trade policy. For example, it gives grounds to resist concluding that apparent trade gains brought about by rules like copyright are an adequate reason to accept those rules. Or, in the United States, it justifies opposing the view that the greater global dominance that further concentration would allow American media conglomerates to gain is a reason to allow that media concentration.

The political order is a major arena in which expressions of preferences can be registered. The same person might choose politically to favor broadcast of domestically produced media content while, when making market purchases, choose imported media products. This political expression may honestly reflect what she wants for herself, at least when expressing herself politically, and not merely what she wants others to hear or see. There is no obvious reason to grant less validity to these political expressions of preferences than to those expressed in the market.

Chapter 4 argued that in a democracy, the political order ought to determine which expressions of preferences the design of institutions and the choice of laws should most strongly seek to satisfy. The law is filled with rules that determine the context in which particular expressions of preferences will be given binding force or that structure institutions', including the market's, response to preferences. Democracy allows people to express politically their preference about which further expressions of wants to prioritize or to determine how legally structured institutions will respond. Given this, the question of whether preferences fulfilled through free trade are more important than those fulfilled through certain restraints cannot be decided by the market or by abstract theory. It is only determined by political decision. People can get the media they want only if they have the right to adopt rules that determine how wants are identified and weighed. These decisions could show that people will obtain the media they want only through rules that interfere with free trade.

Note that this conclusion about the necessarily constructed means for counting expressions of preferences for what a person wants does not provide a justification for a political choice to suppress options. Policies designed to create institutional arrangements that provide people media goods they want might take the form of burdens on imports. However, rules designed to prohibit imports or for the purpose of keeping out imports do not fulfill any preference except for the illegitimate preference of denying someone communications that she wants. Because a person is not forced to consume something merely because it is available, a policy of exclusion seems necessarily directed at preventing fulfillment of desires. Quotas, on the other hand, and most violations of free-trade principles that real-world advocates of "protectionism" have actually supported, often have affirmative, promotional purposes and operate more like subsidies. These measures purposefully benefit local media and only indirectly, not as a rationale, restrict imports.

Finally, there is weighting of preferences. Even accepting market mechanisms of expressing preferences, how much an actual market weights a preference depends on how much a person is willing *and able* to pay. A different distribution of wealth, for example, would produce a different weighting. As noted, sometimes normative reasons support weighting each person's preferences more equally than does the market. Thus, one measure would identify the media people would choose in the market if they all had equal wealth. Another egalitarian weighting would try to fulfill each person's preferences for media products to an equal degree (a much more radical standard than the first). Here I put aside Chapter 4's discussion of the complexities of identifying exactly what equality would mean in this context, a complexity created in part by the public-good aspect (nonrivalrous use) of media goods. A democratic one-person-one-vote criterion is obviously a much more egalitarian criterion than is the market's willingness-and-ability-to-pay. The initial priority of the political allows people to choose when to rely further on this egalitarian preference-counting criterion and when to rely on market weightings. There certainly cannot be a principled objection raised on the ground that the egalitarian measure is less reflective of what people want. Thus, people might choose to rely on this egalitarian criterion to choose politically to receive some media that the market does not provide. If this occurs, there can be no automatic objection that the result is paternalist or nonresponsive to people's actual preferences (although it may be either, depending on the motivations for the use and the specifics of the operation of political power). A decision to favor domestic products could merely reflect a more egalitarian weighting of preferences than would occur if exclusive reliance were placed on free trade. Either can, in a sense, give people what they want; they just differ in how they identify and combine different people's wants in order to get a final outcome.

Even if there is no objectively or logically right answer to the question of what weights should be given different peoples' preferences, like the decision about which expressions of preferences to count, some empirical and normative considerations provide some guidance as to an appropriate approach. For many purposes, a market weighting, at least given a generally (capitalist) market-oriented society, is appropriate. It certainly is for many types of good, including many media goods, especially those valued merely for entertainment. However, a more egalitarian weighting is appropriate for others, especially for those media goods most related to matters such as education, the vote, and maybe the creation of cultural contexts in which people can develop the capacity for autonomous choice. This egalitarian weighting can justify deviations from free trade in order to provide greater and more egalitarian satisfaction of preferences for domestic media that have particular political salience – news and opinion. The egalitarian claim is also stronger when it justifies interventions to preserve or increase diversity over that which the market would provide. Domestic media as a group often fit the second category – domestically relevant news and local cultural materials – in which egalitarian-oriented interventions are justified. Imports more often fit the first category, which justifies more reliance on a market. This observation again supports the conclusion that exclusionary rules are not justified. However, those trade restrictions designed to nurture greater and wider availability of domestic media may embody a justifiable policy of responding to more egalitarian weightings of preferences.

## CHAPTER 11

# Trade, Culture, and Democracy

Economic theory may give reasons to object to free trade in media products, but what about democratic theory? Maybe democratic theory has nothing in principle to say other than countries can decide what they want. Countries routinely limit their own future democratic discretion by means of treaties. When they do, the decision is generally thought to be an exercise, not an abandonment, of their democratic capacities. Any democratic objection to new treaties embodying free-trade rules must relate to something special about media products. The argument must go in at least one of two directions. First, the importance of maintaining decision-making discretion in respect to this type of good might be different than for other goods typically subject to free-trade agreements. Second, and more pointedly, democratic theory might recommend particular substantive media policies. These recommendations might require, or, alternatively, they might conflict, with free trade in these goods. Although this chapter is primarily concerned with the second possibility, I begin with the first.

## MAINTAINING DEMOCRATIC DISCRETION

The preceding chapter emphasized that the public-good aspect of media products – that is, their susceptibility to nonrivalrous use – makes them different than other private goods for purposes of many economic questions. Democratic theory also notes something special about media products, about communications. While other products are often the object of political allocations, discourse or communication, of which media products are (an often commodified) part, is the substance of democratic politics. One central feature of democracy is its responsibility to make deliberative choices about its own institutional embodiments, including making changes as the society's conception of democracy undergoes refinement. In this regard, maintaining discretion to make decisions to improve the media realm would seem centrally important. Entering into international agreements that result in this authority being abandoned should be problematic.

Even if this point were right in theory, if in practice the communications that democracy requires are those that are most likely generated by unrestricted market processes, then an international free-trade regime would seem perfectly appropriate. The thrust of Part II of this book is to discredit this hope. More precisely, Part II claims that the specific ways the market will be found to fail depend on the particular democratic theory to which the critic gives allegiance. Different democratic theories expose characteristically different problems with the market. For example, a serious danger exists that the market will generate, from the republican perspective, too much segmentation or, from the liberal pluralist perspective, too little diversity and partisanship. These alternative perspectives are also likely to find that the market corrupts either the common discourses or segmentation that the theory favors. Complex democracy, implicitly favored in Part II, suggests that any or all of these could be a problem depending on the particular historical and political context. Thus, the complex democrat would find maintenance of deliberative discretion in respect to media policy especially important. All these theories would provide reason to resist automatic reliance on the market. Although specific solutions vary depending on the particular democratic theory, in the language of Part I, the market fails because the products that prevail in the unregulated market often do not adequately serve intense political and informational interests, especially of smaller groups. It also fails because it does not take account of huge positive externalities in speech's contribution to democracy, an institution or practice whose proper functioning people value. And the unregulated market fails because it does not appropriately identify, and it is too inegalitarian in weighing, people's desires for democratically relevant speech. Not only do markets fail generally in this regard; the failure is predictably exacerbated by international trade to the extent that local media are especially central to the media's democratic roles (a point that later in the chapter is contested but then reaffirmed).

Democratic theory's view of the difference between the media and other industries points to another reason to resist treating the media as part of a typical trade agreement – a reason that could be labeled the "don't mix apples and oranges" argument. Trade agreements are a matter of bargaining. The economic interests of one country are often particularly advanced by trade in one category of goods, whereas those of another are most clearly advanced by trade in other goods. Even if all countries benefit from the eventual deal, they do not always like all portions of it. Rather, each country accepts the disliked elements because they are part of the best package it can get and the country benefits overall from the freer trade. Of course, like in most bargaining, what a party (here, a country) gets depends heavily on its power position going into the negotiations. These "facts" may not seem overly troublesome (except, maybe, to those interests sold out by their country's acceptance of the overall agreement or to those countries possessing particularly and, they believe, unfairly weak bargaining positions) as long as the issues involve the same "currency" – economic gain. More questionable is the acceptability of this bargaining when interests of dramatically different normative orders are at stake and a country is being asked to give up something universally considered appropriate for it to maintain.[1] Of course, people make trade-offs between different realms, like between family life and work. Still, it is normatively questionable to place a country in a position where outsiders demand that it give up democracy (as it sees democracy) in return for economic benefits. In any event, this characterization of the situation provides a common objection to trade agreements covering media products.

One response – one that the United States has been inclined toward – is to deny that a trade-off is required. These advocates see an identity, not a conflict, between democracy and free trade, *especially in the communications and cultural contexts*. Earlier I noted reasons to reject this substantive claim. Still, an interesting aspect of the claim is the general stance it exhibits toward the relation of market processes and other values. A repeated pattern within communications policy has been for the United States and Europe to take opposing positions as to whether there is a conflict or identity between the market and democratic or other noneconomic interests. Although now a virtually forgotten history,[2] opposition to commercial broadcasting was intense and almost victorious in the United States during the late 1920s and early 1930s. Within this struggle, advantage was sought rhetorically by proclaiming a commercial system paid for by commercial advertising as the "American plan," often contrasted to the darkly foreign "European plan" or Canadian approach of state support.[3] Educational, cultural, and democratic concerns had led most of the West to adopt a public-service approach that purposefully avoided reliance on advertising. The United States rejected this, implicitly asserting that there was no conflict between these noneconomic values and commercialism.

Similarly, today, a massive battle between Europe and the United States is raging over protection of privacy in digital communications. Gathering of personal data on line apparently has huge commercial value, most obviously for advertising or promotional purposes. Companies such as Double-Click can supply individualized banner ads on the computer screen when a person goes to various web pages, with the ad keyed to the previously gathered information about the users' interests. Like in its approach to public broadcasting seventy years before, Europe has taken the attitude of not sacrificing a noncommercial value, privacy, to the interests of marketing. The currently dominant (but, just as seventy years age, internally very contested) U.S. position seeks to rely on industry self-regulation. Advocates of this position argue that, after a period of commercial experimentation and consumer education, industry will provide the amount of privacy people really want, at least as expressed by their market behavior. This attitude was well expressed by an American lawyer who works with industry on this issue. She remarked, similarly to what could have been said about broadcasting, that providing all these web sites and information that people value is very expensive and then asked, rhetorically, who is going to pay for it if not advertisers.[4] This remark about the Internet is provocative. Especially given the historical analogy to broadcasting, I wonder to what extent the use of the medium and its contribution to different values will depend on how and by whom it is paid for. Note that this conflict between nonmarket values and the consequences of relying on the market is the same conflict that exists in the dispute about free trade in media products. One side asserts cultural value and democratic functioning should not be sacrificed to the market, whereas the other sees no conflict (or argues economic trade-offs are as appropriate here as anywhere).

The rest of this chapter seeks to see what further light the lens of democratic theory can throw on the trade debate. I offer hesitant comments about this in the context of three questions. What has been at issue in the assertion about culture made by those objecting to a free-trade regime? Does democracy in fact *require* free trade in media products as an aspect of the goal of creating a global public sphere necessary to support global democracy? And if imports both create democratic problems and provide vital democratic resources for people in an importing country, what legal regime best responds to this dual quality?

## CULTURE

The normal framing of the media trade policy debate weighs pro-trade claims of economic efficiency against competing protectionist cultural claims. The preceding chapter rejected the pro-trade economic claims. Unfortunately, my discussion cannot do justice to the other side of the debate. "Culture" is rightfully described by Raymond Williams as "one of the two or three most complicated words in the English language."[5] This difficulty in coming to terms with culture reflects more than its ubiquitousness and plasticity[6] and the fact that culture takes different forms – high, ethnic, and popular, among others.[7] Rather the difficulty also reflects that different commentators use the word as a surrogate for very different concerns. Nevertheless, I want to suggest that in the trade debate, first, that the two sides do not effectively join issue in part because they implicitly adopt very different conceptions of culture. And, second, I suggest that democratic theory helps explain the reach and limit of the cultural claims as pressed by liberal advocates of trade restraints.

Many American representatives from the political sphere are hardly respectful of the cultural claim. U.S. Ambassador Carla Hills, for example, called the European quotas for television "blatantly protectionist[,] unjustifiable, and discriminat[ory]."[8] Similarly, U.S. Trade Representative Mickey Kantor characterized the Canadian cultural identity argument as an "excuse" to "protect the financial and economic viability of the Canadian industry."[9] In contrast, scholarly treatments sympathetic to the U.S. free-trade position typically recognize the presumptive legitimacy of the concern with cultural values,[10] although they too often then proceed to denigrate its significance.[11] More interestingly, a close reading of the literature reveals that these pro-trade scholars' implicit conception of culture typically differs from a second conception held by many defenders of national rights. Supporters of free trade typically invoke what I label a "museum," "commodity," or "artifact" conception of culture.[12] Given this conception, free-trade advocates are right to then question whether culture's value justifies trade restraints. Even as they quote and initially purportedly credit foreign claims, however, these scholars do not hear the protectionists' arguments or comprehend the different conception of culture they invoke.

In the artifact view, culture and cultural integrity are relatively static, largely *backward*-looking, and very much *content*-oriented. Cultural integrity involves preservation of the historical content. Undoubtedly, traditional cultural content often merits respect; it would be wrong as well as ungenerous to condemn many efforts at preservation or those who revere these contents.[13] Still, many historical cultures, especially their dominant forms, are vulnerable to severe criticisms. Their social use is also often problematic. Too often, elites manipulate these historical contents to deflect challenges to their rule, to justify historically developed forms of domination, and to stifle liberating change. In the extreme, preservation treats people as constituting a "living museum" in which the "natives" live as exhibits. Sectarian systems are kept pure. Aboriginals, Third World patriarchal cultures, and maybe even Frenchmen are seen as interesting "specimens."[14] Identifying culture with particular content invites the question of whether the culture is worth preserving – as illustrated by a critic of protectionism who, after implicitly asking this question, quoted Canadian "[a]rtists of the cultural industry . . . equat[ing] 'Canadian content' with 'crap.'"[15]

Free trade can threaten the museum contents – the existing historical collection of world cultures. Any liberal commentator, however, even if admitting that the loss of any people's culture impoverishes the world in some respects, must question the justness of forcing preservation when the bulk of the people would like to change, for example, by watching American television. Free-trade advocates observe that although some people within these societies gain by keeping their cultures roughly the way they are, others do not. Thus, the free-trade advocate properly asks how much freedom or wealth should be given up for preservation – how much oppression can be justified in culture's name. She asks who benefits and who pays, often with the implicit suggestion that certain elites benefit and members of the broader public, who are denied the imported cultural goods they want, pay.

Contrast this artifact conception with a second one, which I refer to as the "discourse" or "dialogic" conception of culture.* Discourse or

---

* The distinction is comparable to that made by Will Kymlicka discussed in Chapter 4. Kymlicka identifies two visions of "cultural community." A common view, which Kymlicka associated with communitarians and conservatives such as Lord Devlin – see Patrick Devlin, *The Enforcement of Morals* (New York: Oxford U. Press, 1965) – identifies culture with some specific content and treats it as inherently valuable to preserve. In contrast, Kymlicka argues that the liberal must recognize empirically that membership in a cultural community is often crucial for individual identity and enabling for individual agency. The (liberal) value of cultural community lies in its being a necessary context of choice. This value justifies efforts to maintain that community's distinct

dialogue makes participants, rather than content, central to culture. In discourse, it matters who the speaker and who the audience are. The speaker and audience typically struggle with the same concerns. The primary audience of a cultural product is other members of the speaker's community, although, as with public discourse, others can certainly listen and, if able, appreciate the discussion. Members' speech to other members of the community often is contextually specific, even if universal meanings can sometimes be found in the particulars. In contrast, content with an overtly universal orientation – the U discussed in the preceding chapter – is frequently devoid of much relevance for the cultural discourse. In this dialogic conception, culture is necessarily a living practice. Like all practice, discourses of identity and value require a context, which makes a cultural heritage crucial. Thus, this second conception treats culture as the integration of a specific heritage into a current behavioral discourse. Addition, development, and, sometimes, rejection of particular cultural content are inherent in this dialogic conception of culture.

Rather than preserving specific, backward-looking content, the relevant protectionist goal is to assure an adequate context for participation in cultural, social, and democratic dialogue and to provide resources needed for dialogic participation by all members of the cultural community. Protection of culture in this conception includes the goal of assuring that members of the cultural community have meaningful opportunities to be cultural "speakers."[†] Culture as dialogue emphasizes both a past as context and a present as an arena for affirming, critiquing, and transforming individual and collective identity. Democracy in any participatory sense involves popular self-determination of people's collective world. Thus, in his discussion of

---

vitality. But if serving "choice" is the cultural community's value, then the importance of providing for the existence of a context of choice cannot justify denying choice. Rather, members of a cultural community should have the right to be constantly changing the community's specific content. See Will Kymlicka, *Liberalism, Community, and Culture* (New York: Oxford U. Press, 1989), 168–70, 196.

[†] Any reader familiar with my prior work on freedom of speech will recognize a similarity. See, e.g., C. Edwin Baker, *Human Liberty and Freedom of Speech* (New York: Oxford U. Press, 1989); C. Edwin Baker, "Of Course, More Than Words," *University of Chicago Law Review* 61 (1994): 1181, reviewing Catharine A. MacKinnon, *Only Words* (1993). I have emphasized freedom of speech as an aspect of individual liberty – the right of a speaker to speak and a listener to listen to willing, protected speakers. This liberty focus can be contrasted with a marketplace of ideas theory in which content is crucial – in which "[w]hat is essential is not that everyone shall speak, but that everything worth saying shall be said." Alexander Meiklejohn, *Political Freedom* (New York: Oxford U. Press, 1965), 26.

the four values that he saw justifying freedom of speech, Thomas Emerson argued that one reason to protect speech freedom is because it is "essential to provide for participation in decision making by all members of society" a right that embraces "participating in the building of the whole culture."[16] Culture in this discourse sense is both a primary means and central result of democratic participation.

This discourse conception of culture is implicit in most defenses of a cultural exception to free-trade principles. It has been a constant, for instance, in Canada. As noted in the previous chapter, even in the 1920s a Canadian editorial by Frederick Paul argued that "[n]ational periodicals allow people in the different parts of [the country] to understand one another's viewpoints, which is the first step towards co-operation and the removal of grievances. . . . If we depend on the[] United States . . . for our reading matter we might as well move our government to Washington."[17] In the 1990s Raymond Chretien, the Canadian ambassador to the United States, saw the trade issue as centering on "the ability to maintain viable, home-grown cultural industries that tell us about ourselves."[18] A Canadian law that the WTO found to violate GATT prohibited Canadian advertisers from placing advertising directed toward Canadians in split-run (basically foreign) magazines.[19] In approving the law and rejecting the WTO analysis, Ted Magder, a Canadian-born communications scholar, explained that "the Canadian government made a choice between the speech rights of Canadian magazine publishers addressing Canadian readers, and the speech rights of Canadian advertisers."[20] Similarly, in describing the fundamental importance of the Canadian broadcasting system, former Canadian minister of communications Flora McDonald asserted that "[i]t plays a major role in defining our national, regional, local[,] and even our individual identities."[21] As Magder explained, "[m]ost of all, culture is an ongoing dialogue, a conversation about who we are and who we want to be."[22]

The Europeans have implicitly emphasized the same dialogic conception. In attempting to explain "the European mind," an American academic, although critical of the European Community's Television without Frontiers Directive,[23] noted that the Europeans resist total domination of market forces in part because of "the vital role broadcasting has played in the development of informed democratic political discourse."[24] French President François Mitterrand argued that the question raised by free trade "is the right of each country to *forge* its imagination and to *transmit* to future generations the representation of

252

its own identity."[25] "Forging" is an active, here an essentially dialogic process that, Mitterrand emphasized, must involve the people of the country. "Transmitting" does not imply forcing an artifact on future generations that they must then preserve, but rather giving them access to a heritage. The fact that culture is crucial to identity does not imply a need to preserve any specific cultural content. Rather, culture is required as a historically developed *context* in which those whose identity is at stake can draw upon and change. Moreover, "the right of each country" does not require (or arguably even permit) limits on the cultural possibilities considered by the participants. As a report of an international group of mostly ministers of culture from various countries indicated in 1998, the watchwords of cultural protectionists were pluralism, diversity, citizen opportunity, choice, creativity, and participation.[26] Similarly, the earlier Stockholm Action Plan of an Intergovernmental Conference on Cultural Policies for Development, assuming an attitude to culture very different from the commodity perspective promoted by the United States, states that "cultural goods and services [are] . . . not like other forms of merchandise," and emphasized the need for governments to support "the development of a local, creative and participatory cultural life and pluralistic management of diversity."[27] Illustrating a dialogic conception of culture, the Stockholm Plan implicitly emphasizes the desirability and necessity of people considering or forging identity in a grounded and internally accepted manner.

Cultural discourse arguably is distorted and its helpfulness to people is reduced to the extent that profit needs of market-oriented firms, rather than creative and normative impulses of human creators, determine its content. Note that this view of distortion does not assume that a culture has an essentially "right" content or a specific historical essence that merits preservation. Rather, the focus is on the integrity of the cultural process. The normative claim is that, whatever its evolving content, culture should reflect more the discourse of civil society and the lifeworld than the self-directed logic of the economic subsystem.[28] A properly "living culture" embodies judgments that grow out of people's own experiences and their efforts at self- and world-understanding. Critics of market influences claim that the market, in contrast, generates culture to serve its internal system needs – that is, profit maximization. More concretely, critics often conclude that the market mainly promotes commodified cultural content that celebrates materialist values. Properly designed forms of trade protectionism

(often also involving subsidies to domestic nonmarket cultural products) could help a country restrict this market colonization of culture
and empower less market-dominated bases of discourse. Thus, an international meeting of cultural ministers observed that "the production
and distribution of cultural works cannot be left to the marketplace
alone"; the Greek minister of culture argued that "some protection [is
needed] in order to respect and preserve political, aesthetic and ideological *liberalism*."[29]

International (and American) critics of U.S. media products regularly deplore their consumerist, individualist, and materialist orientation, as well as their cultural shallowness. As the preceding chapter
showed, these ideological tilts may be predictable economic consequences of producing media for international distribution. Under the
rubric of defending the importing country's domestic culture, "protectionists" may, in part, be resisting that particular ideological orientation. Still, this content-based objection is hardly the only ground to
defend domestic culture. The defense can reflect a view about the
appropriate discursive or internal process of national cultural life as
much or more than any claim about domestic cultural life's "superior"
content. Thus, Daniel Hallin implies the substantive content critique
when he notes "[t]he claim . . . that global cultural industries are
pushing all human cultures toward the culture of consumer capitalism."
However, he then relies on the process value of the dialogic conception
of culture when he treats as obvious "that issues of access, voice, the
representation of diverse social interests and the creation of dialogue
among them[] belong today at the forefront of the agenda for . . . media
politics."[30]

Trade restraints favoring domestic cultural industries are no panacea.
An international legal order that permits protectionism hardly
guarantees that a country will regulate to prevent the commercial
distortion or destruction of its own culture. At best, the protectionist
option allows and invites each country to struggle over the extent and
form of commercialization of its cultural spheres. The optimistic hope
is that, given this option, a country will then proceed to design an
optimal regulatory regime. The regime should seek to increase the
independence of diverse, domestic public spheres from both governmental and market distortions.

State regulatory regimes sometimes merely replace market distortion
with governmental distortion. However, a free-trade regime may do
little to alleviate this danger. Governments that would impose content

censorship presumably could do so on a geographically nondiscriminatory basis, thereby adhering to free-trade mandates. Some device other than free trade – in the United States, reliance is partially placed on the First Amendment – is needed to block censorious governmental distortions.

A free-trade regime, however, can seriously undermine the struggle to create less distorted, more robust public spheres. Free-trade rules may enable foreign commercialized media to overwhelm domestic non-commercialized media. They can also make subsidization much more expensive if it is allowed at all.[31] Moreover, as compared with international commercialization, even unimpeded domestic commercialization may be more responsive to internal needs and domestically salient issues. Domestic commercialization typically focuses on specifically domestic demand and embodies the background experience and interests of local people, who domestic firms are more likely than foreign media to employ to create content. Thus, both domestic nonmarket and domestic market media are likely to contribute to a "discursive" culture – that is, a dynamic reflection or meditation on identity and on collective problems, values, policies, and ambitions that is grounded in a particular heritage.

The policy implications of the dialogic conception of culture are very different from those of the artifact or museum view. Its goal is to maintain (or create) a dynamic local cultural discourse. This goal requires preserving (or creating) local cultural industries. It could justify both direct and indirect subsidies – for example, screen or broadcast percentage quotas providing guaranteed space for domestic products – as well as some discriminatory burdens on imports, especially burdens designed to enhance opportunities for domestic cultural products. Nevertheless, because the value of culture lies in its being a "context for choice," any categorical exclusion of imports should not be allowed. Exclusion would stunt discourse. Accordingly, a Canadian government advisory group, while proclaiming governmental policy objectives of developing "Canadian cultural content" and ensuring that it "is available to all Canadians," properly emphasized that this should be done "without limiting [Canadians'] access to foreign cultural products."[32]

In contrast, the artifact conception's aim is to preserve heritage. At most, it permits conforming additions that illuminate and maintain that heritage. Preservation could require fanatical protectionism. Exclusion of all "polluting" outside content would be necessary. Interestingly, this illiberal practice might be more comprehensible to free-trade advocates, who often attribute this goal to cultural protectionists, than to actual protectionists, who instead defend a national cultural discourse. Although contrary to free traders' interests, being a commodity pure of outside pollutants makes sense from a free traders' perspective of viewing culture as a potentially possessable and, thereby, salable content.[33] Conveniently for these free traders, however, the extremism of a purity goal – and the inevitable ineffectiveness of its implementation – make this notion very vulnerable to their critiques.

The museum or artifact conception of culture is constantly in evidence in free traders' arguments. Each of their five main critiques of a cultural exemption from trade agreements implicitly assumes the artifact conception but loses force against protectionists who value the dialogic conception. First, some commentators question the positive value and pedigree of "national" culture. Eli Noam, for example, argues that the emphasis on national culture is largely a nineteenth-century innovation used by elites to manipulate subject populations and to extract loyalty.[34] The primary beneficiaries of allegiance to national culture, he argues, are political elites who use it to prop up their rule by generating hostility and sometimes violence against outsiders. Noam's observations have obvious worth[35] and are related to why the merits of nationalism as a social phenomenon are a matter of continuing controversy. His objection has great force against particular conceptions and uses of a national culture – those that see it as a historical artifact and defend it against challenge. His historical observation, however, hardly amounts to an objection to protecting a historically grounded dialogic practice of a group of people, especially a juridical group, trying to make sense of themselves in a modern world. Nothing about the evils of nineteenth-century nationalism makes this dialogic cultural discourse problematic.

In any event, the imminent disappearance of either nation-states or nationalism is doubtful. (I here use "nation-state" as the equivalent of "sovereign country" and intend to imply nothing about the relation or lack of relation of "state" and "nation.") Although forms of participatory global politics may develop, for the foreseeable future any democratic politics will be grounded largely in independent sovereign states and in subgroups and subjurisdictions of these states. As long as this situation holds, the policy question should concern the necessary conditions for a "good" or "liberal" – that is, a more open and more democratic – nationalism. Surely these conditions include the preservation (or creation) of both national and local subgroup discourses.[36] This dialogic conception of culture discredits oppressive historical uses of national cultural politics. From this dialogic perspective, the issue becomes how to distinguish protectionism that supports an open and vibrant discourse from protectionism that undermines the discourse's openness and fairness.

Second, free-trade advocates often question the richness or depth of distinctly national culture. Their characterizations can reduce Canadian culture to two guys sitting before a map of Canada, talking about beer and hockey.[37] Given the multiplicity of nations and cultures in Europe, commentators similarly wonder whether the European Community's directive for individual countries to adopt minimum requirements for *European*-produced television can possibly be premised on a concern for domestic culture rather than merely on advantage for European cultural industries.[38] They observe that the directive still allows dominance by a few huge media conglomerates that can ignore the many specific cultures contained in Europe. Thus, Eli Noam suggests that the motives behind "[e]fforts to create a common European cultural front against Hollywood . . . have often been suspiciously economical."[39] Critics of protectionism question the reality of this European culture. They ask whether Spain actually has more in common culturally with Sweden than with Argentina.[40]

These criticisms assume culture as specific content – an object or artifact. The critics are right that a great deal of England's cultural content, including its language, is more like that in the United States than in Greece. A dialogic conception, however, answers these objections. If Europe hopes to forge governmental and other collective institutions in which people relate on grounds of equality and respect, then it needs to foster a European discourse. For that purpose, people in Greece *are* especially relevant to the British. The legitimacy of protecting a country's (or the European Community's) discourses against domination by global trade – the premise that allows legal protection of "European" culture – also authorizes additional domestic laws protecting Europe's many, more local, national cultures. Dialogues oriented to forging and understanding "national" identity (or identities), whatever the current depth of these identities, are crucial for a democratic political order.

Free-trade advocates' third claim argues that "[u]sing the nation as a cultural unit is to some extent arbitrary."[41] Protectionism makes little sense on cultural grounds because "[c]ulture is often more alien across social classes and age groups than across borders."[42] Cultures, such as youth culture or proletarian culture, provide many people with their central foci.[43] This point has considerable force descriptively. Still, here, the most immediate way the artifact and discourse conceptions diverge is their respective reaction to this descriptive point. As a matter of consumption items, as artifacts, the point seems right – with the youth culture becoming as global as Nike or popular music. As a matter of identifying cultural discourses requiring and meriting self-conscious nurture, the critique of the arbitrariness or accuracy of a national culture focus is more questionable. National and subnational cultures may not be intrinsically a more vital part of a person's life than various transnational categories. Nevertheless, the nation as a cultural unit is hardly arbitrary if the concern is the discourse of people living in the same area, especially people who potentially participate in the same political order and who are bound by the same laws. The nation can provide a central, grounded locus of dialogue about identity, values, and politics. Moreover, only national sovereignty authorizes market interventions to protect or enhance subgroup identity and dialogue as a means of supporting a meaningful pluralist or multicultural democracy. Thus, from a dialogic perspective – and certainly from the perspective of either republican or complex democracy – the importance of a national democratic discourse justifies resistance to automatic acceptance of free-trade rules.

Free-trade advocates also suggest that the protectionists' focus on the nation is arbitrary because ethnic culture does not track national borders.[44] Cultural integrity is an arbitrary value, they argue, because few cultures are pure; rather, specific cultures are themselves mixtures of other cultures.[45] W. Ming Shao's focus on culture as an artifact with particular content as opposed to a discourse is also evident in his complaint about the difficulty of "delineat[ing] a particular culture at a given time."[46] Again, this point has force only if the protectionists' concern is with the quality or purity of a museum culture, of some particular historical artifact. True, "any governmental trade measure aiming at cultural specificity [is arbitrary]."[47] The claim that "a Canadian from Toronto has more in common with a Bostonian than with someone from Alberta"[48] is surely right for some purposes – at least, for *some* people in Boston and Toronto. Nonetheless, even when they disagree, the Toronto *citizen* has much more in common with the person in Alberta if the issue is selecting a prime minister and probably if the issue is considering relations with the First Nations peoples, determining whether health insurance is a national or regional issue, or deciding how to relate to the United States. In other words, the Toronto and Alberta residents have in common the issues themselves. They have in common that the answers to these issues pertain to them both. If Canada is to exist as a country, it almost certainly is more important for the person from Toronto to hear the views of people from Alberta and Quebec than from people in Boston.[49] The crucial concern is with the maintenance and quality of a participatory discourse – the heart of pluralist, republican, or complex democracy.

Free traders' fourth criticism is that even if cultural integrity is worth protecting, protectionist measures are generally ill-designed to achieve that goal.[50] From the museum view of culture, this objection is correct. The European Community's local-content requirement, for example, may be "entirely ineffective at encouraging programs produced in Europe or elsewhere that promote European culture."[51] American programming, such as an American documentary on European art, "may promote European culture more than European programs."[52] Thus, the local content requirement appears to relate more to employ-ment than to meaningful cultural content. This criticism, however, clearly assumes a concern with "content" rather than with "discourse." For example, a quality American film on the French Revolution could contribute more as an accessible representation of French history, even for the French, than a French knock-off of an American game show.[53] European television quotas that advantage the latter over the former seem particularly ill-suited for preserving historically French culture. From the perspective of preserving space for people engaged in a national discourse, however, the rules make sense even if the quality of the resulting discourse is sometimes questionable (and often questioned).

Fifth, protectionism purportedly encourages parochialism in a country's cultural industries, whereas free trade allegedly allows these domestic industries to show the world their quality as well as to induce them to produce more popular, and hence more desirable, material, which they then can sell to the world.[54] Although Chapter 10 casts con-siderable doubt on the economic plausibility of this recommendation, the point here is the recommendation assumes that the value of culture lies in the universal appeal of its content rather than in its appeal to and use by domestic audiences. If cultural value lies specifically in members of a national community speaking to other members, which is the claim of the discourse theory, the proposal is unhelpful. *Even if* free trade enabled or induced a nation to export plenty of cultural goods, this very effect of free trade could itself contribute to an impoverishment of domestic cultural dialogue if it caused the nation's cultural industry to change its content to compete better internationally but to speak less directly or subtly to domestic audiences.

Thus, free-trade advocates purport to recognize the protectionists' concern for culture. The two groups, however, mostly talk about very different things – a museum or artifact culture on the one hand and a dialogic culture on the other. Unsurprisingly, the two conceptions of culture have very different policy implications. As particular content, cultural products are ultimately valued or disvalued because of good or bad features of their content. Protection of culture under this museum or artifact conception requires rules that block outside content or at least limit its availability sufficiently to prevent successful challenges to a country's traditional cultural content. To serve their purpose, protectionist policies would have to be draconian and, even then, are likely to fail. In this approach, not only is protection of culture often contrary to many people's desires (the economic objection to protectionism), it is inherently contrary to any open, participatory form of democracy and popular choice. Free traders are correct that, historically, some authoritarian – often sectarian – regimes have tried to protect or promote culture as conceived here, although usually not only with censorious import restrictions but also with equally severe internal limits on expressive freedoms. More important, free traders are right to object to the elitism that this conception supports.

The free traders' critique, however, misses the point from the perspective of the dialogic conception. Here, the cultural concern is with protecting internal creative and discursive processes as well as the conceptual resources that a local heritage makes available for such processes. The key policy implication is the need to maintain and nourish domestic media. Outside content cannot be excluded, however. It too can contribute usefully to local discursive processes about national and subgroup identities and relate to people's social and political needs. Given this goal, the often-observed fact that countries seldom have a pure or monolithic culture does not support – indeed, is not even relevant to – the critique of trade restrictions. Rather, from the discourse view, border restraints are legitimate if they help to protect diverse internal sources from decimation without excluding outside content. From the perspective of complex democracy, intelligent democratic media policy probably also requires institutions, policies, and subsidies to support nonmarket communications helpful to subgroups' self-understanding and their participation within the country's overall cultural and political processes. Unrestricted international free trade could block some policies to promote both national and subgroup public spheres that rely heavily on local products. Moreover, by reducing the ranks of people employed in domestically oriented media production, competition from global media products could undermine the economic viability of participation by professional communicators – writers, journalists, film producers – in national discourses. In other words, if the target were as they conceive it, many of the free traders' objections to cultural protectionism are well taken, but their arrows completely miss most protectionists' legitimate concerns.

## AN INTERNATIONAL PUBLIC SPHERE?

A reader might suspect that I am skeptical of international trade specifically and globalization generally. I am. But that skepticism is not the point here or in the preceding chapter. All the economic and democratic arguments here have been media-specific. These arguments have related to special, identifiable aspects of media products that could justify restraints even given general approval of free-trade principles. Still, critics may argue that especially my democratic analysis is antiquated in its focus on existing sovereign states. Many astute observers conclude that globalization – the code word of the 1990s – is inevitable. If so, the following quite plausible, *media-specific* argument *may favor* free trade:[55]

1. Economic globalization is already a fact and is rapidly expanding. The major economic players today are multinational corporations that produce tremendous wealth and tremendous profits. With more revenue than most nation-states' domestic products, these multinational corporations are owned and operated internationally.
2. As the United States discovered a century ago with respect to domestic trusts and corporate giants, unregulated economic entities often turn lawless. Even when they do not, they often exercise power in socially disastrous ways, ranging from their treatment of labor to their effect on the environment (as well as their corruption of democratic politics).

261

3. Therefore, only legal regulation coming from government, preferably a democratic government, can successfully limit these disas-
   ters and channel corporate power into more benign uses.
4. These multinational corporations' power and their capacity to
   exploit the opportunities of international markets have nevertheless left traditional nation-states with increasingly little room to
   maneuver in performing regulatory or even traditional welfare-
   state tasks. In many respects, these corporations are the world's
   new sovereigns.
5. Given these multinationals' power, enhanced by the mobility of
   capital, to evade nation-states' regulations and to make most
   attempts to regulate disastrous for the regulating country, the
   world today vitally needs global governmental bodies with the
   reach and power to monitor, regulate, and control global corporations and global capital. To some extent these global bodies are
   already taking shape, albeit usually as bodies of experts with little
   democratic or popular control.
6. This nondemocratic aspect of evolving global bodies is troubling.
   A partial solution might be greater transparency. Still, transparency is hardly enough if bodies, such as the World Bank, the
   International Monetary Fund, or the World Trade Organization,
   feel free to do largely as they wish despite public exposure. In
   any event, any believer in democracy and self-government must
   favor global political structures that are more democratically
   responsive.
7. Just as public spheres are absolutely crucial for nation-state
   democracies, a global public sphere where public opinion is developed and brought to bear on "democratic will formation"[56] is
   absolutely essential for any global democracy.[57]
8. The mass media are possibly the most crucial institutional
   element of the modern national public sphere. The need for
   global public spheres implies the need for global media and
   global circulation of media. Thus, as compared with other trade
   restraints, restrictions on trade and the international operations
   of the mass media and the "cultural industries" are especially
   objectionable.

There is force to this argument. To begin, I find unassailable the
points about the extent and dangers of global capitalism and the need
to subject it to democratic political control. Nevertheless, two main

weaknesses in the overall argument should lead to rejecting its final conclusion. The first criticism relates to the fourth and fifth points about the inadequacy of traditional governments and the necessity, as well as possibility, of global democratic bodies. The second criticism questions whether even the goal of global democratic bodies served by appropriate public sphere(s) implies the eighth point, regarding the desirability of avoiding national restraints on trade in media products.

Certainly, a democrat can be sensibly pessimistic about the near-term prospects for an effective and democratic world government. Working to improve the long-term chances of such a government is surely a possible goal. More immediately, worthy efforts, ranging from the use of new communications technologies such as the Internet to participation in street demonstrations, can be directed toward empowering popular input into international decision making and toward creating more populist or democratic international institutions and agencies. Still, given reasonable grounds for pessimism about if, when, and the extent to which these efforts will bear fruit, a more immediate political strategy may be to work to maintain and increase the power of nation-states to control multinational corporations, especially as these corporations operate in or affect that nation-state.

Although the structural capacity of multinational corporations to move jobs and capital across borders may inevitably limit national power, continual invocations of this disempowerment of nation-states can become a defeatist self-fulfilling prophecy. The room for nation-states to maneuver may depend significantly on political will within the state. Of course, this political will is itself often blunted by multinational corporations' domestic political power, the bases of which range from general ideological dominance to huge campaign contributions as well as their often legally unrestrained capacity to threaten (or promise) economic acts, such as moving capital and jobs. Still, multinational corporations' political power is unlikely to be any less influential within currently possible international bodies. Rather, the more democratic structure of nation-states should make resistance easier there. Opposition to misbehavior by multinational corporations and opposition to their ideological hegemony can be a crucial part of partisan domestic politics. This politics should aim at slowing down the evisceration of national sovereignty, except when the reduction serves democratic principles, such as grants of power to international bodies to protect human rights, or when the reduction serves other democratically determined interests.

This strategy calls for selective opposition to trade agreements. And it calls for demands for treaties to include elements empowering local forces such as labor or environmentalists. My claim is that this strategy also requires demands for provisions to protect domestic media. This general position has been pushed by many progressive activists in the United States and Canada over the past decade, as illustrated by their reservations about or opposition to NAFTA or the Multilateral Agreement on Investment. In fact, one of the major political defeats of President Clinton's second term related to his request in 1997 for fast-track trade authority relating primarily to the planned Multilateral Agreement on Investment. The effective, and to the mainstream press, surprisingly strong, opposition – especially of labor, but also environmentalist and other activist groups – stemmed not from general opposition to international trade but rather from objections regarding the undemocratic manner in which they saw it being structured.[58] For those conscious of this battle, the huge demonstrations and activist workshops in Seattle in December 1999, which again took most of the press and the political elites by surprise, were entirely predictable.

It may be that many functions of local democracy eventually will be replaced by global democratic institutions. This does not contradict the conclusion that the best *current* political strategies require opposition to any international changes that weaken currently existing domestic democracy. If so, this approach means avoiding any policy that would weaken domestic public spheres and the media on which they depend. Of course, a major claim of this chapter is that free trade in media or cultural products is such a policy.

If the first objection is largely pragmatic, the second is more theoretical. It accepts the democratic aspiration for global democratic governmental bodies and recognizes their dependence on appropriate public spheres. These premises, however, do not lead automatically to the eighth point, that the ideal of global democracy is best furthered by a regime of international free trade in media products. It may not even imply the seventh point, that the most needed public spheres, other than that of the "strong" public within the global parliament itself, are themselves global in dimension.[‡] Without a doubt, global democ-

---

[‡] As used here, a "strong public" refers to a more institutionalized group capable not only of deliberation but also of reaching determinative decisions that have some force – will formation – such as legislation. A "weak public" is less formal, allows basically unrestricted entry, engages in deliberation and a search for the better argument, but has output that takes the form of "public opinion," not law.

racy requires global circulation of information for intelligent opinion formation about issues. This circulation may be adequately achieved in a world with considerable trade restraints in the media field, especially if censorship is prohibited, as required by basic human rights norms. Global circulation of information can result from practices of international news services and from local media's collection of and editing of globally available information using technologies ranging from the mail to the Internet as well as through the local media's own correspondents. It can also result from commercial entry of foreign media, which restrictive trade law would still permit even though the entry could be burdened, and from noncommercial circulation of information, as promoted by nongovernmental organizations (NGOs). In comparison with likely global media, strong domestic media may do as well or better in promoting public awareness and discussion of globally relevant information. Certainly, global democracy and global public spheres do not require the leveling of cultural differences or the merging of cultures any more than national public spheres require this leveling within the multiethnic nation-state.[59]

As suggested in Part II, unadorned reliance on markets has been inadequate for the public spheres democratically required by traditional nation-states. Democracy within a country is better served by appropriate government interventions in the media order. This need to deviate from pure reliance on trade is likely to be equally true in any global democracy. This conclusion, of course, leaves open the question of whether a global democratic government itself (when such an entity exists) or smaller political units, specifically, nation-states (as long as they continue to exist), will best be able to formulate appropriate interventions. In any event, instinctive reliance on free trade hardly seems appropriate.

Both the type of needed interventions and the level of government best able to design and implement these interventions can be informed by a consideration of the nature of the public sphere(s) that would best serve a global democracy. Obviously, no global discourse can meaningfully involve all individuals within a single discourse. The physical capacity of the Internet, or any other version of a global public sphere, has little to do with the limited number of people who can meaningfully interact in an actual single discussion. Part II's discussion of complex democracy becomes important here. Meaningful discourse within a single state – whether a multicultural state or a state divided by class, gender, race, or religion – requires that subgroups first be able to engage in internal discourses to formulate their own visions. Subgroups must then be able to present those visions powerfully in negotiations with other groups that have different visions as well as in discourses of self-understanding and justice with governing bodies and the rest of society. The same surely is true within a global democracy. Any absence of well-developed group discourses leaves the overarching public sphere open to easy domination by elites, whether corporate, technical, or governmental. Within nation-state democracies, a major defect of the market is its empirical failure to provide adequate media for the discourse and political functions of the otherwise marginalized subgroups of society – failure to provide for what Nancy Fraser calls "subaltern counterpublics."[60]

This problem is likely to be the same or worse on the global stage under conditions of free trade. Even groups that have not previously been marginalized domestically will likely be marginalized under conditions of global free trade. Thus, for a global democracy to represent anything other than domination by powerful elites requires protection of counterpublics and subpublics from the ravages of free trade. The composition of these subpublics will be diverse, encompassing subaltern groups within an individual country and labor, social movement, and ethnic groups that cross national boundaries. A major focus, however, will be on nourishing general public spheres of smaller *political* entities, especially of the smaller or developing nation-states.[61] This requires that they be able to resist free trade when needed. Similarly, interventions by these states are likely to be the best hope for nourishing their smaller internal subgroups. In other words, global democracy requires national capacity to restrain and supplement free trade precisely in the ways called for here – interventions designed to assure vigorous domestic media serving national, cultural, and political discourse functions.

## WEAK PROTECTIONISM AND HUMAN RIGHTS

Part III has argued that free trade will not provide the media products that people in various countries desire or that their democracies require. As a consequence, governments will need to intervene in ways that violate free-trade principles. This conclusion by itself does not indicate what type of interventions are needed. Trade certainly provides access to media content valuable to both consumers and citizens. Consequently, some forms of protectionism surely could be worse than free trade. The policy goal should be to identify the types of interventions that would be appropriate and, even better, to devise ways for the international legal order to increase the prevalence of these good interventions while reducing the occurrence of objectionable forms of protectionism.

In thinking about this issue, Oliver Goodenough makes a useful distinction. He contrasts "strong protection," which has an exclusionary goal, with "weak protection," which is designed to promote choice by keeping domestic products in existence.[62] When he eventually condemns cultural protectionism, he clearly means strong protectionism, as evidenced by his continued defense of the propriety of weak protection, such as subsidies intended to preserve choice.[63]

Both this and the preceding chapter parallel Goodenough in condemning strong protection while recognizing a useful role for weak protection. Weak protectionism can serve culture and democracy when culture is conceived of as a context of choice. In contrast, strong protectionism contradicts this democratic reason for valuing culture. Only the museum conception of culture justifies the exclusions required by strong protection. Similarly, an economic focus on providing consumers with what they want can hardly justify strong protectionism's exclusion of media products that consumers clearly wish to receive. It can, however, justify weak protectionism's concern with properly pricing imports and with rules designed to ensure the continued availability of valued local cultural materials. Each section of Chapter 10 described circumstances in which "free" markets would fail to maximally provide for people's media preferences. The obvious policy recommendation is to provide the desired products – hence the propriety of subsidies. Still, other, more complex policies may be even more useful and economically justified. Sometimes, consumers might be better off, on balance, with trade restrictions that cause them to get fewer imported media products if the result is that they get more products that they value more but otherwise would not obtain. Trade restrictions can also produce net benefits if they burden media imports either that have significantly more negative than positive externalities or that have a worse balance of positive and negative externalities than the domestic products they replace. In a sense, the trade burden requires consumers to pay for some of the negative externalities and competitively advantages media products that have more positive externalities. Neither subsidies nor these limited impact restrictions are designed to be exclusionary, and they are unlikely to be so in practice. These policies attempt to expand or empower choice and, thus, do not fit the notion of strong protection. In fact, given that weak protectionism and *only* weak protectionism seems justifiable, it might be surprising if a democracy ever attempts anything else.

Thus, Goodenough's categories are fine. The difficulty comes with their interpretation and implementation. For example, Goodenough treats many Canadian policies as involving strong protectionism, especially the Canadian tariff's flat prohibition on importing split-run magazines[64] and the 80 percent tax on Canadian advertising in those split-run magazines printed in Canada.[65] Like most American commentators, Goodenough seems ready to sign on to the 1997 decision by the WTO declaring that Canada's provisions violated GATT.[66]

This characterization of the tariff prohibition and the advertising tax is wrong. Canada did not try to exclude any foreign magazines, that is, magazines printed and sold outside Canada. Imports were welcomed. Rather, the tariff only required that when magazines come in, the magazines have basically the same advertising that they had when sold in other national markets or, more precisely, that the magazines not have different advertisements "directed to a market in Canada."[67] This requirement is hardly an attempt to keep out foreign ideas or foreign magazines. Instead, its obvious purpose was "to ensure that Canadian [and Canadian-oriented] advertising expenditures support Canadian magazines."[68] In that sense, the tariff was a legal arrangement designed to get Canadians, specifically Canadian businesses that advertise, to subsidize Canadian magazines – a clear example of weak protectionism.

These measures to get Canadian advertisers to subsidize Canadian magazines could be vital to the survival of Canadian magazines. Advertising provides about 60 percent of Canadian magazine revenue.[69] Canadian magazines' reported operating profit is 2.5 percent of revenues (compared with 12 percent for U.S. magazines).[70] The Canadian Magazines Publishers Association has "estimated that the entire magazine industry's profits could be wiped out completely with only a [3 percent] shift in [Canadian advertising] dollars to American publications."[71] According to a Canadian government task force, allowing the U.S. split-run magazines to include advertising directed at their Canadian readers could reduce advertising revenue for Canadian magazines by almost 40 percent.[72] This predicted decline is similar to the 40 percent of total Canadian magazine advertising revenue captured by Canadian editions of American magazines around 1960 before the adoption of protectionist measures.[73] Small wonder that observers suggest that implementing the WTO decision is likely to be devastating for Canadian magazines. At various times in the past, without protection, American magazines have held roughly 80 percent of the Canadian market.[74] In 1992, a time when laws were in effect that aimed not at keeping American magazines out but at keeping them from taking advertising away from Canadian magazines, Canadian magazines obtained more than two-thirds of the Canadian circulation.[75]

Canadian magazines potentially can make crucial contributions to the Canadian political order in ways valued by all theories of democracy and to Canadian discourses of identity valued at least by republican and complex theories. These magazines potentially represent precisely the type of product that this chapter argues is central for a dialogic conception of culture and that Chapter 10 argues may fail competitively even though it produces positive externalities and even though it is more valued by consumers than the import that replaces it. That is, experience shows that these domestic magazines often will fail, but not because Canadian audiences will not purchase them if American magazines are available; they will lose out competitively because of price. If American and not Canadian magazines receive the subsidy provided by Canadian advertising dollars, then the Canadian magazines will be priced too high, relative to the American ones, for the Canadian magazines to succeed. Canada's attempt to ensure that Canadian advertising goes to Canadian magazines, however, does not and is not intended to exclude imports. Rather, the Canadian law attempts to divert the subsidy to Canadian magazines. This subsidy is justifiable weak protectionism. Canada's view that its advertisers are a resource that should support Canadian media products is hardly unreasonable. Nevertheless, not only did the panel and appellate body of the WTO find that the Canadian effort violates GATT provisions, but Goodenough also concluded that it is exclusionary. Why did they all go wrong?

This question points to my final suggestion. Professional orientations of trade law practitioners are likely to tilt toward more commodified analyses. After all, commodification is the premise of trade. Given this orientation, these trade law practitioners are likely to focus on a law's effect on commodity exchange. They are likely to attribute unacceptably protectionist purposes to regulatory policies even when other important, legitimate justifications exist for such policies.[76] Predictably, trade law practitioners will misapply even properly formulated trade principles to make them more restrictive of national sovereignty in the media context than is desirable, just as Goodenough misapplied his useful notion of strong protectionism. If this bias is a regular feature of practice within a trade law regime, the question is whether there is any way for the legal order to do better. Despite the real evils of strong protectionism, possibly the best hope of most often getting justifiable results is to leave all decisions related to media products solely to national discretion – that is, to exempt cultural materials from all free-trade agreements. The contrary approach, applying free-trade rules to media products, is, in practice, likely to prevent democratic countries from adopting economically and democratically justified regulatory programs more often than it would thwart objectionably strong protectionism.

An even better option would be to develop international law principles that allow domestic regulation of trade in media products but block at least the worst cases of strong protectionism. As noted, strong protectionism has no economic or democratic legitimacy despite its allure for undemocratic authoritarian or traditional elites. The international norms that strong protectionism most obviously violates, however, are not economic ones, but rather are human rights principles concerning freedom of information. In fact, strong protectionism usually aims to exclude what a regime considers "impure" communications. Pursuit of that goal, however, usually avoids offense to free-trade principles because it is best accomplished by content-based censorship that applies equally to domestic and foreign media goods. As to such a law free-trade principles would be irrelevant. Instead, the global community would need to use international human rights law, not trade law, to identify impermissible national burdens or restraints on imported media products. In many respects this result parallels the American use of the First Amendment to forbid objectionable restrictions on communications while allowing governmental structural regulation of the communications industries.

This human rights strategy admittedly creates serious strategic dangers. Internally in the United States, corporate media firms regularly try to pervert First Amendment doctrine to protect their economic interests. If human rights law were effective globally, corporate media interests would predictably try to appropriate it for their own purposes.

History suggests such an attempt will occur. During the late 1970s and early 1980s, UNESCO studied national and world media structures from the perspective of serving the legitimate interests of all nations. This effort culminated in the MacBride Commission Report,[77] written under the leadership of Sean MacBride, an Irish diplomat, a Nobel Peace Prize winner and, as the American press often noted, a Lenin Peace Prize winner. As noted earlier, this report and UNESCO's focus on communications structures became possibly the main reason for the U.S. withdrawal from UNESCO in 1985. But what was the problem? One non-American commentator correctly observed, "not a single paragraph in all the NWICO [New World Information and Communication Order] resolutions included restrictions or censorship for Western mass media, and . . . both the Mass Media Declaration and the resolution of the MacBride Report reaffirmed the principle of freedom of information as a basic human right."[78] An equally accurate summary description of the MacBride Commission Report, given in a law review comment, is that it "advocated the elimination of governmental interference and censorship, the decentralization of the mass media, high standards of professionalism for journalists, and a better balance in the contents and coverage of mass media reporting."[79]

Look at that summary again. Surely, such a report should delight anyone committed to a free press and a sound communications order. So what did the author of this summary conclude? Without reference to any language in the report, he stated that a "proposal based on the MacBride Report's recommendations conflicts with both the First Amendment and international standards because a major component of such a proposal involves governmental control over the flow of information and ideas."[80] This misguided evaluation might be merely the fantasy of a confused, young law student. But it is not. Also without textual reference to anything within the MacBride Report, Leonard J. Theberge, chair of the American Bar Association Section of International Law's Committee on International Communications, described the Third World view purportedly represented by the report as one in which "the state has a duty . . . to censor incoming and outgoing news."[81] He accused the MacBride Commission and UNESCO of "deviat[ing] from earlier international legal precepts based on protecting individual rather than governmental rights."[82] To prove his point about earlier precepts from which the MacBride Report purportedly deviates, Theberge quotes language, which he approves, from Article 19 of the Universal Declaration of Human Rights.[83] He inexplicably fails to note that the language he quotes is virtually identical to language in Conclusion 3 of the MacBride Report, which asserts that "communication is a basic individual right" and that "[f]reedom of information – and, more specifically the right to seek, receive and impart information – is a fundamental human right."[84]

An article prepared under the direction of Sarah Goddard Power, a deputy assistant secretary in the State Department, echoed Theberge's points and emphasized that the United States "strongly oppose[s]" some of the eighty-two recommendations.[85] Elsewhere, James Buckley, under secretary of state for security assistance, science, and technology, is described as seeing "NWICO as a serious threat to First Amendment values."[86] Newspapers in the United States exhibited the same hostility. The six-week Belgrade UNESCO conference that considered the MacBride Commission Report mostly engaged in extensive work in a vast array of other areas. The National News Council found that American newspaper coverage of the conference completely ignored all of this work except that the newspapers contained 173 news stories and 181 editorials on the debate over communications policy. All the editorials expressed apprehension, with 158 being strongly hostile and the other 23 critical but moderate in tone; the news reports generally were edited to reinforce the editorial perspective.[87]

This vilification by the State Department and Bar Association leaders and misreporting by the media might be hard to understand if First Amendment values, which the MacBride Commission Report largely embodied, were the critics' real concern. The American objection, however, may have had little to do with censorship. Apparently more troubling to the critics was the MacBride Commission's conclusion that, in many parts of the world, governments would need to play a significant role in promoting a better communications order. Curiously, none of these critics appear to note that this is precisely what the United States did in the late eighteenth and nineteenth centuries by using the postal service to provide major subsidies to newspapers, with the subsidies designed to help structure the industry in a manner that purposefully favored certain types of newspapers and, thereby, certain types of content.[88] Indeed, the United States and virtually all democratic countries continue expensive state efforts to enhance the quality of the communications order.

American commentators found especially objectionable the MacBride Commission Report's recommendation that "in expanding communication systems, preference should be given to non-commercial forms of mass communication" and suggesting that "public funds might be made available for this purpose," as they are for education.[89] Of course, this recommendation looks little different than a national policy in Britain to expand the British communications system by creating the British Broadcasting Corporation[90] or little different than tax exemptions for nonprofits given in the United States. The American Bar Association representative Leonard Theberge condemned the MacBride Commission Report for having a "clear bias against private sector involvement in communications,"[91] although no portion of the Report suggested any limitations on the freedom of privately owned media. As evidence of this purported bias, Theberge instead cited a statement by UNESCO Director General M'Bow, who commented that " 'an increasing concentration of media in the hands of a few private or public enterprises' is a major issue."[92] The U.S. Department of State likewise considered the same statement to be a "major troublesome aspect of the [UNESCO] Director-General's comments."[93] I assume it is troublesome because the U.S. State and Commerce Departments favor media concentration,[94] despite its undemocratic nature and its conflict with First Amendment principles.[95] For example, the State Department's Sarah Goddard Power called further attempts to decentralize the media simply "unacceptable to the U.S."[96]

What happened? Probably the best assessment is that the U.S. response to NWICO was totally captured by an intersection of corporate interests and Cold War fears. The United States seemed to equate corporate interests – free trade and commercial dominance – with the meaning of the First Amendment and international human rights. Corporate interests and the U.S. government opposed the possibility that noncommercial media elsewhere in the world would receive substantial public support or that antitrust-like principles or other laws would restrict commercial media's unfettered rule. Similar attempts to characterize human rights as pro-market or pro-corporate are likely to recur. Attempts, however, do not mean success. In the past, American corporate media argued unsuccessfully that applying general labor laws or antitrust laws to the press entities violates the First Amendment.[97] They regularly made similar claims in litigation against *media-specific* structural regulation, but those arguments also routinely failed before the Supreme Court.[98] Although commercial media interests undoubtedly will invoke international human rights law as the basis to oppose trade restrictions designed to support local media, the challenge should fare no better than it did when based on the First Amendment in the Supreme Court. On the other hand, when national legislation really is exclusionary and censorious, human rights law is the proper field of dispute. Challenges to such legislation should prevail, although their success may require considerable development of the effective force and reach of international human rights law.

Thus, my suggestion is that human rights law, unlike trade law, provides a legal context likely to lead interpreters to be sensitive both to countries' need to nourish their own media and to the human rights mandate that countries not isolate their citizens from diverse viewpoints and troublesome ideas. Reliance on human rights law might even have a positive side effect. Given the prospect of multinational media corporations operating on the world stage, it would be a happy event if the structure of the legal order made corporate interests more dependent on a fuller, more effective development of international human rights law than on further invocations of trade law that simply enlarge the rule of multinational capital.

## TRADE AND PRINCIPLE

The U.S. willingness to stand up for principle in the new global order is good. Although free trade in media products obviously provides great benefits for American media businesses, most American advocates of free trade see their position as based on principle – giving consumers access to the communication and cultural products they desire and promoting the free flow of information that is fundamental to human rights. On closer inspection, Chapter 10 concludes that the first, essentially economic argument is wrong in its economics. Chapter 11 concludes that the second, democratic claim assumes a naive conception of the relation of media and democracy. Applying free-trade rules to media products often would thwart both consumers and citizens – both those located around the globe and those in the United States.

Chapter 11 also suggests that the American position often attributes to foreign advocates of protectionist measures a commodified rather than a discourse conception of culture, improperly portraying these foreign advocates as elitist rather than democratic. This attribution was both self-serving and ideological. It allowed American advocates to avoid the real and principled bases of the protectionist position. Legitimate principle calls here not for strict free trade, but rather for limited forms of protectionism and for support of a different body of law – international human rights law – to address concerns about censorship. Continued American insistence on strict free-trade rules in the area of cultural products would make the United States into an international bully, not a world leader in the realm of freedom of expression.

# Conclusion

Jerome Barron used the title of a superb book to ask a key question: "Freedom of the Press for Whom?"[1] Although possibly intended to be rhetorical, supplying a meaningful answer to this question is not that simple. In a rant against corporate control of the media "debasing democracy," Ronnie Dugger asserted that constitutional law had been "perverted" by "entrenched corporate seizures of the First Amendment." According to Dugger, it is the "reporter, for the dissemination of whose work the press is supposed to be free."[2] A journalist himself, Dugger's answer to Barron's question probably represents the view of many journalists. That may be a better answer than the alternative he considered, corporate owners, but the answer is not adequate. Whether the First Amendment gives journalists any special privileges is a very debated and controversial issue. But assuming, as I do, that it does and should and that it does and should protect media entities in ways that it does not protect other business entities, the reason cannot be because journalists can rightfully claim a class of citizenship denied other people or that media entities are valuable in themselves. Special privileges for journalists or the media make sense, if at all, because the press serves particularly important functions in society and that granting these special privileges (whether constitutionally or policy based) increases the likelihood that the press will be able to successfully serve those functions. We can and should value individuals in themselves, each as uniquely valuable and meriting certain fundamental rights – among them rights of free expression and of respect for their equality and dignity. In contrast, institutions, like the press, are human creations. Any secular conclusion is that they should be valued only for how they serve human needs and values. So a better answer to Barron's question might be, as Barron intended: "freedom of the press is for the people."

Unfortunately, that answer is also inadequate – too imprecise or underdeveloped for guidance. What does "for the people" mean? What are the people's rights relative to the press? People play different roles, for example, both those of consumers and citizens. Good arguments can be made that the press should be "for" the people in both roles. Part I argued that the market did not adequately provide for people in the first role. Generally, in our and most other democracies, people believe that economic entities ought to benefit the people. If they do not now provide well, legislative interventions intended to improve matters are possible and are little constrained by the Constitution. But interventions are not so unconstrained in the media context. Smokestack pollution can be prohibited but intellectual pollution cannot be. Thus, this *consumer* notion of "for the people" does not lead unambiguously to the First Amendment. It does not explain why the Constitution would, as it does, constrain Congress when acting as the people's agent in regulating the press.

The other answer – a press freedom is "for the people" as citizens – is more promising. Many constitutional provisions merely set up the structure of government and, in a sense, carry out various housekeeping tasks. The Constitution, for example, determines the number, minimum age, and term length of members of the House. In addition to these setting-up-government tasks, other provisions provide guarantees or protections for fundamental individual rights, which I just suggested is not the key to the Press Clause because it refers generally to collective entities such as newspapers or broadcasters, not to individuals. Finally, some provisions are designed to make the structure work both better and more legitimately. Provisions specifying a separation of powers and federalism fit this rubric. Building on the observation that a free press is almost universally recognized as an essential element of democracy, a "fourth estate," the Press Clause should be interpreted in a manner directed to furthering the legitimacy and effectiveness of democratic government. In that respect, the Press Clause can be seen as crucially "for the citizen." So the answer seems to be: "the press" is for the people. The institution's freedom is valued for its contribution to the people in both their roles as consumers and citizens. However, the constitutional guarantee of "freedom of the press" is for the citizen.*

---

* This framework combines the insights of Parts I and II of this book. The two notions – that the press is for the people but that the constitutional guarantee is added for the citizen – suggest,

But what does this mean? "For the citizen" is still inadequate as guidance. Barron apparently had an answer. One of his objectives was to claim a right of access for people outside the media to have their statements printed or broadcast, at least in certain circumstances. That would be one way for the freedom to be "for" the people. But press freedom could also be "for" the people if the Constitution protected the press's independence against outsiders – the government or self-anointed publicists – if rights for these outsiders would interfere with the press's capacity to provide properly for the people as recipients of communications. Citizens have different roles: as participatory speakers or as readers, listeners, and potential voters needing to be informed. It is not clear for which of these roles the Constitution protects the press. Only the second interpretation leads to Dugger's claim – that, in practice, the protection is for the journalist. Press freedom is ultimately protected *for* the benefit of the citizen but concretely it is the *journalist's freedom* that needs constitutional protection.

Even this relatively conventional answer is insufficient in two ways. First, it ignores the problem of identifying the conditions under which even dedicated journalists will be able to perform their professional democratic role. And the answer ignores the issue of what government actions or market structures threaten these conditions. As Part I emphasized, good media content depends not just on dedication and skill of journalists or other media professionals and on the absence of government censorship. It also depends on resources and directives of owners. Journalists and editors produce less when unemployed! And when employed, the market or ideological interests can lead owners to distort or restrict the assignments they give editors or journalists, thereby distorting or restricting the content that editors and journalists deliver and, in a sense, limiting their freedom. The same is true for cultural media. Thus, an obvious question is whether the freedom of the press requires, permits, or prohibits government structural interventions to promote journalists' and editors' freedom and protect the freedom from private threats.

Assume, as I argued in Chapter 9, that the answer to this question is that freedom of the press at least permits if it does not require such structural interventions. Still, the question of specifically what needs to

first, that government interventions that undermine the press's democratic role are ruled out. However, both the theory of democracy and the goal of serving people as both consumers and citizens should then guide other interventions, which would be permitted to the extent not ruled out by the first premise.

be protected, as opposed to the vague answer that some freedom needs protection from both government and market, needs consideration. As Part II showed, any real answer here requires a theory of democracy. Whether outsiders should have a legal or constitutional right to have their views included in the media may be "yes" under one view of democracy – a republican and, under some circumstances, the more realistic complex democratic theory – and "no" under others, an elitist or liberal pluralist theory. More generally, if the democratic roles of the press are plural, an adequate interpretation of press freedom being "for" the citizen must carry out several tasks. It must describe those roles and consider how they are threatened. It must face the issue of whether and when legislative efforts to create conditions supportive of one role would undermine other democratic roles. If such a conflict occurs, it must decide which roles are most important or how the conflict can be avoided or resolved. That was what Part II attempted.

Then there is the question of how can society get to where it needs to go in terms of the media – how can it get the media that people want and citizens need. I am not here about to offer any programmatic strategy of how to achieve reform. Still, a concluding observation, addressed to a subset of this book's potential readers, may be appropriate.

One of the great attributes of journalists is their almost religious insistence on independence. Historically, this has manifested itself equally in heroic resistance to interference into journalism by the business side of the press and resistance to any government tampering. Sadly, I believe, it will be hard to move beyond those basically good instincts. American journalists are not academic sociologists or economists. Their stories customarily center on individuals. When they turn their attention to the problems facing journalism today and recommending solutions, they follow this professional orientation. Their solution is individualistic. What is needed is for individuals (here journalists) to stand tough by principle – to get *their house* in order.[3] This advice, repeatedly and inspirationally given by leading journalists, often on ceremonial occasions or on their retirement, should be heeded.

Still, this advice is grossly inadequate. It duplicates the journalistic tendency to focus on stories of the good and bad fortunes of individuals and their struggles for good over evil. The almost exclusive reliance on individualistic solutions – which, when possible, are certainly important for individuals to embrace – fails to make an adequate response when the problems individuals face require changes in legal, economic, and social structures. When journalists turn this misconstruction to their own situation, it produces a sad result. The profession, whose "freebooting" quality is nurtured by its mantra of the First Amendment, is doubly deceived. They are misled by both their professional ethos of a constitutionally based independence and by their professional story-telling practice.

Nevertheless, these media professionals are surely the most significant constituency dedicated to press freedom and quality. Corporate owners are too often only interested in press freedom to the extent it contributes to the bottom line. Political parties and the public usually place other issues much higher on the agenda. Media professionals – writers, journalists, editors – are often not merely professionally committed to providing the media the public needs. Often they are in effect activists in their self-sacrificing efforts to see that this is provided. Tragically, their own ethos and practice leads them to become politically quietistic as to the economic and legal structural changes on which greater success for their journalistic efforts depend. When this happens, both they and the public that relies on them are the losers.

Considerable reflection is required to describe a properly ordered house (e.g., Part II). My thesis is that, even with this knowledge and a professional commitment to providing it, a major factor determining what media content gets produced is the structure of economic and legal support for the media (Part I), not just journalists' integrity, skill, and commitment. Whatever the integrity of the journalist, when a paper's Washington bureau is cut from ten to two reporters for economic reasons, that cut will affect what content the journalists can create and distribute. When the bureau's reporting is eliminated entirely in favor of cheaply available press releases that the home office takes off the Internet, content will again be affected. Journalists concerned about their profession need to be concerned with economic structure and with the legal rules and government actions that partly determine and could improve that economic structure.

If I am right in Parts I and II of this book, really serving democracy, as well as successful resistance to perverting pressures from the business side, will require two things, one substantive and the other in a sense procedural. In substance, the press needs a structurally mixed system, as suggested in Chapter 8, with different economic bases and different goals for different portions of the press. This mixed system could effectively respond both to the press's multiple and sometimes conflicting assignments in a democratic society and to the danger that reliance on a single basis of support leaves the press too vulnerable to being undermined by either the government, market, or private power.

Procedurally, this result requires involvement by government, not in censoring and not in everyday running of media entities – both of which journalists properly resist just as the constitution generally prohibits – but in intelligent and properly oriented structuring of the media, creating a mixed system, and providing it adequate support. Pressure for this to happen will not come primarily from media owners nor from outsiders, although democratic activists would be wise to make this a high priority. Hope for freedom of the press as envisioned here depends on journalist professionals abandoning at least some of their instinctual opposition to government involvement and turning some of their dedication toward structural change.

# The Internet and Digital Technologies

A reader might think that however relevant this book would have been twenty years ago, the Internet and the new digital technologies, hardly mentioned here, change everything. They create an abundance that eliminates any need for government interventions.[1]

This reader would surely be right that much will change but is equally and more emphatically wrong that these changes undermine any of the critical claims or policy recommendations made in this book. Without pretending to survey the legal and policy issues raised by the new communications technologies,[2] which would require at least another book, I want to explain why whatever changes the new technologies will bring, and I can only inadequately speculate about their substance, the changes will not eliminate the problems with the market and the need to think about our democratic commitments.

Like a printing press or plow, a typewriter or table, a telephone or airplane, the Internet and related digital computer technologies are tools. Tools can make doing some things easier, so much easier that people will now do new things. But the Internet is not ideas, not knowledge; it is not passion or values; nor is it wisdom or meaning. It may increase the creation, occurrence, or distribution of these things that it is not. But that depends on its use.

At least to my relatively naive eyes, this tool does three things particularly relevant to the media concerns of this book. Computer technologies and the Internet make the assembly, storing, searching, and copying of data that exists in digital form easier and cheaper by such a magnitude that whole new realms of information use become possible. Second, they allow new, easy ways to manipulate data to create new "content." Finally, they dramatically reduce the cost and difficulty of distributing communications. Singularly or in combination, these tools open up dramatic possibilities. Nevertheless, in order to view their significance from the perspective of the issues discussed in this book, I here want to note, first, what has not changed for the media realm; second, what benefits these tools have brought or are likely soon to bring to consumers or citizens who rely on media products; and, third, the extent that these changes and related benefits potentially create new problems or raise new issues that need to be considered from the perspective of consumers and citizens.

Much has not changed. A great journalist, Sydney Schanberg, put it simply: "a good story is still a good story." Digital technologies have not changed the need for good reporting. They have not eliminated the need to create reliable news, quality commentary, and meaningful cultural content. Moreover, the new technologies only modestly and selectively change the capacity to do these things. Schanberg continued: "A good story must be carefully and rigorously reported. . . . Only then can you plug in the new toys and send the story across the world in a nanosecond."[3] Although the new technologies may make the nanosecond delivery easier, they do not get members of the public to read, hear, or view the content. Finally, media content has impact on the social order through complex social processes. The Internet has not changed the centrality of having this impact – that is, it has not changed the importance of communication's social efficaciousness. Whether it will have changed the social processes for better or worse, will have reduced or magnified the efficaciousness of various types of content, is a matter of investigation.

The new technologies expand the universe of people offering information, opinion, and other communicative content to strangers. They may empower "volunteers," unpaid individuals who construct web pages and create content solely out of a desire to create, report, and communicate, whether for personal expressive, political, charitable, or more narrowly self-interested reasons. These people are likely to become more important participants in the communications realm. Nevertheless, to the extent these volunteers' web pages or postings are no more read than were their earlier leaflets when distributed on street corners, the fact that they now can self-publish may make less difference than they often naively hope. In any event, I will temporarily put them aside. The concerns of this book have focused primarily on communicative content created by people who depend on being paid to create it.

My assumption is that society benefits from having professional creators of fictional, opinion, and news content, and that they will require support, whether from the market, the government, or elsewhere. That is, I assume that the amount, quality, and distribution of these professionals' creations will continue to be important to consumers and citizens. It is doubtful, for example, that if people suddenly had free access to the home movies of millions of amateur moviemakers whom they do not know, they would quickly lose their interest in the products of Hollywood. Likewise, I assume that the value of investigative journalism will not go away and that the expense of such journalism will usually not be born by volunteers. In other words, my assumption is that an economic base for media content will continue to be important and that what is produced will depend largely on the nature of this economic base. The availability of valued media content will continue to depend largely on the market, taxes, subsidies, intellectual property rules, industry structure, and the various other factors discussed in this book. Even after the creation of a great new tool, the Internet and digital technologies, people will continue to need auto workers and health professionals to provide them with cars and health care. Similarly, I assume that both consumers and citizens will continue to need quality journalists, writers, and video producers to help provide for their news and cultural needs. These points, I believe, will hold whether, as I suspect, the traditional media formats – physical versions of newspapers and books as well as (digitalized) films in movie houses – continue to be a major part of the social world, although importantly supplemented by new forms distributed over the new media, or whether the world moves to content delivered over the new media largely replacing older media forms. If my assumptions hold – and could it be otherwise? – then the question will continue to be: what set of market arrangements and governmental interventions will lead to production of the content that best serves people both in their roles as consumers and citizens?

In at least four ways, the new tools have the potential to improve dramatically what consumers and citizens receive. First, digital technologies and the Internet may reduce the cost of both copying and delivering material, thereby reducing the cost to the consumer. Second, they can reduce the difficulty (or cost) of finding and selectively retrieving computer-stored information that a person wants. Third, they can reduce the cost of certain content by making it easier (cheaper) for media professional creators to gather, assemble, and manipulate inputs and turn them into the product these professionals want (or are paid) to create. Fourth, digital technologies can reduce bottlenecks presently created by the necessity of receiving approval of editors or publishers and bottlenecks caused by distribution costs. This reduction of gatekeeper problems can lead to the availability of content, sometimes desired by consumers or citizens, and provided either by people who previously were unable to sell their content but can do so now over the Internet or by people who are willing to create and offer content without being paid.

These are all significant benefits. Nevertheless, each gain also contributes to potential new dangers. Most important, the gains do not eliminate the concern about how the structure – which is a combination of legal, technological, and economic arrangements[4] – determines what content is created, about who is able to distribute and receive the content, and about how the media affects actual social practices that use this content. Each of the three concerns merits attention.

## CONTENT CREATION

Copying and delivery contribute to the cost of a media product. The normal effect of reducing the cost of a "product" is to increase the amount that will be sold – if it is cheaper, more people will buy. Thus, decreased costs of distribution and individualization might be expected merely to increase the universe of available media material. Some media content previously not produced because demand would not pay for its cost will now be produced. More and potentially more diverse media content will be commercially viable. The reduced costs will also make noncommercial "voluntaristic" publication more possible. The number of products and their availability is increased not only due to lower distribution costs for the creator-providers, the "push" side; it is also increased by recipients' technological capacity to seek out and obtain material they choose, the "pull" side. Digital technology allows people to design their own newspaper or otherwise access types of cultural products they like (or think they like or have liked in the past). They can more easily (cheaply) find sellers of the products they want. At first it might seem that all is for the best: the range of selection, the capacity to select, and diversity have all increased.

Nevertheless, the story is more complicated. The competitive success of some new products is likely to cause the failure of other media products, a consequence of the monopolistic competition discussed in Part

I and illustrated in Part III in the international trade context. Although at first reducing costs may seem unambiguously to mean "more" – which certainly few Americans complain about – once it is seen that the new environment causes some old publications to fail and some communication practices to decline, the matter requires more careful analysis. When it is not merely a matter of adding the new but of replacing some old with some new, "more" or "better" becomes a contestable claim. At least it is contestable absent an agreed-upon scale to measure or compare the gain with the loss. Of course, this scale must contain a quality or weighting dimension. Just having more "bits" matters little. Many people would experience a net loss if they gained access to hundreds of randomly selected street corner speakers (or these speakers' web pages) but lost access to the *New York Times*. Whether the result will actually constitute a gain depends not merely on people's preferences or on the permissibility of offering content in a market but also on additional elements of the background structure – for example, tort rules, intellectual property rights, taxes, direct and indirect subsidies, and even such obscure matters as the Internet's "architecture" or protocols. Getting the best (most preferred) result requires a means to assess which background legal structure to favor.

I challenge later the hypothesis that the new technology necessarily increases diversity, individualization, and the amount of quality products effectively created and distributed. Even granted the hypothesis, there are at least two reasons not to be too sanguine. First, many culturally or politically valuable media contents are expensive to produce – well-edited papers or investigative journalism, for example. Unless people significantly increase the money (and time) devoted to media consumption, new specialized or individualized communications will spread revenue and audiences more thinly, probably too thinly to support some socially valuable but expensive contents – the "ruinous competition" that Chapter 2 showed could reduce consumer welfare. Already, mushrooming cable channels reduce audiences for network programming, although I suspect the networks could reduce their huge expenditures, at least those spent on the "stars" of entertainment programming or on news anchor personalities, without exacerbating the justified despair about television quality. Still, virtually all newspaper editors believe that decreasing editorial resources reduces newspaper quality. Certainly, it is not obvious that either consumers or citizens would be well served if the result of the new technology is that people have access to press releases on a much wider range of subjects from more (self-interested) sources than ever before but that newspapers no longer receive sufficient support and revenue to pay for investigative reporting (or even the resources to minimally check the validity of the press releases). Even now, newspapers are not adequately compensated for the positive externalities produced by performing the democratically crucial watchdog function (Chapters 3 and 6). The new technologies could spread audiences and revenues, leaving the media even less equipped to perform this function.

Second, having everyone receive her own individualized media content could cause concern on another level – a concern possibly described as either a negative externality or a democratic threat. The danger is starkest from the perspective of republican democracy. Cass Sunstein, for example, describes a media nightmare that is the equivalent of Robert Putman's account of bowling alone.[5] The nightmare is about an individualization that circumvents, possibly eliminates, a common public realm of discourse. The sociological effect of fragmenting media and discussion among self-identifying groups may give additional reasons for worry. Social science evidence shows, Sunstein reports, that when people discuss an issue primarily with other like-minded individuals, their views move toward the extreme position. For the overall society, this leads to polarization rather than any coming together. Individualization and segmentation, made possible by cheap delivery and reduced costs of finding desired content, may undermine any general public sphere and the discourses that lead to finding common ground. Republicans should worry – and complex democrats may worry, depending on whether at the time they believe the bigger problem is inadequate collective discourse or insufficient undominated subgroup discourse.

Despite these worries, and even if the new technologies result in a massive increase in generally available "stuff," whether its dominant effect will be audience fragmentation and superdiversity is not clear. Both history and economic theory give reason for doubt. Historically, for example, did the reduction of delivery and reproduction costs by the advent of the then new technologies of the phonograph and motion pictures increase or decrease the actual number of different plays produced or songs performed and the diversity in their content? Did these reduced costs increase the time people spent with music or drama and distribute audiences over a larger number and variety of cultural creations or did they mostly concentrate people's attention on fewer broadly available songs and plays – possibly ones with greater appeal due to resources lavished on their initial production or their promotion? Observe that these lavish expenditures and a possible resulting concentration are economically viable only because the reduced distribution and copy costs allow these first-copy costs (or an advertising budget) to be spread cheaply over the larger population. Even if the total time consumers spent with music or performance increased, the net result could be less diversity of professionally produced content, fewer professionals involved in creating and performing, and less total time spent either with nonmainstream content or with noncommercial (noncommodified) content. In this scenario, the Internet world will produce a huge increase in web sites but a concentration of "hits" onto a limited number of sites and an increasingly limited number of commercially successful providers of various types of content.

Economic theory explains why the answers are difficult to predict. Here I only note why the initial hypothesis of an inevitable "more" is doubtful. When comparatively large portions of the cost of individual access to content (or a performance) lie in the delivery or copying (or an actual live performance), some incentive exists to design unique content to suit the interests or needs of specific audiences. In percentage terms, the extra expenditure on individualizing does not increase the cost much but could increase the product's appeal a lot. In contrast, greatly reduced distribution and reproduction costs mean that products' cost becomes concentrated in the creation of the original content – and allows, as described in Chapter 1, virtually nonrivalrous use. Now the only profitable expenditures are likely to be those that increase the products' reach. Dividing the audience – which is what providing unique material does – creates a proportionately huge increase in per-person cost. Thus, low copy and delivery costs greatly increase the economic incentive to provide everyone with the *same* good (or, more realistically in the media context, with *fewer* original works delivered *more* broadly).

To get people to focus their consumption on this narrower range requires that either the seller be able to reduce the price or increase the appeal of products in this narrower range as compared with its competitors. The public-good quality of non-rivalrous-use goods allows for either strategy. The media firm could make greater expenditures on the first copy or could reduce the price for each copy. However, if in competition with other producers trying to reach a large audience, with both competitors willing to sacrifice some profits to succeed, a firm is likely to try to distinguish itself at least in part by making higher expenditures on the first copy. The resulting concentration of preferences on these lavishly produced products, in turn, tends to reduce diversity, as reflected in the discussion of the monopolistic competition described in Chapter 2. (Note that low copy and distribution costs' tendency to create an incentive for decreased individualization could even spill over into the noncommercial world. If the only way to write a letter is by hand, the norm would be individualized letters. But if copy costs are negligible, the temptation increases to send the same letter to multiple "friends.") This incentive to sell broadly because copies are costless also creates a parallel incentive to orient content toward that which is more universally understood – the factor that Chapter 10 invoked to explain the bias in global media products toward sex, violence, or simple stories of good versus evil and to sacrifice contextually or culturally specific content (or, more generally, a bias toward what Chapter 10 described as $U$ as opposed to $D$ content). In these ways, the economics of reduced copying and distribution costs, rather than unambiguously resulting in "more," could reduce the diversity of commercially produced and widely received content even as it also increases the number of largely unread volunteer publishers, the leafletters of the Internet realm.

Even if concentration is a dominant effect of the new technology, the matter of assessment remains. Few people want to return to a world without film (now video) or sound (now digital) recordings. Even if in some sense the culture industries concentrate people's attention on fewer songs or performances, copy and distribution technologies have surely broadened dramatically the diversity of musical and video performances available to any one individual. Thus, surely the new technologies' reduction of the costs of copying and delivery is in itself a human good. Probably even the most Luddite commentators' critique of the social consequences of television or computers[6] is much more about the uses of the technology than about the new capacity to do various things more cheaply and more easily. Nevertheless, not merely the existence of the technologies but also public policy and its structuring of market incentives influence people's uses. Thus, the question of whether the change is an unambiguous good should be recast. The issue is under what circumstances it is a good (or the most good). If not an unambiguous good under current market and legal arrangements (which seem "natural," if they do, only because they are current), the additional question is, Are there any policy moves that can reduce the bad and increase the good? Of course, this is precisely the type of questions asked throughout the book. Thus, Part I showed that products that prevail competitively sometimes undermine the commercial basis of other communicative content that people value even more – in which case some policy response is appropriate. Moreover, as Part II explained, depending on the theory of democracy (or, using Part I's framework, depending on externalities and an appropriate weighing of preferences), this monopolistic competition could cause substantial harms by reducing diversity. From the perspective of a liberal pluralist or complex democracy theory, for example, a reduction in diverse, professional quality, subgroup-oriented media content would be a serious problem.

At this point, I have described two possible but opposing effects on content – more diversity and more concentration – and discredited the claim that prevailing in a free market shows what is best. Abstractly it will be hard to sort out which tendency will dominate either with or without conscious legal or policy intervention. Consider a speculative hypothesis. Given reliance on markets, the new technologies will generate three results. (1) Reduced costs of copying and distributing will allow many "volunteer" creators to produce and make available content not previously available, and some people will want and receive this new, diverse content. (2) These reduced costs, combined with some money-backed, highly focused demand will result in some new media products being produced for special segments, often commercial segments, of the public. (3) Overall, as compared with the situation before, more consumer time and consumer resources will be expended on fewer media products and on the products of fewer content providers; economically successful providers will be those who spend the most on their product and on promoting their web sites; depending on their ability to extract revenue from audiences, either directly by payment or indirectly through advertising or commercial tie-ins, the amount these relatively few providers will spend on content will be a lot or a little. In this scenario, one key factor relating to the extent of the first two results as compared to the third will be the degree that people desire unique products. However, the actual outcome would not merely reflect audience preferences. Instead, what media content people get will depend on the costs of fulfilling these desires as these costs exist *given* the technologies and *given* a particular legal universe that has no natural or inherent content. Thus, any claim that an outcome is best will depend on evaluations of the consequences of those "givens."

Too much store should not be placed in this speculative hypothesis. Evidence from current observations of the Internet world support various contradictory predictions. Many commentators unconsciously blind themselves to half the evidence in order to support their own favored characterizations. The digital world is just too new – commercial and cultural practices are too much in developmental flux – for any great certainty. Still, I can say three things with some confidence. First, policy choices – whether made consciously or by default – will affect the actual mixture of content produced and then pushed to or pulled by audiences. Second, no such thing as a pure market process exists. The digital, Internet media market is dependent, for example, on policy choices concerning intellectual property law, the scope and liability for various potential on-line torts, or the enforceability of various agreements. For instance, will "click-wrap" contracts, where a party purportedly agrees to terms about her own privacy or about intellectual property's further use when clicking the mouse to gain access to the content, be enforced.[7] Even if there were a "pure" market, there would be absolutely no reason to expect that it would produce the best results from the perspective of either consumers or citizens. Finally, the analyses developed in this book would be useful for any intelligent assessment of policy alternatives.

One final observation about the content to which the new technologies will lead must be made. The capacity, cheaply, quickly, and often anonymously, to copy and distribute obviously has huge consequences both for the type of intellectual property rights that are abstractly desirable and the legal framework in which these rights would be effective. Predictions about the impact of the new technologies range from claims that they will inexorably lead to the death of copyright – authors or owners will no longer be able to control or receive direct financial benefit from reproduction – to fears that it will lead to dramatic expansions of copyright's domain. The second, increased owner control, might result both directly through changes in intellectual property law or through use of contract, combined with encryption technology and legal prohibitions. Some of these legal prohibitions are already embodied in the Digital Millennium Copyright Act, which outlaws circumventing encryption or providing devices or code that enables unauthorized circumvention.[8] The legal framework that most effectively provides for the preferred set of intellectual property rights could have huge additional consequences for other matters ranging from privacy, political expression, access to information, and even national security. Again, the point here is merely that the economic and democratic analyses initiated in this book should be central to thinking through the new intellectual property issues generated by the new technologies.

## ACCESSIBILITY TO SPEAKERS AND AUDIENCES

Extraordinary capacity to search for and retrieve content or routinely and almost costlessly to deliver content at first would seem to make content much more accessible to audiences as well as make audiences more available to speakers. Of course, the second involves a debatable gain – not everyone wants to be more accessible to all senders of content. "Spam," usually commercial content sent out to huge numbers of people who have not requested it, is not universally desired. And although there are technological "fixes" for this technologically created problem, each fix has its own downside. The question here, however, is twofold. Is the gain in access uniformly available to all content providers and all audiences? And what are the consequences for the media realm of any limits on access availability?

Consider each point where some entity potentially could exercise some degree of control over speakers' cyber access to audiences or audiences' access to cyber content. Any such point becomes a location where corporate (or governmental) entities may have either ideological or economic incentives to create significant bottlenecks. Those potentially able to create bottlenecks include setters of usage protocols or standards, owners of transmission facilities, equipment providers, and most obviously Internet service providers, search engine operators, owners of popular subnetworks, and providers of discussion or chat room locations. Competition creates some incentive to better serve at least the economically exploitable users. The result is competing incentives, one to create and exploit bottlenecks and one to reduce bottlenecks, with other contextual (and legal) factors determinative of which incentive operates most powerfully.

Entities that own and market content obviously have an incentive to favor their own content. When these entities also own widely relied upon transmission facilities, they will have some ability to create obstacles for speakers or producers of competing content. An obvious solution is for the government to require enterprises that sell both content and transmission services (or that have any other power over any potential bottleneck, e.g., Microsoft) to maintain open and fair access. To do so, however, can create almost insurmountable regulatory burdens. Accounting and physical practices can easily hide unequal treatment of outsiders. Uncovering discriminations requires great effort; evidence and conclusions will be disputable, creating delays and errors. In any event, a good society should not be in the business of *unnecessarily* creating work lives, the point of which is merely to monitor the work of others. In contrast, prohibiting enterprises that own and operate transmission facilities from also owning and marketing media content is a clean, structural solution that does not require constant regulatory monitoring and largely eliminates this incentive to block or burden outsiders' expression. In many situations, this separation should be the preferred policy response.[9]

This approach led to sensible legal prohibitions on telephone companies owning and selling (as opposed to carrying) cable programming. By requiring phone companies only to carry content, the incentive for the phone companies was to drum up business for carriage services, thereby reducing bottlenecks and increasing communications flows. Then regulation was only needed to prevent the phone company from charging monopoly rates. Phone companies, however, used a misconceived First Amendment theory to attack this prohibition in the courts before they prevailed more directly in Congress.[10] Virtually the same issue of combining ownership of transmission with the sale of content exists in AT&T's takeover of TCI and Media One, major cable companies, to whose cable offerings AT&T is adding carriage of its own Internet service as well as phone service. AT&T predictably asserts that it should not be legally required to allow other Internet service providers equal access to the cable. Similar incentives explain Microsoft's alleged attempt to use its virtual monopoly in personal computers' operating systems as leverage to gain power in the browser market. Disney/ABC and Time-Warner had agreements for the latter's cable systems to deliver the former's broadcasts and cable channel offerings. In early 2000, the two were unable to negotiate a new contract. This led briefly to Time-Warner removing ABC from its cable system – and producing an immediate (and effective) public backlash. Some evidence suggests that the real negotiating blockage related to Disney's fear that when Time-Warner merged with AOL, Time-Warner would use AOL as a delivery system to favor Time-Warner content over Disney content.[11] In each of these examples, the danger is that an owner of one part of the communications system will both be able and have an incentive to disfavor the media content of outside entities.

These illustrations have focused on blockages that economic entities can impose on speakers. Although I only flag the issue, an additional problem is that the Internet also does not eliminate bottlenecks at the recipients' end. Many people do not and are not likely soon to have equal or even meaningful access to the Internet. Cultural or educational as well as economic conditions can make any medium unavailable (or only minimally available) to many people. For the likely long "short-run," the so-called digital divide could increase inequality in access to cultural and informational content.[12] Moreover, new transmission technologies can exacerbate problems of access. If they reduce reliance on old forms of communications, their introduction could cause a rise in the per-person cost or a lowering of the quality of the content available in the old media. That is, if outcomes are left to markets, new communications technologies do not uniformly lead to more availability, but rather lead to more availability for some (in this case, predictably those already comparatively advantaged) without benefiting, and potentially even disadvantaging, others.[13] Any concern with either people getting what they want or citizens getting the media they need would justify policy-based government interventions.

### COMMUNICATION-ORIENTED SOCIAL PRACTICES

The press produces "commodities" – communications that are sold or that have commercial value for other reasons, such as for selling viewers and readers to advertisers. This "thing" focus has been central so far in my discussion of new technologies. The issue has been what content (a "thing" or "object") is created and how is this content distributed. This commodity orientation also dominates much popular commentary about the Internet. Constant references are to "information," for example, in slogans such as the "information age" or the "information economy," rather than to dialogue or discussion. Despite its public-good aspect, "information" is something a single individual can *possess*, as opposed to "discussion," which requires more than one person and is something people *do*. "Communications" is more ambiguous. It can refer either to the commodity or the activity. Stories about the new technologies on newspapers' business pages are usually about the commodity or about the business of facilitating communications. In contrast, in sociology or philosophical tracts, the term usually refers to the activity. In any event, the commodity orientation is too reductionist. Any public policy toward the Internet that considers what is of value about that communications realm must consider its impact on activities.

It took an anthropological or sociological approach to investigate the significance for people's daily activities of the express highways that linked suburbs and city centers, including their implications for the nature and quality of life in the center city. Similarly, an activity focus is needed to predict and evaluate likely effects of the Internet on forms of life. An important initial observation is that a useful communications order is about much more than a consumer obtaining and a seller making available expressive content in either the marketplace of ideas or of goods. Even as to what individual users value about media "products," often an activity perspective can be more informative than a commodity perspective. A standard observation is that the Internet allows for easy individualization of content, which makes for more choice. This option is presumptively desirable within a commodification perspective. Recipients of content, however, do not uniformly desire more choice. The couch potato may not want to be bothered. Others want to rely on the informed judgment of trusted, professional editors. Or they may place value less on the content than on their receiving the same content received by their friends, associates, and fellow citizens with whom they want to be able to engage in a common discourse. That is, people sometimes want to be part of media consumption communities. For such reasons, psychological theory, focusing on people's activities rather than increased market opportunities, predicts that the mass audience is not about to totally disintegrate.[14]

Any vision of mere private consumption of "digital bits" also presents an incredibly narrow view of the value and role of media "objects" in people's lives. Despite e-book fanatics' belief that the attitude is a curious cultural oddity soon to be abandoned, book lovers seem to have a quaint desire to hold and possess actual books, a desire that apparently goes beyond having easy access to "information." The emphasis on availability of information, whether "free" or merely easily findable on the web, also ignores significant educational, social, or societal roles played by the context of access – a point relevant for both on-line and off-line access. People sometimes go to a book or music store, possibly with a friend, as an enjoyable diversion into a public space – an experience nicely romanticized in Italio Calvino's *If on a Winter's Night a Traveler*. Observers who see this as basically a waste of time have bought into a commodity rather than activity paradigm. The singing along with the artist near the finale of a live performance involves an experience, sometimes of solidarity, sometimes inspirational, that is not easily accounted for in a tale about consumption of bits. The commodity paradigm grounds the attitude displayed by many commentators who largely ignore the interactive or dialogic uses of the new technologies – e-mail, discussion groups, bulletin boards, and the like – and instead, if they extend their gaze at all beyond merely e-commerce, focus only on access to information. These commentators see search engines and informational web pages as providing people with a product, information, and as locations to place advertising or to have users be manipulated, diverted, or linked to commercial sites or products.

A commodity orientation is part of what misled many popular commentators to think the main media policy problem in the pre-Internet world was "scarcity" of channels or other scarcity-producing bottlenecks. Although serious criticisms of the media system abound, an inadequate quantity of choice is at best a minor theme. Are there really too few books published – or, instead, is the problem that commercial incentives and people's limited time cause too few of the excellent published books to be found, read, and discussed? How many people – of course, I admit there are some – are frustrated by having too few choices at Tower Records, as opposed to the number frustrated by not knowing which compact discs to choose or frustrated by a culture that does not produce and value better music? Cyber music stores, like cyber book stores, can increase the choice over Tower Records. Individually established web sites allow for unlimited outlets. But even if cyberspace increases the technical availability of diverse sources, the primary issue involving the communications order is less the availability of diverse products than the quality of the diversity or, the point emphasized here, the social or political consequences of the materials' presentation and use.

The central concern of an activity orientation is not with the availability of "information" but with what is done with information, with the social salience of its receipt, possession, and use. Moreover, because these activities inevitably occur within particular contexts, the concern is also necessarily with these contexts. For many evaluative and policy discussions, this activity orientation provides the more useful beginning point. Leftist critics of the closed or censorious nature of the present corporate-controlled communications environment abound. But their complaint is less about the technical unavailability of diverse information – they regularly draw from published accounts in media sources to illustrate the stories the media do not tell.[15] Rather they argue that the media do not present vitally important material *in a publicly effective manner.* Too often the media publish but bury the most significant stories.[16] Meaningful presentation often requires intelligent decision making by *skillful, independent,* and *financially backed* media professionals – a difficult-to-find combination. Moreover, the political and cultural salience of "meaningfully presented" content may require attention within a public sphere as a place where people actually access or discuss or act on that content. The question about the new technologies is how they do or could reduce or magnify these problems of salience. Merely updating news highlights in real time on video screens may accomplish little other than provide viewers to sell to advertisers.

I use two contexts to illustrate the importance of an activity focus. The first, concerning investigative journalism, further illustrates the Internet's implications for the *media*'s capacity to serve consumers or citizens. The second concerns how different mixtures of commodified and noncommodified communications serve or misserve consumers and citizens.

Chapter 3 discussed positive externalities produced by investigative journalism and the consequent inadequate market support. Chapter 6 noted crucial contributions to democracy of investigative journalism and the press's watchdog role. How will a move toward cyber journalism affect these performances? Earlier, I gave reasons to fear that the move might further undermine the economic base for the "commodity" – quality content produced by investigative journalism. An activity focus provides an additional ground to worry.

To think clearly about this issue requires an understanding of how investigative journalism feeds nonmarket practices or, more specifically, political practices. Contrast two images of how investigative journalism makes its contribution. In the first, investigative reporting (i) produces stories that are then (ii) read and valued by an interested public (iii) who becomes enraged by the exposés, (iv) leading that public to demand and often to obtain (v) reformist political responses. In this scenario, the main issue concerning cyber media is only whether they will adequately support investigative journalism. Although journalists often complain that they do a story and nothing happens, public officials' reformist responses are frequently of the sort predicted in this scenario. Still, this picture may be overly simplistic. An empirical study of investigative journalism found that often the middle steps, an outraged public demanding change, was missing and unnecessary. Investigative reports did produce responses by officials, but often the officials planned these responses before the story became public and the reform went forward even if the public largely ignored the story.[17] Responsiveness apparently only required that the officials knew the story would be published. This scenario raises the interesting possibility of a second image. Maybe in our political order the mass media often function less as informers of the public than *as the public*, the public to which public officials respond. If so, the value of investigative journalism lies more in being a part of this process than in being a consumer product. As Michael Schudson observes, "[t]he news constructs a symbolic world that has a kind of priority, a certification of legitimate importance."[18] Thus, it is still possible that the reformist response to the media *as the public* depends on public officials' (and the public's?) knowledge that the investigative report is publicly and prominently presented by a respectable media entity that is received by an important segment of the population. Schudson argues that "[s]o long as information is publicly available, political actors have to behave *as if* someone in the public is paying attention."[19]

This second account, however, creates a new worry about cyber journalism. The destruction of mass media in favor of individually consumer-designed information/news retrieval systems, even if widely used, could undermine the presently most politically salient public – the publicly presented press. Markets provide no mechanism even to identify much less to respond to this social loss. This inadequacy follows because the issue is largely not about supplying commodities wanted by consumers but about the nature of the public political process – in economic language, a positive or negative externality of the context of people's commodity consumption. A response to this potential loss will come, if at all, either from new informal norms and customarily developed activities or from public policies, that is, government interventions, designed to assure conditions in which investigative journalism both exists and has appropriate public force.

Enough on the relevance of an activity focus for a policy analysis of journalism. Although this book is about the products of mass media, not about the activity of communications, the economics of Part I and the democratic theory of Part II are also relevant to assessing what communicative activities people want and need. Digital technologies facilitate (and occasionally undermine) the general category of communications as well as its subcategory, mass media. Possibly the most important but mostly ignored policy story about digital communications is the governmental and technological choices that will determine its differential enhancement (or blockage) of commodified versus noncommodified, "voluntaristic" generated communications.[20] In this respect, the benefit of an activity as opposed to a commodity focus is that the second almost automatically channels thought about digital technologies into considering its impact on media products, whereas an activity focus is more open to broader issues concerning both commodified and noncommodified communications.

An analytic division can be made between communications that are one to one, one to many, many to one, and many to many. One to one communications encompasses the realm of individual noncommodified interaction as well as the more commodified realm of professional services – lawyering, therapy, medicine, accounting, as well as direct sales transactions and many other business activities. The mass media's terrain is the second – one to many – as is the typical terrain of teaching, preaching, and various forms of performance (although the "one" here may be a group, ensemble, or team composed of a number of people). Survey research and polling as well as petitioning or letter writing campaigns directed at, for example, a senator, illustrate the third – many to one. But the last category – many to many – could be viewed as paradigmatic for participatory political discourse. It is definitive of the notion of a public sphere. Prior communications technologies have centered on the first three relationships: telephone and mail – one to one; broadcasting and other mass media – one to many. Various traditional tools further the third. Each of these relations supported by prior technology is facilitated by individualized sales or has major commodified uses. Commodified versions, however, have not been common for the "many to many" relation. At least in the past, "many to many" communications have been largely limited to discursive meetings rather than commodity-related functions (although meetings can be commodified to an extent by having professional facilitators and even commercial "party hosts"). In this communications relationship, it is difficult to separate what people receive from what they do.

Digital technologies can have important political uses. They allow people to get information out quickly. Rather than depend on the *New York Times* and *Washington Post*, both of which are potentially subject to control by injunction,[21] Daniel Ellsberg could today post the *Pentagon Papers* on the web. Action alerts can be sent out quickly and effectively, especially to members of pre-established groups. However, in the past telephones, newsletters, and the press have served these functions of information transmittal relatively well. The potential use for "many

to many" discourse is possibly the most politically significant innova-
tive feature of the new technologies. This potential may have been
central for the Internet's early utopian democratic cachet. The Internet
allows "many to many" communications to escape the necessity of
assembling people at a particular real-world place or even assembling
at a particular time. Some observers suggest that the central scarce
resource for democratic participation is not lack of information but lack
of discussion and, even more, lack of motivation – people not being
concerned or committed. Although there are no guarantees, "many to
many" communications hold the potential of providing public spheres
that respond to these scarcities. However, this communicative form,
though studied by sociologists or anthropologists, is mostly ignored in
business page reports on the information economy and within more
commodity-oriented thinking of many Internet-oriented policy circles.
Nevertheless, possibly the most significant policy issues involve the
ways and extent policy favors or disfavors activity, and especially noncommodified, orientations. The analyses in Parts I and II of this book
do not uniformly point in a single direction concerning these choices.
Still, these analyses will constantly be relevant to careful consideration
of these policy issues.

Intellectual property law currently provides the chief battleground
over different visions of the communications order. Because digital
technologies provide the capacity to make countless copies and to transmit or distribute them broadly, with each copy being then a possible
locus for more copying and distribution, and with anonymous remail-
ers and other technological devices potentially making tracing difficult,
the threat to intellectual property is obvious. However, because intellectual property is only an instrumentally justified device designed to
promote valued communication, the policy implications of the threat
are not obvious.

Intellectual property issues arise constantly. Often particular settlements in retrospect will, in Whiggish fashion, seem obvious and
inevitable. The significance of any challenge will often be seen to have
been overstated. Still, at the risk of being dated, consider the world
from the time when Napster arrived on the scene. Napster is the name
of an on-line service and code that permits any on-line computer user
to listen to or obtain copies of computer files of recorded music located
on the hard drive of anyone participating in the "sharing." Is it – or
similar technologies or codes – good or bad? And are there legal or

technological ways to control it? Here is not the place to answer these questions, but a few comments immediately suggest that considerations such as those covered in this book are relevant.[22]

Napster technology obviously reduces control by the copyright owner over copying and distribution – and hence reduces control of access by potential listeners. Like with the earlier use of xerox machines, tape recorders, and video cassette recorders to copy copyrighted material, the extent of the use of this technology to evade market purchases is hard to predict. In the most extreme scenarios, Napster or similar technology will destroy the recorded music industry as we know it today. Assume that happened. To the extent high-quality content depends on this industry, this destruction could be a serious consumer and cultural loss. The destruction would also eliminate a major source of compensation for people who now make their living as musicians – or at least the few stars who receive substantial record label income – and also for many other people connected with the recording and distribution business. Bad overall? Not clear. Greater accessibility of recordings does not eliminate the availability of *performance* income to support music professionals. The reduced (or eliminated) power of the major record labels and the new methods of communication that music fans would inevitably develop, including methods dependent on digital technologies, to communicate and compare evaluations of different recordings could widen the focus of demand for music. Many currently obscure musicians, who receive little or nothing from recording royalties, would receive greater exposure and potentially more payments in the performance realm, possibly even more sales of their presently virtually unmarketed recordings. Are these benefits, to which should be added the reduced cost and wider availability of music to consumers due to elimination of many middlemen and of payments for copies, greater than the loss of quality music due to greatly reduced recording-based economic incentives currently provided star recording artists? This question is obviously relevant from the perspective of audiences' getting what they want. Both systems generate some, but different, positive externalities. Evaluations of the nature of monopolistic competition and how it distorts the results people get in the market are relevant. Democratic theorists, especially republican and complex democrats who in different ways are concerned with culture's discourse of self-understanding and identity, would also find the question important. Those concerned with empowered diversity, especially complex democrats, may be more sympathetic to a Napster world than would be republicans who are more concerned to maintain a common dialogue.

Although not necessarily dispositive of the Napster issue, a view I am sympathetic to is a presumption toward a greater public domain in the resources for further communications – that is, a public domain in prior communications – and especially toward greater opportunities for new noncommercial, noncommodifying users. Such a presumption should prevail unless the advantages of a contrary approach can be shown with convincing clarity and unless the intellectual property claim is strictly limited to what has been justified. Readers familiar with standard First Amendment doctrine will recognize that this is essentially a claim that the scope of copyright, which is a legal mechanism for restricting the content of other people's expression, be subject to a rigorous First Amendment test of heightened scrutiny.[23]

The policy significance of the contrasting emphases on commodified or noncommodified digital expression affects many areas beyond copyright. Normally, a publisher, whether presenting her own expressive work or instead merely reporting someone else's speech or carrying someone else's advertisement, is liable for any defamatory or obscene content. Even booksellers or other vendors can be liable if they have actual knowledge of the illegal content.[24] Should, for similar reasons, liability be similarly imposed on Internet service providers who provide the locus of and access to communications that are, for example, posted on its computer bulletin boards or in chat rooms it maintains? Of course, imposition of liability for speech always disfavors the covered speech and disfavors the entity on which liability is imposed. Nevertheless, in the imposition of liability for defamation, society presumably intends to disfavor the offending speech and to impose legal responsibility on certain purveyors. In analogy to both the newspaper and bookseller, the Internet service provider, who provides the "original" defamatory speaker access to audiences, is located in the best position to exercise control over these speakers.

The value of promoting noncommodified speech, however, leans heavily in favor of Congress's decision to exempt Internet service providers from liability.[25] This can be seen by comparing the impact of the opposite decision on the speech available over the Internet. Imposing liability on the service provider is unlikely to deter it from carrying the speech of (solvent) commercial entities – including these entities' media content, whether sold or provided free, their advertisements, or their other messages and web page connections. A plaintiff normally will go after the source, but even if the plaintiff also sues the service provider, the provider could require indemnity from the commercial entity in its original contractual agreement. The consequences would be very different for service providers' attitude toward the speech of individual users and most noncommercial entities. As to those speakers, the only effective way the service provider could protect itself from general publisher liability would be either to monitor their speech, a potentially very expensive task that presumably would have to be passed on in charges to the noncommodified speakers, or to shut down the loci where their unmonitored speech got included. Here, publisher liability greatly disfavors uncommodified speech.

Similarly, a possible response to on-line indecency is to require content ratings, presumably with the rating coded into the digital content. The rating creates the potential for recipient computers to easily exclude the content or filter access. Or the law could mandate that anyone providing or offering access to indecent or "adult" content require its recipients to verify their age by use of means such as credit cards. Putting aside serious questions of the effectiveness of these techniques, the nature of the burden these rules would impose on the "speaker" is something that commercial communicators are likely to be much better equipped to bear than noncommercial speakers. Although the Supreme Court has invalidated Congress's first attempt and a lower court has invalidated its second attempt to restrict indecent material available to minors on the Internet, Congress in the second act responded to one of the Court's earlier criticisms by having the statute apply only to communications made for commercial purposes, an effort implicitly recognizing the undesirability of imposing the same burdens on noncommodified communications.[26] In other words, it is clear that even now, at least when the power of intellectual property owners is not too dominant, policy makers recognize the need not to sacrifice non-commodified communications.

These comments describe merely the iceberg's tip and do not intend to be definitive of any policy conclusions concerning the digital communications. The comments illustrate several related points. Different legal arrangements favor different types of Internet communications. One important difference between arrangements is the degree they favor commodified or noncommodified communications when the two are in conflict. I also suggest that no quick end to old forms of communication can be expected; these will continue to be important, and the analysis in the book will continue to be relevant to them.

However, no matter how dominant the new technologies become, the main point of this postscript is to argue that no blind reliance on some imagined "market" or on an unregulatable technological progression is appropriate. Rather, economic, democratic, and other normative analyses of the general type developed in this book will be as crucial to an intelligent public response to the possibilities created by these new technologies as they will continue to be for responding to the traditional media.

# Notes

## Preface

1. *Butler v. Michigan*, 352 U.S. 380 (1957). Cf. *FCC v. Pacifica*, 438 U.S. 726 (1978) (broadcasting), *Young v. American Mini Theatres*, 427 U.S. 50 (1976) (movies), *Ginsberg v. New York*, 390 U.S. 629 (1968) (magazines), with *Reno v. American Civil Liberties Union*, 521 U.S. 844 (1997).
2. *Whitney v. California*, 274 U.S. 357, 375 (1927) (Brandeis, with Holmes, concurring).
3. Cf. Kenneth L. Karst, "Boundaries and Reasons, Freedom of Expression and the Subordination of Groups," *Illinois Law Review* (1990): 95.

## Part I

1. See Thomas G. Krattenmaker & L. A. Powe Jr., "Converging First Amendment Principles for Converging Communications Media," *Yale Law Journal* 104 (1995): 1719, 1725.
2. See ibid.
3. Mark S. Fowler & Daniel L. Brenner, "A Marketplace Approach to Broadcast Regulation," *Texas Law Review* 60 (1982): 207, 210.
4. Ibid., 211.
5. Caroline E. Mayer, "FCC Chief's Fears: Fowler Sees Threat in Regulation," *Washington Post* (Feb. 6, 1983): K6.
6. See, e.g., Telecommunications Act of 1996, Pub. L. No. 104–104, 110 Stat. 56 (1996); *Chesapeake & Potomac Tel. Co. v. United States*, 830 F. Supp. 909 (E. D. Va. 1993), *vacated and remanded to determine if moot*, 116 S. Ct. 1036 (1996); U.S. Department of Commerce, *Globalization of the Mass Media* (Washington, D.C.: GPO, 1993).
7. But cf. Bruce M. Owen, *Economics and Freedom of Expression: Media Structure and the First Amendment* (Cambridge: Ballinger, 1975) 189 (emphasizing the propriety of government regulation of the transmission system but not the structurally distinguishable editorial or content creation system); C. Edwin Baker, "Merging Phone and Cable," *Hastings Communications and Entertainment Law Journal* 17 (1994):

309

97, 116–17 (arguing for separation of control over content and delivery where possible).

8. Pub. L. No. 104–104, 110 Stat. 56 (1996).

9. Committee on Commerce, Science, & Transp., 104th Cong., Report on Telecommunications Competition and Deregulation Act of 1995, S. Rep. No. 104–23, at 1 (1995).

10. Ibid., 67 (Hollings); 70 (dissent).

11. Because I have discussed interpretations of the Press Clause as well as some of the history of government intervention elsewhere, I do not explore those issues here. See, e.g., C. Edwin Baker, *Advertising and a Democratic Press* (Princeton: Princeton U. Press, 1994), ch. 5; C. Edwin Baker, "Private Power, the Press, and the Constitution," *Constitutional Commentary* 10 (1993): 421; C. Edwin Baker, "Turner Broadcasting: Content Regulation of Persons and Presses," *Supreme Court Review* (1994): 57. See also Cass R. Sunstein, *Democracy and the Problem of Free Speech* (New York: Free Press, 1993).

12. See Fowler & Brenner, "Marketplace Approach."

13. See C. Edwin Baker, "The Ideology of the Economic Analysis of Law," *Philosophy & Public Affairs* 5 (1975): 3; C. Edwin Baker, "Posner's Privacy Mystery and the Failure of Economic Analysis of Law," *Georgia Law Review* 12 (1978): 475.

14. See Margaret Jane Radin, *Contested Commodities* (Cambridge: Harvard U. Press, 1996).

## Chapter 1

1. For example, (1) reliance on market allocation accepts the existing distribution of wealth as a given when it should be changed or is contested; (2) the market stimulates undesirable desires precisely because they can be profitably fulfilled; (3) the market encourages (rewards) undesirable interpersonal behavior and undesirable personality traits; and (4) the market promotes optimal preference satisfaction only if, contrary to reality, most goods are made available at their marginal cost; moreover, too much production of a good properly priced at its marginal cost will occur when it improperly substitutes for a good improperly priced above its marginal cost and too little will occur when the properly priced good is replaced by a good priced below its marginal cost. These problems suggest a more modest policy-making role for traditional economic analysis, especially for the standard model described here, than many of its practitioners recognize.

2. See, e.g., Richard C. Edwards, *Contested Terrain: The Transformation of the Workplace in the Twentieth Century* (New York: Basic Books, 1979).

3. The point is somewhat overstated. Many goods function like public goods only within limits. For example, more users eventually interfere with the quality of the park – the crowd begins detracting from others' enjoyment or otherwise imposes marginal costs, like extra cleanup or wear-and-tear costs. Still, once goods like defense of national borders or media content are produced, multiple people can consume them without significant increased costs.

4. I make little direct use of nonexcludability, although the concept could apply to (positive) externalities taken up in Chapter 3. In common usage, nonexcludability as an aspect of a public good usually refers to situations where any purchaser and

each nonexcluded beneficiary get roughly the same type of benefit from the good, whereas the concept of externalities is most commonly used where the benefit or burden on nonexcluded third parties is of a different sort than that which enticed the purchaser.

5. The claim here is that this public-good element in media products is sufficiently large and its significance sufficiently variable among media products that economic and policy analyses ought to take it explicitly into account. The difference here between media products and other goods is at most a matter of degree. Virtually all mass-produced products include what I here call a "public-good" element – most obviously, the "design cost." This always creates some tension in the standard competitive market model. The market encourages efficient amounts of research on practices or product design only to the extent that the research is aimed at creating products over which the researcher will have something approaching monopoly power – for example, if it obtains a patent or trade secret – and will have an ability to price discriminate in its sale. This helps explain, for example, why the market encourages research expenditures on drug therapies *even if* the marginal improvement of health, say the marginal reduction of death from cancer or heart disease, would be much greater from research dollars spent on developing non-patentable "public health" or environmental health methods (although this is only one cause of the skewing of research expenditures). One solution is to socialize research – providing government funding, often times within a university.

6. An early study calculated that the value to Americans of free over-the-air television was at least $20 billion, which was roughly ten times the advertising revenue then produced. See Roger G. Noll et al., *Economic Aspects of Television Regulation* (Washington, D.C.: Brookings Institution, 1973), 23. The authors concluded that "by traditional criteria of consumer welfare, not only another network but a very large expansion of television is warranted." Ibid., 30.

7. See C. Edwin Baker, *Advertising and a Democratic Press* (Princeton: Princeton U. Press, 1994), ch. 2.

8. See Linda Lawson, *Truth in Publishing: Federal Regulation of the Press's Business Practices, 1880–1920* (Carbondale: Southern Illinois U. Press, 1993). The requirement that advertising be identified may have conformed to the competitive economic interests of some, especially the quality, papers. The law also required papers to publish the identity of their owners in the expectation that public knowledge of ownership would allow greater ability to resist manipulation. In both respects, the law required some editors to print what they would prefer not to print. See *Lewis Publ'g Co. v. Morgan*, 229 U.S. 288, 296 (1913) (upholding the law against a First Amendment challenge); cf. *Miami Herald Publ'g Co. v. Tornillo*, 418 U.S. 241, 254–55 (1974) (invalidating a Florida statute requiring newspapers that attack a political candidate's character to print the candidate's reply).

9. U.S. Constitution, Art. I, Sec 8. The Court repeatedly emphasizes this point. Copyright "is a means by which an important public purpose may be achieved." The right is created "in order to benefit the public." It "is intended to increase and not to impede the harvest of knowledge" and "serve[s] its intended purpose [by] inducing the creation of new material." *Harper & Row, Publishers v. Nation*, 471 U.S. 539 U.S. 539, 545–46 (internal quotes from *Sony v. Universal Studios*, 464 U.S. 417, 429, 477) (opinions of Stevens for the Court and Blackmun, dissenting).

10. Yochai Benkler, "Free as the Air to Common Use: First Amendment Constraints on Enclosure of the Public Domain," *New York University Law Review* 74 (1999): 354.

11. See James Boyle, *Shamans, Software and Spleens: Toward the Construction of the Information Society* (Cambridge: Harvard U. Press, 1996), 51–60.

12. See Dan Cox, "Soaring Star Salaries Induce Labor Pains," *Variety* (Sept. 11, 1995): 1; Richard Harwood, "Extinct Stained Wretches?" *Washington Post* (Nov. 2, 1995): A31.

13. See Leo Bogart, *Commercial Culture: The Media System and the Public Interest* (New York: Oxford U. Press, 1995), 182.

14. See James Fallows, *Breaking the News* (New York: Pantheon Books, 1996), 157–59.

15. Bogart, *Commercial Culture*, 186.

16. *Cohen v. Coles Media*, 501 U.S. 63 (1991). This raises interesting issues in the context of current debates about privacy and the Internet. Cf. Jerry Kang, "Information Privacy in Cyberspace Transactions," *Stanford Law Review* 50 (1998): 1193. I believe the key step is to see that regulation of how commercial enterprises other than the press obtain, use, and sell information poses problems largely outside the concern of the First Amendment.

17. See Edward S. Herman & Noam Chomsky, *Manufacturing Consent: The Politics of the Mass Media* (New York: Pantheon Books, 1988), 18–25.

## Chapter 2

1. The classic work on monopolistic competition is Edward H. Chamberlin, *The Theory of Monopolistic Competition: A Re-orientation of the Theory of Value*, 8th ed. (Cambridge: Harvard U. Press, 1962). This section extends an analysis that I developed in C. Edwin Baker, *Advertising and a Democratic Press* (Princeton: Princeton U. Press, 1994), 9–13, 73–76. The general type of phenomenon I describe here is explained in Clement G. Krouse, *Theory of Industrial Economics* (Cambridge: B. Blackwell, 1990), 190–218, and applied to a media context in Bruce Owen & Steven Wildman, *Video Economics* (Cambridge: Harvard U. Press, 1992).

2. This subsection is based on Baker, *Advertising and a Democratic Press*.

3. Leo Bogart reports that in Sunday papers, more readers report regularly reading ad inserts (46%) than reading sports (42%), comics (40%), business (29%), and most other sections except for hard news. On any day in 1986, about 38% of newspaper readers looked at classified ads for either real estate, cars, or employment. And 75% of men and 84% of women say they like to look at ads even when they do not plan to buy. Leo Bogart, *Press and Public*, 2d ed. (Hillsdale, N.J.: L. Erlbaum Associates, 1989), 49–50, 166–68, 319–20.

4. See, e.g., Bruce Owen, *Economics and Freedom of Expression: Media Structure and the First Amendment* (Cambridge: Ballinger, 1975).

5. Martin Mayer, *Making News* (Boston: Harvard Business School Press, 1993), 84–85.

6. This bundling in effect constitutes a method of price discrimination that has also been profitable in cable systems' sale of channel packages. See Owen & Wildman, *Video Economics*, 132–35, 218–22, 246.

7. See Baker, *Advertising and a Democratic Press*, 17–20.

8. See Gloria Steinem, "Sex, Lies & Advertising," *Ms.* (July–Aug. 1990): 18.

9. The argument in this section generally follows Krouse, *Theory of Industrial Economics*. See also Owen & Wildman, *Video Economics*.

10. See *Carroll Broad. Co. v. FCC*, 258 F.2d 440, 440–44 (D.C. Cir. 1958). This doctrine has been largely abandoned. See 3 F.C.C.R. 638, 638 (1988).

11. See Communications Act of 1934, 47 U.S.C. §303 (1991). Obviously, denial of a license under this reasoning would result in the government preventing someone from broadcasting for reasons other than physical scarcity of airwaves. The Supreme Court noted but said nothing about this point in *Red Lion Broadcasting Co. v. FCC*, 395 U.S. 367, 401 n.28 (1969). Cf. C. Edwin Baker, "Turner Broadcasting: Content Regulation of Persons and Presses," *Supreme Court Review* (1994): 54 (arguing that authority to structure rights to broadcast in order to provide a better communications order, not scarcity, explains government constitutional power in this area).

12. This phenomenon has been often noted. See, e.g., Owen & Wildman, *Video Economics*; Matthew L. Spitzer, "Justifying Minority Preferences in Broadcasting," *Southern California Law Review* 64 (1991): 293, 304.

13. See, e.g., *Los Angeles v. Preferred Communications, Inc.*, 476 U.S. 488, 488–97 (1986).

14. An ACLU suit challenging Kansas City's elimination of a public-access channel raised this claim among others. The issue was not decided when the city settled in favor of the plaintiff. See Marc A. Franklin & David A. Anderson, *Mass Media Law*, 5th ed. (Westbury, N.Y.: Foundation Press, 1995), 759 (I participated in the discussions leading up to the complaint in this litigation).

15. See *Chesapeake & Potomac Tel. Co. v. United States*, 830 F. Supp. 909, 909–32 (E.D. Va. 1993), *vacated and remanded to determine if moot*, 116 S. Ct. 1036 (1996).

16. See Telecommunications Act of 1996, Pub. L. No. 104-104, 110 Stat. 56 (1996). But see C. Edwin Baker, "Merging Phone and Cable," *Hastings Communications and Entertainment Law Journal* 17 (1994): 97–136 (criticizing the First Amendment challenge and arguing that the earlier law, which required phone companies to be only carriers, not sellers, of programming, is more likely to result in competition and diversity in programming).

17. Owen, *Economics and Freedom of Expression*.

18. Thomas Hazlett points to cases where cable competition produces better service and/or lower prices. See Thomas W. Hazlett, "Duopolistic Competition in Cable Television: Implications for Public Policy," *Yale Journal on Regulation* 7 (1990): 65, 90–113.

19. Allowing phone companies to carry cable programming, as was to be allowed under the "video dialtone" rules, does not speak to whether the phone company should be allowed to be the owner and marketer of the programming. See Baker, "Merging Phone and Cable," 100.

20. Bogart, *Commercial Culture*, 200.

21. William B. Blankenburg, "Newspaper Scale & Newspaper Expenditures," *Newspaper Research Journal* 10 (1989): 97, 101.

22. See Robert M. Entman, *Democracy without Citizens* (New York: Oxford U. Press, 1989), 91–101.

23. See C. Edwin Baker, *Ownership of Newspapers: The View from the Positivist Social Science*, Shorenstein Barone Center of JFK School of Gov., Harvard U. (Cambridge, 1994).

24. See Ben H. Bagdikian, *Media Monopoly*, 4th ed. (Boston: Beacon Press, 1992); Leo Bogart, *Press and Public*, 2d ed. (Hillsdale, N.J.: L. Erlbaum Associates, 1989), 352–53.

25. See Bagdikian, *Media Monopoly*, 201–2; John C. Busterna et al., "Competition, Ownership, Newsroom and Library Resources in Large Newspapers," *Journalism Quarterly* 68 (1991): 729; Gerald L. Grotta, "Consolidation of Newspapers: What Happens to the Consumer?" *Journalism Quarterly* 48 (1971): 245, 248. Lower prices or higher newsroom budgets in competing papers may also reflect short-run strategies of deep-pocketed companies that operate at a loss while seeking to become the surviving monopolist. See *Michigan Citizens for an Indep. Press v. Thornburgh*, 868 F.2d 1285, 1285–1306 (D.C. Cir. 1989).

26. This effect is in addition to blockbusters' capacity to produce monopoly or "winner-take-all" profits, which creates inefficient incentives to invest in producing blockbusters. See Robert H. Frank & Philip J. Cook, *The Winner-Take-All Society* (New York: Free Press, 1995).

## CHAPTER 3

1. See Margaret Jane Radin, *Contested Commodities* (Cambridge: Harvard U. Press, 1996).

2. Government decision making based on promoting some people's interest in what other people read has sometimes been considered an improper reliance on external preferences. Cf. Ronald Dworkin, *Taking Rights Seriously* (Cambridge: Harvard U. Press, 1977), 275–76. Even if properly characterized as an "external preference," reliance is proper for some purposes such as funding a library – in fact, concern for what others read or view can be central to individual and collective self-determination – but is not proper as a basis for suppressing "others'" liberty. See C. Edwin Baker, "Counting Preferences in Collective Choice Situations," *UCLA Law Review* 25 (1978): 381, 381–416.

3. Cf. C. Edwin Baker, "Harm, Liberty, and Free Speech," *Southern California Law Review* 70 (1997): 979 (arguing that preventing harm or injury to others is virtually never a *sufficient* basis for restricting people's liberty – although emphasizing that this claim is only plausible given particular formal conceptions of liberty).

4. From a suitably abstract perspective, the discussion here resembles issues considered in Chapter 2. There, only disablingly high transaction costs blocked price discrimination sufficient to achieve "efficient" outcomes. Here, the same is true. Still, externalities or third-party effects are often commonly recognized and treated separately from public-good effects.

5. Mark S. Fowler & Daniel L. Brenner, "A Marketplace Approach to Broadcast Regulation," *Texas Law Review* 60 (1982): 211.

6. Of course, regulation or other legal changes can make things worse; a response to one problem, one externality, often creates other problems. Likewise, regulatory rent seeking typically tries to mask itself in the rubric of the public interest. However, as long as even the theoretically ideal market is inadequate at providing socially desirable results, intellectual and political energy should be spent on improving, not merely disparaging, political and governmental processes – the *only*

realm in which appropriate solutions are possible. That effort, however, is beyond the scope of this book.

7. See Ruy A. Teixeira, *Why Americans Don't Vote: Turnout Decline in the United States, 1960–1984* (New York: Greenwood Press, 1987), 88 (decline in newspaper reading can account for two-thirds of net voter decline in 1968 to 1980 and one-third of the socioeconomic status adjusted total).

8. Justin Lewis, "What Do We Learn from the News?" *Extra!* (Sept. 1992): 16, 17 (publication of Fairness and Accuracy in Reporting).

9. C. Edwin Baker, *Advertising and a Democratic Press* (Princeton: Princeton U. Press 1994), 31–32 (reviewing literature).

10. In a survey of research findings, John Murray observes, "Despite decades of research, there is a perception that the research evidence on television violence is unclear or contradictory. This perception is incorrect." John P. Murray, "The Impact of Televised Violence," *Hofstra Law Review* 22 (1992): 809, 810. Murray's conclusion is best summarized by Leonard Eron's testimony to Congress: "There can no longer be any doubt that heavy exposure to televised violence is one of the causes of aggressive behavior, crime, and violence in society." Ibid., 823; but cf. L. A. Powe Jr. & Thomas G. Krattenmaker, "Televised Violence: First Amendment Principles and Social Science Theory," *Virginia Law Review* 64 (1978): 1123, 1134–70. The best, comprehensive treatment, roughly along the lines suggested here, is James T. Hamilton, *Channeling Violence* (Princeton: Princeton U. Press, 1998).

11. For an early development of this point, see George Gerbner & Larry Gross, "Living with Television: The Violence Profile," *Journal of Communications* 26 (1976): 173.

12. See *Beauharnais v. Illinois*, 343 U.S. 250, 263 (1952).

13. See Charles R. Lawrence III, "If He Hollers Let Him Go: Regulating Racist Speech on Campus," *Duke Law Journal* (1990): 431, 457–66. This harm includes the injury both to the people disparaged and to those who adopt the view implicit in the disparagement – although, to the extent members of this second group do not experience this influence as a harm, or at least do not at the time it occurs, how the effect should be characterized by a nonpaternalistic analysis of giving people what they want is ambiguous. See Chapter 4.

14. Cass Sunstein, *Republic.com* (Princeton: Princeton U. Press, 2001), 94–96.

15. See Vincent Blasi, "The Checking Value in First Amendment Theory," *American Bar Foundation Research Journal* (1977): 521, 539. Blasi develops the checking function as central to interpreting both the Speech and the Press Clause, but arguably it makes most sense as a reason for and as guidance in an independent interpretation of the Press Clause. See C. Edwin Baker, "Press Rights and Government Power to Structure the Press," *University of Miami Law Review* 34 (1980): 819.

16. Potter Stewart, "Or of the Press," *Hastings Law Journal* 26 (1975): 631; William J. Brennan Jr., "Address," *Rutgers Law Review* 32 (1979):173.

17. See Amartya Sen, "Freedom and Needs," *New Republic* (Jan. 10 & 17, 1994), 31; Amartya Sen, "The Economics of Life and Death," *Scientific American* (May 1993), 40.

18. Sen notes that areas suffering the most devastating famines often export food due to starving groups' lack of income with which to purchase available food stocks. See Amartya Sen, *Poverty and Famines* (New York: Oxford U. Press, 1981), 161.

19. Given the non-copyrightability of facts, the media entity that uncovers the information often must effectively share with other media entities the revenue produced by selling this "news."

20. James Fallows, *Breaking the News* (New York: Pantheon Books, 1996), 57–60.

21. See Todd Gitlin, *The Whole World Is Watching* (Berkeley: U. of California Press, 1980), 78–123.

22. Abrahum H. Miller, ed., *Terrorism, the Media, and the Law* (Dobbs Ferry, N.Y.: Transnational Publishers, 1982); David E. Long, *The Anatomy of Terrorism* (New York: Free Press, 1990); M. Cherif Bassiouni, "Media Coverage of Terrorism," *Journal of Communications* 32 (1982): 128.

23. See Thomas C. Leonard, *Power of the Press* (New York: Oxford U. Press, 1986), 91–96.

24. See James Curran, "Capitalism and Control of the Press, 1800–1975," in James Curran et al., eds., *Mass Communication and Society* (London: Edward Arrold, 1977), 195, 202.

25. See Leo Bogart, *Press and Public*, 2d ed. (Hillsdale, N.J.: L. Erlbaum Associates, 1989), 54–55.

26. See *Lewis Publ'g v. Morgan*, 229 U.S. 288, 314–16 (1913) (newspapers); 47 U.S.C. §§317, 508 (1994) (broadcasting).

27. *SEC v. Wall St. Publ'g Inst.*, 851 F.2d 365, 376 (D.C. Cir. 1988).

28. Of course, what is deceptive is not the admitted fuct that superimposed images are advertising but that they are not present at the place of the event – hence the media's implicit claim to be presenting a "real" picture of the event is false. On the increasing use of computer images in sports, see Alex Kuczynski, "On CBS News, Some of What You See Isn't There," *New York Times* (Jan. 12, 2000): A1. On policy relating to product placements, see Baker, *Advertising and a Democratic Press*, 103–5, and sources at 176–77 n.73.

29. Bill Carter, "CBS Is Divided over the Use of False Images in Broadcasts," *New York Times* (Jan. 12, 2000): C1.

30. Marc Lacey with Bill Carter, "In Trade-Off with TV Networks, Drug Office Is Reviewing Scripts," *New York Times* (Jan. 13, 2000): A1.

31. See *In re Policies & Rules Concerning Children's Television Programming*, 6 F.C.C.R. 2111 (1991); Newton N. Minow & Craig L. LaMay, *Abandoned in the Wasteland* (New York: Hill and Wang, 1995), 21.

32. See, e.g., Diane Zimmerman, "Requiem for a Heavyweight: A Farewell to Warren and Brandeis's Privacy Tort," *Cornell Law Review* 68 (1983): 291; John Sabini and Maury Silver, *Moralities of Everyday Life* (New York: Oxford U. Press, 1982); Max Gluckman, "Gossip and Scandal," *Current Anthropology* 4 (1964): 307; *Anderson v. Fisher Broadcasting*, 300 Or. 452, 712 P.2d 803 (1986) (noting that while some editors tailor content to public tastes, others wish to challenge majority orthodoxy).

33. See *Branzburg v. Hayes*, 408 U.S. 665, 690–91 (1972).

34. See Vince Blasi, "The Newsman's Privilege: An Empirical Study," *Michigan Law Review* 70 (1971): 229, 262.

35. See C. Edwin Baker, *Human Liberty and Freedom of Speech* (New York: Oxford U. Press, 1989), 242–49.

36. See Joseph H. Kaufman, "Beyond *Cohen v. Cowles Media Co.*: Confidentiality Agreements and Efficiency within the 'Marketplace of Ideas,'" *University of Chicago Legal*

*Forum* (1993): 255, 259–68; "The Supreme Court, 1990 Term – Leading Cases," *Harvard Law Review* 105 (1991): 177, 277–87.

37. See *Cohen v. Cowles Media Co.*, 501 U.S. 663, 673 (1991) (Blackmun, J., dissenting).

38. The best treatment, suggestive on points made here, is Lilli Levi, "Dangerous Liaisons: Seduction and Betrayal in Confidential Press-Source Relations," *Rutgers Law Review* 43 (1991): 609.

39. See Jerome A. Barron, "*Cohen v. Cowles Media* and Its Significance for First Amendment Law and Journalism," *William & Mary Bill of Rights Journal* 3 (1994): 419, 452–56. An editor's exercise of a power to break promises of anonymity can hurt the journalist by limiting her future effectiveness to the extent she will now have a bad reputation among potential sources.

40. Cf. *Cohen v. Cowles Media*, 501 U.S. at 670, criticized in C. Edwin Baker, "Turner Broadcasting: Content Regulation of Persons and Presses," *Supreme Court Review* (1994): 57, 119–22.

41. "How Confidentiality Ceases to Be Binding," *New York Times* (Jan. 17, 2000): C9.

42. See *KOVR-TV, Inc. v. Superior Court*, 37 Cal. Rptr. 2d 431, 432–33 (Cal. Ct. App. 1995).

43. 18 U.S.C. §2511 (1994).

44. Constitutional challenges claiming that these bans interfere with news gathering have been upheld in particular contexts, but more often are rejected. See Marc A. Franklin & David A. Anderson, *Mass Media Law*, 5th ed. (Westbury, N.Y.: Foundation Press, 1995), 408–11, 581–82.

45. *Branzburg v. Hayes*, 408 U.S. 665, 672 (1972).

46. Generally reporters have no special constitutional right to trespass, see, e.g., *Wilson v. Layne*, 526 U.S. 603 (1999); *Food Lion v. Capital Cities*, 194 F.3d 305 (4th Cir. 1999). Nevertheless, state statutory or common law, under certain circumstances, has given reporters limited special rights to trespass, for example, under a theory of fictional implied consent. See, e.g., *Florida Publishing Co. v. Fletcher*, 340 So. 2d 914 (Fla. 1976).

## Chapter 4

1. The mere use of economic terms such as externalities to discuss these issues runs the danger of contributing to improper commodification. See Margaret Jane Radin, *Contested Commodities* (Cambridge: Harvard U. Press, 1996), 174–76, 178, 180–83. But see my introduction to Part I.

2. Ibid., 1–15.

3. See C. Edwin Baker, "Property and Its Relation to Constitutionally Protected Liberty," *University of Pennsylvania Law Review* 134 (1986): 741, 751–53.

4. See Mark Kelman, "Consumption Theory, Production Theory, and Ideology in the Coase Theorem," *Southern California Law Review* 52 (1979): 669, 686–87.

5. The claim is "in part" – both in the sense that participants in the commercial media often are also serving nonbusiness ideals and in the sense that some mass-media entities will not be businesses. Any broader claim would ignore the contested nature of the organization of the mass media. McChesney, for example, documents the struggle over the commercialization of television in this country. Robert W.

McChesney, *Telecommunications, Mass Media, and Democracy* (New York: Oxford U. Press, 1993).

6. Some evidence supports the empirical claim that noncommodified media forms are both more common and more empowering under conditions of scarcity of commodified media. See Ullamaija Kivikuru, "Peripheral Mass Communication: Rich in Contradictions," in Kaarle Nordenstreng & Herbert I. Schiller, eds., *Beyond National Sovereignty* (Norwood, N.J.: Ablex, 1993), 145.

7. Radin, *Contested Commodities*, 95–103. Cf. C. Edwin Baker, "Counting Preferences in Collective Choice Situations," *UCLA Law Review* 25 (1978): 381, 404–8 (describing how some choices affect the world in an "additive" and others in a "determinative" manner and arguing that there is greater justification for collective control over the second).

8. See C. B. Macpherson, *The Political Theory of Possessive Individualism* (Oxford: Oxford U. Press, 1961); C. Edwin Baker, *Human Liberty and Freedom of Speech* (New York: Oxford U. Press, 1989), 198–206.

9. Radin, *Contested Commodities*, 97.

10. This claim may reflect only one possible way of characterizing or seeing culture specifically or the social world more generally. If a person's preference is for less commercialization of sex (or less homosexual sex), then each person's choice adds to or detracts from the result she prefers. However, if her preference is to live in a world where those practices never occur, one other person's practice can determine the world in an objectionable way. Thus, more normative argument is required to show why the first, "liberal" way of seeing the world should prevail, at least in policy contexts. See C. Edwin Baker, "Counting Preferences in Collective Choice Situations," *UCLA Law Review* 25 (1978): 381.

11. Radin, *Contested Commodities*, 98.

12. See Yochai Benkler, "Free as the Air to Common Use: First Amendment Constraints on Enclosure of the Public Domain," *NYU Law Review* 74 (1999): 354.

13. Potter Stewart, "Or of the Press," *Hastings Law Journal* 26 (1975): 631.

14. The same point can also be made about which commodified forms and which noncommodified forms will be chosen. Thus, Michael Madow argues that rejecting rights of publicity – property rights in one's identity – would have the beneficial effect of favoring culturally experimental and nonmainstream cultural commodities over monopolistic, more tightly controlled cultural commodities, as well as having beneficial distributive consequences, including some empowerment of more marginal producers of cultural commodities. Michael Madow, "Private Ownership of Public Image: Popular Culture and Publicity Rights," *California Law Review* 81 (1993): 125.

15. At least when being careful, economists do not claim that a perfectly working market fulfills the most preferences; they certainly do not claim that it maximizes "utility." At best, their claim is that market maximizes fulfillment of preferences "given the existing distribution of wealth" or they avoid interpersonal comparisons by claiming only that the perfectly working market creates a "Pareto optimal" result, not that it best or maximally satisfies preferences. Eventually recognizing the disconnect between efficiency and utility, Richard Posner once explained that society's real normative concern should not be with utility (or happiness) but with "wealth,"

which he defined in terms of what would be paid in a perfectly functioning market. See Richard Posner, "The Ethical and Political Basis of the Efficiency Norm in Common Law Adjudication," *Hofstra Law Review* 8 (1980): 487; cf. C. Edwin Baker, "Starting Points in the Economic Analysis of Law," *Hofstra Law Review* 8 (1980): 939, 948–53 (critiquing Posner's analysis).

16. *Shapiro v. Thompson,* 394 U.S. 618, 632–33 (1969) (footnote omitted).

17. Michael Walzer, *Spheres of Justice: A Defense of Pluralism and Equality* (New York: Basic Books, 1983), 65 (emphasis added).

18. Ibid., 68.

19. See C. Edwin Baker, "Outcome Equality or Equality of Respect: The Substantive Content of Equal Protection," *University of Pennsylvania Law Review* 131 (1983): 933.

20. Of course, even if in principle different, distinguishing between educational, political, and cultural media on the one hand and entertainment media on the other creates difficult, possibly for some purposes insurmountable, line-drawing problems. See *Hannegan v. Esquire,* 327 U.S. 146 (1946) (refusing to allow the Post Office to enforce distinctions among magazins for getting second-class postal rates).

21. 512 U.S. 622, 637–41 (1994).

22. See C. Edwin Baker, "Turner Broadcasting: Content Regulation of Persons and Presses," *Supreme Court Review* (1994): 57, 93–114.

23. Richard B. Kielbowicz, *News in the Mail: The Press, Post Office, and Public Information, 1700–1860s* (New York: Greenwood Press, 1989), 33–34. The structure of mail rates favor particular types of papers, with corresponding political consequences, and this fact was well reflected in the legislative debates. The result was a compromise but one that arguably most favored the city papers, with their presumably nationalizing content, over the local or county papers. In addition to these overt policy issues, the cynic might see in the subsidy more overt rent seeking by a favored industry.

24. See generally Jonathan Weinberger, "Broadcasting and Speech," *California Law Review* 81 (1993): 1103.

25. See, e.g., *FCC v. National Citizens Committee for Broadcasting,* 436 U.S. 775 (1978) (upholding selective limitation on newspaper's cross-ownership of broadcast stations); *Committee for an Independent P-I v. Hearst Corp.,* 704 F.2d 467 (9th Cir. 1983) (upholding the Newspaper Preservation Act against challenge that it favored some papers at the expense of others). See generally Baker, "Turner Broadcasting," 93–114.

26. Sometimes it is argued that the First Amendment protects only or primarily political speech from suppression. Not only is this claim descriptively contrary to judicial doctrine and properly rejected on straight normative premises (see Baker, *Human Liberty and Freedom of Speech,* ch. 2), but the distinction between the categories is too problematic to allow censorship or suppression of "merely" entertaining speech. Zechariah Chafee Jr., "Book Review," *Harvard Law Review* 62 (1949): 891, 895–901. Criticisms such as Chafee's apparently led Alexander Meiklejohn to modify his early views that limited the First Amendment to political speech. See Alexander Meiklejohn, "The First Amendment Is an Absolute," *Supreme Court Review* (1961): 245, 255.

27. *Hannegan v. Esquire, Inc.*, 327 U.S. 146, 148 (1946), quoting 39 U.S.C. §226 (1946). The statute also denied second-class mailing rates to a second content-based category – "publications designed primarily for advertising purposes."

28. The simplicity as to voting may be superficial. The "effectiveness" of a person's vote depends, in addition to the number of voters in the district, on the relation of the voter's specific political orientation to the political orientation of other voters within her district. The second part of this relationship means that the effectiveness of a person's vote *always* depends on how the district lines have been drawn (gerrymandered). Moreover, the first part of the relationship means that even within a single district different people will experience the effectiveness of their vote differently. For example, a person on the far left or right may want a strong majority for her party so that she can influence who in the party gets the "safe" seat. In contrast, a centrist may have a more effective voice if candidates of roughly equal parties have to vie for her vote, a context that denies any effectiveness to the far right or left. Thus, a one-person–one-vote, winner-take-all system cannot provide voters with the "equally effective voice" that the Court sometimes says the Constitution demands. *Reynolds v. Sims*, 377 U.S. 533, 565 (1964). Nothing but proportional representation could come close. Still, one-person–one-vote does provide formal equality, which is the only equality properly required constitutionally. See C. Edwin Baker, "Neutrality, Process, and Rationality: Flawed Interpretations of Equal Protection," *Texas Law Review* 58 (1980): 1029, 1072–84.

29. Cf. *San Antonio Indep. Sch. Dist. v. Rodriguez*, 411 U.S. 1 (1973).

30. This paragraph is based on C. Edwin Baker, *Advertising and a Democratic Press* (Princeton: Princeton U. Press, 1994), 66–69.

31. 383 U.S. 663 (1966).

32. See ibid., 670.

33. Cf. *Rodriguez*, 411 U.S. at 36 (noting that a right to a minimum amount of education may be implicit in the right to vote).

34. See Will Kymlicka, *Liberalism, Community, and Culture* (New York: Oxford U. Press, 1989), 175–76.

35. Ibid., 164.

36. Ibid., 165. For similar reasons, Jürgen Habermas argues that "[a] correctly understood theory of [individualistically designed] rights requires . . . [protection of] the life contexts in which [an individual's] identity is formed." Jürgen Habermas, *The Inclusion of the Other* (Cambridge: MIT Press, 1998), 208; see also 220–21.

37. Kymlicka, *Liberalism, Community, and Culture*, 165, quoting John Rawls, *A Theory of Justice* (Cambridge: Harvard U. Press, 1971), 440.

38. Ibid.

39. See ibid., 169, 177.

40. Ibid., 166.

41. Habermas, *The Inclusion of the Other*, 210 (emphasis added).

42. Ibid., 210.

43. Kymlicka argues that the liberal project crucially depends on a distinction between "context" and "choice." A person has no complaint if her own choices frustrate her life plan but does if she more than others is disadvantaged by context. Thus, liberal theorists properly favor compensating for disadvantages that are not "chosen" but

reflect context – for example, a person's social environment or natural endowments. Likewise, the legal order treats people unequally if it disadvantages them because of their cultural heritage, which it does if it does not equally support that heritage. Kymlicka, *Liberalism, Community, and Culture*, 186–89.

44. See Jürgen Habermas, "Three Normative Models of Democracy," *Constellations* 1 (1994): 1; and my Chapter 6.

45. For more stringent criticisms of Kymlicka's thesis along the line suggested in the text, see Andrei Marmor, "Equality and Minority Culture," *Democratic Culture* 3 (2001).

46. See *Planned Parenthood v. Casey*, 505 U.S. 833, 872 (1992).

47. A prominent economist once told me that the market provides the only reliable source of information about preferences – about demand. Consider, however, an ugly shirt in the back of my closet. Does the fact that I never wear it or the fact that I paid $25 for it when I bought it in a drunken stupor provide the best evidence of the content and strength of my preferences? The economist might say the purchase, but a noneconomist might simply say that I made a mistake about my "real" preferences.

48. See Cass Sunstein, "Social Norms and Social Rules," *Columbia Law Review* 96 (1996): 903, 928–31. Emphasizing how social roles, norms, and meanings affect preferences, Sunstein generates a powerful critique of law and economics methodology. His primary point is that preferences are not autonomous and are often effectively changed by government action. Ibid., 947–52; see also Cass Sunstein, *Behavioral Law and Economics* (Cambridge: Cambridge U. Press, 2000). Here, Sunstein generalizes and empirically supports a long-standing criticism of standard law and economics methodology – namely, that one reason the methodology is inherently indeterminate in identifying "efficient" rules is that its analysis must take a set of preferences as given, but often part of the issue in the choice of rules is to decide which preferences should count and which are desirable. Moreover, because the rule chosen will affect the preferences people develop, reliance on any particular set for this choice seems arbitrary. See, e.g., C. Edwin Baker, "Posner's Privacy Mystery and the Failure of Economic Analysis of Law," *Georgia Law Review* 12 (1978): 487–93. Consequently, as a positive analysis, the economics analysis will necessarily be inadequate. Either rule that could have been chosen may, if chosen, create the preferences that in retrospect make it appear efficient. See Baker, "Starting Points in Economic Analysis of Law," 966–68.

49. Sunstein, "Social Norms and Social Rules," 933.

50. Lee C. Bollinger, "The Rationale of Public Regulation of the Media," in Judith Lichtenberg, ed., *Democracy and the Mass Media* (Cambridge: Cambridge U. Press, 1990): 355, 366.

51. Ibid., 366–67; see also 363–64.

52. See, e.g., C. Edwin Baker, "The Ideology of the Economic Analysis of Law," *Philosophy & Public Affairs* 5 (1975): 3; Bollinger, "The Rationale of Public Regulation of the Media."

53. See Harry Frankfurt, "Freedom of the Will and the Concept of a Person," *Journal of Philosophy* 68 (1971): 5, 7.

54. See Steven H. Shiffrin, *Dissent, Injustice, and the Meaning of America* (Princeton: Princeton U. Press, 1999).

55. Steven Shiffrin, "The First Amendment and Economic Regulation: Away from a General Theory of the First Amendment," *Northwestern University Law Review* 78 (1983): 1212, 1281.

56. See Michael Schudson, *Advertising, The Uneasy Persuasion* (New York: Basic Books, 1984), 5–6, 209–33.

57. See John Stuart Mill, *On Liberty* (London: J. W. Parker & Son, 1859), ch. 5. Mill argued that society might legitimately want to regulate the commercial promotion of various preferences – for instance, for commercialized sex or drugs.

58. *Virginia State Board of Pharmacy v. Virginia Citizens Consumer Council*, 425 U.S. 748 (1976). See Baker, *Human Liberty and Freedom of Speech*, ch. 9.

59. See Baker, *Advertising and a Democratic Press*, 44–70; Joseph Turow, *Breaking Up America: Advertising and the New Media World* (Chicago: U. of Chicago Press, 1997).

60. See Turow, *Breaking Up America*, 22.

61. Reportedly 6 million people planned to participate in TV Free America's fifth annual week where participants are supposed to turn off their televisions and engage in other activities and forms of entertainment. Christine Walker, "Event Helps Turn Kids Off TV," *Sun Sentinel* (Fort Lauderdale, Fla.) (Apr. 22, 1999): 4B.

62. Reid Calvin, "Verso: Sales Up; Marketing Marx," *Publishers Weekly* (Feb. 2, 1998).

63. A second element of "brand" identity – including serial publications, story serialization, stars, prominence of book authors or movie directors – is its capacity to reduce the audience's informational search costs, a reduction based on the premise that the brand continuity correlates with quality continuity. This feature gives products with the brand identity a competitive advantage, although the advantage may not correspond to the media products that the audience would have wanted advantaged if they did not have to worry about search costs. This point, although related, is separate from the concern discussed in the text about the economic incentive to create preferences for particular types of content.

64. See Madow, "Private Ownership of Public Image," 191–96.

65. Leo Bogart, *Commercial Culture: The Media System and the Public Interest* (New York: Oxford U. Press, 1995), 227.

66. Ibid., 228 (quoting recording executive). The law helps structure this drift toward a star system by, for example, recognizing a "right of publicity." See Madow, "Private Ownership of Public Image," 130.

67. See Robert H. Frank & Philip J. Cook, *The Winner-Take-All Society* (New York: Free Press, 1995), 101–23; Madow, "Private Ownership of Public Image," 216–17.

68. *Miami Herald Publ'g Co. v. Tornillo*, 418 U.S. 241, 258 (1974).

69. *Associated Press v. United States*, 326 U.S. 1, 20 (1945).

## CHAPTER 5

1. See *United States v. UAW*, 352 U.S. 567, 570–75 (1957) (discussing history of restrictions on corporate political contributions); Louise Overacker, *Money in Elections* (New York: Arno Press, 1932), 177–88; Earl R. Sikes, *State and Federal Corrupt-Practices Legislation* (Durham: Duke U. Press, 1928), 108–13.

2. Compare *Austin v. Michigan State Chamber of Commerce*, 494 U.S. 652, 660 (1990) (upholding statute prohibiting corporations from making independent

expenditures on behalf of political candidates from corporate treasury), with *First Nat'l Bank v. Bellotti*, 435 U.S. 765, 795 (1978) (striking down statute prohibiting corporations from making expenditures to influence the outcome of referendum not affecting the corporation's property, business, or assets).

3. C. Edwin Baker, "Campaign Expenditures and Free Speech," *Harvard Civil Rights–Civil Liberties Law Review* 33 (1998): 1, 4–9 (listing examples of regulations upheld); cf. *Buckley v. Valeo*, 424 U.S. 1 (1976) (striking down regulation of expenditures on campaign-oriented speech).

4. See *New York Times Co. v. Sullivan*, 376 U.S. 254, 279–80 (1964).

5. See *Mills v. Alabama*, 384 U.S. 214, 220 (1966); see also *Landmark Communications, Inc. v. Virginia*, 435 U.S. 829, 838 (1978) (protecting publication of truthful information regarding confidential Judicial Inquiry and Review Commission proceedings). Before the development of modern First Amendment jurisprudence, prohibitions that served very partisan positions were treated as constitutionally much less problematic. See *Patterson v. Colorado*, 205 U.S. 454, 463 (1907) (Holmes, J.) (upholding contempt citation of newspaper for publishing political cartoons and denying the paper an opportunity to defend by proving truth). Cf. *Hustler Magazine v. Falwell*, 485 U.S. 46 (1988).

6. See *Brown v. Hartlage*, 456 U.S. 45 (1982); *Eu v. San Francisco County Democratic Central Committee*, 489 U.S. 214 (1989).

7. See Richard B. Kielbowicz, *News in the Mail: The Press, Post Office, and Public Information, 1700–1860s* (New York: Greenwood Press, 1989), 20–24. Newspapers' political power may have led to subsidies, especially postal subsidies – many early postmasters were newspaper publishers. Originally, in addition to newspapers, the more common users of the mail were apparently other businesses, not individuals engaged in noncommercial communications. Hence, the postage expenditures of these other businesses probably paid most of the newspaper subsidy.

8. See Richard B. Kielbowicz, "Origins of the Second-Class Mail Category and the Business of Policymaking, 1863–1879," *Journalism Monographs* 96 (1986): 1, 4, 13, 20.

9. See 5 U.S.C. §552 (1994).

10. See ibid. §552(a)(4)(A)(ii)(II), (iii).

11. See Danny Schecter, "Fresh Airwaves," *Nation* (Feb. 14, 2000), 6–7.

12. See Karl Erik Gustafsson & Stig Hadenius, *Swedish Press Policy* (Stockholm: Swedish Institute, 1976), 78; Goran Hedebro, "Communication Policy in Sweden: An Experiment in State Intervention," in Patricia Edgar & Syed A. Rahim, eds., *Communication Policy in Developed Countries* (Boston: Kegan Paul International, 1983), 137; Lennart Weibull & Magnus Anshelm, "Indications of Change: Developments in Swedish Media 1980–1990," *Gazette* 49 (1992): 41.

13. Newspaper Preservation Act, Pub. L. No. 91-353, 91 Stat. 353 (1970).

14. See, e.g., Thomas E. Humphrey, "The Newspaper Preservation Act: An Ineffective Step in the Right Direction," *Boston College Industrial & Commerce Law Review* 12 (1971): 937.

15. See, e.g., Leo Bogart, *Commercial Culture: The Media System and the Public Interest* (New York: Oxford U. Press, 1995), 174–75; Doug Underwood, *When MBAs Rule the Newsroom* (New York: Columbia U. Press, 1993), 59–66.

16. See, e.g., C. Edwin Baker, *Ownership of Newspapers: The View from the Positivist Social Science*, Shorenstein Barone Center of JFK School of Gov., Harvard U. Cambridge, 1994, 9–12 (review of literature); William B. Blankenberg & Gary W. Ozanich, "The Effects of Public Ownership on the Financial Performance of Newspaper Corporations," *Journalism Quarterly* 70 (1993): 68, 70–71, 74; David Pearce Demers, "Corporate Structure and Emphasis on Profit and Product Quality at U.S. Daily Newspapers," *Journalism Quarterly* 68 (1991): 15, 23; John Busterna, "How Managerial Ownership Affects Profit Maximization in Newspaper Firms," *Journalism Quarterly* 66 (1989): 302, 302, 307, 358.

17. Author interview with Warren Phillips, CEO, *Wall Street Journal*, Fall 1992; see also Bill Kovach, "Big Deals, with Journalism Thrown In," *New York Times* (Aug. 3, 1995): A25.

18. C. K. McClatchy, *How Newspapers Are Owned – and Does It Matter?*, Press Enterprise Lecture Series No. 23 (1988), 8.

19. See, e.g., "Cereal Killing," *New Yorker* (July 24, 1995): 4 (discussing the closing of *New York Newsday* by the former General Mills executive put in charge of *Times Mirror Company*).

20. Both legal and customary factors could cause *control* to diverge from *ownership* and even to devolve lower down the corporate structure, moving from central management to editors or journalists. The extent and nature of employee associations, of unionism (and hence of labor law), and the content of contract and corporate law will significantly affect the locus of actual control. Sensitive attention to this is crucial for intelligent media policy. For example, Jerome Barron based his analysis of *Cohen v. Cowles Media*, 501 U.S. 663 (1991), in part on how the decision would affect decision-making control within media organizations. See Jerome A. Barron, "*Cohen v. Cowles Media* and Its Significance for First Amendment Law and Journalism," *William & Mary Bill of Rights Journal* 3 (1994): 419; see also Gail L. Barwis, "Contractual Newsroom Democracy," *Journalism Monographs* 57 (1978): 1.

21. See Werner J. Severin, "The Milwaukee Journal: Employee-Owned Prizewinner," *Journalism Quarterly* 56 (1979): 783.

22. See, e.g., Commission on Freedom of the Press, *A Free and Responsible Press* (Chicago: U. of Chicago Press, 1947), 79–80.

23. These media-specific concentration rules have been routinely upheld by the Supreme Court when challenged even though some place restrictions on constitutionally favored media entities, such as newspapers, restrictions that are not imposed on nonmedia businesses. The Supreme Court also allowed the FCC to distinguish among newspapers, requiring divestiture of their local broadcast licenses in sixteen "egregious" cases, but not in others. See *FCC v. National Citizens Comm. for Broad.*, 436 U.S. 775, 793 (1978); see also *United States v. Storer Broad. Co.*, 351 U.S. 192, 203 (1956) (upholding national concentration limits on broadcast licenses).

24. See, e.g., *Policy Statement on Comparative Broadcast Hearings*, 1 F.C.C.2d 393 (1965). The FCC's readiness to approve sale of the license by the party that wins the comparative proceeding to a party that could not have prevailed in the proceedings arguably doomed this policy from the start. See ibid., concurring statement of Commissioner Robert E. Lee (it's a "hell of a way to run a railroad").

25. See *National Broad. Co. v. United States*, 319 U.S. 190, 224–27 (1943) (upholding rules against statutory and constitutional challenge).

26. See U.S. Department of Commerce, *Globalization of the Mass Media* (Washington, D.C.: GPO 1993), 124.

27. See Telecommunications Act of 1996, Pub. L. No. 104-104, 110 Stat. 56 (1996).

28. See James N. Dertouzos & Kenneth E. Thorpe, *Newspaper Groups: Economies of Scale, Tax Laws and Merger Incentives* (Santa Monica, Calif.: RAND Corp., 1982), 55–87. One policy justification for recent changes in inheritance laws was to reduce the pressure on families to sell their media properties. See ibid. at 72–75.

29. See Robert W. McChesney, *Telecommunications, Mass Media, and Democracy: The Battle for the Control of U.S. Broadcasting, 1928–1935* (New York: Oxford U. Press, 1993), 121–50.

30. This explains why corporate special interest groups' power to obtain policies that sacrifice the public interest should not motivate an interpretation of the First Amendment that keeps government out of the arena of press policy. See C. Edwin Baker, "Private Power, the Press, and the Constitution," *Constitutional Commentary* 10 (1993): 421, 432 (arguing that courts have properly rejected this approach to the Press Clause).

31. See Ben H. Bagdikian, *Double Vision* (Boston: Beacon Press, 1995), 239.

32. See C. Edwin Baker, "Mergerphobia," *Nation* 257 (Nov. 8, 1993): 520, 521.

33. See James Curran, "Mass Media and Democracy Revisited," in James Curran & Michael Gurevitch, eds., *Mass Media and Society*, 2d ed. (New York: St. Martin's Press, 1996), 81.

34. See John P. Murray, "The Impact of Televised Violence," *Hofstra Law Review* 22 (1992): 809.

35. For a rare, thoughtful attempt to consider serious structural responses to media portrayals of violence, see Stephen J. Kim, " 'Viewer Discretion Advised': A Structural Approach to the Issue of Television Violence," *University of Pennsylvania Law Review* 142 (1994): 1383.

36. See, e.g., *Gitlow v. New York*, 268 U.S. 652, 672 (1925) (Holmes & Brandeis, JJ., dissenting); see also *American Booksellers Ass'n v. Hudnut*, 771 F.2d 323 (7th Cir. 1985) (harm caused by pornography does not justify suppression), *aff'd*, 475 U.S. 1001 (1986). Likewise, a liberty theory asserts that harm does not itself justify suppressing speech. See C. Edwin Baker, "Harm, Liberty, and Free Speech," *Southern California Law Review* 70 (1997): 979.

37. See *Brandenburg v. Ohio*, 395 U.S. 444 (1969). An appellate court relied on this theory to hold that the district court should not dismiss the complaint charging liability against the publisher of *Hitman: A Technical Manual for Independent Contractors. Rice v. Paladin Enterprises*, 128 F.3d 233 (4th Cir. 1997).

38. See C. Edwin Baker, "Of Course, More than Words," *University of Chicago Law Review* 61 (1994): 1181, 1205–6 (critiquing Catherine MacKinnon in part for not taking women's and men's agency seriously).

39. See Amy Adler, "What's Left? Hate Speech, Pornography, and the Problem for Artistic Expression," *California Law Review* 84 (1996): 1499; see also Lili Levi, "The Hard Case of Broadcast Indecency," *NYU Review of Law & Social Change* 20 (1992–93): 49.

40. See Carlin Meyer, "Sex, Sin, and Women's Liberation: Against Porn-Suppression," *Texas Law Review* 72 (1994): 1097, 1100–1.
41. See Kenneth L. Karst, "Boundaries and Reasons: Freedom of Expression and the Subordination of Groups," *University of Illinois Law Review* (1990): 95, 95–99.
42. See C. Edwin Baker, *Human Liberty and Freedom of Speech* (New York: Oxford U. Press, 1989), ch. 5.
43. See *FCC v. Pacifica Found.*, 438 U.S. 726, 765–77 (1978) (Brennan and Marshall, JJ., dissenting) (noting the "depressing inability [of the Court's majority] to appreciate that in our land of cultural pluralism, there are many who think, act, and talk differently from the members of this Court, and who do not share their fragile sensibilities").
44. Cf. *Board of Educ. v. Pico*, 457 U.S. 853, 868–69 (1982) (holding the First Amendment imposes limitations on a school board's discretion to remove books from junior and senior high school libraries).
45. See *Butler v. Michigan*, 352 U.S. 380, 383 (1957).
46. See *FCC v. Pacifica Found.*, 438 U.S. 726, 750–51 (1978); see also *Ginsberg v. New York*, 390 U.S. 629 (1968) (print media); *Sable Communications v. FCC*, 492 U.S. 115 (1989) (telephone). The Court also emphasized not decreasing availability when it first upheld physical zoning of adult movie theaters, noting that the zoning was designed to decrease negative externalities and was unrelated to any interest in restricting access to communicative content. See *Young v. American Mini Theaters*, 427 U.S. 50, 62–63 (1976).
47. See C. Edwin Baker, "The Evening Hours during Pacifica Standard Time," *Villanova Sports & Entertainment Law Journal* 3 (1996): 45, 55–60. *Pacifica* itself is consistent with a constitutionally permissible attempt to enhance parental authority. However, the later governmental decision to prohibit indecency between 6 A.M. and 12 P.M., upheld in *Action for Children's Television v. FCC*, 58 F.3d 654, 669 (D.C. Cir. 1995) (en banc), improperly accepted a majoritarian purpose of molding people. The key difference between Kennedy's majority opinion and Breyer's dissent in *United States v. Playboy Entertainment Group*, 120 S.Ct 1878 (2000), was that the majority only credited the state interest in aiding parental control, for which the law seemed unnecessary, while the dissent credited a governmental interest in preventing children from viewing certain material, an interest that arguably justified the law.
48. See William P. Marshall & Susan Gilles, "The Supreme Court, the First Amendment, and Bad Journalism," *Supreme Court Review* (1994): 169, 207–8.
49. See *Medico v. Time, Inc.*, 643 F.2d 134, 137 (3d Cir. 1981).
50. See William Glaberson, "Publication of a Unabomber's Tract Draws Mixed Response," *New York Times* (Sept. 20, 1995): A16.
51. See, e.g., Alex P. Schimd & Janny de Graaf, *Violence as Communication* (Beverly Hills, Calif.: Sage, 1982), 33–42.
52. Some countries, for example, Germany, use this procedure although it has not been adopted in the United States. See Gary S. Lutzker, "Dat's All Folks: *Cahn v. Sony* and the Audio Home Recording Act of 1991 – Merry Melodies or Looney Tunes?" *Cardozo Arts & Entertainment Law Journal* 11 (1992): 145, 183; cf. *Sony Corp. v. Universal City Studios*, 464 U.S. 417, 456 (1984).
53. See 47 U.S.C. §317(a)(i) (1994) (imposing on broadcasters a duty to identify payee as advertiser); *Lewis Publ'g Co. v. Morgan*, 229 U.S. 288, 313–14 (1913) (upholding

against First Amendment challenge a statute that imposed this requirement on newspapers receiving second-class mail privileges). Cf. *SEC v. Wall Street Publishing Institute*, 851 F.2d 365 (D.C. Cir. 1989).

54. Max Frankel, "Words and Images; Plots for Hire," *New York Times* (Feb. 6, 2000): G6 (magazine); Marc Lacey and Bill Carter, "In Trade-Off with Network, Drug Office Is Reviewing Scripts," *New York Times* (Jan. 14, 2000): A1.

55. See Edward S. Herman & Noam Chomsky, *Manufacturing Consent: The Politics of the Mass Media* (New York: Pantheon Books, 1988), 21.

56. See *Metro Broadcasting v. FCC*, 497 U.S. 547 (1990). Here, Brennan in his last opinion as a justice, found for the Court that greater diversity in content was a sufficiently important government purpose to justify an affirmative action program. See C. Edwin Baker, "Turner Broadcasting: Content Regulation of Persons and Presses," *Supreme Court Review* (1994): 57, 125–27.

57. Sometimes the law directly supports this bias against outsiders. Privileges in the libel area permit easier reliance on or reportage of statements by a public official or charges made by "a responsible, prominent organization . . . regardless of the reporter's private views regarding their validity." *Edwards v. National Audubon Soc'y, Inc.*, 556 F.2d 113, 120 (2d Cir. 1977).

58. The Court suggested that the content-based, discriminatory tax scheme invalidated in *Arkansas Writers' Project v. Ragland*, 481 U.S. 221, 232–33 (1987), might have been constitutional if it could plausibly have been understood as designed to help "fledgling" publications.

59. See *Syracuse Peace Council v. FCC*, 867 F.2d 654, 669 (D.C. Cir. 1989).

60. See *Time Warner v. FCC*, 93 F.3d 957 (D.C. Cir. 1996).

61. See Richard B. Kielbowicz & Linda Lawson, "Reduced-Rate Postage for Nonprofit Organizations: A Policy History, Critique, and Proposal," *Harvard Journal of Law & Public Policy* 11 (1988): 347, 348–49.

62. See *Regan v. Taxation with Representation*, 461 U.S. 540, 549–50 (1983).

63. See *In re Review of Stephen Paul Dunifer*, 11 F.C.C.R. 718 (1995) (upholding ban on low-power radio station); "Rebels Hoist Challenge to Radio Rules," *Chicago Tribune* (Aug. 5, 1996): Bus. 7; Luis J. Rodriquez, "Rappin' in the 'Hood; Rebel Radio," *Nation* (Aug. 12, 1991): 192; Michael Wines, "An Internet Service Is Denied Access to the Capitol," *New York Times* (Feb. 26, 1996): D7 (relating story about Vigdor Schreibman, a leftist nonprofit Internet news service publisher who was denied access to congressional press galleries because his venture was not commercial); Craig R. Smith, ed., *Silencing the Opposition: Government Strategies of Suppression of Freedom of Expression* (Albany: State U. of New York Press, 1996).

64. 47 U.S.C. §315.

65. The statute required that all other candidates get equal access when one candidate got to "use" the broadcast station. In 1975 the FCC changed its interpretation of "use" of a broadcast station in a way that permitted broadcasters to televise debates sponsored by the League of Women Voters even though not all legally qualified candidates were invited to participate. See *Chisholm v. FCC*, 538 F.2d 349, 366 (D.C. Cir. 1976). Televising the earlier Kennedy-Nixon debates had only been permitted, given the interpretation of "use" accepted at that time, because of special congressional legislation. Ibid., 360.

66. In 1996 the major networks sought exemption from the equal-opportunities requirement so that it could provide free time for "*major* presidential candidates, as determined by the Commission on Presidential Debates." Public Notice, FCC Seeks Comment on Issues Relating to Broadcaster Proposals to Provide Time to Presidential Candidates; Will Hold En Banc Hearing (May 13, 1996).

67. 523 U.S. 666 (1998). Justice Stevens, writing for four dissenting justices, did not object to this discretion. However, in order to prevent partisan abuse of discretion and to assure the exclusion did not occur for impermissible reasons, Stevens would have required the station to exclude legally qualified candidates only on the basis of "narrow, objective, and definite [written] standards."

68. But cf. *Saloomey v. Jeppesen & Co.*, 707 F.2d 671, 676–77 (2d Cir. 1983) (allowing recovery for plane crash due to inaccurate flight chart, analogizing chart to a product, and using products liability doctrine).

69. Although the Supreme Court consistently protects the media from liability for publication of truthful information, it has refused to accept the media's suggestion that it "hold broadly that truthful publication may never be punished consistent with the First Amendment." *Florida Star v. B.J.F.*, 491 U.S. 524, 532 (1989).

70. Cf. *Milkovich v. Lorain Journal*, 497 U.S. 1, 17–20 (1990).

71. See Diane L. Zimmerman, "Requiem for a Heavyweight: A Farewell to Warren and Brandeis's Privacy Tort," *Cornell Law Review* 68 (1983): 291, 362.

72. Because both the positive and negative third-party effects can easily exist whether or not the information is true, the different treatment of true and false information may reflect distributional or fairness concerns rather than mere efficiency matters. But this turns out to be more complex. For instance, there may be inefficiencies in a system that promotes the creation and spread of false information. These may provide an efficiency reason to make the distinction.

73. Even where recognized, the tort requires that the information not only be "highly offensive" but also be of "no legitimate public concern." See *Haynes v. Alfred A. Knopf, Inc.*, 8 F.3d 1222, 1232 (7th Cir. 1993); see also *Restatement (Second) of Torts* §652D (1981).

74. See Note, "And Forgive Them Their Trespasses: Applying the Defense of Necessity to the Criminal Conduct of the Newsgatherer," *Harvard Law Reveiw* 103 (1990): 890, 893–903. Compare *Florida Publ'g Co. v. Fletcher*, 340 So. 2d 914, 918 (Fla. 1976), with *Stahl v. State*, 665 P.2d 839, 841 (Okla. Crim. App. 1983). Allowing the trespass might reflect the prediction that, if not for insurmountable transaction costs, permissions would be obtained, sometimes with and sometimes without a charge – such that the rule reaches a Kaldor-Hicks result. However, sometimes a permissive approach to trespassing seems to reflect a view of the value of news gathering that should outweigh the interest in a private property owner in suppressing information even when the owner would deny permission or charge an amount larger than the media would be willing to pay.

75. The law on this issue is still in dispute. Most recently, in *Food Lion v. Capital Cities/ABC*, 194 F.3d 505 (3d Cir. 1999), the Court of Appeals found that it is unconstitutional, in the context of that case, to impose damages that result from the publication of information of public importance gained by trespass. Compare *Dietman v. Time*, 449 F.2d 245 (1971) (allowing enhancement of damages by publication) with *Costlow v. Cusimano*, 311 N.Y.S.2d 92, 97 (1970) (not allowing

enhancement). A closely related but presumably easier question is whether the First Amendment prohibits liability for communicating the contents of illegally intercepted information by those who did not participate in or encourage the illegal interception. Although here liability should surely be inappropriate – and is inconsistent with *Food Lion* – the issue has split the circuits. See *Bartnicki v. Vopper*, 69 U.S.L. W. 3748 (2001) (on narrow facts, protecting publication and rejecting liability).

76. A law making it criminal to record without the consent of all parties was upheld against the claim that recording aided the accuracy of reporting and provided potential corroboration in a suit for defamation. See *Shevin v. Sunbeam Television Corp.*, 351 So. 2d 723, 727 (Fla. 1977).

77. See Duncan Kennedy & Frank Michelman, "Are Property and Contract Efficient?" *Hofstra Law Review* 8 (1980): 711.

78. Some research indicates that viewers of violent sexual videos, as compared to nonviewers, have more aggressive attitudes toward women and unsympathetic attitudes toward rape victims, but if the viewing is followed by appropriate debriefing, the viewers have greater sensitivity toward issues of violence toward women than they had before seeing the videos. See Daniel Linz & Edward Donnerstein, "The Effects of Counter-Information on the Acceptance of Rape Myths," in Dolf Zillman & Jennings Bryant, eds., *Pornography: Research Advances & Policy Considerations* (Hillsdale, N.J.: L. Erlbaum Associates, 1989): 259, 263–67, 284.

79. See Joseph N. Cappella & Kathleen Hall Jamieson, *Spiral of Cynicism* (New York: Oxford U. Press, 1997).

80. See Frank Rich, "The Idiot Chip," *New York Times* (Feb. 10, 1996): A23. But cf. Clyde H. Farnsworth, "Chip to Block TV Gore Popular in Canada Test," *New York Times* (Feb. 28, 1996): A2 (discussing the V-chip's popularity in Canada).

81. See Lawrie Mifflin, "U.S. Mandates Educational TV for Children," *New York Times* (Aug. 9, 1996): A16.

82. *Turner Broadcasting v. FCC*, 512 U.S. 622, 680, 684 (O'Connor, J., dissenting) (1994). Actually, the Court did not conclusively uphold the law for another three years. *Turner Broadcasting v. FCC*, 520 U.S. 180 (1997).

83. Cf. *West Coast Hotel v. Parrish*, 300 U.S. 379 (1937) (characterizing the absence of a minimum-wage law as a "subsidy for unconscionable employers").

84. Cf. Robert Pitofsky, "The Political Content of Antitrust," *University of Pennsylvania Law Review* 127 (1979): 1051, 1051 (calling for the courts to consider not only the economic approach to antitrust, but a political values approach as well).

85. See Anthony T. Kronman, "Contract Law and Distributive Justice," *Yale Law Journal* 89 (1980): 472.

86. To be more precise, because the government always intervenes at least to the extent of creating and enforcing a legal framework of property rights, this purported nonintervention benefits those who profit most from interventions conventionally seen from a status quo perspective as noninterventions.

## PART II

1. *Craig v. Harney*, 331 U.S. 367, 383 (1947) (Murphy, J., concurring). Moreover, this view of the press is widely accepted internationally. See, e.g., Henricus G.

Schermers, "International Human Rights in the European Community and in the Nations of Central and Eastern Europe: An Overview," *Connecticut Journal of International Law* 8 (1993): 313, 316 ("Freedom of the press is an essential element of democracy"). See generally Pnina Lahav, "An Outline for a General Theory of Press Law in Democracy," in Pnina Lahav, ed., *Press Law in Modern Democracies* (New York: Longman, 1985), 339.

2. *Associated Press v. United States*, 326 U.S. 1, 28 (Frankfurter, J., concurring).
3. Letter from James Madison to W. T. Barry (Aug. 4, 1822), reprinted in Gaillard Hunt, ed., *The Writings of James Madison*, vol. 9 (New York: G. P. Putnam's Sons, 1910), 103, 103.
4. Thomas Jefferson, *Democracy*, ed. Saul K. Padover (New York: D. Appleton-Century Co., 1939), 150–51, quoted in *Dyson v. Stein*, 401 U.S. 200, 208 n.6 (1971) (Douglas, J., dissenting).
5. The argument for this claim is complex, but it has been a theme in recent works of Jürgen Habermas and Frank Michelman. See Jürgen Habermas, *Between Facts and Norms* (Cambridge: MIT Press, 1996); Frank I. Michelman, "Justification (and Justifiability) of Law in a Contradictory World," in J. Roland Pennock & John W. Chapman, eds., *Justification*, NOMOS XXVIII (New York: New York U. Press, 1985), 71. Roughly the thesis is that public liberty can only result from choices of autonomous agents whose autonomy is constituted by private liberties, and the necessary content of private liberties can only be determined (and secured) collectively by exercises of public liberty.
6. This attempt at a descriptive or scientific theory is a characteristic common among elite democrats and is also proclaimed by many pluralist or interest-group theorists. See, e.g., Robert A. Dahl, *A Preface to Democratic Theory* (Chicago: U. of Chicago Press, 1956); David B. Truman, *The Governmental Process* (New York: Knopf, 1951).
7. See, e.g., Edmund Burke, *Reflections on the Revolution in France* (London: J. Dodsley, 1790), reprinted in L. G. Mitchell & William B. Todd, eds., *The Writings and Speeches of Edmund Burke*, vol. 8 (Oxford: Clarendon, 1989), 53, 111 ("The science of constructing a commonwealth, or renovating it, or reforming it, is, like every other experimental science, not to be taught a priori. Nor is it a short experience that can instruct us in that practical science . . .").
8. See C. B. Macpherson, *The Life and Times of Liberal Democracy* (New York: Oxford U. Press, 1977), 77–92.

## Chapter 6

1. Walter Lippman, *Public Opinion* (New York: Free Press, 1965), 197. See also ibid., 157, 250–51; Joseph A. Schumpeter, *Capitalism, Socialism, and Democracy* (1942; New York: Harper & Row, 1976), 260–62.
2. Vincent Blasi, "The Checking Value in First Amendment Theory," *American Bar Foundation Research Journal* (1977): 521, 562.
3. Schumpeter, *Capitalism, Socialism, and Democracy*, 285. Even as to this limited form of democracy, Schumpeter argues that its advantages are empirical and only exist under certain, specifiable conditions. See ibid., 290.

4. This empirical claim is heavily indebted to the work of Weber. See generally Max Weber, *Economy and Society*, ed. Guenther Roth & Claus Wittich (Berkeley: U. of California Press, 1978). The claim obviously requires more support, and may turn out to be wrong or more complicated in various circumstances. See, e.g., Alan Hyde, "The Concept of Legitimation in the Sociology of Law," *Wisconsin Law Review* (1983): 379, 385 (asserting that "the Weberian model . . . at best is problematic and unproven and at worst is probably wrong"). But for present purposes, the claim's actual truth is less relevant than is the belief in its truth by theorists of elite democracy.

5. See Schumpeter, *Capitalism, Socialism, and Democracy*, 258.

6. Robert A. Dahl, *A Preface to Democratic Theory* (Chicago: U. of Chicago Press, 1956), 6.

7. David Held identifies Max Weber and Joseph Schumpeter as his exemplar democratic elitists, noting that some commentators find a point-by-point correspondence between their views of democracy. David Held, *Models of Democracy*, 2d ed. (Stanford: Stanford U. Press, 1996), 179. Held argues that "virtually the only role [Weber] envisaged for the electors" was "being able to dispense with incompetent leaders." Ibid., 173. Held also argues that, for Schumpeter, the "essence of democracy was . . . the ability of citizens to replace one government by another," a capacity that checks "the threat of tyranny." Ibid., 179. C. B. Macpherson observed that, after Schumpeter's identification of this capacity as key and his general critique of participatory democratic theory, there is little left for democracy "except the sheer protection-against-tyranny function." C. B. Macpherson, *The Life and Times of Liberal Democracy* (New York: Oxford U. Press, 1977), 91.

8. Vince Blasi treats the checking function, which he sees as following from the democratic theories of John Locke and Joseph Schumpeter, as a major purpose of both the First Amendment's Speech and Press Clauses. Blasi, "Checking Value," 542. On both theoretical and historical grounds, I have argued that this checking function is primarily relevant to an understanding of the Press Clause. C. Edwin Baker, *Human Liberty and Freedom of Speech* (New York: Oxford U. Press, 1989), 225–49; see Potter Stewart, "Or of the Press," *Hastings Law Journal* 26 (1975): 631. My own view is that the constitutional right of speech freedom has been and should be primarily about individual liberty rather than about serving an instrumental political function.

9. See Blasi, "Checking Value," 538–41.

10. Ibid., 538.

11. Although market competition provides some check on incompetency, it is less clear that it checks, rather than encourages, many forms of illegality, corruption, and inefficient although profitable externalizing of costs onto members of the public.

12. Blasi, "Checking Value," 539.

13. *Turner Broadcasting System v. FCC*, 512 U.S. 622, 685 (1994) (O'Connor, J., concurring in part and dissenting in part).

14. Mark Hertsgaard, *On Bended Knee: The Press and the Reagan Presidency* (New York: Farrar, Straus, Giroux, 1988), 54–76 (attributing the problem in part to the press's dependence on the very officials it is supposed to be checking); see also Mark Hertsgaard, "Media Matters: The Star Wars Mirage," *Nation* (June 24, 1996): 10 (describing palace court journalism).

15. It has also received considerable social science criticism. See generally Peter Bachrach, *The Theory of Democratic Elitism: A Critique* (Lanham, Md.: U. Press of America, 1980) (arguing that democratic elitism is unsound in theory and has failed to meet contemporary political needs in practice).

16. Cf. Hyde, "The Concept of Legitimation," 384 (critiquing the descriptive persuasiveness of this notion of legitimacy).

17. H. L. A. Hart, *The Concept of Law* (Oxford: Clarendon Press, 1961), 79–88.

18. Ronald Dworkin, *Taking Rights Seriously* (Cambridge: Harvard U. Press, 1977), 274. This view also seems implicit in Ackerman's conception of neutrality. See Bruce Ackerman, *Social Justice in the Liberal State* (New Haven: Yale U. Press, 1980), 11, 43. In choosing principles of justice in the original position, Rawls excludes knowledge of people's differing conceptions of the good and their comprehensive doctrines. His emphasis on the priority of the right over the good and his emphasis on organizing society based on principles that are primarily distributive – equal basic liberties and other primary goods allocated by institutions designed to embody the difference principle – likewise seem to endorse the view that society should not favor one view of the good over another, except for its appropriate disfavoring of views inconsistent with justice. See John Rawls, *A Theory of Justice* (Cambridge: Belknap Press, 1971), 504–11. But see C. Edwin Baker, "Outcome Equality or Equality of Respect: The Substantive Content of Equal Protection," *University of Pennsylvania Law Review* 131 (1983): 933, 949–59 (arguing that Rawls' interpretation of justice is irrational partly because of its discounting of political expression of people's conceptions of the good). More recently, Rawls seems to hold this view of neutrality in respect to issues to be decided by "public reason," especially concerning the conception of justice and constitutional essentials, but not to other matters of law and government in respect to which citizens can vote their nonpolitical values based on their (reasonable) comprehensive doctrines of the good. John Rawls, *Political Liberalism* (New York: Columbia U. Press, 1993), 212–54.

19. Cf. John Hart Ely, *Democracy and Distrust* (Cambridge: Harvard U. Press, 1980), 80–82.

20. *Harper v. Virginia Bd. of Elections*, 383 U.S. 663, 667 (1966), quoting *Yick Wo v. Hopkins*, 118 U.S. 356, 370 (1886). For a view that this statement can be better read as supportive of a constitutive discourse rather than a liberal bargaining, see Frank I. Michelman, "Conceptions of Democracy in American Constitutional Argument: Voting Rights," *Florida Law Review* 41 (1989): 443, 480–85; C. Edwin Baker, "Republican Liberalism: Liberal Rights and Republican Politics," *Florida Law Review* 41 (1989): 491, 506–7.

21. *United States v. Carolene Prods. Co.*, 304 U.S. 144, 153 n.4 (1938).

22. See Ely, *Democracy and Distrust*, 82, 151–53.

23. See Jürgen Habermas, *Between Facts and Norms* (Cambridge: MIT Press, 1996), 333–34 (discussing the difficulty of economic theories of democracy in accounting for the phenomenon of voting, and arguing that "the empirical evidence sp[eaks] against all models [of voting] that were premised on egocentric decision making").

24. Developing and defending institutional designs aimed at aiding people's ability as well as reinforcing their inclination to act politically in the direction of a public good has been a central theme in much of Cass Sunstein's scholarly work. See, e.g., Cass Sunstein, *Republic.com* (Princeton: Princeton U. Press, 2001).

25. The difference between these two critiques of elite democracy is repeated in two critiques of a dominant law and economics methodology. In identifying "efficient" legal rules or dispute settlements, the economic methodology typically takes some hypothesized existing distribution of wealth and set of preferences as given. Parallel to the liberal pluralist critique of elite democracy, the first critique emphasizes that the distribution is precisely what cannot be taken as a given since it is both undetermined and part of what is at issue in the choice of legal rules or the settlement of disputes. The analogue to the republican agrees but asserts that the content of the preferences is also unsettled and appropriately at issue. Both critiques show that efficiency is a theoretically indeterminate criterion because the choice of rule or settlement will affect the distribution of wealth and the generation of preferences, often in ways that make the choice appear efficient even though the opposite choice would have had distributive and preference effects that would have made it also appear efficient. The efficiency criterion appears determinative only if the analyst first makes normative assumptions about what distribution and what set of preferences to identify as "existing" or as otherwise appropriate to employ. See C. Edwin Baker, "The Ideology of the Economic Analysis of Law," *Philosophy & Public Affairs* 5 (1975): 3, 27–33; C. Edwin Baker, "Posner's Privacy Mystery and the Failure of Economic Analysis of Law," *Georgia Law Review* 12 (1978): 475, 493.

26. Sheldon Wolin, "Democracy & Counterrevolution," *Nation* (Apr. 22, 1996): 22, 24.

27. Jim Pope takes this feature of openness to distinguish true republican politics (and republican moments) from, for example, practices of the Klan – that is, political activism designed to silence opponents. See James Pope, "Republican Moments: The Role of Direct Popular Power in the American Constitutional Order," *University of Pennsylvania Law Review* 139 (1990): 287, 313–15.

28. See ibid., 311–15.

29. John Dewey, *The Public and Its Problems* (New York: H. Holt, 1927).

30. Ibid., 207.

31. Ibid., 209. Dewey observes that "[t]he world has suffered more from leaders and authorities than from the masses." Ibid., 208.

32. Ibid.

33. Ibid.

34. Ibid., 147.

35. Ibid., 146.

36. Obviously, an act done to further a common good of which the actor is also a beneficiary is not necessarily entirely altruistic; however, it is altruistic (or an embodiment of a claim of solidarity) to the extent that the direct benefit to the actor is less than its direct cost to the actor. In this circumstance, the act can be, and experientially is, justified by the benefit to the group. The claim that the act is still not altruistic because the actor's identity is tied to the benefited group (or, if the act benefits a stranger, because the actor's identity is tied to humanity) and, therefore, the actor benefits because and to the extent that the group (or stranger) benefits from *her* act, is not – at least for my purposes – a refutation of altruism, but rather an argument that places solidarity as opposed to self-interest at the core of a person's being. Similarly, observations from game theory about the rational response in circumstances of repeat performances can as easily be interpreted as showing that in many spheres of social life, attitudes and practices of solidarity are

likely to prevail and to be mutually beneficial than as showing that people are basically self-interested. Likewise, deviations in the direction of even greater solidarity can be interpreted as behavior indicating people's underlying self-conception.

37. Nancy Fraser effectively develops most elements of what I call complex democracy in her critique of Habermas' original formulation of the notion of the public sphere, although I find Habermas' position, especially as developed in his more recent discussion of democratic theory, fully consistent with Fraser's approach. See Nancy Fraser, "Rethinking the Public Sphere: A Contribution to the Critique of Actually Existing Democracy," in Craig Calhoun, ed., *Habermas and the Public Sphere* (Cambridge: MIT Press, 1992), 109, 137; cf. my text accompanying note 49.

38. Todd Gitlin, *The Twilight of Common Dreams* (New York: H. Holt, 1995), 217.

39. Ibid., 35, 44. Gitlin notes the pervasiveness of this theme on the left. In addition to citing Dewey, Carl Sandburg, Paul Robeson, Frank Capra, and Woody Guthrie, he quotes Communist Party leader Earl Browder: "Communism is twentieth century Americanism." Ibid., 56.

40. I emphasize this because some people who consider themselves liberal pluralists or republicans will think my description overly flat; some will view the conception described here as complex democracy to be closer to their self-described republican or liberal views.

41. See Rawls, *Political Liberalism*, 10, 36–38, 131–72. Although many see the later book as representing a change from his earlier *A Theory of Justice* (1971), an alternative reading sees them as congruent but as engaged in different tasks. The earlier book is a philosophical argument that "justice as fairness" is the best (liberal) account of justice, whereas the later takes up the important political or pragmatic task of arguing to a pluralist society that the acceptability of "justice as fairness" is not dependent on its liberal pedigree.

42. To the extent that the "good" conflicts with principles of justice, like the "good" of the sadist, a justifiable democracy would try to rule out or suppress, rather than bargain over, the practice of that conception of the good. See, e.g., C. Edwin Baker, "Counting Preferences in Collective Choice Situations," *UCLA Law Review* 25 (1978): 381.

43. John Stuart Mill, *On Liberty* (1859; Indianapolis: Bobbs-Merrill, 1956), 19–67.

44. Ibid., 28, 53.

45. Ibid., 82.

46. Ibid., 77.

47. Robert Post argues that attempts to structure public discourse predictably lead to this result – that is, the improper rule of dominant perspectives. Post's observations are relevant as objections to censorship and persuasive as objections to limitations on individual autonomy. However, when leveled against Cass Sunstein's arguments for a more managerial approach to the mass media, in Robert C. Post, *Constitutional Domains* (Cambridge: Harvard U. Press, 1995), 268–89, Post risks ignoring the fact that media institutions are inevitably legally structured and that this legal structuring historically often has been and should be oriented toward conceptions of the good in general and toward serving favored conceptions of democracy in particular. C. Edwin Baker, "Turner Broadcasting: Content-Based Regulation of Persons and Presses," *Supreme Court Review* (1994): 57. For these reasons, blanket

objections to a managerial approach are misguided. Instead, the need in the mass-media context is for principles that limit managerial abuse and democratic theory that guides managerial input. Sunstein's approach may be entirely consistent with the perspective of complex democracy described here. He emphasizes the democratic value of "disagreement and heterogeneity" – that is, "diverse perspectives, and contributions to democratic discourse made by people differently situated." Cass Sunstein, *Democracy and the Problem of Free Speech* (New York: Free Press, 1993), 242. Nevertheless, Sunstein often seems to value this diversity much as Mill seemed to value freedom of speech: as an aid to a common discourse useful in reaching appropriate conceptions of a truly common good (or, in Mill's case, of the truth). See Mill, *On Liberty*, 19–67. To this extent, Sunstein's conception of democracy is more aligned with what I have labeled republican democracy than with complex democracy.

48. Fraser also emphasizes the contribution of a plurality of public spheres to a desirable, egalitarian, multicultural society. See Fraser, "Rethinking the Public Sphere," 120–25. In other words, these partial public spheres are valuable both as a means and as an end.

49. See generally Jürgen Habermas, "Three Normative Models of Democracy," *Constellations* 1 (1994): 1. This theme reoccurs at many points in Habermas' major recent book on legal theory. See, e.g., Habermas, *Between Facts and Norms*, 166–67, 180, 283–86, 296–302.

50. Habermas, *Between Facts and Norms*, 97. Here, "moral" refers to more universal normative principles, whereas "ethical," although also referring to normative principles, is more culturally and historically specific, more overtly open to choice and variation among societies.

51. Ibid., 5; see also 452.

52. For an excellent study of ways the press is an institutional part of the governing process, including in ways not discussed in this chapter, but reaching conclusions similar to those here about the need for conscious design of the press to best and most fairly perform these functions, see Timothy E. Cook, *Governing with the News* (Chicago: U. of Chicago Press, 1998).

53. See C. Edwin Baker, *Advertising and a Democratic Press* (Princeton: Princeton U. Press, 1994), 41–43; Michael E. McGerr, *The Decline of Popular Politics* (New York: Oxford U. Press, 1986), 116–35 (describing the role of the partisan press in making the political world seem accessible, exciting, and important, thus generating higher voter turnout).

54. Sunstein, *Democracy and the Problem of Free Speech*, 20, 22; see also 251.

55. See Kenneth Karst, "Boundaries and Reasons: Freedom of Expression and the Subordination of Groups," *University of Illinois Law Review* (1990): 95, 109–16.

56. Charles T. Salmon & Theodore L. Glasser, "The Politics of Polling and the Limits of Consent," in Theodore L. Glasser & Charles T. Salmon, eds., *Public Opinion and the Communication of Consent* (New York: Guilford Press, 1995), 437, 440–41. Salmon and Glasser contrast plebiscitary democracy, implicit in opinion polling, with a preferred alternative that amounts roughly to what I describe as republican democracy. Ibid., 449.

57. "1999 State of the First Amendment Survey: Questionnaire," questions 25 and 26, <http:/www.freedomforum.org/first/sofa/questionnaire.as> (visited 4/21/00).

335

58. Harry C. Boyte, "Public Opinion as Public Judgment," in Glasser & Salmon, *Public Opinion and the Communication of Consent*, 417, 417.

59. See Elisabeth Noelle-Neumann, "Public Opinion and Rationality," in Glasser & Salmon, *Public Opinion and the Communication of Consent*, 33, 34, 47–48 (describing the two main concepts of public opinion as rationality and social control, and maintaining that polling is relevant mostly to the second). The classic critique of polling is Herbert Blumer, "Public Opinion and Public Opinion Polling," *American Sociology Review* 13 (1948): 542.

60. John Durham Peters, "Historical Tensions in the Concept of Public Opinion," in Glasser & Salmon, *Public Opinion and the Communication of Consent*, 3, 10–11.

## CHAPTER 7

1. Commission on Freedom of the Press, *A Free and Responsible Press: A General Report on Mass Communication: Newspapers, Radio, Motion Pictures, Magazines, and Books* (Chicago: U. of Chicago Press, 1947) (hereafter Hutchins Commission Report); see also Everette E. Dennis, "Internal Examination: Self-Regulation and the American Media," *Cardozo Arts & Entertainment Law Journal* 13 (1995): 697, 698–99 (stating that many media executives and critics have subscribed to the Hutchins Commission Report, and that it has been used as a text for journalism schools and media ethics courses). But cf. Lee C. Bollinger, "Why There Should Be an Independent Decennial Commission of the Press," *University of Chicago Legal Forum* (1993): 1, 1–2 (claiming that the commission's report has "assumed only minor status within the history of freedom" but urging that it merits much wider influence).

2. Fred S. Seibert, Theodore Peterson, & Wilbur Schramm, *Four Theories of the Press: The Authoritarian, Libertarian, Social Responsibility, and Soviet Communist Concepts of What the Press Should Be and Do* (Urbana: U. of Illinois Press, 1956).

3. Colin Sparks, "Media Theory after the Fall of European Communism, in James Curran and Myung-Jin Park, eds., *De-Westernizing Media Studies* (London: Routledge, 2000), 35, 36.

4. Paolo Mancini, "Political Complexity and Alternative Models of Journalism: The Italian Case," in Curran and Park, *De-Westernizing Media Studies*, 265.

5. See Seibert et al., *Four Theories of the Press*, 74–103; cf. John C. Nerone, ed., *Last Rights: Revisiting Four Theories of the Press* (Urbana: U. of Illinois Press, 1995), 1 (describing *Four Theories of the Press* as "an influential classic in communications theory"); Jerilyn S. McIntyre, "Repositioning a Landmark: The Hutchins Commission and Freedom of the Press," *Critical Studies in Mass Communications* 4 (1987): 136, 137 (suggesting that the commission has had its "greatest circulation and influence" by way of Peterson's social responsibility theory).

6. Hutchins Commission Report, 21, 23, 26–28; see also Theodore Peterson, "The Social Responsibility Theory of the Press," in Seibert et al., *Four Theories of the Press*, 87–91.

7. See Peterson, "Social Responsibility Theory," 74. In addition to its political role, the commission noted the press's role as an advertising medium and an entertainment medium, and its need, as an ongoing entity, to be financially sound.

8. Ibid., 90, quoting Norman Isaacs, "A Small Town Paper Has One Supreme Ethical Duty – To Print the News," *Quill* (Dec. 1953): 7, 15.
9. Ibid., 91.
10. Ibid., 101.
11. Cf. ibid., 83 (pointing out that during the twentieth century publishers began to speak "not merely of their right to exercise their freedom but also of the responsibilities attached to its exercise").
12. Cf. "Introduction" to Seibert et al., *Four Theories of the Press*, 5.
13. Hutchins Commission Report, 25.
14. Ibid., 28.
15. The Hutchins Commission does note that the republic involves "conflict and conscious compromise among organized groups." Ibid., 20. I see no evidence, however, that the Hutchins Commission relies on this observation in its assignment of tasks to the media.
16. Ibid., 25.
17. Ibid., 21, 28.
18. Ibid.
19. Peterson, "Social Responsibility Theory," 102–3, quoting Hutchins Commission Report, 113 (emphasis added).
20. Ibid., 101. The press does not need to present "preposterous" ideas. Ibid.
21. For example, for several years, a progressive magazine, *Lies of Our Time* (or "*LOOT*"), published monthly from 1989 to 1994 by the Institute for Media Analysis (New York), was devoted largely to exposing the distortions, errors, and "lies" of the *New York Times*.
22. Hutchins Commission Report, 22.
23. See, e.g., Joseph N. Cappella & Kathleen Hall Jamieson, *Spiral of Cynicism: The Press and the Public Good* (New York: Oxford U. Press, 1997), 209–28; James Fallows, *Breaking the News* (New York: Pantheon Books, 1996), 7.
24. See, e.g., Arthur Charity, *Doing Public Journalism* (New York: Guilford Press, 1995); Davis Merritt, *Public Journalism and Public Life* (Hillsdale, N.J.: L. Erlbaum Associates, 1995).
25. Jay Rosen, *Getting the Connections Right: Public Journalism and the Troubles in the Press* (New York: Twentieth Century Fund, 1996), 16; see also 13, 50, 69.
26. Robert M. Steele, "The Ethics of Civic Journalism: Independence as the Guide," in Jay Black, ed., *Mixed News: The Public/Civic/Communitarian Journalism Debate* (Mahwah, N.J.: L. Erlbaum Associates, 1997), 162, 162.
27. Rosen, *Getting the Connections Right*, 74, quoting Davis Merritt, "Public Journalism: Defining a Democratic Art," *Media Studies Journal* 9 (Summer 1995): 131.
28. Ibid., 50, quoting David Mathews, *Politics for People: Finding a Responsible Public Voice* 40 (Urbana: U. of Illinois Press, 1994). David Mathews is president of the Kettering Foundation.
29. See ibid., 2, 82.
30. Theodore L. Glasser & Stephanie Craft, "Public Journalism and the Prospects for Press Accountability," in Jay Black, ed., *Mixed News: The Public/Civic/Communitarian Journalism Debate* (Mahwah, N.J.: L. Erlbaum Associates, 1997), 120, 121.

31. See Jürgen Habermas, *The Structural Transformation of the Public Sphere: An Inquiry into a Category of Bourgeois Society* (Cambridge: MIT Press, 1989); James W. Carey, "The Mass Media and Democracy: Between the Modern and Postmodern," *Journal of International Affairs* 47 (1993): 1.

32. See Rosen, *Getting the Connections Right*, 83 ("People have to participate, so that they'll want and need to become informed"); see also 20. Cf. Michael Schudson, *The Power of News* (Cambridge: Harvard U. Press, 1995), 27 ("Political activity leads people to follow the news. News does not ordinarily lead people to political activity").

33. Of course, there can be tension between serving democratic ideals and serving profit. Arguably, using well-designed public (taxpayer) support to reduce its dependence on market-based profits could improve public journalism's performance. See Theodore L. Glasser & Stephanie Craft, "Public Journalism and the Search for Democratic Ideals," in Tamar Liebes & James Curran, eds., *Media, Ritual, and Identity* (London: Routledge, 1998), 203, 215–16 (suggesting that, like libraries, museums, and schools, public journalism serves the public good and may deserve public support).

34. See Ben H. Bagdikian, *The Media Monopoly*, 4th ed. (Boston: Beacon Press, 1992), 119, 265–66 (describing an average 17.1% return on equity for publicly traded newspaper companies in 1980 and a five-year average profit margin of 18.3%).

35. See Gerald J. Baldasty & Jeffrey B. Rutenbeck, "Money, Politics and Newspapers: The Business Environment of Press Partisanship in the Late 19th Century," *Journalism History* 15 (1988): 60, 66.

36. The development of a separate editorial page may have been a response to market advantages of emphasizing objective news, a consideration that even led the *New York Times* and the *New York Herald* to consider dropping their editorial pages. See Michael Schudson, *Discovering the News: A Social History of American Newspapers* (New York: Basic Books, 1978), 98.

37. See Gerald J. Baldasty, *The Commercialization of News in the Nineteenth Century* (Madison: U. of Wisconsin Press, 1994), 127–34; see also C. Edwin Baker, *Advertising and a Democratic Press* (Princeton: Princeton U. Press, 1994), 28–29.

38. See Rosen, *Getting the Connections Right*, 70, 72–73.

39. Glasser & Craft, "Public Journalism and the Prospects for Press Accountability," 123, quoting Charity, *Doing Public Journalism*, 11.

40. Rosen, *Getting the Connections Right*, 72, quoting Osborn Elliott, former editor of *Newsweek* and former dean of Columbia University's journalism school.

41. See ibid., 21–22 (discussing how the media coverage of politics has contributed to a drop in public confidence in the press); see also Cappella & Jamieson, *Spiral of Cynicism*, 209–28; Fallows, *Breaking the News*.

42. Christopher Conte, "Angels in the Newsroom," *Governing* (Aug. 1996): 22; cf. Charity, *Doing Public Journalism*, 86–87 (noting that 22,000 people responded to an Akron paper's question of what can be done about racism in the city).

43. See Conte, "Angels in the Newsroom," 23.

44. Glasser & Craft, "Public Journalism and the Prospects for Press Accountability," 124.

45. Conte, "Angels in the Newsroom," 24.

46. Mike Hoyt, "Are You Now, or Will You Ever Be, a Civic Journalist?" *Columbia Journalism Review* (Sept.–Oct. 1995): 27, 27.

## CHAPTER 8

1. See generally Lucas A. Powe Jr., *American Broadcasting and the First Amendment* (Berkeley: U. of California Press, 1987), 216–47 (making this type of argument with respect to broadcasting and cable television).

2. Public-good and collective-action problems prevent markets from properly taking into account these preferences for equality even as weighted by the market's criterion of willingness and ability to pay. Harold M. Hochman & James D. Rodgers, "Pareto Optimal Redistribution," *American Economic Review* 59 (1969): 542, 542–43. Markets are even more inappropriate to the extent that the preferences should be democratically weighted. See my Chapter 4.

3. See Mike Hoyt, "Are You Now, or Will You Ever Be, a Civic Journalist?" *Columbia Journalism Review* (Sept.–Oct. 1995): 32 (noting fears that public journalism leads to a "softness" of newspapers and the avoidance of controversy, out of fear of offending readers); Carl Sessions Stepp, "Public Journalism: Balancing the Scales," *American Journalism Review* (May 1996): 38, 40 (describing the danger of the press's losing its outsider status); Mike Tharp, "The Media's New Fix," *U.S. News & World Report* (Mar. 18, 1996): 72, 74 (noting the fears that papers will become too cozy with a community's elite). But cf. Jay Rosen, *Getting the Connections Right: Public Journalism and the Troubles in the Press* (New York: Twentieth Century Fund, 1996), 2, 82.

4. Mark Hertsgaard, *On Bended Knee: The Press and the Reagan Presidency* (New York: Farrar, Straus, Giroux, 1988), 54.

5. Editors identify a high proportion of staff-written content to wire service or feature material as a major criterion of a good paper. See Leo Bogart, *Press and Public*, 2d ed. (Hillsdale, N.J.: L. Erlbaum Associates, 1989), 253–65.

6. See Edward S. Herman & Noam Chomsky, *Manufacturing Consent: The Political Economy of the Mass Media* (New York: Pantheon Books, 1988), 26–28.

7. See Clarice N. Olien et al., "Conflict, Consensus, and Public Opinion," in Theodore L. Glasser & Charles T. Salmon, eds., *Public Opinion and the Communication of Consent* (New York: Guilford Press, 1995), 301, 305.

8. Cf. *Turner Broadcasting System v. FCC*, 512 U.S. 622, 685 (1994) (O'Connor, J., concurring in part and dissenting in part).

9. See Randall P. Bezanson, "The New Free Press Guarantee," *Virginia Law Review* 63 (1977): 731, 732 (making an analogy to the Establishment Clause). On that basis, Bezanson concluded that the Constitution created a presumptive principle that the press could not be singled out for either benefits or burdens. Ibid., 733–34.

10. This statute is codified at 15 U.S.C. §§1801–4 (1994).

11. But see *Committee for an Indep. P-I v. Hearst Corp.*, 704 F.2d 467, 481–82 (9th Cir. 1983) (noting Congress's realization that the act imposes a competitive burden or cost on some papers when it provides a benefit to others).

12. See James D. Squires, *Read All About It!* (New York: Times Books, 1993), 123; see also Lucas A. Powe Jr., *The Fourth Estate and the Constitution* (Berkeley: U. of California Press, 1991), 219–20.

13. *El Dia, Inc. v. Rosello*, 165 F.3d 1406 (9th Cir. 1996); *North Mississippi v. Jones*, 951 F.2d 652 (5th Cir. 1992).

14. *Sherrill v. Knight*, 569 F.2d 124 (D.C. Cir. 1977).

15. Potter Stewart, "Or of the Press," *Hastings Law Journal* 26 (1975): 634; see also William J. Brennan Jr., "Address at the Dedication of the S. I. Newhouse Center for Law and Justice in Newark, New Jersey" (Oct. 17, 1979), *Rutgers Law Review* 32 (1979): 173.

16. See C. Edwin Baker, *Human Liberty and Freedom of Speech* (New York: Oxford U. Press, 1989), 234–40 (describing and defending Stewart's approach to protecting the institutional integrity of the press by providing constitutional "defensive" but not "offensive" rights on behalf of news gathering). This distinction between defensive and offensive rights explains Stewart's rejection of special press constitutional rights of access to information or claimed rights to violate normal criminal laws such as trespass, speeding, or wire-tapping laws in order to get a story.

17. *Branzburg v. Hayes*, 408 U.S. 665, 725 (1972) (Stewart, J., dissenting).

18. See ibid., 731; see also *Zurcher v. Stanford Daily*, 436 U.S. 547, 573 (1978) (Stewart, J., dissenting).

19. See Vincent Blasi, "The Pathological Perspective and the First Amendment," *Columbia Law Review* 85 (1985): 449, 449–50.

20. James Fallows, *Breaking the News* (New York: Pantheon Books, 1996), 240, 243. Fallows explicitly sees the tension between what I have called republican democracy and elitist democracy – or, as he describes it, between the views of John Dewey, whom he prefers, and those of the early Walter Lippman, whom Fallows characterizes as believing that the "only hope for effective modern government lay in cultivating a group of well-trained experts, who would manage the country's journalism as well as its governmental affairs." Ibid., 236.

21. Ibid., 31.

22. See Rosen, *Getting the Connections Right*, 2, 5, 13–15, 82; see also C. Edwin Baker, *Advertising and a Democratic Press* (Princeton: Princeton U. Press, 1994), 41–43.

23. See Todd Gitlin, "Public Spheres or Public Sphericules?" in Tamar Liebes & James Curran, eds., *Media, Ritual, and Identity* (London: Routledge, 1998), 168; Elihu Katz, "And Deliver Us from Segmentation," in Roger G. Noll & Monroe Price, eds., *A Communications Cornucopia* (Washington, D.C.: Brookings Institution Press, 1998), 99, reprinted from *Annals of the American Academy of Political and Social Science* 546 (1996): 22.

24. See Oscar H. Gandy Jr., *The Panoptic Sort* (Boulder, Colo.: Westview, 1993); Joseph Turow, *Breaking Up America: Advertisers and the New Media World* (Chicago: U. of Chicago Press, 1997).

25. Katz, "And Deliver Us from Segmentation," 104–10.

26. Ironically, one interpretation argues that the recent Yugoslav violence resulted, in part, as a rebound against the former Communist state's manipulative and authoritarian attempt to suppress segmented discourse. Cf. Thomas I. Emerson, *The System of Freedom of Expression* (New York: Random House, 1970), 7 (noting, as one of four values of the system, the maintenance of a balance between stability and change). Certainly, nationalistic political entrepreneurs during the breakup of Yugoslavia manipulated the press to promote the Yugoslav ethnic animosity and conflict. See Warren Zimmermann, "The Captive Mind," *New York Review of Books* (Feb. 2, 1995): 3, 3. According to the "suppressed-diversity" perspective, the problem was in part the vulnerability of people to manipulation because they had had no prior free pluralism that could have developed their ability to understand both their

differences and commonalities. Zimmerman, however, implicitly adopts a social responsibility perspective and rejects pluralistic media, twice mentioning with undisguised horror proposals to create politically opposing or ethnically separate broadcast services in Serbia. See ibid, 6. Interestingly, he noted that a survey found nine out of ten viewers opposed to this segmentation. See ibid. See also Monroe E. Price, *Journeys in Media Space: Identity, Law and Technology in the Global Environment* (forthcoming), ch. 9.

27.  *Miami Herald Publ'g Co. v. Tornillo,* 418 U.S. 241, 256 (1974).
28.  See Baker, *Advertising and a Democratic Press,* 61.
29.  *Miami Herald Publ'g Co. v. Tornillo,* 418 U.S. 241, 258 (1974). More recently, the Court has given *Miami Herald* an even more restrictive interpretation as concerned only with content-based regulation. C. Edwin Baker, "Turner Broadcasting: Content-Based Regulation of Persons and Presses," *Supreme Court Review* (1994): 54.
30.  *Associated Press v. United States,* 326 U.S. 1, 20 (1945).
31.  David L. Protess et al., *The Journalism of Outrage: Investigative Reporting and Agenda Building in America* (New York: Guilford Press, 1991), 276–77. Including both the percentage that listed each possibility as either their first and second choices gave the following results: a reformer in you satisfied (78%), increased freedom over time or assignments (54%), personal recognition (36%), journalism awards (17%), monetary benefits (8%).
32.  Cf. Lee C. Bollinger Jr., "Freedom of the Press and Public Access: Toward a Theory of Partial Regulation of the Press," *Michigan Law Review* 75 (1976): 1.
33.  See Jonathan Weinberg, "Broadcasting and Speech," *California Law Review* 81 (1993): 1101.
34.  See *NBC v. United States,* 319 U.S. 190, 224–27 (1943) (sustaining various FCC regulations concerning the relations between broadcasters and networks).
35.  See 47 U.S.C. §312(a)(7) (1994) (granting reasonable access); ibid. §315 (requiring equal opportunity). The "equal opportunity" requirement was in the 1934 act; "reasonable access" was added to §312 in 1972.
36.  *Red Lion Broad. Co. v. FCC,* 395 U.S. 367 (1969) (upholding the Fairness Doctrine); *Syracuse Peace Council v. FCC,* 867 F.2d 654 (D.C. Cir. 1989) (upholding the FCC's repudiation of the Fairness Doctrine on statutory grounds). The problem with the Fairness Doctrine arguably was deterrence of coverage resulting from the mandate that any issue covered be covered in a balanced fashion. The political candidate's reasonable access right is relatively definite, which means that adding an equal opportunity requirement in this context (unlike the Fairness Doctrine's balance requirement) could not deter the broadcaster from making access available. If so, then this equal opportunity requirement is much less constitutionally problematic.
37.  Cf. Stewart, "Or of the Press," 636 ("[I]f there were no guarantee of a free press, government could convert the communications media into a neutral 'market place of ideas' ").
38.  See *Red Lion,* 395 U.S. at 382–86 (noting that Congress surely could have chosen this alternative if it wished); cf. *CBS v. Democratic Nat'l Comm.,* 412 U.S. 94, 121–32 (1973) (holding that neither the Communications Act nor the First Amendment requires broadcasters to accept paid editorial advertisements).

39. MacKinnon argues that pornography both silences women and makes their speech inaudible to others. See Catharine A. MacKinnon, "Pornography, Civil Rights, and Speech," *Harvard Civil Rights–Civil Liberties Law Review* 20 (1985): 1, 63; see also Frank I. Michelman, "Conceptions of Democracy in American Constitutional Argument: The Case of Pornography Regulation," *Tennessee Law Review* 56 (1989): 291; Cass R. Sunstein, "Pornography and the First Amendment," *Duke Law Journal* (1986): 589.

40. Arguably the constitutional evil of racial segregation struck down in *Brown v. Board of Education*, 347 U.S. 483 (1954), if one could grant the counterfactual assumption of materially equal facilities, lies in the meaning or message expressed by segregation as a purposeful practice and the impermissibility of the state giving expression to that message. See Charles R. Lawrence III, "If He Hollers Let Him Go: Regulating Racist Speech on Campus," *Duke Law Journal* (1990): 431, 438–44.

41. Stewart, "Or of the Press," 636.

42. Letter from James Madison to W. T. Barry (Aug. 4, 1822), reprinted in Gaillard Hunt, ed., *The Writings of James Madison*, vol. 9 (New York: G. P. Putnam's Sons, 1910), 103, 103.

43. See National Telecommunications and Information Administration, U.S. Dept. of Commerce, *Final Report of the Advisory Committee on Public Interest Obligations of Digital Television Broadcasters: Charting the Digital Broadcasting Future* (Washington, D.C.: Secretariat, 1998), 17–33.

44. *Carroll Broadcasting v. FCC*, 258 F.2d 440 (D.C. Cir. 1958) (approving such a doctrine, thereby recognizing economic problems with too much fragmentation). In the recent deregulatory environment, the *Carroll* doctrine has been largely abandoned but not constitutionally rejected. *In re Policies Regarding Detrimental Effects of Proposed New Broadcast Stations on Existing Stations*, 3 F.C.C.R. 638 (1988).

45. Cf. *Los Angeles v. Preferred Communications*, 476 U.S. 488 (1986) (cable franchise monopolies may be unconstitutional, at least where there is "sufficient excess physical capacity and *economic demand*"; emphasis added).

46. See Doug Underwood, *When MBAs Rule the Newsroom: How the Marketers and Managers Are Reshaping Today's Media* (New York: Columbia U. Press, 1993), 14–25; Iver Peterson, "The Bottom-Line Publisher of the Los Angeles Times Faces the Hard-Line Skeptics," *New York Times* (Mar. 9, 1998): D7.

47. See 47 U.S.C. §317 (1994) (requiring radio station broadcasters to identify sponsors); *Lewis Publ'g Co. v. Morgan*, 229 U.S. 288 (1913) (upholding against a First Amendment challenge a law requiring newspapers receiving second-class mail rates to identify advertising materials); 47 C.F.R. §76.221 (1998) (requiring cable origination programming to identify sponsorship); 47 C.F.R. §73.1212 (1998) (requiring broadcasters to identify sponsors). Despite merely requiring information, these rules will predictably cause some potential advertisers not to purchase some ads and others to change the content of their advertisement.

48. See *Time Warner Cable v. Bloomberg*, 118 F.3d 917, 927–28 (2d Cir. 1997) (upholding an injunction preventing a city from placing commercially produced business and news services on public-access cable channels).

49. Cf. *CBS v. Democratic Nat'l Comm.*, 412 U.S. 94, 123–24 (1973) (noting that a system that allocates media access on the basis of financial resources would not necessarily serve the public interest). An alternative possibility, which might also

appeal to complex democrats, is to require each media entity to announce publicly its policies concerning ads and then be legally obligated to accept any ad not ruled out by the policy. This approach increases access and openness while permitting a media entity to identify itself either as a partisan voice or as an inclusive medium, but an inclusive medium that continues to conform to express standards of civil discourse.

50. See Robert Cirino, "An Alternative American Communications System," in Donald Lazere, ed., *American Media and Mass Culture: Left Perspectives* (Berkeley: U. of California Press, 1987), 568, 574–75 (proposing four independent publicly supported networks, one for each perspective: socialist, liberal, conservative, and libertarian).

51. See John Stuart Mill, *On Liberty*, ed. Currin V. Shields (1859; Indianapolis: Bobbs-Merrill, 1956), 45.

52. Ben H. Bagdikian, "Conquering Hearts and Minds: The Lords of the Global Village," *Nation* (June 12, 1989), 805, 807. Bagdikian reported in the first edition of *The Media Monopoly* published in 1982 that most of the major media were owned by 50 corporations, but that this number had declined to 20 when the fourth edition was published in 1992. See Ben H. Bagdikian, *The Media Monopoly*, 4th ed. (Boston: Beacon Press, 1992), ix; cf. ibid., 21 (listing the change as being from 46 to 23). The handful of media giants may be more of a family than oppositional competitors. Extensive joint ventures link each giant with most of its competitors. See Edward S. Herman & Robert W. McChesney, *The Global Media* (Washington, D.C.: Cassell, 1997).

53. U.S. Department of Commerce, *Globalization of the Mass Media* (Washington, D.C.: GPO, 1993).

54. See Chapter 2; Bruce M. Owen & Steven S. Wildman, *Video Economics* (Cambridge: Harvard U. Press, 1992), 99–100 (emphasizing that whether monopoly or competition and whether reliance on advertising or viewer support will be welfare maximizing depends on complex relations between the distribution of viewer preferences and the number of channels available); Matthew L. Spitzer, "Justifying Minority Preferences in Broadcasting," *Southern California Law Review* 64 (1991): 293, 304–17.

55. To raise this challenge does not mean it cannot be met. For the beginning of a reply, see C. Edwin Baker, *Ownership of Newspapers: The View from Positivist Social Science*, Shorenstein Barone Center of JFK School of Gov., Harvard U. (Cambridge, 1994), 15–20.

56. I take these terms and much of the discussion in the next few paragraphs from Jürgen Habermas, *The Theory of Communicative Action*, vol. 2, trans. Thomas McCarthy (Boston: Beacon Press, 1987), 113–52.

57. See Zechariah Chafee Jr., *Free Speech in the United States* (Cambridge: Harvard U. Press, 1967), 38–51 (discussing the Espionage Acts of 1917 and 1918).

58. Of course, the First Amendment has not always been an effective safeguard. See *Masses Publ'g Co. v. Patten*, 246 F. 24, 38–39 (2d Cir. 1917) (rejecting a First Amendment challenge to the exclusion of left-wing literature from the U.S. mail).

59. This hypothetical draws on Baker, *Advertising and a Democratic Press*, 66–70.

60. James Curran, "Capitalism and Control of the Press, 1800–1975," in James Curran et al., eds., *Mass Communication and Society* (London: Edward Arnold, 1977), 195, 225.

61. The text has described the role of income and advertising in corrupting segmentation. In addition, competition for advertising revenue creates market incentives to ignore particular types of content – content offensive to those members of the targeted audience or content that provides information or promotes policies contrary to advertisers' interests. Thus, advertising corrupts not only segmentation but also discourse within segments. See Baker, *Advertising and a Democratic Press*, ch. 2.

62. A targeted audience's ability to treat particular media consumption as a deductible business expense also distorts segmentation. The government partially subsidizes that segment while the targeted groups' customers or clients pay the rest. Here again, the market and the government, not the lifeworld, develop and reinforce segmentation.

63. See *Arkansas Writers' Project, Inc. v. Ragland*, 481 U.S. 221, 232 (1987).

64. See Richard B. Kielbowicz, "Origins of the Second-Class Mail Category and the Business of Policymaking, 1863–1879," *Journalism Monographs* (April 1986): 6, 14, 20.

65. See Richard B. Kielbowicz & Linda Lawson, "Reduced-Rate Postage for Nonprofit Organizations: A Policy History, Critique, and Proposal," *Harvard Journal of Law & Public Policy* 11 (1988): 347, 352. For a set of proposals to reduce the corrupting effects of advertising, see Baker, *Advertising and a Democratic Press*, 83–117.

66. The Postal Reorganization Act, adopted in 1970, was premised on the notion that, after an adjustment period, each class of mail would bear its full costs. Nevertheless, postal subsidies never died out, a result aided by having regular rates include a portion of all postal service costs while reduced rate categories pay only the costs attributable to carrying that category. See 39 U.S.C. §3622(b)(2)-(3) (1994); Randall P. Bezanson, *Taxes on Knowledge in America* (Philadelphia: U. of Pennsylvania Press, 1994), 234–36 ("To this day, Congress continues to appropriate funds annually in the form of subsidies for reduced rates charged newspaper and magazine publishers and nonprofit groups").

67. See Baker, *Advertising and a Democratic Press*, 94–96; Peter J. Humphreys, *Mass Media and Media Policy in Western Europe* (New York: St. Martin's Press, 1996), 106.

68. See Humphreys, *Mass Media and Media Policy in Western Europe*, 105 (Italy), 106 (Finland). Humphreys notes that the aim to assure readers access to diverse sources of information was "an aim of (direct and indirect) state press subsidies across Europe." Ibid., 104.

69. Gerald J. Baldasty, *The Commercialization of News in the Nineteenth Century* (Madison: U. of Wisconsin Press, 1994), 132.

70. See Spitzer, "Justifying Minority Preferences," 334–46 (arguing that both theory and empirical data suggest that minority ownership may increase minority-oriented programming).

71. See *Metro Broad., Inc. v. FCC*, 497 U.S. 547, 552 (1990). The Court later rejected *Metro Broadcasting*'s holding concerning the appropriate standard of review for congressionally approved racial preferences. *Adarand Constructors, Inc. v. Pena*, 515 U.S. 200, 235–37 (1995). Still, the specific holding of *Metro Broadcasting* currently stands. The case exhibits the doctrinal anomaly of apparently using the importance of supporting particular media content (content reflecting minority interests) to justify violating the equal-protection principle against race-based discrimination,

while using the importance of serving minority interests to justify violating the First Amendment principle against content discrimination. See Baker, "Turner Broadcasting," 125.

72. See Humphreys, *Mass Media and Media Policy in Western Europe*, 139–43.

73. Tax law makes investments in advertising a deductible current business expense while treating investments in tangible capital as deductible on the basis of depreciation over time. Lawrence Summers notes that this difference distorts investing to favor expenditures on advertising rather than on the tangible capital that more directly relates to productivity, jobs, and international competitiveness. Lawrence Summers, "A Few Good Taxes: Revenue without Tears," *New Republic* (Nov. 30, 1987): 14.

74. Robert B. Gunnison & Greg Lucas, "Governor Signs Bills Increasing Taxes," *San Francisco Chronicle* (July 1, 1991): A1.

75. Royal Commission on the Press, *Final Report Appendices* (1977), 108, table C.4.

76. Cf. Spitzer, "Justifying Minority Preferences," 304–46.

77. See Thomas E. Humphrey, "The Newspaper Preservation Act: An Ineffective Step in the Right Direction," *Boston College Industrial & Commercial Law Rev.* 12 (1971): 937, 954.

78. But cf. *Syracuse Peace Council v. FCC*, 867 F.2d 654, 659–64 (D.C. Cir. 1989) (noting evidence that the balance requirement deterred the initial airing of controversial matters).

79. The rosy view that this new technology will eliminate all the old inadequacies of the media seems distinctly implausible. See, e.g., Michael Schudson, *The Power of News* (Cambridge: Harvard U. Press, 1995), 1–2; C. Edwin Baker, "New Media Technologies, the First Amendment, and Public Policy," *Communications Review* (1996): 315, 326–27. See also my Postscript.

80. Cf. R. Randall Rainey & William Rehg, "The Marketplace of Ideas, the Public Interest, and Federal Regulation of the Electronic Media: Implications of Habermas' Theory of Democracy," *Southern California Law Review* 69 (1996): 1923, 1949–72.

81. Ibid., 1982.

82. Ibid., 1983 n.138.

83. B. J. Bullert, *Public Television: Politics and the Battle over Documentary Film* (New Brunswick, N.J.: Rutgers U. Press, 1997), 153, quoting Canby and Ebert.

84. See Lee C. Bollinger, *Images of a Free Press* (Chicago: U. of Chicago Press, 1991), 116–20; Bollinger, "Freedom of the Press and Public Access," 26–37, 42.

85. James Curran, "Mass Media and Democracy Revisited," in James Curran & Michael Gurevitch, eds., *Mass Media and Society*, 2d ed. (New York: St. Martin's Press, 1996), 81, 105–6.

86. Ibid., 105.

87. Ibid., 109, citing O. Hulten, *Mass Media and State Support in Sweden*, 2d rev. ed. (Stockholm: Swedish Institute, 1984).

88. See ibid., 109–10.

89. But see my Chapters 2–4.

90. Curran, "Mass Media and Democracy Revisited," 112.

91. See my Chapter 3. In addition to underproduction related to positive externalities, the public-good aspect of media products and the egalitarian claim for access to

the essentials of political participation suggest that the market will selectively fail to provide adequately for various democratic functions.

92. Baker, *Advertising and a Democratic Press*, ch. 4.

## Chapter 9

1. *Lochner v. New York*, 198 U.S. 45 (1905), struck down as a violation of due process a maximum-hour law for bakers. Its repudiation, most clearly in *West Coast Hotel v. Parrish*, 300 U.S. 379 (1937), ushered in the modern era of constitutional law in which the government has presumptive authority to regulate in the economic sphere.

2. C. Edwin Baker, *Human Liberty and Freedom of Speech* (New York: Oxford U. Press, 1989), 272–83.

3. See C. Edwin Baker, "Turner Broadcasting: Content-Based Regulation of Persons and Presses," *Supreme Court Review* (1994): 57, 72–79.

4. See Warren Hoge, "Murdoch Halts a Book Critical of China," *New York Times* (Feb. 28, 1998): A5.

5. See Richard Harwood, "When Downsizing Hits the Newsroom," *Washington Post* (Apr. 2, 1996): A13 (discussing the elimination of 3,100 daily newsroom jobs from a peak of 56,900 between 1990 and 1996).

6. David E. Rosenbaum, "A Financial Disaster with Many Culprits," *New York Times* (June 6, 1990): A1 (citing General Accounting Office figures).

7. Ken Bode, "Where the Streets Are Paved with Depositors," *New York Times* (May 16, 1993): 7, reviewing Kathleen Day, *S & L Hell: The People and the Politics Behind the $1 Trillion Savings and Loan Scandal* (New York: W. W. Norton, 1993).

8. "Fraud in Welfare Put at $1 Billion," *New York Times* (Dec. 7, 1987): A25 (citing a report by the inspector general of the Department of Health and Human Services about fraud in the AFDC program).

9. James Curran, "Mass Media and Democracy Revisited," in James Curran & Michael Gurevitch, eds., *Mass Media and Society*, 2d ed. (New York: St. Martin's Press, 1996), 89.

10. The Puerto Rican government withdrew $4.5 million a year of advertising in a newspaper after the paper published a negative evaluation of the first 100 days of the governor's second term. "Newspaper Is Suing Puerto Rico's Governor," *New York Times* (Dec. 10, 1997): A26. A court, however, properly found this to be unconstitutional. *El Dia, Inc. v. Rosello*, 165 F.3d 1406 (9th Cir. 1996). See also *North Miss. Communications, Inc. v. Jones*, 792 F.2d 1330, 1337 (5th Cir. 1986).

11. See Monroe E. Price, "The Market for Loyalties: Electronic Media and the Global Competition for Allegiances," *Yale Law Journal* 104 (1994): 667, 689; Matthew L. Spitzer, "The Constitutionality of Licensing Broadcasters," *New York University Law Review* 64 (1989): 990, 1050–51.

12. In contrast to the denial of interviews, courts may be able to monitor the reasons for denial of access to press facilities or press conferences. See, e.g., *Borreca v. Fasi*, 369 F. Supp. 906, 911 (D. Haw. 1974) (giving a disliked reporter the right to attend press conferences on the same basis as other reporters).

13. Although some writers appear to suggest such a wall – see, e.g., Randall P. Bezanson, "The New Free Press Guarantee," *Virginia Law Review* 63 (1977): 731,

732 – it is, in fact, quite implausible and has never been historically approached. The wall can be breached by manipulating "carrots" as well as by employing "sticks." However, a government that did not offer the press "carrots" in the form of interviews with public officials, press releases, access to some records, maybe press galleries and press facilities or press passes, hardly seems plausible. Other privileges, ranging from the mail subsidies to reporter-source shield laws have been historically routine and seem generally desirable.

14. Ibid. 733–34. In contrast, after noting the American (I would say, elite democrat) tendency to hold this view, Pnina Lahav argues "that a special press law in itself constitutes a threat to press freedom" only under an authoritarian press regime, and observes that the Swedes see a "specialized press regime as both a manifestation and a guarantee of press freedom." Pnina Lahav, "An Outline for a General Theory of Press Law in Democracy," in Pnina Lahav, ed., *Press Law in Modern Democracies* (New York: Longman, 1985), 339, 346.

15. But cf. *CBS v. Democratic Nat'l Comm.*, 412 U.S. 94, 118 (1973) (Brennan & Marshall, JJ., dissenting).

16. See Cass Sunstein, *Democracy and the Problem of Free Speech* (New York: Free Press, 1993), 36–37, 45 (observing that "broadcasters are given property rights in their licenses by government, and their exercise of these rights is a function of law," and could therefore be viewed as state action). In a nonmedia context, both the majority and dissent rejected this approach to state action in *DeShaney v. Winnebago County Dep't of Soc. Servs.*, 489 U.S. 189 (1989), where the state failed to intervene to protect a child from a violent parent. Rather than find state action in nonaction, the dissent emphasized the state's affirmative actions in creating DeShaney's dependence on the social service agency.

17. See Baker, "Turner Broadcasting," 93–114 (describing historical examples and theoretical justifications for content-motivated interventions).

18. See Baker, *Human Liberty and Freedom of Speech*, 225–49 (arguing that the Press Clause should protect "defensive rights" such as a "press privilege" from mandated disclosure of its sources or work product).

19. *Minneapolis Star & Tribune Co. v. Minnesota Comm'r of Revenue*, 460 U.S. 575, 586 (1983).

20. At least in the United States, potentially damaging reports are often made with little effect unless they are developed and endorsed by the major media. Even a report made by the major media is often sufficiently buried so that it has no effect.

21. *CBS v. Democratic Nat'l Comm.*, 412 U.S. 94, 124 (1973). But see Vincent Blasi, "The Checking Value in First Amendment Theory," *American Bar Foundation Research Journal* (1977): 521, 623–31.

22. If, however, monopoly status is embedded deeply enough in the economic context, then the pluralist democrat might give up on the ideal of each group having its own media and accept pluralism within a single forum as the only partisan possibility available.

23. This approach obviously fits what has happened in the broadcasting context. It even suggests a basis for the view held by Justices White, Blackmun, and Powell in *CBS v. Democratic National Committee* that the government could choose not to provide access even if state action were found, although there are other possible routes to this conclusion.

24. *Miami Herald Publ'g Co. v. Tornillo*, 418 U.S. 241 (1974).
25. *Red Lion Broad. Co. v. FCC*, 395 U.S. 367, 369 (1969).
26. *CBS v. Democratic Nat'l Comm.*, 412 U.S. 94 (1973).
27. *Miami Herald Publ'g Co. v. Tornillo*, 418 U.S. 241, 258 (1974).
28. Ibid., 256, 257.
29. See *Turner Broadcasting Sys. v. FCC*, 512 U.S. 622, 656 (1994) ("Moreover, in con-trast to Tornillo, no aspect of the must-carry provisions would cause a cable oper-ator or cable programmer to conclude that 'the safe course is to avoid controversy,' and by so doing diminish the free flow of information and ideas" [citation omitted]); Baker, "Turner Broadcasting," 113–14. An additional ground for distin-guishing *Miami Herald* was the difference between cable systems and newspapers. Although hardly necessary for its holding, the Court in *Buckley v. Valeo*, 424 U.S. 1 (1972), also characterized the flaw of the law in *Miami Herald* not as an intrusion into editorial control but as a "legislative restraint" on the newspaper's freedom to criticize a candidate. *Buckley*, 424 U.S. at 51.
30. Reasons internal to the decision also suggest that the penalty-deterrence rationale in *Miami Herald* was primary. Only this primacy would explain Brennan's concur-rence (joined by Rehnquist), suggesting that the majority's decision did not imply a view about a statute giving a libeled plaintiff a right to require a printed retrac-tion. See *Miami Herald*, 418 U.S. at 258 (Brennan & Rehnquist, JJ., concurring). Such a statute would intrude into editorial control. It would not, however, impose a penalty or deter "protected" speech (since the libel is not protected).
31. *Syracuse Peace Council v. FCC*, 867 F.2d 654, 659–64 (D.C. Cir. 1989).
32. *CBS v. Democratic Nat'l Comm.*, 412 U.S. 94, 172 (1973) (Brennan & Marshall, JJ., dissenting).
33. Although this factual characterization may be persuasive as applied to network tele-vision (as involved in this case), it is less applicable to cable and other portions of broadcasting, such as community radio, which presumably is also covered by the ruling.
34. See *CBS v. Democratic Nat'l Comm.*, 412 U.S. at 121 (Burger, C.J., Stewart, J., & Rehnquist, J.).
35. *San Antonio Indep. Sch. Dist. v. Rodriguez*, 411 U.S. 1, 36 (1973).
36. I have argued that the press has the same speech rights as individuals and that, in addition, the Constitution protects the press as an institution. As Justice Potter Stewart explains, in "Or of the Press," *Hastings Law Journal* 26 (1975): 631, this pro-tection requires defensive rights, such as reporters' testimonial privileges, that protect their work product, but not offensive rights that would give the press special constitutionally founded rights of access or rights to violate otherwise applicable laws. See Baker, *Human Liberty and Freedom of Speech*, 225–49.
37. Stewart, "Or of the Press," 636.
38. See *Richmond Newspapers, Inc. v. Virginia*, 448 U.S. 555, 579–80 (1980). Cf. *Pell v. Procunier*, 417 U.S. 817, 833–34 (1974) (upholding a restriction on access to prisons); *Saxbe v. Washington Post Co.*, 417 U.S. 843, 850 (1974) (same).
39. Cf. Aviam Soifer, "Freedom of the Press in the United States," in Lahav, *Press Law in Modern Democracies*, 79, 105 (noting that the United States has at least 100 federal statutes and countless agency rules either prohibiting or limiting disclosure or authorizing nondisclosure of specified information).

40. In colonial America, printers were jailed for printing the laws and for publishing the votes or proceedings of colonial assemblies without a license. See Leonard W. Levy, *Legacy of Suppression* (Cambridge: Belknap Press, 1960), 24, 44–46, 76 (noting various cases in which printers were charged in criminal proceedings for printing the laws of the colonies); see also Thomas C. Leonard, *The Power of the Press: The Birth of American Political Reporting* (New York: Oxford U. Press, 1986), 63–65; Michael Schudson, *The Power of News* (Cambridge: Harvard U. Press, 1995), 46–47.

41. See Robert C. Cottrell, *Izzy: A Biography of I. F. Stone* (New Brunswick, N.J.: Rutgers U. Press, 1992), 5; see also Michaela Jarvis, "Sunday Interview," *San Francisco Chronicle* (Sept. 3, 1995): 3/Z3, quoting Ben Bagdikian, who said he "read I. F. Stone, whose chief impact was in saying 'Look, here are these documents that exist in government that are very important, and nobody's reporting on them.'"

42. *United States v. Nixon*, 418 U.S. 683, 713 (1974).

43. Cf. *Senate Select Comm. on Presidential Campaign Activities v. Nixon*, 498 F.2d 725, 733 (D.C. Cir. 1974) (en banc) (holding that the president's defeasible, constitutionally based privilege prevails even over the Senate committee's subpoena).

44. Christopher Lasch, "Journalism, Publicity and the Lost Art of Argument," *Gannett Center Journal* 1 (1990): 1.

45. *Harper & Row v. Nation Enters.*, 471 U.S. 539, 545 (1985). Copyright also furthers various private interests, especially people's pecuniary interests. These private interests, however, do not have constitutional status in justifying the existence of copyright. Copyright can also support a person's nonpecuniary interest in creative control or personal privacy. Even a writer interested solely in spreading her message has an interest in stopping "free" copying. Often, only her ability to transfer rights involving her work will induce a publisher to publish and promote her message.

46. The most interesting examination of copyright through the lens of democratic theory is in Neil Weinstock Netanel, "Copyright and a Democratic Civil Society," *Yale Law Journal* 106 (1996): 283, and in Neil Weinstock Netanel, "Asserting Copyright's Democratic Principles in the Global Arena," *Vanderbilt Law Review* 51 (1998): 217. The text attempts to extend Netanel's work by emphasizing that the specific content of democratic theory has implications for the proper reach of copyright.

47. The arguments in favor of narrowing copyright protection suggest reasons that other legal practices, most importantly contract, should also not be allowed free reign to again limit the use of intellectual creations. See Julie E. Cohen, "Lochner in Cyberspace: The New Economic Orthodoxy of 'Rights Management,'" *Michigan Law Review* 97 (1998): 462.

48. See Alexander Meiklejohn, *Political Freedom: The Constitutional Powers of the People* (New York: Oxford U. Press, 1965) (reprinting the 1948 article); Alexander Meiklejohn, "The First Amendment Is an Absolute," *Supreme Court Review* (1961): 245.

49. See Amy Adler, "What's Left: Hate Speech, Pornography, and the Problem for Artistic Expression," *California Law Review* 84 (1996): 1499, 1502 ("Race, gender, and sexual orientation have become the subjects of art, and art has become a central medium to activists concerned with achieving equality in these realms").

50. Rosemary J. Coombe, "Authorial Cartographies: Mapping Proprietary Borders in a Less-Than-Brave New World," *Stanford Law Review* 48 (1996): 1357, 1357.

51. This point is implicit in the word "shamans" in the title of James Boyle, *Shamans, Software, and Spleens: Law and the Construction of the Information Society* (Cambridge: Harvard U. Press, 1996).

52. Michael Madow, "Private Ownership of Public Image: Popular Culture and Publicity Rights," *California Law Review* 81 (1993): 125, 144.

53. *San Francisco Arts & Ath., Inc., v. United States Olympic Committee,* 483 U.S. 522 (1987).

## PART III

1. See Thomas M. Murray, "The U.S. Dispute over GATT Treatment of Audiovisual Products and the Limits of Public Choice Theory," *Maryland Journal of International Law & Trade* 21 (1997): 203, 207 (1997) (cultural products are second after aerospace and aviation; American entertainment industry produced $18 billion of foreign revenues and generated a $4 billion trade surplus in 1992). Statistics list the United States net surplus in 1993 for international film rentals to be $2.48 billion: Organization for Economic Co-operation and Development, *Services: Statistics on International Transactions: 1970–1994* (Paris: OECD, 1996), 99 (table A-21). Trade is vitally important to some American media industries, with foreign markets providing about half of the revenue for U.S. film and television products. Steven S. Wildman & Stephen E. Siwek, *International Trade in Films and Television Programs* (Cambridge, Mass.: Ballinger, 1988), 1.

2. Ted Magder, *Franchising the Candy Store: Split-Run Magazines and a New International Regime for Trade in Culture* (Orono, Maine: Canadian-American Center, U. of Maine, 1998), 8, quoting Frederick Paul, Editorial, "National Periodicals or Annexation," *Saturday Night* (Toronto) (Mar. 20, 1926): 2.

3. Unless context indicates otherwise, I use "cultural products" and "media products" interchangeably to refer to types of products that would receive First Amendment protection in the United States, for example: film, television, music and other audio recordings, video recordings, text materials, live performances, and, somewhat more controversially, advertising.

4. W. Ming Shao, "Is There No Business Like Show Business? Free Trade and Cultural Protectionism," *Yale Journal of International Law* 20 (1995): 105, 107 & n.9.

5. Bernard Weinraub, "The World Trade Agreement," *New York Times* (Dec. 15, 1994): D1.

6. Newspapers reported that "France defeated the film moguls of Hollywood"; and Prime Minister Edouard Balladur told the French Parliament that "[t]he European cultural identity has been saved." "Gentlemen, We Have a Deal," *Daily Mail* (Dec. 15, 1993): 10; Scott Kraft, "In French Parliament, A Resounding 'Oui' for Accord," *Los Angeles Times* (Dec. 16, 1993): A19.

7. NAFTA followed the earlier Canada–United States Free Trade Agreement, Jan. 2, 1988, Can.-U.S., art. 2005, 27 I.L.M. 281, 396, in not covering trade in cultural products. See North American Free Trade Agreement, Dec. 17, 1992, 32 I.L.M. 605, 701, 702, art. 2106, annex 2106.

8. The United States withdrew from UNESCO on January 1, 1985, citing UNESCO's communication initiatives as one of its main reasons. See Colleen Roach, "*American Textbooks v NWICO* History," in George Gerbner, Hamid Mowlana, &

Kaarle Nordenstreng, eds., *The Global Media Debate: Its Rise, Fall, and Renewal* (Norwood, N.J.: Ablex, 1993), 35, 43–46.

9. See World Trade Organization Report of the Appellate Body, *Canada – Certain Measures Concerning Periodicals*, June 30, 1997 <http://www.wto.org/wto/ddf/ep/public.html>.

10. See, e.g., Robin L. Van Harpen, "Note: Mamas, Don't Let Your Babies Grow Up to Be Cowboys: Reconciling Trade and Cultural Independence," *Minnesota Journal of Global Trade* 4 (1995): 165, 187–89.

11. See Immanuel Kant, "Perpetual Peace: A Philosophical Sketch" (1795), in Hans Reiss, ed., H. B. Nisbet, trans., *Kant's Political Writings* (Cambridge: Cambridge U. Press, 1970), 93, 114.

12. Fred H. Cate, "The First Amendment and the International Free Flow of Information," *Virginia Journal of International Law* 30 (1990): 371, 407.

13. See, e.g., Amy E. Lehmann, "The Canadian Cultural Exemption Clause and the Fight to Maintain Identity," *Syracuse Journal of International Law & Commerce* 23 (1997): 187, 206–13; Van Harpen, "Trade and Cultural Independence," 174–80. But cf. Murray, "GATT Treatment of Audiovisual Products," 223–24 (concluding that the French protectionist position was public-good-oriented, not rent-seeking, from the perspective of public-choice theory).

14. A few of the best articles on these trade disputes do challenge the simple economic argument as I have presented it. See, e.g., Shao, "Free Trade and Cultural Protectionism"; Oliver R. Goodenough, "Defending the Imaginary to the Death? Free Trade, National Identity, and Canada's Cultural Preoccupation," *Arizona Journal of International & Comparative Law* 15 (1998): 203; Richard L. Matheny III, "In the Wake of the Flood," *University of Pennsylvania Law Review* 147 (1998): 245. In each case, however, the author is more averse to protectionism than is appropriate (though less averse than many others), often because of inadequacies in his development of the economic critique.

## Chapter 10

1. See Michael Walzer, *Spheres of Justice* (New York: Basic Books, 1983), 64–91.

2. Steven S. Wildman & Stephen E. Siwek, *International Trade in Films and Television Programs* (Cambridge: Ballinger, 1988), 4–7.

3. See The World Trade Organization, Agreement on Implementation of Article VI of the General Agreement on Tariffs and Trade 1994, pt. I, art. 2 (Apr. 15, 1994), reprinted in H. R. Doc. No. 103–316, vol. 1, at 1463 (1994) (Sup. Docs. No. Y1.1/7:103–316/V.1); John H. Jackson & Edwin A. Vermulst, eds., *Anti-Dumping Law and Practice: A Comparative Study* (Ann Arbor: U. of Michigan Press, 1989).

4. See Wildman & Siwek, *International Trade in Films*, 3–4; W. Ming Shao, "Is There No Business Like Show Business? Free Trade and Cultural Protectionism," *Yale Journal of International Law* 20 (1995): 105, 124.

5. Wildman and Siwek create a simple economic model that largely predicts actual trade patterns in media products based on this public-good quality combined with several other obvious assumptions, such as the existence of some preference for domestic culture and language. See Wildman & Siwek, *International Trade in Films*, 2–3, 67–77. In contrast, Noam merely creates confusion when he treats trade in

audiovisual products as functionally equivalent to trade in traditional private goods such as Swiss watches and New Zealand kiwi fruits. See Eli Noam, *Television in Europe* (New York: Oxford U. Press, 1991), 15. Why Noam suggests this equivalence is difficult to understand. Maybe he refuses to note the public-good aspect of media products because to do so would undermine his attempt to deny the structural economic advantage that U.S. firms, that is, "Hollywood," have in the audiovisual arena. Unlike Wildman and Siwek, Noam finds the export success of Hollywood's high-cost producers "paradoxical." He tentatively explains the success by invoking various other factors such as the concerns of Americans being universal, thus having foreign appeal, or the United States being particularly good (technically) at filmmaking just as France is at winemaking. See ibid., 21–23.

6. After putting aside countries with nonmarket economies, such as China, Wildman and Siwek show that English speakers are both the largest and wealthiest market and that among English-speaking markets, the United States is clearly dominant. See Wildman & Siwek, *International Trade in Films*, 85.

7. See ibid., 22–26.

8. Ibid., 42–43.

9. See ibid., 13–48, 83–98, 170–75. This economic logic need not be the only factor contributing to American dominance. Some commentators describe imperialistic American foreign policy initiatives as having contributed to the prevalence of U.S. products. Others less persuasively attribute the popularity of U.S. products in part to Americans just being better at this form of service production. See, e.g., Noam, *Television in Europe*, 22.

10. See Noam, *Television in Europe*, 18. Of course, as all television network programmers and Hollywood studio heads know, popular tastes are sufficiently unpredictable that any modeling will be quite primitive.

11. Henceforth, I mostly ignore foreign content, *F*, because structurally there is seldom reason for a producer who sells either primarily domestically or both domestically and internationally to include it. Of course, sometimes a producer will create content initially for a primarily foreign market, especially a lucrative foreign market. Some Canadian companies as well as some U.S. companies operating in Canada for labor or locational reasons sometimes produce content primarily for the U.S. market. Similarly, many multinational media companies sell content that is domestic, *D*, within a country in which they produce it, even though it is *F* to the corporation's place of incorporation and to where the bulk of its equity owners live. Mostly, this and related complexities raise issues of corporate globalization more than of trade law. See generally Edward S. Herman & Robert W. McChesney, *The Global Media: The New Missionaries of Global Capitalism* (Washington, D.C.: Cassell, 1997). Of course, domestic-trade law must still decide whether to characterize particular products as imports or local.

12. See, e.g., *Turner Broadcasting System v. FCC*, 512 U.S. 622, 642 (1994) (a content-discriminatory law is presumptively unconstitutional); cf. Susan H. Williams, "Content Discrimination and the First Amendment," *University of Pennsylvania Law Review* 139 (1991): 615, 619–20 (arguing that facially neutral laws that have significant content-discriminatory effects should be treated constitutionally as content discriminatory). Contrary to strong dicta in *Turner*, as long as a law's purpose is not to *suppress* certain content, content-oriented media laws have,

historically and appropriately, been regularly upheld against First Amendment challenges; the merits of such laws should be judged as a policy matter. See C. Edwin Baker, "Turner Broadcasting: Content-Based Regulation of Persons and Presses," *Supreme Court Review* (1994): 57, 93–114.

13. See Wildman & Siwek, *International Trade in Films*, 4–7.

14. The lower price of the imports should cause an increase in the total size of the market for media products. Unusual circumstances could be imagined where this expansion could result in some increase in demand for local media, a point suggested by Gerry Neuman in conversation. Still, at least as long as the cost of producing local media goods does not go down, the cheaper (or otherwise successful) imports normally will partly replace, rather than increase demand for, local products.

15. See George Gerbner, "The Hidden Side of Television Violence," in George Gerbner, Hmid Mowlana, & Herbert I. Schiller, eds., *Invisible Crisis: What Conglomerate Control of Media Means for America and the World* (Boulder, Colo.: Westview, 1996), 27, 32.

16. See "Aircraft Subsidies, Audiovisuals Remain Barrier to US-EC Accord," *International Trade Reporter (BNA)* 10 (Dec. 8, 1993): no. 48, 2038; J. E. Ferry, "Seeking Same Subsidies," *Financial Times* (Dec. 20, 1993): 12.

17. This policy created a major controversy when embodied in a European Community Directive in 1989. See John David Donaldson, "Television without Frontiers: The Continuing Tension between Liberal Free Trade and European Cultural Integrity," *Fordham International Law Journal* 20 (1996): 90, 92–93. Countries such as Australia, Canada, France, Italy, Mexico, and Spain have adopted domestic-content requirements for broadcast programming. See Cultural Industries Sectoral Advisory Group on Int'l Trade, *Canadian Culture in a Global World: New Strategies for Culture and Trade* (1999), 18–19, available at <http://www.infoexport.gc.ca/trade-culture>. France, Mexico, and Spain are among those that impose minimum film-screening requirements for domestic films. See ibid., 19.

18. Various countries, including Australia, Canada, France, Israel, and South Africa, impose domestic-content requirements on radio broadcasts of popular music. See Sectoral Advisory Group, *Canadian Culture in a Global World*, 10, 18; Tim Cohen, "After Hours – SA Music Goes Number One with a Rocket," *Business Day* (South Africa) (May 14, 1999): Music, 1 (attributing the increased taste for and sales of South African music in part to the government's 20% domestic content requirement for radio music broadcasts); "Hebrew Melodies, Please," *New York Times* (Dec. 23, 1998): A3 (reporting on a new Israeli law requiring that one out of two songs broadcast over public radio stations be in Hebrew).

19. See, e.g., *Philadelphia v. New Jersey*, 437 U.S. 617, 623–24 (1978).

20. See, e.g., *Exxon Corp. v. Governor of Md.*, 437 U.S. 117, 125–29 (1978); *Minnesota v. Clover Leaf Creamery*, 449 U.S. 456 (1981).

21. See Daniel C. Hallin, "Broadcasting in the Third World: From National Development to Civil Society," in Tamar Liebes & James Curran, eds., *Media, Ritual and Identity* (London: Routledge, 1998), 153, 165.

22. The notion that such Enlightenment ideas are "foreign" to non-Western developing societies may itself be one of the elitist mistakes made by many Western

intellectuals. See Martha C. Nussbaum, *Women and Human Development: The Capabilities Approach* (Cambridge: Cambridge U. Press, 2000).

23. Even a democratic regime that censors certain content, such as pornography, may find free trade difficult to police, particularly if the products are imported by individual customers. See Amy Harmon, "Internet Sales of Nazi Books in Germany Assailed," *New York Times* (Aug. 9, 1999): C12.

24. Larry Gross, "Minorities, Majorities and the Media," in Liebes & Curran, *Media, Ritual and Identity*, 87, 87–88.

25. Annebelle Sreberny, "Television, Gender and Democratization in the Middle East," in James Curran and Myung-Jin Park, eds., *De-Westernizing Media Studies* (London: Routledge, 2000), 63, 74–77.

26. See Baker, "Turner Broadcasting."

27. See C. Edwin Baker, "Counting Preferences in Collective Choice Situations," *UCLA Law Review* 25 (1978): 381, 399–413.

28. Cultural taboos and interpretative practices relating to sex may make this assertion problematic. Countries may be clustered in how sexual content is understood and valued. I make no claims to sort out this issue.

29. See American Psychological Association, *Summary Report of the American Psychological Association Commission on Violence and Youth* 1 (Washington, D.C., 1993); Committee on Communications, American Academy of Pediatrics, "Media Violence," *Pediatrics* 95 (1995), 949; James T. Hamilton, *Channeling Violence* (Princeton: Princeton U. Press, 1998): 20–30 (reviewing numerous studies on the effects of violent television programs on individuals).

30. See Annabelle Sreberny-Mohammadi, "The Global and the Local in International Communications," in James Curran & Michael Gurevitch, eds., *Mass Media and Society*, 2d ed. (New York: St. Martin's Press, 1996), 177, 192–93.

31. Of course, international law seems to permit, if not require, such censorship of certain racist material and perhaps other purportedly equality-denying speech, such as pornography. In this book, I take no position on such restraints. But see C. Edwin Baker, "Of Course, More Than Words," *University of Chicago Law Review* 61 (1994): 1181, 1181–1211 (arguing that, properly understood, constitutional norms of both equality and autonomy reject the suppression of "equality-denying" speech).

32. See Wildman & Siwek, *International Trade in Films*, 19.

33. Ibid., 42–44.

34. See, e.g., Sectoral Advisory Group, *Canadian Culture in a Global World*, 30–32; see also International Meeting on Cultural Policy, *Final Report: Putting Culture on the World Stage* (Quebec: Department of Canadian Heritage,1998), 16 (statements of the Italian and South African ministers).

## Chapter 11

1. The last clause in this sentence distinguishes giving up democracy (as a country plausibly conceives it) from giving up its practice of engaging in human rights violations. Applying economic pressure to do the latter seems more acceptable even though it crosses "currency" categories.

2. The leading legal casebook on the media law could state, in a Whiggish history completely contrary to the facts, that the "AM band developed and was filled before the concept of noncommercial broadcasting entered the picture. As a result, the FCC made no specific allotment of such stations on the AM band." Marc A. Franklin & David A. Anderson, *Mass Media Law*, 5th ed. (Westbury, N.Y.: Foundation Press, 1995), 738. In fact, with huge numbers of noncommercial broadcasters on the air, one of the major original roles of the Federal Radio Commission (later to become the FCC) was to clear these stations off the spectrum in favor of commercial broadcasters. Nevertheless, huge public efforts opposed commercial broadcasting. At different times during this initial development of the AM band, Congress considered proposals to reserve 15%, 25%, 50%, or all channels for noncommercial or governmental stations. See generally Robert W. McChesney, *Telecommunications, Mass Media, and Democracy: The Battle for the Control of U.S. Broadcasting, 1928–1935* (New York: Oxford U. Press, 1993).

3. Ibid., 99–106, 242–43, 264.

4. Remark of Susan Crawford, workshop leader, Salzburg (Austria) Seminar (Aug. 6, 2000).

5. Raymond Williams, *Keywords: A Vocabulary of Culture and Society* (New York: Oxford U. Press, 1985), 87.

6. Cf. John David Donaldson, "Television without Frontiers: The Continuing Tension between Liberal Free Trade and European Cultural Integrity," *Fordham International Law Journal* 20 (1996): 90, 147 ("Without doubt, culture is one of the most difficult and problematic English terms to define due to its amorphous and inherently subjective nature").

7. Oliver R. Goodenough, "Defending the Imaginary to the Death? Free Trade, National Identity, and Canada's Cultural Preoccupation," *Arizona Journal of International & Comparative Law* 15 (1998): 203, 209–10.

8. Quoted in Donaldson, "Television without Frontiers," 109.

9. Quoted in Shawn McCarthy, "U.S. Challenges Our Magazine Law: Asks World Trade Group to Kill Tax on Split-Run Editions," *Toronto Star* (Mar. 12, 1996): D2.

10. See, e.g., W. Ming Shao, "Is There No Business Like Show Business? Free Trade and Cultural Protectionism," *Yale Journal of International Law* 20 (1995): 105, 136–37.

11. For example, Eli Noam does not deny that culture is "worthy of support," but explains that his aim is to create skepticism and to show that these notions are "not necessarily benign; they may well mask a form of information protectionism that serves entrenched interests." Eli Noam, *Television in Europe* (New York: Oxford U. Press, 1991), 25. Similarly, Donaldson exhibits considerable skepticism when he writes: "Few will argue that cultural integrity and preservation are not worthy goals, but . . ."; and "While cultural concerns *may be* legitimate, . . ." Donaldson, "Television without Frontiers," 169 (emphases added).

12. I use these terms interchangeably as context suggests. Their common feature is that each treats the crucial aspect of culture as identifiable content. The notion of "museum" emphasizes historical claims made on behalf of that content. "Commodity" emphasizes that culture consists of items or intellectual property containing specific content that can be possessed, valued, and (presumably) transferred. "Artifact" may be the more general term, suggesting both of these elements.

13. Cf. Patty Gerstenblith, "Identity and Cultural Property: The Protection of Cultural Property in the United States," *Boston University Law Review* 75 (1995): 559; Sarah Harding, "Justifying Repatriation of Native American Cultural Property," *Indiana Law Journal* 72 (1997): 723.

14. After I defended trade restrictions in cultural products at a conference in 1998 sponsored by the Cultural Environment Movement, a participating economist, in a private side remark, rhetorically asked: "Surely you don't think the French are worth preserving, do you?"

15. Amy E. Lehmann, "The Canadian Cultural Exemption Clause and the Fight to Maintain Identity," *Syracuse Journal of International Law & Commerce* 23 (1997): 187, 200, quoting Hester Riches, "Faith in the Future," *Vancouver Sun* (Mar. 22, 1995), B2.

16. Thomas I. Emerson, *The System of Freedom of Expression* (New York: Random House, 1970), 7.

17. Quoted in Ted Magder, *Franchising the Candy Store: Split-Run Magazines and a New International Regime for Trade in Culture* (Orono, Maine: Canadian-American Center, U. of Maine, 1998), 7–8. Of course, free trade might be hoped to do the same at the global level, but even the fulfillment of this aspiration would not reduce the essential need to promote understanding and cooperation within smaller political units.

18. Andrew M. Carlson, "The Country Music Television Dispute," *Minnesota Journal of Global Trade* 6 (1997): 585, 609.

19. Split-run magazines are magazines produced in two or more editions with all or mostly the same editorial content. The primary difference usually is advertising directed at a different group of consumers – for example, a Canadian edition of an American magazine would have Canadian advertising plus maybe one or two Canadian stories or a Canadian cover.

20. Magder, *Franchising the Candy Store*, 50. He explained that magazines "are an important forum for the expression of the ideas, attitudes and values of the reading communities they represent." Ibid.

21. Quoted in Lehmann, "Canadian Cultural Exemption Clause," 197.

22. Ted Magder, "Going Global," *Canadian Forum* (Aug. 1999): 11, 15.

23. The 1989 Directive, among other elements, specified that television broadcasting in member states should contain at least 50% European content, as therein defined and subject to certain exceptions. See Lawrence G. C. Kaplan, "The European Community's Television without Frontiers Directive: Stimulating Europe to Regulate Culture," *Emory International Law Review* 8 (1994): 255, 256.

24. Donaldson, "Television without Frontiers," 145.

25. Quoted in Shao, "Free Trade and Cultural Protectionism," 137–38 (emphasis added).

26. See International Meeting on Cultural Policy, *Final Report: Putting Culture on the World Stage* (Quebec: Department of Canadian Heritage, 1998).

27. Ibid., 28, 27.

28. On the notion of market corruption of segmentation, see Chapter 8. Jürgen Habermas argues that pathologies occur due to colonialization of aspects of the lifeworld and public sphere by the system realms of the market and bureaucratic power. He shows that "[u]nlike the material reproduction of the lifeworld, its sym-

bolic reproduction cannot be transposed onto foundations of system integration without pathological side effects." Jürgen Habermas, *The Theory of Communicative Action*, trans. Thomas McCarthy (Boston: Beacon Press, 1987), 2:322–23; see also 304–5, 311–12, 330, 345. The liberating cultural and political potential of the mass media, with feet in both the lifeworld and the systems worlds of the state and economy, is undermined to the extent that the imperatives of the latter control its role in the former. See Jürgen Habermas, *The Structural Transformation of the Public Sphere*, trans. Thomas Burger (Cambridge: MIT Press, 1989), 389–91.

29. International Meeting on Cultural Policy, *Final Report*, 14, 16 (emphasis added).

30. Daniel C. Hallin, "Broadcasting in the Third World: From National Development to Civil Society," in Tamar Liebes & James Curran, eds., *Media, Ritual and Identity* (London: Routledge, 1998), 153, 164, 162.

31. In the GATT negotiations, the United States offered to compromise its stance concerning the illegitimacy of film subsidies if the subsidizing country would agree to give its subsidies to Hollywood too! See Julie Wolf, "GATT Talks Stumble on Films and Flying," *Guardian* (London) (Dec. 8, 1993): 15; "French Do Not See Culture as a Good to Be Bought and Sold," *Irish Times* (Dec. 9, 1993): 6. In earlier trade negotiations with Canada, "the US entertainment industry objected to public funding of the [Canadian Broadcasting Corporation], Telefilm Canada, and the [Canadian National Film Board]." Peter Karl Kresl, "The Political Economy of Canada's Cultural Policy: The 1990s," in *Language, Culture and Values in Canada at the Dawn of the 21st Century* (Ottawa: International Council for Canadian Studies and Carlton University Press, 1996), 223, 236.

32. Cultural Industries Sectoral Advisory Group, *Canadian Culture in a Global World: New Strategies for Culture and Trade* (1998), 3 (emphasis omitted), available at <http://www.infoexport.gc.ca/trade-culture>.

33. Thus Magder suggests that Jack Valenti views "culture as something that is fixed and immutable." This view allows Valenti to conclude that Hollywood's products, despite their appeal, would not "tear a nation's allegiance from its culture," and thus that free trade would not create any problem. Magder, "Going Global," 15, quoting Valenti, head of the Motion Picture Association of America.

34. See Noam, *Television in Europe*, 23. Noam also observes that sometimes protection of national culture is used as a mask for "information protectionism that serves entrenched interests." Ibid., 25. See also Monroe E. Price, "The Market for Loyalties: Electronic Media and the Global Competition for Allegiances," *Yale Law Journal* 104 (1994): 667.

35. For current examples, Noam easily could refer to Serbian and other Balkan nationalisms. In an excellent, sensitive article, Oliver Goodenough notes that having a foreign threat may be useful or even necessary for nation building. The battle over cultural protectionism, for example, could itself help establish the United States as the enemy and create a Canada, defined as "not United States." Goodenough, "Defending the Imaginary," 247–49. Accordingly, the "real point of the fight [over cultural protectionism] is the fight itself." Ibid., 247. Goodenough concludes, however, that this strategy is fatally flawed. By accepting the legitimacy of cultural protectionism and of the protected identity as a basis of nationhood, he argues, cultural protectionists justify the unraveling of Canada, first as Francophone Quebec secedes and then as the First Nations peoples exit. See ibid., 250–52.

36. See Will Kymlicka, *Liberalism, Community and Culture* (New York: Oxford U. Press, 1989); Nancy Fraser, "Rethinking the Public Sphere: A Contribution to the Critique of Actually Existing Democracy," in Craig Calhoun, ed., *Habermas and the Public Sphere* (Cambridge: MIT Press, 1992), 109, 109–42.
37. See Lehmann, "Canadian Cultural Exemption Clause," 201. Lehmann illustrates her complaint that no one "has verbally articulated what [Canadian] identity is," with the Canadian joke that "define[s] a Canadian as an unarmed American with Medicare." Ibid., 200.
38. See Donaldson, "Television without Frontiers," 154.
39. Noam, *Television in Europe*, 24.
40. See, e.g., ibid.; Donaldson, "Television without Frontiers," 150; Shao, "Free Trade and Cultural Protectionism," 140.
41. Noam, *Television in Europe*, 23.
42. Ibid.
43. See Shao, "Free Trade and Cultural Protectionism," 140.
44. See Noam, *Television in Europe*, 23; Donaldson, "Television without Frontiers," 151; Shao, "Free Trade and Cultural Protectionism," 146.
45. See Noam, *Television in Europe*, 22; Shao, "Free Trade and Cultural Protectionism," 140.
46. Ibid.
47. Ibid.
48. Nina Munk, "Culture Cops," *Forbes* (Mar. 27, 1995): 41, 42, quoted in Goodenough, "Defending the Imaginary," 253 n.153.
49. Cross-border connections are not always irrelevant. Because some groups within a state will identify with those outside, some forms of protectionism – for example, a Canadian law restricting access to "foreign" French culture – might seriously hamper some Canadians' participation in internal Canadian discourse.
50. See Donaldson, "Television without Frontiers," 174–75 & n.491; Shao, "Free Trade and Cultural Protectionism," 140.
51. Donaldson, "Television without Frontiers," 174–75.
52. Ibid., 175 n.491, citing Clint N. Smith, "International Trade in Television Programming and GATT," *International Tax & Business Law* 10 (1994): 97, 134.
53. See Donaldson, "Television without Frontiers," 170–71.
54. See Lehmann, "Canadian Cultural Exemption Clause," 217–18.
55. This argument roughly parallels an analysis offered by Habermas. See Jürgen Habermas, *The Inclusion of the Other* (Cambridge: MIT Press, 1998), 105–61. Curiously, I have not seen this argument for free trade clearly articulated in the U.S. scholarship favoring free trade in media products. The argument may be too visionary and too dependent on speculative developments for the purportedly pragmatic American authors who write on media free trade. Or it may be too anti-corporate. Still, intuitive belief in the argument might influence some people's thinking on the subject. Thus, addressing it explicitly seems warranted.
56. Ibid., 153, 160.
57. See ibid., 124, 127, 153, 160–61. Unfortunately, these assertions, usually concluding Habermas' analyses, do not discuss in detail the appropriate form of these public spheres.

58. See, e.g., David Moberg, "Global Economy Needs Regulating," *Newsday* (Dec. 9, 1997): A41. The *New York Times*, often considered the paper of record in the United States, had a virtual blackout on news about negotiations concerning the Multilateral Agreement on Investment. A search of the Lexis data base for non-U.S. publications during 1997–98 shows 1,054 stories including this term, and during this period it was included in 712 stories in the Lexis major papers data base, but the *New York Times* referred to it only three times, in each case only in passing.

59. Habermas' critique of identifying the nation-state with a mythical ethnic people rather than with democratically legitimatized law involves a similar rejection of the necessity of leveling cultural differences. In contrast, critics of a European democratic government often assume that a single ethnic culture or at least a single people is necessary for democratic government but impossible to achieve at a European level. See Habermas, *Inclusion of the Other*, 105–61.

60. Fraser, "Rethinking the Public Sphere," 123 (emphasis omitted).

61. This concern with the impact of trade on the cultural industries of weaker economies is quite intense internationally. Representative are views such as those of Mia Bottley, minister of education, youth, and culture from Barbados, who suggests that larger countries "lack sensitivity to the particular needs of small island states," International Meeting on Cultural Policy, *Final Report*, 16, and Abdelbaki Hermassi, cultural minister of Tunisia, who argues that international trade agreements pose a much greater threat to countries in the South, where they could have a "devastating effect." Ibid., 17. This is true also in the intellectual property context. Wildman suggests that copyright law has been responsive to developing countries' needs relating to materials relevant for educational development purposes, Steven S. Wildman & Stephen E. Siwek, *International Trade in Films and Television Programs* (Cambridge: Ballinger, 1988), 143. However, the primary effort in this respect, the 1976 Stockholm Protocol Regarding Developing Nations, which included low-cost compulsory licenses in appropriate cases, was rejected after opposition by many industrialized nations. See Sam Ricketson, *The Berne Convention for the Protection of Literary and Artistic Works: 1886–1986* (London: Kluwer, 1987), 598–620; Neil Weinstock Netanel, "Asserting Copyright's Democratic Principles in the Global Arena," *Vanderbilt Law Review* 51 (1998): 217, 235, 277–78; Sunny Handa, "A Review of Canada's International Copyright Obligations," *McGill Law Journal* 42 (1997): 961, 966. Netanel persuasively argues that developing countries' democratic and educational needs require currently unlikely modifications of the existing international copyright regime. Netanel, "Copyright's Democratic Principles," 327–28.

62. Goodenough, "Defending the Imaginary," 211 (emphasis omitted). Goodenough includes "economic subsidies and affirmative quotas for Canadian production" as examples of weak protectionism and lists "flat prohibitions, negative quotas, and other significant barriers on imports" as illustrations of strong protectionism. Ibid. Later, given Goodenough's functional definition of the two categories, I quarrel with the way he characterizes various policies.

63. Ibid., 252. Goodenough is quite clear that subsidies have important and defensible uses. Ibid., 235–36.

64. Tariff Code 9958 prohibited importation of "a split run or a regional edition[] that contained an advertisement that was primarily directed to a market in Canada, and that did not appear in identical form in all editions . . . distributed in [the

periodical's] country of origin." Customs Tariff, ch. 49, sched. VII, code 9958, 1987 S.C. 3308, 3310 (Can.). See also Goodenough, "Defending the Imaginary," 213 n.44 (quoting Tariff Code 9958).

65. Bill C-103 closed a possible loophole: printing the Canadian edition in Canada and thereby not engaging in importation. The bill imposed an 80% excise tax on the Canadian advertising of such a locally produced split-run publication. See Goodenough, "Defending the Imaginary," 214.

66. Although much about the WTO decision's *legal* analysis can be criticized, and although it seemed to adopt much too much of a commodity orientation in its notion of "comparable" goods and its analysis of "directly competitive or substitutable products," a critique of the legal reasoning is not needed for the purposes of this chapter. For a mostly effective legal critique, see Richard L. Matheny III, "In the Wake of the Flood," *University of Pennsylvania Law Review* 147 (1998): 245.

67. Customs Tariff, ch. 49, sched. VII, code 9958, 1987 S.C. at 3310.

68. Magder, *Franchising the Candy Store,* 5. As Magder correctly observes, "[n]one of the Canadian measures [struck down by the WTO decision] were designed to block the entry into Canada of foreign magazines with foreign content." Ibid., 49.

69. Ibid., 49.

70. Ibid., 28.

71. Robin L. Van Harpen, "Note: Mamas, Don't Let Your Babies Grow Up to Be Cowboys: Reconciling Trade and Cultural Independence," *Minnesota Journal of Global Trade* 4 (1995): 165, 173–74 (citation omitted).

72. Magder, *Franchising the Candy Store,* 28–29.

73. Ibid., 10.

74. Although the quality of the data is unclear, U.S. magazines reportedly held more than 80% of the Canadian market in the 1920s. See ibid., 7. Likewise, in the late 1960s roughly 130 million out of 160 million copies of magazines (81%) sold in Canada were American. See ibid., 12–13.

75. See ibid., 13.

76. This is similar to the tendency of lawyers, who represent corporations challenging facially neutral state regulations as violations of the Commerce Clause, to find and attribute protectionist purposes to the challenged laws. Even though the challenged law has the effect of discriminating mostly against out-of-state goods, the Supreme Court consistently refuses to invalidate on this ground if, as is usually the case, there is also some plausible nonprotectionist justification for the law.

77. International Commission for the Study of Communication Problems, *Many Voices, One World* (New York: Unipub, 1980) [hereafter referred to as the MacBride Commission Report].

78. Wolfgang Kleinwachter, "Three Waves of the Debate," in George Gerbner, Hamid Mowlana, & Kaarle Nordenstreng, eds., *The Global Media Debate: Its Rise, Fall, and Renewal* (Norwood, N.J.: Ablex, 1993), 13, 16. See also A. H. Raskin, "U.S. News Coverage of the Belgrade UNESCO Conference," *Journal of Communication* 31, no. 4 (Autumn 1981): 164, 171, quoting observation of John G. Massee, a staff member of the MacBride Commission, that "nothing coming out of the MacBride Report or UNESCO . . . suggests a curtailment of news flow."

79. Michael J. Farley, "Conflicts over Government Control of Information – the United States and UNESCO," *Tulane Law Review* 59 (1985): 1071, 1076.

80. Ibid., 1088.
81. Leonard J. Theberge, "U.N.E.S.C.O.'s 'New World Information Order': Colliding with First Amendment Values," *American Bar Association Journal* 67 (1981): 714, 715–16.
82. Ibid., 718.
83. Ibid.
84. See Michael Traber & Kaarle Nordenstreng, eds., *Few Voices, Many Worlds* (London: World Association for Christian Communication, 1992), 46, reprinting the "Conclusions and Recommendations" of the MacBride Commission Report.
85. Sarah Goddard Power, "The US View of Belegrade," *Journal of Communications* 31, no. 4 (Autumn 1981): 142, 143.
86. William Fitzmaurice, "Note, The New World Information and Communication Order: Is the International Programme for the Development of Communication the Answer?" *New York University Journal of International Law & Policy* 15 (1983): 953, 979.
87. Raskin, "Coverage of the Belgrade UNESCO Conference," 164, 166–67; George Gerbner, "UNESCO in the U.S. Press," in Gerbner et al., *The Global Media Debate*, 111, 117–20. Raskin, a former assistant editor of the *New York Times* editorial page and associate director of the National News Council, is hardly some anti-press radical.
88. See, e.g., Richard B. Kielbowicz, *News in the Mail: The Press, Post Office, and Public Information, 1700–1860s* (New York: Greenwood Press, 1989); Richard B. Kielbowicz, "Origins of the Second-Class Mail Category and the Business of Policy-making, 1863–1879," *Journalism Monographs*, no. 96 (April 1986).
89. Fitzmaurice, "Note, The New World Information and Communication Order," 980 n.97, quoting and condemning the report's recommendation.
90. The eventual consequence of the increasing presence of private commercial television, authorized over the past twenty years in liberal democracies outside the United States, is still unsettled. James Curran, for example, has challenged Elihu Katz's view that this development will erode public support for continued large government subsidies for and viewership of public broadcasting, with a consequent splintering of the audience and a weakening of the public sphere required for liberal democracy. Compare Elihu Katz, "And Deliver Us from Segmentation," *Annals of the Amercian Acadamy of Political & Social Sciences* 546 (1996): 22 (arguing that with public television broadcasting giving way to commercial broadcasting, "[w]e have all but lost television as the medium of national political integration"), with James Curran, "Crisis of Public Communication: A Reappraisal," in Liebes & Curran, *Media, Ritual and Identity* (taking issue with Katz's position and arguing that "only by opening up [broadcasting] to more voices will it be possible to strengthen public identification with the broadcasting system").
91. Theberge, "U.N.E.S.C.O.'s New World Information Order," 716.
92. Ibid.
93. Power, "The US View of Belegrade," 144. Power also duplicated Theberge in stating that the "MacBride Report . . . exhibits a clear bias against the involvement of the private sector in communications." Ibid.
94. A preference for media concentration has recently been the quite explicit policy of the Commerce Department, at least when considering international trade. See

National Telecomm. & Info. Admin., U.S. Department of Commerce, Special Pub.
No. 93–290, *Globalization of the Mass Media* (Washington, D.C.: GPO, 1993).
95. See *Associated Press v. United States*, 326 U.S. 1, 20 (1945).
96. Power, "The US View of Belgrade," 144.
97. See *Associated Press v. United States*, 326 U.S. 1 (1945) (antitrust laws); *Associated Press v. NLRB*, 301 U.S. 103, 130–33 (1937) (labor laws).
98. See *FCC v. National Citizens Committee for Broadcasting*, 436 U.S. 775 (1978) (limits on newspaper ownership of broadcast stations); *Lewis Publishing v. Morgan*, 229 U.S. 288 (1913) (requirement that newspapers receiving second-class mail privilege publish information identifying ownership and identifying advertisements); *Committee for an Independent P-I v. Hearst Corp.*, 704 F.2d 467 (9th Cir. 1983) (the Newspaper Preservation Act, which gives certain newspapers a limited exemption from antitrust laws despite injury to other newspapers); C. Edwin Baker, "Turner Broadcasting: Content-Based Regulation of Persons and Presses," *Supreme Court Review* (1994): 57, 93–114.

## CONCLUSION

1. Jerome Barron, *Freedom of the Press for Whom? The Right of Access to the Mass Media* (Bloomington: U. of Indiana Press, 1973).
2. Ronnie Dugger, "The Corporate Domination of Journalism," in William Serrin, ed., *The Business of Journalism* (New York: New Press, 2000), 27, 34–35.
3. See, e.g., Sydney H. Schanberg, "Journalism Lite," in Serrin, *The Business of Journalism*, 117, 137–39.

## POSTSCRIPT

1. This section draws heavily on C. Edwin Baker, "New Media Technologies, the First Amendment, and Public Policies," *Communications Review* 1 (1996): 315; and Ed Baker, "Private Censorship on the Net and the Need for Corrective Policies" (1999), at <http://webserver.law.yale.edu.censor/baker.htm>.
2. For an excellent introduction to policy issues raised by the new technologies, see Lawrence Lessig, *Code and Other Laws of Cyberspace* (New York: Basic Books, 1999).
3. Sydney H. Schanberg, "Journalism Lite," in William Serrin, ed., *The Business of Journalism* (New York: New Press, 2000), 117, 131.
4. Lessig's mantra emphasizes social norms as well as the other three elements as a determinant and I certainly do not disagree. Lessig, *Code*. I merely would not describe social norms as structure but rather argue that results reflect the combination of structure, norms, and individual initiative. See Yochai Benkler, "Communications Infrastructure Regulation and the Distribution of Control over Content," *Telecommunications Policy* 22 (1998): 183.
5. Cass Sunstein, *Republic.com* (Princeton: Princeton U. Press, 2001); Robert D. Putman, *Bowling Alone: The Collapse and Revival of American Community* (New York: Simon & Schuster, 2000).
6. Theodore Roszak, *The Cult of Information*, 2nd ed. (Berkeley: U. of California Press: 1994); Neil Posman, *Amusing Ourselves to Death: Public Discourse in the Age of Show*

*Business* (New York: Viking, 1985); Jerry Mander, *Four Arguments for the Elimination of Television* (New York: Morrow, 1978).

7. See Julie E. Cohen, "Lockner in Cyberspace: The New Economic Orthodoxy of 'Rights Management,'" *Michigan Law Review* 97 (1998): 462.

8. Digital Millennium Copyright Act of 1998, 17 U.S.C.A. 1202. See Yochai Benkler, "Free as the Air to Common Use: First Amendment Constraints on Enclosure of the Public Domain," *New York University Law Review* 74 (1999): 354.

9. Bruce M. Owen, *Economics and Freedom of Expression: Media Structure and the First Amendment* (Cambridge: Ballinger, 1975); Leo Bogart, *Commercial Culture: The Media System and the Public Interest* (New York: Oxford U. Press, 1995), 320; C. Edwin Baker, "Merging Phone and Cable," *Hastings Communications and Entertainment Law Journal* 17 (1994): 97.

10. *Chesapeake & Potomac Telephone v. United States*, 42 F.3rd 1181 (4th Cir. 1994); Baker, "Merging Phone and Cable."

11. Bill Carter, "Blackout of ABC on Cable Affects Millions of Homes," *New York Times* (May 2, 2000): C1.

12. Colin Sparks, "The Internet and the Global Public Sphere," in Lance Bennett & Robert Entman, eds., *Mediated Politics: Communication in the Future of Democracy* (Cambridge: Cambridge U. Press, 2001), 75.

13. See Robert Britt Horwitz, *The Irony of Regulatory Reform: The Deregulation of American Telecommunications* (New York: Oxford U. Press, 1989).

14. W. Russell Neuman, *The Future of the Mass Audience* (Cambridge: Cambridge U. Press, 1991).

15. Project Censored has annual awards identifying the major stories significantly underreported in the mainstream press, with an annual book describing the "winning" stories, and using other methods of trying to publicize information about both the stories and the story of their being underreported. See <http://www.projectcensored.org/intro.htm>.

16. Edward S. Herman & Noam Chomsky, *Manufacturing Consent* (New York: Pantheon Books, 1988), xiv–xv.

17. See David L. Protess et al., *Journalism of Outrage* (New York: Guilford Press, 1991), 18.

18. Michael Schudson, *The Power of News* (Cambridge: Harvard U. Press, 1995), 33.

19. Ibid., 25. Maybe it should not be so surprising that reporters "often act as if their real audience is made up of the other reporters or government officials they consider their peers." James Fallows, *Breaking the News* (New York: Pantheon Books, 1996), 240.

20. This has been a major theme in the work of Yochai Benkler to whom I am much indebted. See, e.g., Benkler, "Free as the Air to Common Use." See also Niva Elkin-Koren & Neil Netanel, eds., *The Commodification of Information: Political, Social, and Cultural Ramifications* (London: Kluwer, 2001).

21. Although even in legal circles the Pentagon Papers case, 403 U.S. 713 (1971), is often taken to be a ringing endorsement of an almost absolute rule against prior restraints (i.e., injunctions against publication), a majority of the Court either approved an injunction in that case or indicated no view about whether such an injunction would be permissible if authorized by a congressional statute.

22. At the time this was being written, the music industry appeared to be winning the legal battle against Napster, *A & M Records v. Napster*, 2001 U.S. App. LEXIS 1941 (9th Cir, Feb. 12, 2001), but the eventual legal and cultural "settlement" remains hard to predict.

23. As a constitutional matter, I do not generally approve of these tests, which I think not only provide too little protection but misguide the inquiry as to whether protection should be granted – see C. Edwin Baker, *Human Liberty and Freedom of Speech* (New York: Oxford U. Press, 1989); C. Edwin Baker, "Turner Broadcasting: Content-Based Regulation of Persons and Presses," *Supreme Court Review* (1994): 57 – but this test may provide a rough description, at least as a policy matter, of the scope that should be given to intellectual property.

24. *Smith v. California*, 361 U.S. 147 (1959) (violates First Amendment to impose liability on bookstore owner for content of which he was not aware in book he was selling).

25. Communications Decency Act of 1996, 47 U.S.C. §230 (exempting Internet service providers from publisher liability). See *Zeran v. America Online*, 129 F.3d 327 (4th Cir. 1997). I do not here endorse any particular legal regime dealing with this issue because approaches much more sensitive to the competing concerns than either absolute exemption from liability or imposition of publisher or bookseller liability are possible.

26. Child Online Protection Act, 112 Stat. 2681 (1998). See 47 U.S.C. §231(1) and §231(e)(6) (limiting law to commercial providers). *Reno v. American Civil Liberties Union*, 521 U.S. 844 (1997); *ACLU v. Reno*, 217 F.3d 162 (3rd Cir., 2000) (upholding preliminary injunction against enforcement of COPA).

# Index